Ransomware, Viruses, Social Engineering, and Other Threats

RANSOMWARE, VIRUSES, SOCIAL ENGINEERING, AND OTHER THREATS

Protecting Your Digital Assets

Kelly C. Bourne

MERCURY LEARNING AND INFORMATION
Boston, Massachusetts

MERCURY LEARNING AND INFORMATION
121 High Street, 3rd Floor
Boston, MA 02110
info@merclearning.com

K. Bourne. *Ransomware, Viruses, Social Engineering, and Other Threats: Protecting Your Digital Assets*. ISBN: 978-1-50152-313-7

Library of Congress Control Number: 2024950426

242526321   This book is printed on acid-free paper in the United States of America.

Our titles are available for adoption, license, or bulk purchase by institutions, corporations, etc.

All of our titles are available in digital format at various digital vendors.

This book is dedicated to my five wonderful grandchildren.

*Jason who knows just about everything about coins,
U.S. Presidents, and history.*

Aylee is so smart, extremely talented, and as brave as can be.

Rosie who is artistic, fun, and an incredibly kind girl.

*Fiona who is independent, determined, and a friend to all the
animals of the world.*

Zoey who's sweet, smiley, and yet a little spitfire.

I love you all!

CONTENTS

PREFACE

About one hundred years ago Albert Einstein had a quote that began "The world is a dangerous place to live." This was true when he wrote it and it's equally true, if not more so today. Physical threats existed then and now, but perhaps even more significant are the electronic threats that exist in our modern world. Everyone can have their property, privacy, reputation and even their identity stolen in the blink of an eye.

Another immense difference between Einstein's world and our own is that threats can now be projected around the world instantly. In the 20th century, a criminal had to be physically close to harm you. In our current world criminals can attack you with ransomware, viruses, or social engineering scams from the other side of the globe. This means that every cybercriminal in every country has the potential to target you.

Einstein's complete quote ends with "not because of the people who are evil, but because of the people who don't do anything about it." This book is my attempt to do something about it. I hope that the information contained in this book will help the reader make their world a little bit less dangerous for themselves and their families, friends and co-workers.

Realistically I don't have anything to offer IT professionals who are cyber-security experts. They're already extremely familiar with the threats that I describe. They also know how to recognize computer-based dangers, protect against them, and recover from cyberattacks. Instead, this book is intended for mainstream computer users. People who use a computer or smartphone every day to browse the web, read their emails, watch videos, play games, interact with friends, make purchases online and keep tabs of their bank accounts or portfolios, but have no cybersecurity training. Whether they know it or not, everyday activities like these that are performed by billions of people around the world are taking them right up to the precipice of danger. After reading this book, I hope people will understand the dangers that exist and take the steps I outline to help protect themselves.

Each chapter in this book provides the reader with important information like:

- Who are the bad guys and what do they want?

- An overview of the surprisingly large variety of cyberthreats facing all computer users.

- Exactly what ransomware is, how it spreads and how it hurts individuals and organizations.

- How social engineering is used by criminals to manipulate their victims.

- The strengths and weaknesses of passwords.

- How multifactor authentication (MFA) can protect your online accounts.

- Anti-virus tools that everyone should be using on their computers and smart phones.

- The importance of applying patches and upgrades promptly.

- Email is used by almost everyone but few people understand its security weaknesses.

- How social media collects more personal information on users than people realize.

- Backups can be your road to recovery.

- Steps to safely browse the Internet.

- How virtual private networks (VPNs) can shield your online activities from prying eyes.

- Why firewalls are needed to limit communications between your computer and the Internet.

- Smart phones and other mobile devices need protection too.

- Why people need to protect their home network even if they don't realize they have one.

▣   How encryption can be used to protect your privacy.

▣   What the Internet of Things (IoT) is and how little protection it has.

▣   Reducing your personal information's exposure on the Internet

I've enjoyed writing this book and hope that readers will find it both interesting and useful. Even more, I hope that this book will motivate readers to take some steps to protect their digital assets. In these dangerous times we all need all of the awareness and protection that we can acquire.

Kelly C. Bourne
January 2025

ACKNOWLEDGMENTS

I want to thank Steven Elliot at Mercury Learning and Information for giving me the opportunity to write this book. Jennifer Blaney has been great to work with as the book's project manager. Kelly Lee for doing an excellent job as copy editor. Velraja M at BrioWorkx for refining the composition aspects of the book.

Who Are the Bad Guys?

Before learning how to protect oneself against ransomware, viruses, and other kinds of threats, it is useful to have an idea of the dangerous people who would utilize such technologies. Who are the nefarious actors who might be trying to break into electronic devices? What are their motives?

One of the most common names for a cybercriminal is a *hacker*. It might be a surprise to most readers that in the 1960s, this term was actually considered positive. A hacker was someone who was able to write efficient code for mainframe computers (basically, hackers made programs work with fewer lines of code). In the days when computers had less memory and were much slower than they are today, this was a much-admired skill.

THE MOTIVATION OF HACKERS

There are various types of hackers, each with different motivations and goals. Hackers are typically defined according to the "color" of their "hat" (just like the characters in old Western movies, where the hero wore a white hat and the villain wore a black hat). These different colors refer to the motivations of the hackers.

a. *White hat hackers* use their skills to identify and help repair flaws in software and computer systems that they have the consent to work on.

b. *Black hat hackers* typically intend to harm individuals or organizations by installing malware, stealing intellectual property, and damaging computers.

c. *Gray hat hackers* are somewhere between white and black hat hackers. They may have beneficial intentions, but do not always follow the rules when accessing computer systems.

Hackers with Colorful "Hats"

a. *Blue hat hackers* are penetration testers who have been engaged by an organization to test the security of its products before they are released to the public.

b. *Red hat hackers* act as vigilantes against black hat hackers (or *cyber criminals*). They have positive intentions, but do not always follow the law and this can cause problems with the authorities. An example of red hat hackers is the hacktivist group Anonymous.

c. *Purple hat hackers* hack their own systems to improve their skills without threatening computer systems belonging to someone else.

d. *Green hat hackers* are in the field of cybersecurity and are continuing to develop their skills. Their goal is to become white hat hackers, but they are still improving their knowledge and experience.

Other Types of Nefarious Actors

a. *Script kiddies* are inexperienced hackers who rely on pre-written scripts. Although they may lack significant experience, this group can still cause problems for their victims because many dangerous scripts and tools are available for them to use.

b. *Hacktivists* are hackers who are motivated by their political beliefs. Some hacktivist groups fight government censorship, promote freedom of speech, and attempt to undermine corporations they feel are abusive.

c. *Elite hackers* have many years of experience and are considered the innovators and influencers in the field.

d. *Nation-state hackers* are motivated by nationalism. They may be acting for themselves or on behalf of the nation they belong to. Threats posed by this group are often referred to as *Advanced Persistent Threats* (APT).

The Dangers of Script Kiddies

Do not be deceived by the simple description of script kiddies. Even if these individuals are not able to develop new types of attacks on their own, they can base their attacks on techniques that were pioneered by more experienced bad actors.

It Is Not Always Black and White

Hacker motivations can be complicated, and so most are not entirely "good" or "bad." There are numerous instances of individuals moving between the two ends of the cybersecurity spectrum.

Some black hat hackers changed their lives and devoted their efforts working as white hats. Kevin Mitnick was arguably the most famous hacker in history [CYB23]. Mitnick was arrested by the FBI in 1995 on charges of computer fraud as well as having cloned cellular phone codes and false identification. He always claimed that he did not profit from his activities, and that he was simply trying to learn more about the computer systems that he broke into.

After his release, Mitnick spent the remainder of his career as a trusted white hat penetration tester doing security consulting for Fortune 500 companies [Know23]. He wrote several books about computer security, including *The Art of Deception*, *Ghost in the Wires*, *The Art of Intrusion*, and *The Art of Invisibility*.

Sometimes an individual may be engaged in both good and bad activities simultaneously. One example is the security researcher who single handedly stopped the WannaCry attack in 2017. WannaCry was a ransomware attack that impacted over 200,000 computers in over 150 countries [CLO17]. Marcus Hutchins, a security researcher, reverse-engineered the code and discovered that the virus checked for the existence of a specific Web domain. If the Web site did not exist, the malware would install itself on the victim's computer. If the Web site did exist, then the malware could spread but would not be executed. Hutchins registered the domain and this "kill switch" essentially halted the ransomware attack by himself.

Even though this fix helped protect systems worldwide, Hutchins was later involved in criminal activities. A few months later, he was arrested by the FBI for writing a strain of banking malware called Kronos [GUARD19]. (Hutchins was sentenced to time served and probation instead of 10 years in prison.)

Other Names for Hackers

1. Crackers

2. Phreak

3. Bad actor

4. Threat actor

5. Cyber-terrorist

6. Malicious hacker

7. Cyber criminal

8. Nation-state actors

MOTIVES OF ATTACKERS

Hackers have diverse motives. Originally, the primary motivations were to learn how computer systems worked and to be respected by their peers. While those inspirations still exist, other factors gradually have become more important. Some of the recent inspirations are

a. Money: Hacking can be extremely profitable. A zero-day exploit (see Chapter 2) can be sold for millions of dollars. In 2021, a single ransomware payout of $40 million was made [CYB21]. Worldwide credit and debit card fraud in 2022 was estimated to be over $34 billion [WALL24].

b. Theft of intellectual property: Valuable intellectual property (IP) may be stolen by a cybercriminal. IP can be sold to a rival that wants to bypass the large research and development investments made by companies or countries or a nation/state that wants to strengthen its economic or military competitive position.

c. Personal grudge or revenge: Insider attacks may be motivated by a sense of revenge. If an individual perceives that they have been wronged by an organization or its management, they may use their insider position to strike out against it.

d. Whistleblowing: Some individuals are convinced that the organization they belong to is acting unethically. They might see whistleblowing as the only way to expose the activity.

   e. Political motivations: Hacktivists are motivated by political goals. They will disrupt the Web sites and computer systems of organizations or countries that they oppose.

   f. Cyberwarfare: *Cyberwarfare* is the use of cyberattacks by one nation/state against another nation/state. This could include denial of service (DoS) attacks, zero-day attacks, and computer viruses or cyberattacks against a country's infrastructure (such as the power grid, water systems, or hospitals).

To some, the word "hacker" still sounds respectable instead of being a derogatory term. It implies the person is someone who has endless curiosity as well as the skill and tenacity to learn how computers and systems work.

Many people in the field prefer the term *cracker* when referring to individuals who access computer systems without authorization.

REFERENCES

[CYB21] Schwartz, Samantha, "CAN Financial's reported $40M ransom payment likely a record," available online at *https://www.cybersecuritydive.com/news/cna-financial-ransomware-payment-treasury-sanctions/600591/*, May 21, 2021

[CYB23] Morgan, Steve. "Cybersecurity's Greatest Showman on Earth: Kevin Mitnick," available online at *https://cybersecurityventures.com/cybersecuritys-greatest-show-on-earth-kevin-mitnick/*, January 31, 2023

[CLO17] "What was the WannaCry ransomware attack?," available online at *https://www.cloudflare.com/learning/security/ransomware/wannacry-ransomware/#:~:text=The%20WannaCry%20ransomware%20attack%20occurred,networks%20all%20over%20the%20world*, April 22, 2024

[GUARD19] "Briton who helped stop 2017 WannaCry virus spared jail over malware charges," available online at *https://www.theguardian.com/technology/2019/jul/26/marcus-hutchins-wannacry-ransomware-malware-charges*, April 22, 2024

[KNOW23] "Who is Kevin Mitnick?," available online at *https://www.knowbe4.com/products/who-is-kevin-mitnick/*, April 22, 2024.

[WALL24] Kiernan, John. "Credit Card Fraud Statistics," available online at *https://wallethub.com/edu/cc/credit-card-fraud-statistics/25725*, March 4, 2024

2

CYBERTHREATS

There are many types of cyberthreats that victimize individuals, businesses, and governments. A complete list is difficult to compile because existing threats mutate and new threats continuously arise. The following chapter discusses the most significant types of cyberattacks.

ACCOUNT TAKEOVER (ATO) ATTACKS

Account takeover attacks occur when a bad actor obtains the account ID and password of a legitimate user and uses that information to log into the account as if he were the legitimate user. ATO attacks are increasing in number. A study by Javelin Strategy & Research showed that in 2021, over 15 million adults in the United States were affected by ATO attacks [VERIF22].

Targets of Account Takeover Attacks

The types of accounts that are typically targeted by an ATO include any type of account from which the bad actor can profit. This may include withdrawing funds, making purchases of expensive products that can be kept or resold, cashing in rewards points (e.g., frequent flyer miles for trips). Bad actors also sell stolen account information to other criminals who will exploit it. The following types of accounts are commonly targeted by an ATO attack:

a. Financial accounts like checking accounts, savings accounts, credit card accounts or investment portfolios.

b. Government accounts like Medicare, Medicaid, or welfare benefits.

    c. Frequent flyer accounts.

    d. Loyalty accounts with hotels, casinos, and resorts that provide reward dollars or points.

    e. Social media accounts, which can be hijacked and used to influence friends, followers and contacts.

How Bad Actors Obtain Victim Accounts and Passwords

There are numerous possible sources for obtaining a victim's credentials. The more common ones include the following:

    a. Buying credentials on the dark Web that may have been revealed by data breaches.

    b. Using social engineering techniques to get them directly from the victim.

    c. Credential stuffing. In this case, bad actors use bots (computers they control) to repeatedly attempt to log into accounts using account IDs and passwords that were used for other accounts. Users that reuse passwords are especially vulnerable to this type of attack.

    d. Phishing attacks, which begin with emails, text messages or calls that disguise the source hoping the victim will take actions that are not in their best interests.

    e. Keystroke loggers, which can be hardware devices or software applications that are surreptitiously installed on devices to record keystrokes made on the device. They can capture information like account IDs and passwords.

    f. Using brute force password cracking tools to test all possible passwords for an account.

    g. Fake Web sites that mimic legitimate sites to collect logon credentials of victims.

Outcomes of an ATO Attack

The outcomes of an ATO attack include the following:

    a. Credentials can be used to make high-end purchases on Web sites. The nefarious actor either keeps or sells the products, and the victim pays for them.

b. Identity theft can cost thousands of dollars and continue for years before being corrected.

c. Bank or brokerage accounts can suffer large withdrawals or a transfer of significant assets. The worst-case scenario would be a loss of the victim's life savings.

d. Virtual assets associated with online games can be stolen.

e. Compromised email accounts can be used to send spam to everyone in the victim's contact list.

f. Cryptocurrency held by the victim can be transferred to the nefarious actor's wallet.

Recognizing ATO Attacks

Some of the ways to recognize that an ATO attack has occurred are as follows:

a. Account activity notifications, possibly via text messages, that the account has been logged into when it should not have been.

b. Account activity notifications that indicate that a new device, IP address, or location is involved in a login.

c. A significant number of failed login attempts on the account.

d. The account password was changed.

e. Unrecognized activity, e.g., charges or withdrawals, has occurred.

f. Modified contact information associated with the account (e.g., a new email address or telephone number is now associated with the account).

g. Unusual social media posts or messages associated with the account.

Avoiding an Account Takeover Attack

Some of the ways to avoid being the victim of ATOs are as follows:

a. Use multifactor authentication (MFA).

b. Always use strong passwords.

c. Do not use the same account ID or password for multiple accounts.

d. Change all passwords regularly.

    e. If possible, set limits on the number of failed login attempts that can occur before the account is locked.

    f. Set up notifications to be created when a new device has logged into the account or when any changes are being made to the account.

BOTS

Bots, also known as *zombies*, are computing devices that have been taken over by a bad actor. These compromised devices communicate with a command and control center that sends them instructions. Devices like desktop computers, laptops, smart phones, routers, Web cameras, and Internet of Things (IoT) devices can become bots. A large collection of bots is called a *botnet* or *bot army*. The bad actor that is in control of a botnet is referred to as a *bot herder* or a *bot master*. Botnets are often rented out by their "owners" to other cybercriminals.

Malicious bots are used for numerous criminal activities such as

- Delivering spam
- Distributed denial of service (DDoS) attacks
- Brute force password cracking tools
- Credential stuffing attacks
- Mining cryptocurrency
- Participating in click fraud scams

Computing devices can be turned into bots if malicious software is installed on them. This software can be installed on a computer if the owner opens an infected email attachment, goes to an infected Web site, or installs an application that contains a trojan horse within it.

Red Flags Indicating a Computer Might be a Bot

Some indications that a computer might have been taken over and is acting as a bot are as follows:

    a. The device's fan and hard drive may be running at times that the computer is not being actively used.

    b. It takes longer than normal for the computer to shut down. This might indicate that malware is running in the background.

c. The computer appears to be much slower than normal because most of its resources are tied up with bot-related activities.

d. Access to the Internet is much slower than normal. This could indicate that the computer is part of a DDoS attack or is sending out spam emails.

e. The Windows Task Manager lists applications or background processes that are unfamiliar. Task Manager might also show that a very large percentage of the CPU time is being consumed by unfamiliar processes.

f. The battery charge on a laptop or smart phone does not last as long as it used to. This could indicate that the device has significantly more activity going on than is known.

g. Advertisements pop up on the computer's screen at times when a Web browser is not being used. This could indicate that a background process is connected to the Internet.

h. The computer crashes without any warning.

Preventing a Computer from Becoming a Bot

Steps that can be taken to prevent a computer from becoming a bot are similar to steps to protect it from other malware. These steps include the following:

a. Apply all available updates and patches to the operating systems and browsers.

b. Install antivirus software on the computer.

c. Set up a firewall to protect the device.

d. Adding an ad blocker to the Web browser can prevent potentially corrupt online ads from being seen and possibly clicked.

e. Download software only from reputable Web sites. While this is not a guarantee of protection, it is always safer to avoid Web sites from unreliable sources.

f. Do not open unexpected email attachments, especially ones from unknown senders.

g. Be suspicious of emails that encourage the recipient to click on links embedded in them.

Recover a Computer That Has Become a Bot

a. Disconnect the computer from the Internet.

b. Restart the computer in Safe Mode.

c. Run a current version of a legitimate antivirus software package like Norton, Bitdefender, or Avast. Follow any instructions that the antivirus software instructs be taken.

d. Restart the computer.

e. Make sure the operating system, browser, and applications have all updates and patches.

CREDENTIAL STUFFING ATTACKS

Credential stuffing attacks occur when bad actors attempt to log into a Web site or application using credentials (account IDs and passwords) that have been exposed via a previous data breach. They are relying on users' tendencies for using the same IDs and passwords for multiple places. (Additional details on this form of attack are provided in the "Passwords" chapter of this book.)

CROSS-SITE SCRIPTING (XSS) ATTACKS

A *cross-site scripting* (XSS) attack is set up by a nefarious actor injecting a malicious script or executable code into a legitimate Web site that is vulnerable to this type of malware. Typically, this malware is in the form of JavaScript code that will be run on the unwitting victim's browser when he visits the infected Web site. JavaScript is a programming language embedded in Web pages that runs on the user's browser. It adds functionality and the ability for the Web page to interact dynamically with the user.

For example, a nefarious actor can inject JavaScript into a comment box of a legitimate Web site. When a user goes to that Web site and clicks on the comment field, that will cause the JavaScript code to execute on the victim's computer. In some cases, the user only needs to load the infected page or hover the mouse over a field on the page like a hyperlink to cause the XSS code to execute.

What an XSS Attack Can Do

An XSS attack can result in the following:

a. Capture the victim's activity by sending every keystroke to a Web site that is controlled by the nefarious actor. This can provide access to the victim's bank or credit card account details, including account IDs and passwords.

b. Cause a login form to appear on the Web site. The user could be tricked into thinking that he needs to enter his credentials on it. This would allow the bad actor to learn his account ID and password.

    c. Obtain cookie data from the victim's computer. This could include details like account IDs and passwords for other Web sites.

    d. Perform activities on the Web site that have not been authorized by the user. For example, the XSS code could change the user's password on the site. This would give the bad actor control of the account.

Protecting Against XSS Attacks

The initial line of protection for XSS attacks is for the developer of the Web site to prevent such code from being installed on the Web site in the first place. Steps the owner of a Web site can take include the following:

    a. Ensure the server is running the most recent version of the operating system and Web hosting software.

    b. Website developers should never trust text that is entered into their Web pages by users. Input should always be sanitized to prevent executable code from being uploaded to the web site. Specifically, the input should be scanned to ensure that there is no HTML (Hypertext Markup Language) code in it.

    c. Install a Web Application Firewall (WAF) to protect the Web site.

    d. The organization that owns the Web site should conduct penetration testing to ensure that the Web site is not vulnerable to XSS attacks.

Some precautions that the average user can take to help protect themselves from an XSS attack are as follows:

    a. Ensure that the operating system and browser have the most current updates and patches.

    b. Use a browser that provides additional security. Some of the best browsers are Firefox, Google Chrome, Chromium, and Brave.

CRYPTOJACKING

Cryptojacking is the unauthorized use of another person's electronic devices to mine cryptocurrencies like Bitcoin, Ethereum, Dogecoin, or Monero. Crypto mining code can be installed on a computer if a malicious link is clicked, an infected email attachment is opened, or the browser goes to a Web site with malicious JavaScript code.

The motive for the bad actors to engage in this form of attack is that they get to keep all the profit, i.e. the cryptocurrency coins, while pushing the costs, primarily electricity and computing power, onto the victim. The amount of computing power it takes to earn a cryptocurrency coin has increased so much that it is challenging to make a profit at it using legitimate methods. An article posted on *TechTarget* stated that in 2022, mining just a single bitcoin costs an average of $35,000 [TECH22]. If someone else is responsible for all of the costs, then mining cryptocurrencies can be significantly more profitable.

Personal computers and laptops are not the only devices that can be hijacked to perform crypto mining. Cryptojacking can affect devices like servers, routers, cloud computers, and smart phones.

Instances of cryptojacking are on the rise. According to *SonicWall*, there were a record number of 129.3 million hits in 2022 [SONIC23]. The number of hits by mid-2023 had reached 332.3 million, which was an increase of 399%. It is likely that this lucrative income stream for bad actors will continue to grow in the foreseeable future.

Effects of Cryptojacking

a. The device's CPU may be running at a higher-than-normal rate.

b. Response times on the device will be slower than normal.

c. It leaves the device susceptible to other malware.

d. Costs for additional electricity and cooling requirements will accrue for the victim.

e. Devices can wear out more quickly than normal.

f. The additional load can lead to instability and possible errors like a "blue screen."

g. The electronic device may be running at full capacity any time it is turned on.

h. The computer may overheat. If its fan is constantly running, that may be a sign of infection.

Avoiding Cryptojacking

Steps to avoid being the victim of cryptojacking include:

a. Follow the advice listed later in this chapter to prevent phishing attacks.

b. Periodically review the software running on the device.

c. Update default passwords for devices like smart TVs, wireless routers, and Web cameras.

    d. Install an ad blocker on all Web browsers. Cryptojacking scripts frequently are installed though online ads so blocking ads can help protect from this danger.

    e. Install a browser extension that specifically defends against cryptojacking software. Examples of these extensions include minerBlock, No Coin, NoMiner, and Anti Miner.

Removing Cryptojacking Software

If a computer is infected with cryptojacking malware, these steps can help to remove it:

    a. Restart the device in Safe Mode.

    b. Run a current version of a legitimate antivirus software package like Norton, Bitdefender, or Avast.

    c. Restart the device.

    d. Make sure the operating system and all software are current.

DENIAL OF SERVICE ATTACKS (DoS AND DDoS)

Denial of service attacks are when a bad actor attempts to prevent legitimate users from accessing a Web site, application, or organization by overwhelming it with fake traffic. In many instances, the traffic inundating the victim comes from bots, i.e. computers that have been taken over by bad actors. If all of the traffic is coming from a single computer, then the attack is a DoS attack. If the bad actor is using multiple devices to flood the victim, then it is referred to as a *distributed denial of service* (DDoS) attack.

Each contact with the DoS victim's Web site or application has been designed to keep the target as busy as possible. If the target system is kept busy dealing with fake activity, then it will not be able to handle legitimate users or customers. A company that is dependent on e-commerce can be crippled if its customers are prevented from getting to its Web site and making purchases.

Some examples of how cyberattackers can mount a DDoS attack are listed here. This list will always be changing because DDoS attacks evolve constantly. As defenders learn to better deal with existing DoS attacks, new methods of DoS attacks are devised.

    a. Volume-based attacks: The bad actor uses his botnet to overwhelm the site with tens of thousands or hundreds of thousands of legitimate looking requests.

b. Protocol attacks: The bad actor exploits weaknesses in the OSI (Open Systems Interconnection) protocols used to communicate with a Web site. A SYN flood attack overwhelms the target with handshake requests. The victim site attempts to deal with every request but cannot keep up with them.

c. Fragmentation attack: The bad actor breaks legitimate requests into numerous fragments and submits each piece very slowly. The Web site is kept busy waiting for and handling these requests and cannot deal with requests from legitimate users.

Purposes of DDoS Attacks

Some of the reasons that DoS and DDoS attacks are launched vary, but some of the more common motives are as follows:

- *Extortion*: Bad actors extort businesses to pay or threaten that the victim's Web site will be attacked and potentially shut down.
- *Hacktivism*: A group of hacktivists attack the Web sites of businesses, organizations, or governments they dislike.
- *Cyberwarfare*: One nation/state attacks the businesses or government agencies of another nation/state.
- *Competition*: An organization may attack a competitor. If the competitor can be weakened or put out of business, the attacker can gain market share in the industry.
- *Online gaming*: DDoS attacks against gaming sites are common. They are launched to disrupt competitors to either take down a server or slow the victim's games.

Individuals Are Affected Only Indirectly

The average user is not typically the target of a DoS or DDoS attack because targets are usually businesses or Web sites. There are two ways in which a user can be affected by a DoS attack:

1. The Web site or business being accessed is down because of an ongoing DoS or DDoS attack. If this is the case, there is nothing a user can do except be patient. Repeatedly trying to log into the site may make the attack on the site slightly worse.

2. The user's computer has been taken over and is being used as a bot helping to assist in a DDoS attack. In this case, the user should follow the instructions in the "Bots" section of this chapter to remove malware from his computer.

DRIVE-BY DOWNLOAD ATTACKS

A *drive-by download* attack occurs without the user intending or knowing about it. Frequently, it is as simple as going to a Web site that has been compromised or clicking a Web site's link. Drive-by attacks can be particularly challenging because they can occur when visiting legitimate Web sites.

Threats Posed by Drive-By Attacks

Some of the threats that a drive-by attack poses to unsuspecting users are as follows:

a. Adware can be installed on devices. This will lead to pop-up ads and likely a slow-down of the device's performance.

b. Devices can be turned into bots. Bots are computers that have been infected with malware and are controlled by a bad actor. Bots frequently participate in illegal actions like DDoS attacks, sending out spam, participating in credential stuffing attacks, or assisting with click fraud traffic.

c. A keylogger can be installed on the device. This can result in bad actors learning the account IDs and passwords of all Web sites and applications that are logged onto.

d. Ransomware can be installed on the device.

How Drive-By Attacks May Occur

1. A bad actor compromises a Web page by exploiting a security flaw on the website's software.

2. An unsuspecting user uses an Internet browser to view that web page.

3. The malware is downloaded onto the device if its browser and operating system are not capable of defending against this malware.

4. The malware controls the device.

Avoiding Drive-By Attacks

Steps to avoid being the victim of a drive-by attack include:

a. Using a secure browser can also reduce the odds of a drive-by download.

b. Apply all available updates and patches to the operating systems and browsers.

    c. Drive-by attacks can affect mobile devices, so ensure that all updates have been installed on smart phones and tablets.

    d. Install antivirus software onto the computer and keep it updated.

    e. Adding an ad blocker to the Web browser can prevent users from seeing (and clicking on) potentially infected online ads.

    f. Removing any unneeded or obsolete applications, add-ons and plugins from the device reduces its attack surface. This action can help reduce the chances of being the victim of drive-by and other attacks.

    g. Download software only from reputable Web sites. While this is not guarantee of protection, it is always safer to avoid Web sites that are not mainstream.

Preventing Drive-By Attacks for Web Site Owners

Individuals and organizations that set up and host Web sites must take steps to prevent drive-by attacks. The steps they can take include the following:

    a. Ensure that the servers have the most recent patches for the operating system and Web site support software.

    b. Purge the server of any unused software to reduce its attack surface.

    c. Implement a Web Application Firewall (WAF) to monitor and filter Web site traffic.

    d. Set up the Web site to use the secure protocol HTTPS instead of the older and less secure HTTP protocol.

    e. Use strong passwords for administration accounts so bad actors cannot assume control of the site.

INSIDER ATTACKS

An *insider attack* is an incident where a person that is within an organization uses his or her knowledge and access to attack the organization. Insider attacks can be especially damaging because an insider likely has detailed knowledge about the organization's operations. Equifax stated that 60% of data breaches are caused by insider threats [EQUI24].

Insider threats can be either intentional or unintentional. An *intentional* attack occurs when the insider deliberately exploits his position to make the attack occur. An *unintentional* attack is a result of either negligence or an accident but can be just as damaging as an intentional attack. SoftActivity, a company that specializes in employee monitoring software, estimates that two out of every three insider threat incidents are caused by negligence [SOFT24].

People Who Can Be Involved in Insider Attacks

An insider can be in any of the following roles:

a. Employees

b. Board members

c. Contractors

d. Vendors

e. Custodians

f. Repair person

g. Former employees

h. Partners

i. Interns

Recognizing an Insider Threat

Insider threats vary, but exhibit certain associations and characteristics. The following list provides some of these:

a. Insiders who are at risk financially: A person in this position might be likely to look for ways to make extra money. One source of extra income could be by selling his employer's confidential information.

b. An employee who constantly seems to be angry at coworkers and management.

c. Employees who have worked at multiple companies in a short period of time

d. Employees who are downloading an excessive number of files or documents

e. Employees who are in the office or connect remotely at unusual hours. They might be diligent workers, but they also might be stealing corporate secrets due to the lack of oversight.

Minimizing the Damage of an Insider Attack

Some of the steps that can be taken to minimize the damage of an insider attack include the following:

a. Remove access as soon as an employee or contractor quits or is released.

b. If any employee is promoted to a new position, remove any access they no longer need.

c. Periodically audit the access for all employees and stakeholders and reduce it where appropriate.

d. Engage in the ongoing training of employees in "cyber-hygiene."

e. Ensure that all company-provided computers have the proper types of security software and protocols.

f. Minimize all employee and stakeholder access as much as possible. This is referred to as *zero trust approach*.

One final comment on insider threats is that they do not exist only at work. They are possible at home, as well. Many outsiders have access to the average home and potentially have access to all of the electronic devices an employee brings home. Some examples include

a. Friends

b. Children's friends

c. Guests at an event like a party

d. Repairmen

e. Hired help like babysitters, maids, painters, and cleaners

f. House sitters watching a house when the family is on vacation

g. Dog walker

h. Neighbors who can access the Wi-Fi from their homes or properties

MALVERTISING

Many Web sites display advertisements to generate income. *Malvertising* or "malicious advertising" is a cyber threat that infects digital ads displayed on legitimate web sites with malicious code. Targets of malvertising include mobile devices, desktop computers, laptops, and tablets. Examples of exactly how ads can be infected include the following:

a. Text or banner ads can contain malware in them. Even if they are not clicked on, they can infect an unprotected browser or computer.

b. Ads that contain video are a risk because the video file may contain malicious links that, when followed, could infect the device.

c. Ads can contain compromised URLs that lead to corrupted Web sites.

Malvertising Threats

Malvertising poses a number of threats to computers including the following:

a. Browsers can be redirected to malicious Web sites.

b. Malvertising can install ransomware, spyware, viruses, or other malicious software onto a computer.

c. Malvertising code can infect computers and turn them into bots.

d. A computer's performance can be significantly degraded when malicious software is running on it.

Avoiding Malvertising

Steps that should be taken to avoid being the victim of malvertising include the following:

a. Install a pop-up blocker on all web browsers. Doing this will prevent ads from being displayed on the computer.

b. Keep all software, including the operating system and browsers, up to date.

c. Install antivirus (AV) software on all computers. Choose a reputable vendor and once the antivirus has been installed, keep it updated.

d. Do not click on ads that have spelling errors or seem to be unprofessional. Those can be signs that they contain malvertising.

e. Do not click on ads that make offers that are too good to be true.

f. Disable Javascript and Flash from running in the browser.

g. Enable the "click-to-play" plugin feature in the browser. When this is enabled, it gives the user control over which plugins will run on their machine.

Removing Malvertising

Steps to remove malvertising from a computer include:

a. Disconnect the computer from the Internet.

b. Restart the computer in Safe Mode.

c. Run a current version of a legitimate antivirus software package like Norton, Bitdefender, or Avast. Follow any instructions that the AV (antivirus) software provides.

d. Restart the computer.

e. Make sure the operating system, browser, and applications have all updates and patches.

MALWARE

Malware is a term that refers to "MALicious softWARE." Many of the cyber threats described in this chapter are examples of malware. Some types of malwares are as follows:

a. Adware

b. Cryptojacking software

c. Keyloggers

d. Malvertising

e. Ransomware

f. Scareware

g. Spyware

h. Trojan horse

i. Virus

j. Wipers

k. Worms

l. XSS

MAN-IN-THE-MIDDLE ATTACKS (MitM)

Man-in-the-Middle attacks occur when a bad actor is able to intercept communications between two parties without their knowledge, for example between a user's web browser and the website it's connected to. This position allows the criminal to eavesdrop and potentially modify the information being exchanged. Man-in-the-Middle attacks cost about $2 billion in losses annually according to a 2020 report by Accenture [ASTRA23].

Situations that can lead to a Man-in-the-Middle attack include the following:

- Communications between a user and a Web site they have opened
- Two individuals communicating on platforms like Zoom, Facebook Messenger, or WhatsApp
- Communications between two email servers
- Malicious Wi-Fi networks
- Using Web sites that do not employ the HTTPS (Hypertext Transfer Protocol Secure) protocol

Protecting Against MitM Attacks

Steps that can help protect users against MitM attacks are as follows:

- Use a VPN when connecting to Wi-Fi networks, especially public ones.
- Secure home Wi-Fi routers by changing the default password and selecting the WPA2 or WPA3 security protocol. Router firmware should be updated regularly. Check it at least every three to six months. More on this in chapter 16.
- Use MFA (Multifactor Authentication) so if account passwords are guessed or discovered the account will still be secure.
- Do not open or click suspicious links in emails from unknown senders. Many links in emails appear to send victims to legitimate web sites, but they actually lead to sites controlled by the bad actors. These fraudulent web sites may have login screens to capture the victim's credentials.
- Only download mobile applications from trusted sites like the Apple's App Store or the Google Play Store.
- Install malware and virus protection software on all devices and keep it up to date.
- Use only web sites that begin with "HTTPS" and have the locked padlock icon in the browser's address bar.

PHISHING

Phishing is a cyberattack that is a form of social engineering. The attacker sends the victim an email that appears to be coming from a legitimate source, hoping that the victim will take an action that is not in the user's best interest.

Phishing attacks often use *spoofing*, which conceals the sender's true email address and name to trick the user into assuming the email was sent by someone the user trusts or has a pre-existing relationship with. Examples of trustworthy legitimate emails sources often used as disguises by bad actors include the following:

a. Banks

b. The IRS

c. Medical entities like doctor's offices or hospitals

d. Accountants

e. Lawyers

f. Insurance companies

g. Recruiters or employment agencies

h. Political candidates or political parties

i. Charitable organizations

j. Religious leaders or organizations

When a physical letter is sent through the mail, there is no validation done to ensure that the return address on the envelope is accurate. The USPS does not attempt to check that the sender has provided accurate information. Any letter or package can be sent with a return address that appears to be from the IRS, a bank, or the utility company.

Emails have a similar lack of validation regarding who actually sent them. Most email is sent using a convention called the Simple Mail Transfer Protocol (SMTP). SMTP focuses on routing the email to the destination address with minimal emphasis on security. An email may be sent to several intermediate servers before reaching its destination.

Bad actors can send emails using a script instead of an email client like Outlook®. When emails are sent this way, the "Email From" value is not validated. According to Proofpoint, a cybersecurity company that specializes in email security, 3.1 billion emails with a spoofed domain are sent every day [PROOF24].

Typically, the bad actor wants the recipient to open a file that is attached to the email or click on a link in the body of the email. If the attachment is opened, then a virus within it installs itself on the victim's device and executes. If the link in the email is clicked, then the victim is directed to a web site that is identical to the legitimate site but was built by the bad actor. If the victim enters his credentials into the fake login page, then the bad actor is able to log into that account at any time.

Figure 2.1 shows an example of a phishing email that claims to be from the victim's bank. There are numerous "red flags" that show this is a phishing email. The first is that the salutation is generic. Typically, a legitimate email begins with "Dear Mr. Bourne" or a similar type of greeting. The second issue is that the URL link in the email's body does not match the bank's domain. It has the letter "c" instead of "k" in the link: "YourBanc.com" instead of the expected "YourBank.com." These types of discrepancies should be looked for in all emails.

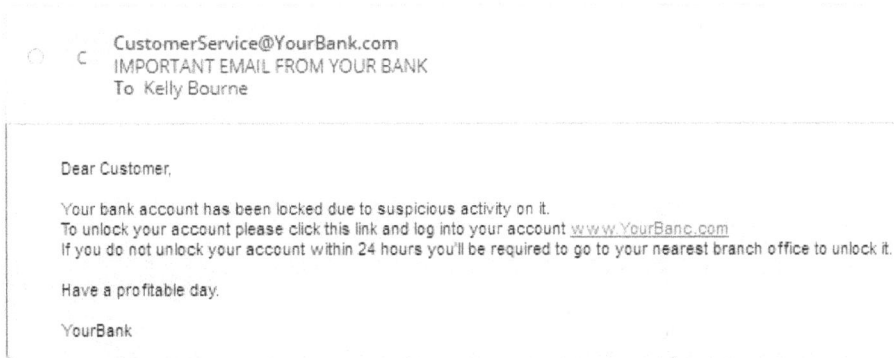

CustomerService@YourBank.com
IMPORTANT EMAIL FROM YOUR BANK
To Kelly Bourne

Dear Customer,

Your bank account has been locked due to suspicious activity on it.
To unlock your account please click this link and log into your account www.YourBanc.com
If you do not unlock your account within 24 hours you'll be required to go to your nearest branch office to unlock it.

Have a profitable day.

YourBank

FIGURE 2.1 Phishing email with a fake URL link

There is a way to learn more about the source of an email. Every email has header information that shows the source IP address as well as each of the steps or hops it took to get to the recipient. Each email provider is a little different, but they all show the header data for every email. For one ISP, the email must be opened, the ellipses on it clicked, and "View source" must be selected. Other vendors have options such as "Show Original," "View Raw Message," "Internet Headers" or "Raw Source."

Figure 2.2 shows the first part of the header for an email recently received from Amazon. Certain parts have been edited to remove personal information.

Mail source: Your Amazon.com order #11-50423-60426

```
Return-Path: <2023030723214857615e7b5b414c50p0na-
c3n8a7nlgm1xas@bounces.amazon.com>
Delivered-To: 3@2670
Received: from imap-director-132.dovecot.ord.rs.oxcs.net ([10.42.5.132])
     by imap-backend-154.dovecot.ord.rs.oxcs.net with LMTP
     id IEfGNg7HB2TdBwAA/hTGKw
     (envelope-from <2023030723214857615e7b5b41c50p0na-
c3n8a7nlgm1xas@bounces.amazon.com>)
     for <3@2672300>; Tue, 07 Mar 2023 23:21:50 +0000
Received: from mx.cox.rs.oxcs.net ([10.42.2.5])
     by imap-director-132.dovecot.ord.rs.oxcs.net with LMTP
     id +HKkNg7HB2R+dAAA+0ibbg
     (envelope-from <202303072321485750p0na-
c3n8a7nlgm1xas@bounces.amazon.com>)
     for <3@2672300.contexts.internal.oxcs.net>; Tue, 07 Mar 2023 23:21:50 +0000
X-original-to:
Received: from cxr-ibgw-5004a.stratus.cloudmark.com (cox.imta.a.cloudfilter.net
[35.174.158.239])
     (using TLSv1.2 with cipher ECDHE-RSA-AES256-GCM-SHA384 (256/256 bits))
     (No client certificate requested)
     by mx.cox.rs.oxcs.net (Postfix) with ESMTPS id 4PWWg25jTvz4x2M0
     for <              >; Tue,  7 Mar 2023 23:21:50 +0000 (UTC)
Received: from a13-45.smtp-out.amazonses.com ([54.240.13.45])
     by cmsmtp with ESMTP
     id ZgcwpHM2wFmcyZgcwpGuPl; Tue, 07 Mar 2023 23:21:50 +0000
X-CX-ORIG-RCPT:
Authentication-Results: cxr-ibgw-5004a.stratus.cloudmark.com;
     dkim=pass header.d=amazon.com header.b=SH5aVqOb;
     dkim=pass header.d=amazonses.com header.b=A6LmbfFm;
     dmarc=pass header.from=amazon.com
X-Authority-Analysis: v=2.4 cv=R6AQpPdX c=1 sm=1 tr=0 ts=6407c70e b=1
cx=a_idp_c a=KG8NcIsl2nfyhfehjbjRxA==:117 a=KG8NRxA==:17
a=vggBfdFIAAAA:8 a=Hgn-wnRn1-cA:10 a=O76VCmqbo-wA:10 a=sWKEhHoA:10
a=hRrdCNPZbloljm5sCd0A:9 a=QEXdDO2ut3YA:10 a=7AhZZqovGUgA:10
a=v3TBYn3wRilA:10 a=DSouV4xLakcA:10 a=YJOkmVJ-hAAA:10 a=SSiAAA:8
```

Close

FIGURE 2.2 Email header data

Understanding email header data is not intuitive or particularly easy. If a user wants to learn this skill, it can be done if they are willing to spend time researching and learning it. An alternative is to use one of the free online tools that will perform the analysis automatically. MxToolBox's Email Header Analyzer is one such tool. Go to the tool's Web site at *https://mxtoolbox.com* and paste the email header data into it. The tool will examine the data and indicate whether the email's source has been spoofed.

Variations of Phishing Attacks

There are several types of phishing schemes. The most common ones are described in the following sections.

Basic Phishing

A basic phishing attack sends phishing emails out to thousands or even hundreds of thousands of potential victims. This approach has no personalized information in the email. For example, if the purported sender is a bank, there is no guarantee that any of the victims actually has an account with that bank. Sending out emails is essentially free, so if the perpetrators are sending thousands of them and even a tiny percentage of recipients fall for this scam, then it is profitable for the bad actors.

Spear Phishing

A spear phishing attack involves additional effort on the part of the bad actors. They spend time researching the potential victim and then customize the details of the phishing email sent to each specific recipient. For example, they could examine the social media presence of the victim and tie the email to his interests. If the victim posts pictures of golf courses on his Facebook page, then the phishing email may be an offer for golf equipment or a reasonably priced round of golf at a local country club. The victim may fall for the scam, believing the sender actually knows him.

Whale Phishing

Whale phishing is an attempt to victimize a high-level officer in an organization or otherwise important individual. The idea being that individuals like this have either more money to steal or access to important information that the average victim doesn't have. Phishing emails sent to this class of victim will be customized similarly to the way a spear phishing attack is prepared.

Vishing

Vishing is a variation of phishing that uses a phone instead of email as the attack vector. The bad actor calls the victim and pretends to be someone else. For example, they might impersonate an employee from the IT department where the victim works or they might claim they are from a bank's fraud department. The goal is to trick the victim into revealing their password or other account information over the phone.

Often, when the bad actor calls the potential victim, the caller ID number will have been spoofed so it appears the call is coming from the bank or whatever legitimate organization the bad actor claims to be a part of. Spoofing a caller ID is not difficult to perform.

Smishing

Smishing is similar to a phishing attack but involves text messages instead of voice or emails. The name "smishing" is a combination of SMS (Short Message Service) and phishing. One reason that smishing attacks are becoming more common is that people are more likely to click on a link in a text message than in an email. A Web page posted by IBM quotes a survey that the click rates for SMS texts are between 8.9 and 14.5% compared to a click rate of 1.33% for emails [IBM23].

Catphishing

Catphishing is a social engineering scam where the bad actor pretends to be someone else in the hope of developing a long-distance relationship with the victim. The perpetrator frequently creates an online presence for their fake persona. Once a relationship has been established with the victim, the bad actor will likely manipulate the victim into loaning or giving them money.

Signs of catphishing emails include the following:

a. The scammer is never willing to meet in person or participate in a video chat session. This is likely because the photograph they posted on their social media accounts almost certainly is of someone else.

b. Early on, they aggressively attempt to deepen the relationship. A relationship that normally would develop over months is compressed into days or weeks.

    c. They always have an excuse for why they cannot meet in person or online in a video session. Their excuses frequently include illness, severe accidents, deaths in the family, catastrophes, and unbelievable amounts of bad luck.

    d. If something seems too good to be true, then it probably is not true. If the potential partner seems too perfect then this is probably a catphishing scam.

Avoiding Phishing Scams

Steps to avoid being the victim of phishing scams include the following:

    a. Be cautious if the email address is not recognized. Even for an email that is from a recognized individual, know there is always the chance that their email account has been taken over by a bad actor.

    b. Look for email address domains that are just a little different or odd. For instance, they might have replaced a letter with a number, e.g., microsoft-supp0rt.com.

    c. Beware of emails from unknown senders that have attachments.

    d. Beware of emails that open with a generic greeting like "Dear Customer."

    e. Beware of emails with attachments from known individuals who have never sent attachments before.

    f. Beware of emails where the recipient is copied on the email, but none of the other recipients are familiar.

    g. Be suspicious of emails that were sent outside of normal business hours for the organization's location.

    h. Beware of emails where the subject line does not seem to match the body of the email.

    i. Be cautious of emails that insist action must be taken immediately.

    j. Be suspicious of emails that refer to a previous email in the thread, but it is not familiar.

    k. Look for attachments with file extensions that are executable like exe, bat, com, or cmd.

l. Look for emails that urge the reader to click on a link or open an attachment.

m. Be cautious with emails with an offer that appears to be too good to be true.

n. Beware emails with links: when the mouse is hovered over these links, the address displayed may not match the Web site it is supposed to take the user to.

o. Be extremely suspicious of requests for personal information like social security numbers, account numbers, and passwords.

p. Be cautious with emails claiming that clicking on a link or opening an attachment will display lewd or embarrassing photos or show enticing information like a list of employee salaries.

RANSOMWARE

Ransomware is a form of malware that encrypts files on the computer or locks up the entire computer until a ransom is paid to unlock it. Chapter 3 covers ransomware in great detail.

ROOTKIT ATTACKS

A *rootkit attack* is one of the most serious types of malware attacks. When installed, a rootkit can give the bad actor complete access to the victim's computer. This includes the ability to turn off antivirus software running on the device. Rootkits are extremely difficult to detect and remove.

An operating system is an extremely complex type of software that allows a computer to respond to users, interact with devices like disk drives, memory, monitors, and the keyboard and mouse. The term "root" in computer programming refers to the highest level of access within the operating system. A rootkit attempts to bury itself as deeply in the operating system as possible. By accessing the highest level of the computer, it can stay hidden and have unlimited ability to cause damage. Being hidden so well allows a rootkit to remain on a computer or network for long periods of time. While it is there, a rootkit might set up a backdoor that allows the bad actor to install additional threats like ransomware or keyloggers or turn the device into a bot.

Well-known Rootkit Attacks

Some of the more infamous rootkit attacks were:

a. Flame targets Windows OS to record audio, screenshots, and keystrokes.

b. GameGuard is a rootkit designed to prevent cheat software from running when games are being played.

c. Machiavelli is the first rootkit that targeted the Mac OS X operating system.

d. NTRootkit is an early rootkit that targeted the Microsoft Windows operating system.

e. Stuxnet is a rootkit that attacked industrial control systems.

f. Zeus is a rootkit that steals banking information by acting as man-in-the-middle malware.

Determining If a Computer Has a Rootkit

Rootkits by their very nature hide themselves well. Some of the possible ways to recognize that a device has a rootkit on it are as follows:

a. Strange Web browser behavior is one way, for example, when the browser is redirected from the intended Web site to another one.

b. Performance of the device has degraded significantly.

c. Internet performance has degraded, as well.

d. Settings on the computer have changed and are unfamiliar.

e. The computer is crashing more frequently than it did in the past.

f. The computer is not responding to mouse or keyboard activity.

Rootkit Defensive Measures

The steps that can be taken to defend against rootkit attacks are similar to many other defensive measures:

a. Keep all software updated.

b. Install antivirus software.

    c. Be aware of phishing attempts and skeptical about opening attachments or clicking on links.

    d. Never attach a USB drive to a device unless there is no doubt that it is safe.

Removing a Rootkit

Removing a rootkit is more difficult than removing other forms of malware like viruses and trojan horses. An expert may be required to remove this form of malware.

If the decision is made to attempt the removal without consulting an expert, then rootkit removal software is needed. Some examples of these tools are Avast One, Sophos Rootkit Removal Tool, McAfee Labs Rootkit Remover, and AVG AntiVirus. Carefully follow the instructions that accompany the rootkit removal tool.

If the rootkit tool does not work, then a more drastic step is to completely rebuild the software on the device. The first step is to reformat the drive to remove all software from it. Then reload everything, including the operating system and all of applications either from scratch or from a previously-made backup. Obviously, this is a serious step, but there might not be any alternatives.

SCAREWARE

Scareware is a type of social engineering attack that tries to trick the victim into thinking there is something wrong with their device when nothing is actually wrong. It frequently takes the form of a pop-up message on the computer screen or phone with a warning that the device has been infected with a virus. The pop-up message claims that a link must be clicked or a call needs to be made to the displayed number immediately to remove the virus, usually for a specified amount of money. In reality, the device is most likely not infected. Clicking on the link provided or calling the listed number typically results in the victim losing money. There is also the possibility of having another form of malware installed on the device. Additionally, many scammers will use the victim's credit card number to make additional unauthorized purchases with the card.

Scareware attacks attempt to frighten the victim into taking an action without taking time to consider whether taking that action is dangerous or not. An extremely common scareware theme is that the computer is infected with a virus. Other common scareware threats that might be encountered are as follows:

a. Child pornography has been detected on the device and that law enforcement agencies will be contacted, but clicking the link on the screen will delete it.

b. Jury duty obligation was missed. If a fine is not paid immediately, the victim will be arrested.

c. Money is owed to the IRS and if it is not paid immediately, the potential victim will be arrested.

d. A warrant for the victim's arrest has been issued by the local police or sheriff's department. Clicking the link or calling the number immediately is the only way to avoid being arrested.

Scareware can happen to anyone at any time. While I was writing this chapter my wife came into my office extremely upset about a message on her iPhone claiming that her phone was infected with a virus. I advised her that it was scareware, and she should just close that screen to solve the problem.

Avoiding Scareware

Some ways to protect against a scareware attack are as follows:

a. Load antivirus software from a reputable vendor on all devices and keep it updated.

b. Make sure that all software, including the browser, on the computer is up to date.

c. Install a pop-up blocker on the browser so these ads won't be displayed.

d. Unsolicited calls from a large vendor's technical support department are never legitimate.

e. When faced with a potential threat take a few moments to consider whether the threat is legitimate. Acting rashly will almost certainly make the situation worse.

f. Back up data regularly so it can be recovered if a scareware's link is accidentally clicked.

g.   Do some research on the Internet about the supposed claim before taking any action. If this is a scam, then something will almost certainly be posted about it on the Internet.

h.   Consult a trusted co-worked, friend or relative about this threat and ask them if they think it is valid.

Managing Scareware

The following steps can help shut down a scareware attack:

a.   Close the browser instead of clicking on the "X" in the upper right corner of the window displaying the scareware threat. This is advisable because some bad actors have coded the "X" button so clicking it actually opens additional pop-up windows.

b.   On a Windows machine, open the Task Manager by right-clicking the Task Bar at the bottom of the screen. If there are any processes listed that are taking a large percent of CPU time (greater than 50%), then delete them.

c.   On a Windows computer, enter "Control Panel" in the Windows search box. Select the "Programs" option. If the most recently installed program is unfamiliar, then select "Uninstall" for it.

d.   On a Mac computer, restart the machine and hold the "Shift" key as it reboots so it starts up in Safe Mode.

e.   Run an antivirus scan on the device. Run the most thorough scan option that is available.

f.   Clear the browser's cache and delete all cookies.

g.   Restart the device.

SPOOFING

Spoofing is when an attacker disguises the origin of a communication with the intent of tricking a victim. Bad actors frequently use spoofing as part of a social engineering attack. They want the potential victim to believe that the communication is legitimate. The following forms of communication can be spoofed.

Emails

It is fairly easy to spoof the "sender" field in an email, so it is wise to never assume that it is accurate. If the email seems unusual or oddly worded, such as encouraging that unusual action be taken or is pressuring for immediate action, then be extremely cautious.

Links

Links in emails and on Web site pages can easily be spoofed. One way to see the actual URL is to position the cursor over the link without clicking it. If the cursor is hovering the mouse over for a couple of seconds the actual URL will be displayed in the bottom left corner of the screen.

Figure 2.3 shows a screenshot of an email the author received while writing this book. At first glance, it appears to be a legitimate email from the Social Security Administration (SSA). It actually says it is from the SSA. It has what looks like the seal or logo of the SSA. The return email address is "@ssa.gov." The text in the body of the email sounds like something that a government agency would send out.

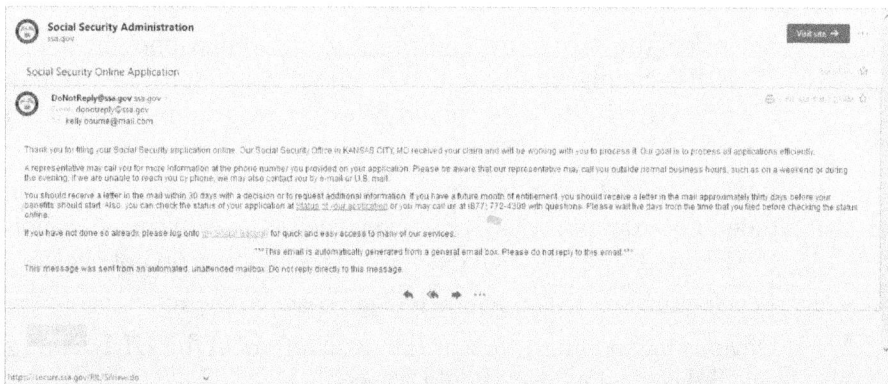

FIGURE 2.3 Spoofed URL

The first clue that this email was malevolent was that I hadn't filed a Social Security application. I following up on my suspicion by hovering over the "my Social Security" link toward the end of the text. The actual URL associated with the link is shown in the left-hand corner of the screen: *https:// secure.ssa.gov/RIL/SiView.do*.

The first part of the link, *secure.ssa.gov*, looks legitimate and the domain of ".gov" makes the email address appear to belong to the SSA. In reality, the *actual* domain in this URL is "SiView.do". If two domains appear to exist in a URL address, as in this example, the actual domain is the one at the end of the string. What appears to be the first domain value is strictly included to trick the viewer. I do not know who "SiView" belongs to, but it only took a quick Internet search to reveal that the ".do" domain refers to the Dominican Republic. Obviously, the U.S. Social Security Administration isn't operating out of the Dominican Republic.

If that link in the email had been clicked, I would have been directed to a Web site that looks just like the SSA login screen. Here, the unwary might enter personal information such as the social security number. This personal information would have been captured and possibly used to submit a false claim or for identity theft purposes.

Spoofed URLs can appear in emails, social media posts, pop-up windows, and on Web sites. In addition to URLs that contain multiple domains, other URLs that might be spoofed or otherwise dangerous include the following:

- URLs consisting entirely of numbers, for example *https://102.102.102.102*.
- Some lengthy URLs are converted to shortened ones by services like TinyURL, Sniply, Cuttly, and Bitly. Since it is impossible to know what the true URL is, the user should be extremely cautious about clicking on them.
- Legitimate Web sites do not usually contain hyphens or other symbols in them. For example, a URL like *www.microsoft-help.com* does not belong to Microsoft. If a link includes characters like this, do not click on it.
- Few legitimate URLs include a blank space in them.
- Obvious misspellings, such as the extra letters in the URL *www.googlee.com* indicate a link that should be avoided.

Text Messages

Text messages (SMS – Short Message Service) can be spoofed so it appears they were sent by someone other than the actual sender. This might be done to make the message appear to be coming from a family member, coworker, boss, friend, or a bank. If there are any suspicions about the source, then be extremely cautious.

Phone Calls

The caller ID shown on phone calls can be spoofed. Some scams utilize the ability to spoof a number to trick the victim into thinking the call is coming from the police, the IRS, a courthouse, or a bank. Once the victim has been tricked regarding the call's origination then a social engineering scam is that much easier to pull off.

Recent improvements in AI software now make it possible to imitate someone's voice with relatively little effort. Examples of peoples' voices may be available online at sites like Facebook or TikTok. One frequent scam that relies on voice impersonation is the "Grandparent" scam. In this swindle, the criminal calls an elderly victim impersonating their grandson or granddaughter. The fake "grandchild" claims to be in jail or being held in a foreign country. Unless the bail, fines, or other fees are paid, their grandchild will remain in jail. All too frequently, the grandparent panics and agrees to pay the fake bail.

Web Sites

A spoofed Web site can be set up to be identical to the Web site that it is mimicking. It is possible to navigate to a spoofed Web site by clicking a link embedded in a phishing email or on a corrupted Web site. The bad actor wants victims to log into this Web site with their credentials. This will allow the bad actor to capture them and likely use them for an account takeover attack.

Avoiding Spoofing

The following practices can help avoid being spoofed. Of course, there may be new ways of spoofing that have not been encountered yet.

a. Install antivirus protection on all electronic devices, including computers and smart phones.

b. Keep software on all electronic devices updated and patched.

c. Never click on URL links in emails. If it is necessary to go to a certain Web site, enter the address into a browser manually or use an address that is in the browser's "Favorites."

d. When being asked to take drastic action, such are pay out a large amount of money, confirm this request with the sender via another type of communication. Ideally speak to them face-to-face.

e. Be skeptical of emails or text messages that warn of dire consequences if the link leading to a Web site is not clicked.

SPYWARE

Spyware is a form of malware that monitors any activity on the device where it has been installed. Information that spyware captures on device will be transmitted to the bad actor without the consent of the device's owner. The monitoring might include

a. tracking all keystrokes made on the device

b. monitoring all Internet activity

c. capturing login credentials for any account that it is logged into

d. capturing credit card account numbers

e. recording the locations that a smart phone has traveled to

f. monitoring all emails being sent and received

How Spyware Gets Installed

Spyware can be secretly installed on a computer or smart phone in many ways. Some of the more common methods are as follows:

a. If the user opens an infected attachment on a phishing email.

b. Clicking on a malicious link in a phishing email or on an infected Web site.

c. Downloading games, movies, or music from a pirated Web site.

d. Downloading software from a Web site that is not trustworthy.

e. Downloading spyware disguised as a useful tool, like a hard disk cleaner.

Avoiding Spyware

Ways to avoid being affected by spyware include:

a. Install antivirus software and make sure it stays updated. Set it to scan the computer regularly, perhaps even daily.

b. Keep all computers and other devices updated and patched.

c. Set the browser on the computer so it does not accept cookies.

d. Do not open attachments or click on links in phishing emails.

e. Only download software from trustworthy sources.

f. Disable the AutoPlay setting on the computer.

g. Be wary of any movie, song, or game that is being offered for free.

h. Adjust the spam filter on the email application to minimize the number of spam emails that get into the inbox.

Spyware Red Flags

Indicators that a computer or mobile phone has been infected with spyware include:

a. The device's performance has slowed down significantly.

b. New icons have appeared in the computer's task bar.

c. The home page for the Internet browser has changed.

d. When browsing the Internet, the web site visited is not the intended destination site.

e. Significantly more pop-up ads are appearing when browsing the Internet.

f. The battery life on a mobile phone is not as long as it used to be.

Removing Spyware

Steps to remove spyware from a device are as follows:

a. Disconnect the device from the Internet.

b. Run a current version of a legitimate antivirus software package like Norton, Bitdefender, or Avast. Follow all the instructions from the antivirus software.

c. Restart the device.

Additional Steps to Take After a Spyware Attack

a. Change any passwords that might have entered on the device since it is very likely that the bad actor has captured them.

b. Anyone who has been a victim of a spyware attack should consider requesting a credit freeze on their credit report. If the bad actor was able to gather enough details about potential victims, then he might attempt to acquire new credit cards in their name. This step will help prevent that.

SUPPLY CHAIN ATTACKS

A *supply chain attack* does not directly attack the computers of users or organizations. Instead, the attack is made against a trusted third-party that is in the supply chain of the victims. The bad actor wants to comprise software or updates that will flow "downstream" to all of that vendor's clients.

The most widely known example of a supply chain attack was in 2020 against a software company named SolarWinds. This vendor provided system management tools for monitoring the computers and networks of their clients. This attack affected more than 18,000 clients using SolarWinds products [Tech23]. Among their clients were both corporations and government agencies.

Avoiding Supply Chain Attacks

A user or organization cannot completely protect itself against a supply chain attack because they have a trust relationship with their vendors. The steps that can be taken to minimize the damage of this form of threat are as follows:

a. Install monitoring tools internally that generate an alert in the event of suspicious behavior and activity on devices and network. This type of software is referred to as an Intrusion Detection System (IDS).

b. Identify and correct any vulnerabilities in computers and networks by conducting vulnerability testing. If necessary, bring in outside experts for this.

c. Encrypt all data. This includes data being moved from one computer to another ("data in motion") as well as data stored on a computer ("data at rest"). This can ensure that bad actors will not be able to use any data that is exfiltrated.

d. Implement a zero-trust model. This security model requires strict identity verification to access any data on the network.

e. Create a complete list of all software and hardware vendors. Have any of them been victims of cyberattacks?

f. On a regular basis, require that vendors assess their security precautions. They may already be performing self-assessment, but this will put them on notice that their clients are taking security seriously.

g. Develop an incident response plan. This step will not prevent a supply chain attack, but can help respond to one, and any other types of cyberattacks, more quickly and effectively.

TROJAN HORSES

The concept of a trojan horse started with the mythical Trojan War between the city of Troy and a coalition of Greek city-states. According to Homer's *The Iliad*, the Greeks laid siege to the city of Troy for 10 years without defeating the Trojans. Odysseus, one of the Greek leaders, devised the ruse of building a huge wooden horse secretly filled with soldiers as a gift to the victorious city of Troy. The remainder of the Greeks sailed their ships out of sight. The Trojans, thinking the war was over, dragged the horse into the city. That night as the city celebrated, Odysseus and the other soldiers exited the horse and opened the city gates for their comrades. The Greeks captured the city and slaughtered the inhabitants of Troy.

A computer related trojan horse, like its namesake, is not what it seems to be. It will present itself as a useful application, tool, or game, but it actually contains malware that will hurt the victim. Once the victim installs the trojan horse, damage is inevitable.

Trojan Horse Attack Examples

Some examples of trojan horse software are as follows:

a. Zeus: a trojan horse attack that attempts to steal banking credentials

b. ILOVEYOU: a trojan horse attack that enticed victims to find out who loved them by opening an email attachment

c. Emotet: another banking-related attack

d. Cryptolocker: a ransomware virus that was distributed as a trojan horse

Preventing Trojan Horse Attacks

Ways to avoid being the victim of a trojan horse attack are as follows:

a. Do not open attachments from unsolicited emails.

b. Do not click on links within an email that might be a phishing attack.

c. Keep the computer's software up to date.

d. Install antivirus software on the computer.

e. Be extremely skeptical of games, utilities, and movies that are available for free.

f. Download applications and games only from reputable sources.

g. Do not click on Web banners or unknown URLs.

h. Install a pop-up blocker on all browsers.

i. Be skeptical and suspicious of anything that seems too good to be true.

Removing a Trojan Horse

Steps to remove trojan horse software from a device are as follows:

a. Disconnect the device from the Internet.

b. Run a current version of a legitimate antivirus software package like Norton, Bitdefender, or Avast. Follow the instructions for the antivirus software.

c. Restart the device.

USB DEVICE ATTACKS

A USB drive (also known as a thumb drive or jump drive) might seem like a safe and convenient storage device, but they can also be targets of attack. They can hold malware that can infect any computer they are plugged into. Examples of the types of malware attacks that a USB drive can initiate are as follows:

a. install ransomware on any computer it is plugged into

b. infect any devices it is plugged into with a virus

c. install a keystroke logger on any device it is plugged into

d. install software to track all browser activity

e. provide the attacker with remote control of the infected computer

f. send a high-voltage surge into the USB port and destroy the computer it is plugged into

g. exfiltrate files or data from any device it is plugged into

AutoPlay Danger

One Windows setting that can make infected USB drives even more dangerous is AutoPlay or AutoRun. If this feature is set to "On," then whenever a device is connected to a Windows computer, executable files on it can automatically start running. Changing this setting to "Off" can help protect against USB malware attacks. Figure 2.4 shows the screen where this setting can be changed on a computer running the Windows 10 operating system. To get to that screen, right-click on the Windows icon in the lower left-hand corner, click on "Search," and enter "AutoPlay" in the search field.

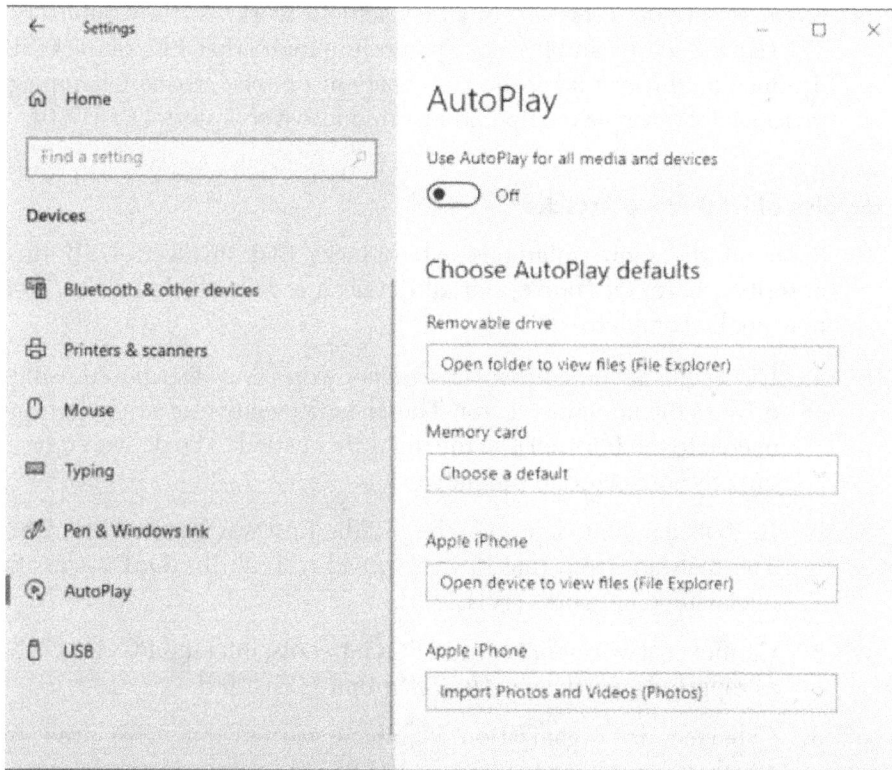

FIGURE 2.4 Changing the AutoPlay setting in Windows 10

USB Infections Move Both Ways

Infections related to USB drives can move in both directions. If a clean USB drive is connected to a computer or network that is infected with a virus, then the USB drive can be infected. Unless precautions are taken, the next computer this USB drive is connected to will also become infected.

USB DROP ATTACKS

A *USB drop attack* is when infected USB drives are scattered near the site that a bad actor intends to attack. The hope is that people will pick up one of the thumb drives and connect it to their personal or work computer. Penetration testers boast that this is an effective way to break into a company they are targeting, but does this sort of attack actually work? A study published in the 37th IEEE Security and Privacy Symposium found that 48% of the USB drives dropped on the ground at the University of Illinois Urbana-Champaign campus actually were picked up and inserted into a computer [ELIE16].

Examples of USB Drive Attacks

Some of the more infamous cyberattacks that involved USB drives are described here. Of course, not all details are definitively known, so this list may not be complete.

a. It is widely assumed that the Stuxnet worm was distributed using a USB drive as the infection vector. The Natanz facility was air-gapped (not connected to the Internet), so the malware needed to be delivered by a device directly connected to the network.

b. In 2008, a military laptop in the Middle East was infected by a USB drive. The malware from that device spread to both the DoD's classified and unclassified networks [WILL08].

c. Conficker, a worm that turned PCs into bots, infected PCs via USB drives, as reported an article in *The Telegraph* [TELE09].

d. Cybersecurity organization Mandiant warned that USB drive malware attacks were spiking in 2023 [TOUL23]. Two of these attacks were named "Sogu" and "Snowydrive."

Avoiding USB Attacks

a. Never insert an unknown USB drive into a computer.

b. Be suspicious of USB drives found or given out for free.

c. Do not use USB devices unless they are from a legitimate, trusted source.

d. Do not use the same USD drive on both work and personal computers.

e. To prevent code on a USB from executing automatically, change the AutoPlay settings on all Windows computers to "Off."

f.   Scan all new USB devices with the antivirus software running on the computer.

g.   If possible, scan USB drives for viruses on a Linux computer instead of a Windows computer.

h.   Scan USB drives on a stand-alone (not networked) computer to prevent infecting the entire network.

VIRUSES

A *virus* is a computer program that spreads itself by infecting files or other parts of a computer. For a virus to execute, a user must take action to initiate it. For example, a user might

a.   Open an infected email attachment.

b.   Click a malicious link in an email or on a web page.

c.   Insert an infected USB drive into a port.

d.   Visit a malicious Web page.

What Can a Virus Do?

When a virus executes, it can cause considerable damage. For example, it can

a.   Destroy files or destroy, i.e. "brick," the computer it is running on.

b.   Install ransomware on the victim's computer.

c.   Monitor activity including tracking keystrokes and web sites visited.

d.   Generate and send out emails in an attempt to spread themselves.

e.   Delete or corrupt files on the computer.

f.   Reformat the computer's hard drive which makes the computer effectively worthless.

Minimizing the Chances of Getting Infected with a Virus

a.   Install antivirus software from a reputable vendor. Make sure that the antivirus is updated and running regularly.

b.   Apply all patches and upgrades to the system, especially the operating system and browser.

    c. Be extremely cautious before opening email attachments.

    d. Avoid clicking on pop-up ads in the browser.

    e. Download files only from trustworthy sites and check all downloaded files for viruses.

    f. Never plug an unknown USB drive into the computer.

    g. Avoid using public Wi-Fi.

    h. Use strong passwords and multifactor authentication (MFA).

Removing a Virus from a Computer

The following steps can help remove a virus. If the antivirus software installed on the computer has different steps, then follow those instructions.

    a. Run a full system scan of the antivirus software that has been loaded onto the computer. Make sure that the antivirus software is updated and running regularly.

    b. Disconnect the computer from the Internet so the virus cannot spread.

    c. Reboot the computer in "Safe Mode."

    d. Run a scan with the antivirus software.

    e. If the antivirus software has identified a virus, then take the option to delete or quarantine it.

    f. Reboot the computer.

    g. Update the operating system and browser running on the computer.

    h. Change the passwords for any account accessed on this computer.

WATERING HOLE ATTACKS

A *watering hole attack* is a variation of a drive-by attack. The difference is that in this variation the bad actor installs malware on Web sites that his victims are likely to visit. For example, if the hacker wants to attack a financial services company, then he might install his malware on Web sites frequented by financial analysts and investment advisers.

The same steps used to prevent drive-by attacks will also help to protect against watering hole attacks.

WIPER ATTACKS

A *wiper attack* is designed to permanently delete data and files on the victim's computer. There is no ransom requested or monitoring of keystrokes, just irreversible destruction. Wiper attacks do not generate profit for the bad actor, so they are most likely initiated by hacktivists or nation-state actors. Wiper attacks are often delivered via phishing emails.

An example of a wiper attack was the Shamoon malware that effected Saudi Aramco in 2012. According to an article by *CNN Business*, 35,000 computers were damaged in just a few hours [CNN15]. Another example of a wiper attack was Dark Seoul in 2013, which attacked South Korean finance and media companies [FORT22].

Protecting Against a Wiper Attack

Precautions against wiper attacks include the following:

a. Have valid backups of all important files.

b. Keep up to date with all upgrades and patches.

c. Install antivirus software on all devices.

d. Keep alert for phishing emails.

WORMS

A computer *worm* is a type of malware that is able to replicate itself and infect other computers while remaining active on infected systems [TECH922]. It is able to do this by exploiting vulnerabilities in the operating systems or other software running on those computers. The biggest difference between worms and viruses is that worms do not require any assistance on the part of users to spread to other systems.

Some of the most infamous worms are as follows:

a. The Morris worm, released in 1988, is considered the first computer worm. It was released on a computer at the Massachusetts Institute of Technology (MIT) by a student. While it did not do any explicit damage, it spread incredibly fast and consumed computer resources so quickly that most computers on the nascent Internet stopped working.

   b. The ILOVEYOU worm, launched in 2000, spread by an email attachment. If the victim opened the email attachment, the worm would resend itself to every contact in the victim's Microsoft Outlook contact list. This worm reportedly affected as many as 45 million users [TECH922].

   c. WannaCry was ransomware that was spread by a worm in 2017. It spread by using a vulnerability in Microsoft Windows to over 200,000 computers worldwide. The cautionary note about the WannaCry attack is that there was *already* a patch available for the vulnerability it exploited, but it had not been installed on the victims' computers.

ZERO-DAY EXPLOITS

A *zero-day exploit* is one that takes advantage of a vulnerability in computer software, firmware, or hardware that has just been discovered. A zero-day vulnerability can be relatively trivial or it can present a massive security risk to software that millions of users and organizations rely upon.

The vulnerability may have existed since the product was first created or it might have been introduced by changes that have been made to the application recently.

Virtually all software has vulnerabilities that have not been discovered yet, so every operating system and application is potentially susceptible to a zero-day attack. Examples of types of software that have impacted by this type of vulnerability include the following:

   a. Operating systems for computers and smart phones

   b. Business application software like Microsoft Word, Excel, and Outlook

   c. Internet browsers like Firefox, Chrome, and Safari

   d. Games

   e. Open-source software

   f. Internet of Things (IoT) devices

Potential victims of zero-day attacks can be any people or organizations using computers or smart phones. This includes the following:

   a. Individuals

   b. Small, medium, and large businesses

c. Government agencies

d. Schools and universities

e. Non-profits and NGOs (non-government organizations)

f. Intelligence agencies

In the best-case scenario, a white hat hacker will uncover a new vulnerability first. He will provide details about it to the vendor so a fix can be developed and distributed to users. Most vendors have a "bounty" program that pays researchers for the zero-day exploits they find. This encourages researchers to reveal bugs to the vendor, instead of allowing them to be exploited by bad actors. Selling zero-days to a vendor can be quite lucrative. Google paid out $10 million via its bounty program in 2023 [VULN24], and $63 million in the last 10 years of its bounty program [MEN23].

In the worst-case scenario, a black hat hacker will uncover a zero-day vulnerability first and will either use that knowledge himself or sell the details to someone else who will take advantage of it. The amount of money being offered by brokers who purchase them is enormous. A startup vendor named Crowdfense is offering millions of dollars for zero-days that can break into iPhones and Android phones as well as vulnerabilities in Chrome and Safari browsers [TECH24].

Can a User Protect Themselves from a Zero-Day Exploit?

Unfortunately, since a zero-day exploit has not been seen before, it is not possible for an individual to protect themselves from zero-day attacks. The best that can be done is to keep all of the software on devices current. This includes operating systems, application software, browsers, and antivirus software. As soon as the affected vendor learns about a new exploit, it will create and distribute a patch to defense against it. Installing these patches as quickly as possible is the best protection that can be taken.

Unfortunately, even after a zero-day vulnerability has been identified and a fix becomes available, not all users choose to install the patches that would protect them from this specific vulnerability. There have been numerous incidents when users or organizations were hit by an exploit for which a patch had been available for some time. The WannaCry ransomware virus affected hundreds of thousands of computers in 2017. That attack occurred even though a patch that would have prevented it had been available for a month [CLOU24].

Some reasons why individuals and organizations do not apply patches immediately after they are available from the vendors are as follows:

a. Applying a patch might cause problems in the system. Some individuals and organizations are not willing to take this chance.

b. Patching a system typically requires that it be taken offline and thus is not available to users during that window of time.

c. Numerous patches are regularly released for all of the software they have. Applying all of them is time consuming.

d. The organization does not have the staff or the expertise to apply patches.

e. Patching is not seen as a priority by management.

There are some situations where no patches for zero-day or any other vulnerabilities exists. One example is if the vendor has gone out of business. Another example is when the product is so old that the vendor no longer supports it. Typically, a vendor will give the customer base years to upgrade to the new version of the product, but some users are reluctant to make the change. According to CMIT Solutions, in January of 2020 nearly 13% of PCs worldwide were still running Windows 7, even though support for it had ended in 2018 [CMIT24].

REFERENCES

[ASTRA23] Palatty, Nivedita James. "How Many Cyber Attacks Per Day: The Latest Stats and Impacts in 2024," available online at *https://www.getastra.com/blog/security-audit/how-many-cyberattacks-per-day/*, December 22, 2023

[CLOU24] "What was the WannaCry ransomware attack?," available online at *https://www.cloudflare.com/learning/security/ransomware/wannacry-ransomware/*, April 18, 2024

[CNN15] Pagliery, Jose. "The inside story of the biggest hack in history," available online at *https://money.cnn.com/2015/08/05/technology/aramco-hack/*, August 5, 2015

[CMIT24] "Do not Ignore Software Updates and Security Patches," available online at *https://cmitsolutions.com/blog/dont-ignore-software-updates-and-security-patches/*, April 19, 2024

[ELIE16] Bursztein, Elie. "Concerns about USB security are real: 48% of people do plug in USB drives found in parking lots," available online at *https://elie.net/blog/security/concerns-about-usb-security-are-real-48-percent-of-people-do-plug-in-usb-drives-found-in-parking-lots*, April 2016

[EQUI24] "Insider Threats Are Becoming More Frequent and More Costly," available online at *https://www.idwatchdog.com/insider-threats-and-data-breaches*, April 18, 2024

[FORT22] Revay, Geri. "An Overview of the Increasing Wiper Malware Threat," available online at *https://www.fortinet.com/blog/threat-research/the-increasing-wiper-malware-threat*, April 28, 2022

[IBM23] "What is smishing (SMS phishing)," available online at *https://www.ibm.com/topics/smishing*, April 16, 2024

[MEN23] Geto, Daniel. "Microsoft paid out USD $63 million in bug bounties," available online at *https://www.menosfios.com/en/microsoft-pagou-usd-63-milhoes-em-recompensas-por-bugs/*, November 23, 2023

[PROOF24] "What Is Email Spoofing," available online at *https://www.proofpoint.com/us/threat-reference/email-spoofing*, April 23, 2024

[SOFT24] "31 Insider Threat Stats You Need to Know in 2024," available online at *https://www.softactivity.com/ideas/insider-threat-statistics/*, April 18, 2024

[SONIC23] Wolff, Amber. "Cryptojacking Continues Crushing Records," available online at *https://blog.sonicwall.com/en-us/2023/08/cryptojacking-continues-crushing-records/*, August 16, 2023.

[TECH22] Barney, Nick. "Cryptojacking," available online at *https://www.techtarget.com/whatis/definition/cryptojacking*, September 2022.

[Tech23] Oladimeji, Saheed. "SolarWinds hack explained: Everything you need to know," available online at *https://www.techtarget.com/whatis/feature/SolarWinds-hack-explained-Everything-you-need-to-know*, Nov 3, 2023

[TECH24]. Franceschi-Bicchierai, Lorenzo. "Price of zero-day exploits rises as companies harden products against hackers," available online at *https://techcrunch.com/2024/04/06/price-of-zero-day-exploits-rises-as-companies-harden-products-against-hackers/*, April 6, 2024

[TECH922] Bedell, Crystal. "Computer Worm," available online at *https://www.techtarget.com/searchsecurity/definition/worm*, September 2022

[TELE09] Beaumont, Claudine. "Windows work being thread through USB memory sticks," available online at *https://www.telegraph.co.uk/technology/microsoft/4322032/Windows-worm-being-spread-through-USB-memory-sticks.html*, January 23, 2009

[TOUL23] Toulas, Bill. "USB drive malware attacks spiking again in first half of 2023," available online at *https://www.bleepingcomputer.com/news/security/usb-drive-malware-attacks-spiking-again-in-first-half-of-2023/*, July 13, 2023

[VERIF22] Hooper, Chris. "What is account takeover Fraud?," available online at *https://www.veriff.com/fraud/news/account-takeover-fraud-statistics*, March 20, 2024

[VULN24] Kovacs, Eduard. "Google Paid Out $10 Million via Bug Bounty Programs in 2023," available online at *https://www.securityweek.com/google-paid-out-10-million-via-bug-bounty-programs-in-2023/*, March 12, 2024

[WILL08] Lynn, William. "Defending a New Domain," available online at *https://apps.dtic.mil/sti/pdfs/ADA527707.pdf*, April 17, 2024

RANSOMWARE

WHAT IS RANSOMWARE?

Ransomware is a version of malware that encrypts critical files, computers, or entire networks. Data remains inaccessible until a ransom is paid. The victim then has to hope that the criminal will actually provide a key to decrypt his assets. The malware frequently leaves the computer operational so the victim can use a browser on it to make the ransomware payment. Figure 3.1 shows an example of how people learn that they are a victim of ransomware.

FIGURE 3.1 Example of a ransomware screen

To maintain their anonymity, the cybercriminal requires that the ransomware be paid in a cryptocurrency, frequently Bitcoin. The bad actor may provide detailed instructions on how to set up a Bitcoin wallet to make paying the ransom easier for the victim. In many cases, if the ransom is not paid by a specified date, then the ransom amount is increased.

Ransomware incidents are a global problem. AAG IT Services estimates that between May 2021 and June 2023, there were 3,640 successful ransomware attacks worldwide [AAG24]. Symantec, a prominent cybersecurity firm, found that ransomware attacks in the fourth quarter of 2024 had increased 36% over the first quarter of the year [SYM24].

Once ransomware has been installed onto a computer or network, it begins encrypting files. They can be encrypted at an astonishingly fast rate. Researchers at Splunk found that the ransomware Lockbit was able to encrypt 100,000 test files in slightly over four minutes [ZDN22]. Other forms of ransomware took up to two hours to encrypt the test files. If an attack took place early in the morning or over the weekend, every file would likely be locked up before anyone could respond. Most likely they would all be encrypted before anyone became aware of the situation.

Examples of files and their extensions that ransomware can encrypt includes

a. Adobe PDF files: any file that has an extension of .pdf

b. Image files: anything with .jpg, .jpeg, .png, .tiff, and .gif extensions

c. Word processing files: such as file extensions of .docx, .doc, .odt, .rtf, .txt, .tex, and .wpd

d. Spreadsheet files: such as file extensions of .xls, .xlsx, and .ods

e. PowerPoint decks: such as files extensions like .ppt, .pptx, .pptm, and .odp

f. Database files: such as file extensions of .db, .dat, .mdf, .mdb, .accdb, and .SQLite

g. Email storage files: such as file extensions like .pst

h. Video files: such as file extensions like .avi, .mov, and mp4

EVOLUTION OF RANSOMWARE

Early versions of ransomware used weak encryption, and in some instances, the encryption used was weak enough that it could be decrypted without the key. In other cases, the same key could be used to unlock files for multiple victims. Unfortunately, recent versions have become more sophisticated. Now encrypted files require a unique password for each victim.

A sophisticated ransomware attack may arrive in waves. The first wave is malware that explores the victim's computers and networks. The victim is not likely to be aware that this phase of an attack has already started. The second wave is when files are actually encrypted and a screen lets the victim know that he has been attacked.

A variation of ransomware, called *doxware* or *leakware*, does not encrypt the victim's files. Instead, it copies the files, and the bad actor threatens to make sensitive data public if a ransom is not paid. This is challenging for a bad actor to accomplish, so this variant of ransomware is less common.

TYPES OF DEVICES BEING ATTACKED

The types of electronic devices that can be impacted by ransomware can surprise most people. Essentially anything built on a computer that is connected to a network is a potential target. Some examples are listed below.

Computers and Tablets

The most common devices that are victims of ransomware are personal computers, both laptops and workstations. As more people use tablets, these devices will increasingly become potential ransomware targets. Any device that is used to read email and surf the World Wide Web can be a potential target for ransomware and other malware.

Mobile Phones

For many people, a mobile phone is the electronic device that they use most frequently. It should not be surprising that bad actors would figure out a way to attack mobile phones with ransomware. Three examples of how ransomware can attack mobile phones are as follows:

1. It locks up the entire phone until a ransom is paid.

2. It encrypts files on a phone. They will not be unlocked until a ransom is paid.

3. It steals personal data from the phone and threatens to publicize it unless a ransom is paid.

For mobile phones, like other devices, the most common infected vector is by tricking the user into clicking on a link or a pop-up ad. Antivirus software can remove viruses and malware, including ransomware, from phones. Some of the well-known vendors are

a. Avast

b. Bitdefender

c. McAfee

d. Norton

Servers

Servers might not be the initial point of contact during a ransomware attack, but they are definitely a target because they hold large amounts of valuable information. After infecting the first computer, many forms of ransomware will move laterally across the organization's network to infect as many devices as it can, including servers. The malware can exploit vulnerabilities in the network to spread itself. At some point, the attack will move from infiltration to actually encrypting files.

Network segmentation, i.e., breaking an organization's network into multiple, smaller networks with limited connectivity between them, is one way to help prevent ransomware from spreading within the organization. For example, network segments might be created for the finance, research and development, legal and HR departments. If a user's computer was infected with ransomware, the infection would (ideally) be limited to just his department.

Kiosks

Interactive kiosks are a regular part of everyday life, and can be found in numerous locations, including airports and malls (even McDonald's has them). Kiosks are typically powered by a computer that runs some version of the Windows operating system, which is also susceptible to ransomware.

Global consumer electronics manufacturer LG found ransomware running on some of its self-service kiosks in South Korea in 2017 [ZDN17]. The kiosks were taken off-line to prevent the malware from spreading.

IoT Devices

It was inevitable that IoT (Internet of Things) devices would be targets of ransomware simply due to the explosion in their numbers. It is estimated that as of 2023, there were about 15.14 billion IoT devices worldwide [COMP23]. IoT devices are also targets because they typically have very limited defenses against any sort of malware.

There is a significant difference between a typical ransomware attack and one on IoT devices. The typical attack locks up the victim's data, while a ransomware attack against IoT devices locks up the devices. Until the ransom has been paid, the devices are not usable.

SmartTVs have already been the targets for ransomware. In 2016, a variant of the Flocker malware attacked some SmartTVs by locking them up until a ransom of $200 worth of iTunes gift cards was paid [TREN16].

An Austrian hotel's system of electronic locks was the target of an IoT ransomware attack in early 2017 [NYT23]. Hotel guests were locked out of their rooms after the cybercriminals took over the electronic system of locks. The hotel paid a ransom of $1,800 in Bitcoin to regain control of the computers.

Other potential IoT devices that have been or could be targets of ransomware include

- smart thermostats
- security cameras
- smart homes
- automobiles
- routers
- medical devices such as pacemakers or insulin pumps
- devices on power grids

WHO ARE THE VICTIMS OF RANSOMWARE?

Everyone is a potential victim of ransomware. One victim might have become ensnared because they happened to go to the wrong Web site and clicked on an ad that looked too good to be true. Another unfortunate person might have had their email address on a list that a cybercriminal purchased on the Dark Web.

Large Corporations

Some potential victims are chosen because it can be assumed that they have the resources to pay a significant ransom: The bigger the company, the more money they have access to is a common belief. According to Trellix Advanced Research Center, more than half of the ransomware victims in the US had an average annual revenue of between $1 million and $100 million [TREL23].

Hospitals

Other victims are chosen because it is assumed that they cannot operate without their data. Hospitals and other healthcare providers fall into this category. In 2023, 46 hospital systems, including at least 141 hospitals, suffered ransomware attacks [HIPA23]. Losing access to their IT systems causes considerable havoc to a hospital. Appointments need to be canceled and rescheduled, bottlenecks can occur in critical departments, and emergency cases had to be redirected to other hospitals. Experts at the University of Minnesota School of Public Health have estimated that between 42 and 67 Medicare patients died between 2016 and 2021 due to ransomware attacks [VOA24].

Government Agencies

Government entities, especially local government computer systems, are frequent victims of ransomware. One example is a ransomware attack on the city of Dallas, TX on May 3, 2023. This attack affected the police department, local courts, utilities, and other services. The city's systems and services were not fully restored until June 13 [TECH23].

Although no one can know for sure, it is likely that government entities are chosen for several reasons.

a. They are assumed to have funds to pay the ransom.

b. It is widely assumed that most government entities, especially the smaller ones, are not well protected against cyberattacks.

c. Government entities often hold sensitive information, e.g., social security numbers, for a large number of citizens. In addition to collecting a ransom, bad actors can exfiltrate this data and sell it on the Dark Web.

School Districts

Local school districts are increasingly becoming the targets of ransomware [EDU23]. Over Labor Day weekend in 2022, the Los Angeles Unified School

District, the nation's second largest school district, was hit with a cyberattack [EDU22]. The attack prevented email access, shut down the district's Web site and interfered with teachers' ability to share lesson plans. Afterward, some of the data stolen during the attack was released online by the criminals. According to cybersecurity firm Emsisoft, it was the fiftieth ransomware attack on the US education sector in the first ten months of 2022 [CNN22].

Professionals

Some organizations seem to be chosen because they hold the intellectual property of their clients [NYS24]. Law firms, accounting firms, and investment firms can fall into this category. A report by Checkpoint Research said cyberattacks, including ransomware, rose by 75% in the first quarter of 2023 compared to the same quarter in 2022 [ABO23]. Lawyers, in particular, need to be concerned about potential liability if ransomware or other cyberattack leads to confidential information being leaked.

Small- to Medium-Sized Businesses

Owners of small- to medium-sized businesses (SMBs) may think that their small size and lack of recognition may keep them safe. Unfortunately, being obscure is no protection against bad actors and their ransomware attacks. In fact, there are several ways in which SMBs are viewed as being even more vulnerable than larger, more well-known organizations. Some of these perceived vulnerabilities are as follows:

a. SMBs are thought to have weaker defenses since they do not have the money to hire experienced cybersecurity staff.

b. SMBs are perceived to be less diligent in backing up their data on a regular basis. Without the ability to recover their data from backups, SMB owners may have no choice other than to pay the ransom.

Survival for an SMB after a ransomware attack is no guarantee. Data protection specialty firm Veeam found up to 60% of small businesses failed after a successful cyberattack [VEEA23]. The reasons for this are a combination of the high costs of recovering their data as well as the costs associated with business interruptions during the attack.

Individuals

If an individual owns a computer or smartphone, then they can potentially get hit with ransomware just like any other potential victim. The vectors of ransomware reaching an individual are the same as those for organizations, primarily phishing emails, corrupt download files, and by visiting infected Web sites.

Advantages of an Individual in a Cyberattack

In some ways, an individual is in a better situation than a large organization. Some advantages that he has are

a. Individuals only have to be responsible for their own actions instead of the actions of everyone in the entire organization. An individual who recognizes the dangers of opening unexpected email attachments can avoid doing it. In a large organization, if a single employee carelessly opens an infected email, then it can affect everyone.

b. The software and data on an individual's computer are almost certainly less complex and smaller in size than what it takes to keep a business running. Few computers, fewer applications, and less data translate directly into a quicker recovery should a ransomware attack occur. If the worst-case scenario happened, an individual could simply purchase a new computer and reload their applications and data onto it. It would take an organization much longer to recover.

c. An individual has less data than an organization. The victim might have music files, photographs, Word documents, spreadsheets, and some databases. This is only a tiny fraction of the data that even a medium-sized organization accumulates over time.

d. The individual has the ability and responsibility to back up their own data. Since the volume of data to be backed up is relatively small, it can be automated and done regularly. The downside of this responsibility is that if the individual neglects making backups, then everything is likely to be lost.

e. An individual does not have to be concerned about "shadow IT." In an organization, if an individual or department acquires hardware, software, or cloud services without the knowledge of official IT channels, it is referred to as "shadow IT." If the organization gets hit with ransomware and needs to completely rebuild the computer environment, the recovery team will not be aware of the shadow IT components that need to be recovered. It is also likely that the group which set up the shadow IT components does not back them up regularly.

Other Ways Individuals Are Affected By Ransomware

Even if an individual's computer is never attacked by ransomware, there are still many ways for him to be affected by a ransomware attack. For example,

a. Their personal data residing on corporate systems can be stolen and sold to other criminals. This can result in identify theft for many individuals. Identify theft can take months or years and cost thousands of dollars to clean up.

b. Businesses that individuals rely upon can be taken down by ransomware. One recent example is the Colonial Pipeline that was attacked in May 2021. The pipeline shutdown reduced gasoline supplies up and down the East Coast. Many drivers had a challenging time locating a gas station where they could fill up their cars.

c. When hospitals are hit with ransomware, then all of its patients can be affected. It could be as minor as rescheduling an appointment or as serious as having to move to another hospital to continue receiving ongoing care.

d. If an individual works for an organization that is hit with ransomware, there can be a significant negative impact on him. The worst case would be if the company goes out of business and the employee loses their job. Another negative impact would be enforced overtime to clean up the ransomware aftermath or time spent dealing with normal work that builds up while the system is unavailable.

e. Customers were unable to pay for their meals with credit cards at over 100,000 restaurants nationwide when NCR was hit with a ransomware attack in April 2023 [CPO23]. The ransomware attack was on a data center which in turn affected NCR's Aloha point-of-sale (POS) system used by independent restaurants and small local chains.

f. Individuals that hold stock in publicly traded companies can take a financial hit if companies they are invested in are the victims of a ransomware attack. The best case would be that stock prices dip for just a short period of time. The worst case is that the company goes out of business and the individual loses their entire investment.

Examples of Recent Ransomware Attacks

Colonial Pipeline

In May of 2021, Colonial Pipeline was attacked by ransomware. The computer systems that were attacked transported petrochemical products from Texas to the East Coast. Operations of the pipeline were impacted for about five days and caused shortages of gasoline, diesel fuel and jet fuel throughout the South and even into the Atlantic coast states. On May 9, 2022, President Biden declared a state of emergency due to the incident. The company paid a ransom of $4.4 million [TECH22].

Las Vegas MGM

MGM Resorts in Las Vegas, NV was the victim of a ransomware attack in October 2023. The impact of the incident included

a. slot machines and ATM machines not working

b. guests not being able to use key cards to enter their hotel rooms

c. bets on sporting events could not be transacted

d. long lines at restaurants, bars, and hotel front desks

e. online reservations were not available

It took the company about ten days to resume normal operations. Estimated losses were around $100 million. MGM refused to pay the ransom demanded by the criminals [NYP23].

Maersk

Maersk, a Danish based shipping firm, suffered a ransomware attack in June of 2017. Maersk is the largest shipping container company in the world. Its losses were estimated to be about $200 - $300 million. It took Maersk ten days to rebuild their IT infrastructure and restore operations [LAT17].

UK National Health System

In May of 2017, the United Kingdom National Health Care system was the victim of a WannaCry ransomware attack. This attack took down critical hospital systems. Almost 20,000 appointments were canceled during this incident. Estimates of the cost to recover from this attack are $116 million [UKP18]. No ransom was paid following this incident.

HOW MUCH WILL IT COST?

The ransom demanded varies widely, but the trend is that the amount is increasing. Sophos, a security solutions company, reported that rates have increased 500% from 2023 to 2024 [SOPH24]. The same white paper found that the average ransom payment increased from $400,000 in 2022 to $2,000,000 in 2023.

The ransom amount that a victim might or might not pay is not the only cost of a ransomware attack. In fact, it might be one of the smaller expenses associated with the incident. IBM has estimated that the global average cost of a data breach in 2023 was $4.45 million [IBM23]. Other costs include

a. Loss of business while the system is down. If the victim organization depends on e-commerce for most or all of its sales, all income could be lost while the files or computers are encrypted. Other victims might be unable to perform basic business functions. Some victims have had to resort to paper- and pencil-based methods to keep the company operating.

b. Damage to a company's reputation once news of the ransomware attack becomes public is significant, but difficult to calculate. For a business that depends on the trust of their customers, being the victim of a cyberattack could encourage many clients to move to a competitor.

c. If PII (Personal Identifiable Information) was exposed during a ransomware attack, the possibility of a class action lawsuit for the company involved is high.

d. In many cases, an organization realizes that it does not have the expertise to deal with a ransomware attack. The decision might be made to bring in a firm that specializes in ransomware remediation. The cost of engaging a team of experts can be significant.

e. A decision that is often made is to bolster the organization's internal IT security team to prevent future ransomware attacks. Hiring cybersecurity specialists is not easy or cheap.

Examples of Significant Types of Ransomware

1. AIDS Trojan (PC Cyborg): In 1989, this was the first type of ransomware.

2. Cryptowall: originally released in 2014; Updated versions are considered to be stealthier.

3. CryptoLocker: a 2013 attack that launched the modern ransomware age and infected up to 500,000 machines at its height

4. WannaCry: spread autonomously from computer to computer

5. Petya: first surfaced in 2016

6. NotPetya: exploited security vulnerabilities to infect computers without needing user intervention.

7. SamSam: SamSam was launched in 2016. It caused numerous outages of services provided by the city of Atlanta, GA.

8. Ryuk: hit newspapers and the North Carolina water utility in 2018 and 2019

9. BadRabbit: spread through drive-by attacks

RANSOMWARE ATTACK VECTORS

The ways that a computer can be infected with ransomware attacks are similar to how most malware is spread. Some of the most significant methods are listed below.

Phishing Emails

According to a survey taken by Barracuda Networks, the most common method of being infected with ransomware is by email. Organizations with more than 250 employees reported that 75% of their ransomware attacks originated with an email [CRED23]. The Verizon 2023 Data Breach Investigations Report found that approximately 33% of all ransomware attacks began with an email [VER23].

Bad actors are experts at creating phishing emails designed to get the recipient to open them. Some examples are

a. promises to get a tax return quicker

b. exceptionally good sale prices, especially on Black Friday or Cyber Monday

c. the offer of a gift or reward

d. claims that the recipient owes or is owed money

e. lucrative job offers

Downloading Infected Files

Any files that are downloaded to a computer can potentially contain malware or ransomware. Files should only be downloaded from trusted sites. Examples of attractive downloads that can hold ransomware include

a. a free game or expansion pack of an existing game

b. a free movie

c. photographs of celebrities

d. a free antivirus program

e. an upgrade to an application

Malvertising

Malvertising (malicious advertising) is the term given when attackers distribute malware (including ransomware) by embedding it in online ads. Anyone unfortunate enough to either go to an infected Web site or click on an infected ad may have some form of malware downloaded to their device. The best defenses against malvertising are setting up a pop-up blocker in the browser and installing antivirus software on the computer.

Drive-By Attack

Clicking on a link in an infected Web page or simply going to an infected Web site can cause ransomware to be downloaded to a computer. Unfortunately, ransomware can be downloaded to a computer as a result of a drive-by attack without the victim realizing that it has happened. Making sure that all computers have up to date antivirus software is a good way to help prevent drive-by attacks.

Scareware Attacks

Tricking victims into believing a scary pop-up message that tells the user their computer is infected with a virus. If they click the link on the pop-up or call the number on the pop-up screen, then instead of fixing their contaminated computer, it is very likely that ransomware will be installed.

Remote Access Software

One of the ways that bad actors can install ransomware on a computer is if they are able to log onto it remotely. One method of doing this is to take advantage of something called Remote Desktop Protocol (RDP). RDP is a network communications protocol developed by Microsoft that allows one to control the destination computer just as if he were sitting right in front of it. It can give users the ability to remotely access their workstations or can allow network administrators to diagnose problems remotely. If bad actors can guess the account ID and password, they can use RDP to connect to a victim's computer and install ransomware on it.

Inserting An Infected USB Drive into A Computer

If a user inserts a USB drive containing ransomware into a computer's USB slot, the computer can become infected. It may not be obvious to the user that anything is happening. To them it appears that everything is fine, right up until the ransomware message is displayed.

DAMAGE CAUSED BY RANSOMWARE

1. All files or entire computer could be locked until the ransom is paid.
2. Other malware can be installed on the computer.
3. Data can be exfiltrated and sold or held for an additional ransom.
4. The organization's reputation could be damaged.
5. An organization may be required to contact their customers, patients, or employees to inform them of the breach.
6. If PII was exposed, then a class action lawsuit against the victim is possible.

Backups Can Be Targeted

Knowing that backup files can be used to restore the encrypted data, some ransomware actually tries to encrypt or destroy backup files. Their rationale is that if all backups can be encrypted or destroyed the victim will have no choice other than to pay the ransom. Two ways to prevent this from happening are to store a copy of the backups off-line or on a Write Once, Ready Many (WORM) device.

Legal Breach Liabilities

Organizations are now required to disclose instances when a data breach affects more than 500 people. A ransomware attack can qualify as a data breach event if there is a chance that data was exfiltrated from the affected computer or system. Data breaches can result in substantial fines for the related company. Two significant pieces of legislation that spell out the consequences of data breaches are listed below. In addition to them, other countries and states may have their own breach notification regulations.

1. The General Data Protection Regulation (GDPR) enforces European regulations on data privacy.

2. The California Consumer Privacy Act (CCPA) enhances privacy rights and consumer protection in California.

Fines levied on corporations related to data breaches can be substantial. Some of the more substantial fines imposed have been as follows:

a. Equifax agreed to a settlement of at least $575 million for failing to fix a critical vulnerability related to the Apache Struts framework.

b. T-Mobile had announced a settlement of $350 million in 2021 related to a class action suit over a data breach.

c. A data breach involving a point-of-sale (POS) system cost Home Depot about $200 million in 2014.

d. In 2016, Uber paid $148 million to settle claims for a data breach involving 600,000 of its drivers and 57 million user accounts.

Additional Challenge: Another Attack

Ransomware is dangerous, and it has other challenges associated with managing it. One very disturbing ransomware trend is for bad actors to hit victims twice. In this increasingly frequent variation, the bad actors copy data or files from a victim's system before encrypting them. The World Economic Forum says this number of cases where data is exfiltrated has risen from 40% in 2019 to 77% in 2020 and is projected to be higher in 2023 [WEF24]. The first ransom demand is to unlock the files. Once that ransom has been paid, the bad actors demand an additional payment so they will not sell or release the confidential data they stole. Of course, there is no way to be sure there will not be a third or fourth demand for more money.

Ransomware as a Service

Ransomware as a Service (RaaS) is a disturbing trend, making ransomware more readily available to criminals. Essentially RaaS is a business model between bad actors who develop the software (RaaS Operators) and their "customers" (RaaS Affiliates) who actually deploy the malware. This allows criminals who are not skilled in developing software to get access to sophisticated malware that can be used to victimize individuals and organizations. There are four ways that the "affiliates" can pay the "operators" for using their software.

1. Pay a monthly flat fee.

2. Paying a monthly fee plus a percentage of the profits, typically around 25%, to the Operators.

3. Pay a one-time licensing fee.

4. Pay a percentage of the profits to the Operators, often 30-40%.

Sophisticated RaaS operators function much like legitimate businesses. They have Web sites that enable their affiliates to make payments and monitor the progress of their ransomware attacks. Operators run marketing campaigns to bring in new affiliates and provide customer support to their affiliates.

RANSOMWARE PAYMENTS: AN ETHICAL AND FINANCIAL CHALLENGE

Every ransomware victim has to make the decision whether to pay the ransom. Research by the World Economic Forum shows that more companies are paying the ransom now than in past years [WEF24]. In 2019, only 10% of companies paid. In 2022, that number had increased to 54%.

Reasons Not to Pay

a. The most obvious reason not to pay is that by paying a ransom, criminal activity is being rewarded. If bad actors can make a profit via ransomware attacks, then they will continue doing it, putting even more people and organizations at risk of becoming victims.

b. Law enforcement agencies discourage victims from paying a ransom. In some countries, including the US, it is technically illegal to pay a ransom

[CISO20]. Additionally, some US states have passed laws making it illegal to make ransomware payments.

c. Even if the ransom is paid, the victim may not get their files back. A blog by Seagate reported that in 2022 46% of the organizations that paid the ransom were able to recover only 61% of their data. Only 4% were able to recover all of their data [SEA24]. A study by data protection specialist Veeam found that in 2023, 80% of ransomware victims paid the ransom, but 25% were not able to recover their data after the attack [VEEA23].

d. Victims that pay the ransom are likely to get attacked again [INVE24]. They are perceived as an easy target by other criminals, since they have already paid once.

Reasons to Pay

a. If an organization either has no backups or the backups were encrypted during the attack, an organization may see no alternative way of recovering the data.

b. If the loss of data could lead to the business' failure, that might lead to the ransom being paid. An e-commerce company faced with the possibility of being off-line for the month leading up to Christmas may decide the loss of those profits would cause the business to collapse.

c. Lives could be at risk if the system is not back online as soon as possible. For example, a hospital might choose to pay to avoid risking its patients' lives.

Mitigating Damage from Ransomware

1. Keep all software, including the operating system, browsers, and significant applications up to date and patched.

2. Install antivirus software on all devices and make sure it is patched.

3. Install pop-up blockers on all Web browsers.

4. Filter email to screen out as many spam and phishing emails as possible, as this reduces the chances of employees clicking on a phishing link that could lead to ransomware being installed.

5. Employee training can help teach workers how to identify and avoid clicking on questionable links in emails or Web sites. Training can include

sending phishing emails to an organization's employees as a training exercise to see how many are clicked.

6. Require that users have strong passwords and use MFA (Multifactor Authentication) whenever possible.

7. Segment the network to make lateral movement difficult. This can limit damage if bad actors gain access to a computer on the system.

8. Keep frequent backups of all files.

9. Keep at least one backup copy offline so they cannot be encrypted or deleted by ransomware.

10. Test backups regularly to ensure that they can be used successfully to rebuild the system.

HOW TO RESPOND TO A RANSOMWARE ATTACK

The steps to responding to a ransomware attack are complex. The situation requires that decisions be made quickly, correctly, and in the proper order. Any list of the steps to be taken in any book or a blog should be taken only as general guidance. The best single piece of advice that can be given here is to contact an experienced professional for assistance.

How to respond to a ransomware situation will differ considerably depending on the size and sophistication of the victim. What works for a medium-sized business is not likely to be appropriate for a school district and certainly will not be correct for an individual. With that caveat in mind, here is a list of common steps that should be taken.

1. As soon as a ransomware attack is recognized, isolate the affected computer(s). This might require physically unplugging the cable that connects it to the network, or it might require that the computer(s) be powered down. This can help prevent any malware from infecting additional machines.

2. If the organization has an IT security team, then contact them immediately (if they are not already involved).

3. If the organization has an incident response plan, then pull it out and start following its instructions. (The time and energy invested in this document will pay off handsomely now.) If a response plan does not exist, then continue with the next step, but schedule time to create an incident response plan as soon as this crisis has been handled.

4. If a cyber insurance policy exists, contact the insurer immediately. It is possible that if the insurance company is not notified as early as possible, the incident will not be covered by the policy. The insurer will probably provide guidance on how to handle the incident or suggest someone that can provide assistance. If there is no coverage, then continue with the next step.

5. If a relationship with a security firm or consultant already exists, then get them involved as early as possible. (If there is no such relationship, then now would is the time to hire a company.) Taking advantage of their experience and expertise is definitely a good idea.

    An additional reason to engage a security firm is that they can help determine how the malware was able to work its way into the system. Knowing this can help prevent similar attacks from succeeding in the future.

6. Consider bringing in a team of experienced ransomware negotiators. Negotiators who have successfully dealt with ransomware situations may be able to reduce the ransom and ensure the files are unlocked. If a cyber insurance policy exists, then insurer may have or recommend an experienced negotiator.

7. Contact law enforcement and the government authorities. They might not be able to provide any meaningful assistance, but documenting the attack can help them to understand ransomware trends. Additionally, documenting the attack with authorities may be required by the insurance provider.

8. The decision has to be made whether to pay the ransom or not. The pros and cons were outlined in an earlier section in this chapter.

9. If possible, identify and learn as much as possible about the particular type of ransomware involved. Researching it may provide understanding on how it spreads, the types of files it attacks and how it can be removed. It can also help to understand whether the bad actors will actually decrypt the files if the ransom is paid.

10. Inform all users of the system about the attack. Everyone being aware of the situation may provide additional insight regarding other areas in the network or organization's computer systems that might have been affected by the attack.

11. Change all login credentials. If the bad actors have been performing reconnaissance on the system, then they might have been able to learn account IDs and passwords for users or administrators. Changing passwords now can prevent them from doing further damage.

12. Run antivirus and antimalware scans to remove the ransomware code. The specific antivirus tool that is being used will provide detailed steps on how to perform a scan and remove any ransomware that it finds.

13. Apply any upgrades and patches to the organization's software that were not applied yet. This includes operating systems, application software, browsers, and security software.

14. Restore data from backups, specifically backups that were kept off-line, if available, to minimize the changes of them being compromised.

15. Understand any applicable breach notification responsibilities. If this incident potentially resulted in PII (Personally Identifiable Information) data being exposed, the organization may be required to contact the affected individuals to make them aware of the breach. If notification requirements are not met, this can result in significant fines for the organization.

REFERENCES

[AAG24] Griffiths, Charles "The Latest 2024 Ransomware Statistics," available online at *https://aag-it.com/the-latest-ransomware-statistics/*, Jan 3, 2024

[ABO23] Nelson, Sharon. "Law Firm Data Breaches Surge in 2023," available online at *https://abovethelaw.com/2023/08/law-firm-data-breaches-surge-in-2023/*, August 1, 2023

[CISO20] CISOMAG. "Paying Ransom is Now Illegal, US Dept. of Treasury Warns," available online at *https://cisomag.com/paying-ransom-is-now-illegal-u-s-dept-of-treasury-warns/*, October 5, 2020

[CNN22] Romine, Taylor. "Cybercriminals behind Los Angeles Unified School District ransomware attack release hacked data, superintendent says," available online at *https://www.cnn.com/2022/10/01/us/los-angeles-unified-school-district-ransomware-attack/index.html*, October 2, 2022

[COMP23] Watters, Ashley. "Top 30+ IoT Statistics and Facts You Should Know for 2023" available online at *https://connect.comptia.org/blog/top-internet-of-things-stats-facts*, July 18, 2023

[CPO23] Ikeda, Scott. "Financial Services Firm NCR Hit by Ransomware Attack, Disrupting Aloha and Back Office Products," available online at *https://www.cpomagazine.com/cyber-security/financial-services-firm-ncr-hit-by-ransomware-attack-disrupting-aloha-and-back-office-products/*, April 25, 2023

[CRED23] Hallo, Steve. "Email is the Most Common Entry Point for Ransomware Attacks," available online at *https://www.cutimes.com/2023/04/18/email-is-the-most-common-entry-point-for-ransomware-attacks/?slreturn=20240426140832*, April 18, 2023

[DBIR23] "Verizon 2023 Data Breach Investigations Report," available online at *https://www.verizon.com/business/resources/reports/dbir/?cmp=knc:ggl:ac:ent:ea:na:8888855284_ds_cid_71700000082347933_ds_agid_58700006959920338&gad_source=1&gclsrc=ds*, April 26, 2024

[EDU22] Klein, Alyso. "Why the Los Angeles Cyberattack is a Wake-Up Call for Every School District," available online at *https://www.edweek.org/technology/why-the-los-angeles-cyberattack-is-a-wake-up-call-for-every-school-district/2022/09*, September 6, 2022

[EDU23] Langreo, Lauraine. "Schools are a Top Target of Ransomware Attacks, and It's Getting Worse," available online at *https://www.edweek.org/technology/schools-are-a-top-target-of-ransomware-attacks-and-its-getting-worse/2023/08*, August 17, 2023

[HIPA23] Alder, Steve. "At Least 141 Hospitals Were Directly Affected by Ransomware Attacks in 2023," available online at *https://www.hipaajournal.com/2023-healthcare-ransomware-attacks/*, January 4, 2024

[IBM23] "Cost of a Data Breach Report 2023," available online at *https://www.ibm.com/reports/data-breach?p1=Search&p4=43700077724064051&p5=p&gad_source=1&gclsrc=ds*, May 1, 2024

[INVE24] Shulmistra, Dale. "6 Reasons Not to Pay the Ransom in a Ransomware Attack," available online at *https://invenioit.com/security/pay-the-ransom/*, June 29, 2024

[LAT17] Leovy, Jill. "Cyberattacks cost Maersk as much as $300 million and disrupted operations for 2 weeks," available online at https://www.latimes.com/business/la-fi-*maersk-cyberattack-20170817-story.html*, August 17, 2017

[MED21] Slabokin, Greg. "Ransomware attacks put availability of medical devices at risk: FDA cyber chief," available online at *https://www.medtechdive.com/news/cyber-attacks-security-medical-devices-kevin-fu-advamed/607483/*, October 1, 2021

[NYP23] Thaler, Shannon. "MGM Resorts loses over $100M after refusing to pay ransom to end cyberattack," available online at *https://nypost.com/2023/10/06/mgm-loses-100m-refused-to-pay-ransom-to-end-cyberattack/*, October 6, 2023

[NYS24] Green, Paula. "Hackers Working for Lucrative Cyber Attack Industry See Law Firms as Rich Targets," available online at *https://nysba.org/hackers-working-for-lucrative-cyber-attack-industry-see-law-firms-as-rich-targets/*, January 19, 2024

[NYT23] Bilefsky, Dan. "Hackers Use New Tactic at Austrian Hotel: Locking the Doors," available online at *https://www.nytimes.com/2017/01/30/world/europe/hotel-austria-bitcoin-ransom.html*, January 30, 2017

[SEA24] "How Do Ransomware Attacks Work?," available online at *https://www.seagate.com/blog/how-do-ransomware-attacks-work/*, March 28, 2024

[SOPH24] "The State of Ransomware 2024," available online at *https://assets.sophos.com/X24WTUEQ/at/9brgj5n44hqvgsp5f5bqcps/sophos-state-of-ransomware-2024-wp.pdf*, April 2024.

[SYM24], Symantec Threat Hunter Team, "Ransomware: Attacks Once More Nearing Peak Levels," available online at *https://www.security.com/threat-intelligence/ransomware-attacks-rebound*, September 12, 2024

[TECH22] Kerner, Sean. "Colonial Pipeline hack explained: Everything you need to know," available online at *https://www.techtarget.com/whatis/feature/Colonial-Pipeline-hack-explained-Everything-you-need-to-know*, April 26, 2022

[TECH23] Waldman, Arielle. "10 of the biggest ransomware attacks in 2023," available online at *https://www.techtarget.com/searchSecurity/news/366564303/10-of-the-biggest-ransomware-attacks-in-2023*, December 21, 2023

[TREL23] "Uncover the Hidden Story of Ransomware Victims – They're Not Who You Think," available online at *https://www.trellix.com/blogs/research/uncover-the-hidden-story-of-ransomware-victims/*, July 31, 2023

[TREN16] Duan, Echo. "Flocker Mobile Ransomware Crosses to Smart TV," available online at *https://www.trendmicro.com/ru_ru/research/16/f/flocker-ransomware-crosses-smart-tv.html*, June 13, 2016

[UKP18] House of Commons. "Cyber-attack on the NHS," available online at *https://publications.parliament.uk/pa/cm201719/cmselect/cmpubacc/787/787.pdf*, March 28, 2018

[UNIT42] "2023 Unit 42 Ransomware and Extortion Thread Report," available online at *https://start.paloaltonetworks.com/2023-unit42-ransomware-extortion-report-success.html?sfdcCampaignID=7014u000001VVbzAAG&languageCode=com&gtm=Unit42&acc=granted*, May 3, 2024

[VER23] Verizon's "Data Breach Investigations Report" available online at *https://www.verizon.com/business/resources/reports/dbir/2023/*, Apr 2, 2024

[VEEA23] Hanks, Colin. "Small Business Ransomware: What You Need to Know," available online at *https://www.veeam.com/blog/small-business-ransomware.html*, January 24, 2024

[VOA24] Jahic, Dino. "Ransomware Attacks: Death Threats, Endangered Patients and Millions of Dollars in Damages," available online at *https://www.voanews.com/a/ransomware-attacks-death-threats-endangered-patients-and-millions-of-dollars-in-damages/7520952.html*, March 10, 2024.

[WEF24] "3 trends set to drive cyberattacks and ransomware in 2024," available online at *https://www.weforum.org/agenda/2024/02/3-trends-ransomware-2024/*, Feb 22, 2024

[ZDN17] Palmer, Danny. "WannaCry ransomware attack at LG Electronics takes system offline," available online at *https://www.zdnet.com/article/wannacry-ransomware-attack-at-lg-electronics-takes-systems-offline/*, August 21, 2017

[ZDN22] Palmer, Danny. "This is how fast a ransomware attacks all your files," available online at *https://www.zdnet.com/article/this-is-how-fast-a-ransomware-attack-encrypts-all-your-files/*, March 22, 2022

4

SOCIAL ENGINEERING

WHAT IS SOCIAL ENGINEERING?

Social engineering is using human interaction, i.e., social skills, to deceive or manipulate victims into divulging information or taking actions that will be harmful to them or their organization. A social engineering attack may be carried out face-to-face, via email, on a phone call, or via text messages.

A successful social engineer does not have to be a programming expert or a network guru. His expertise is dealing with people: He is an expert in manipulating people using psychology. Once a social engineer understands how to overcome his victim's defenses, then technical skills may be used to further the attack. For example, the objective might be the victim's account ID and password. Once that information has been obtained, the cybercriminal will use an account takeover attack to impersonate the victim.

A skilled social engineer is not likely to ask the victim for all of the desired information at once. He may contact the victim multiple times or may contact more than one individual at the organization and piece together what he needs from all of the contacts.

During a social engineering attack, the bad actor may portray himself as a person of authority. Sometimes he may impersonate a high-ranking company executive, a fire inspector, or an auditor. He may claim to be an employee of the same organization but from a different department or office.

SOCIAL ENGINEERING AND EMOTIONS

Social engineering attacks depend on human emotions to be effective. The seven emotions that are triggered during a social engineering attack according to cybersecurity firm Defendify are as follows [DEF24]:

Fear

Fear can be used to induce a feeling of panic in a victim. Once a person has panicked, they are unlikely to be thinking clearly and can be more easily manipulated. An email stating that the recipient's bank account has been compromised could motivate the recipient to click on the link in the email to update their password and protect their account.

Curiosity

Curiosity can be used to influence email recipients into opening attachments and clicking on embedded links that they normally would not consider doing. The ILOVEYOU worm that was spread via emails with "ILOVEYOU" in the subject field is a perfect example of using peoples' inherent sense of curiosity to propagate malware. In May 2000, this worm spread to an estimated 45 million users in about ten days [TEC21]. The estimated damages from this virus were around $10 billion.

Helpfulness

Helpfulness is an attribute that people are encouraged to have from an early age. Unfortunately, social engineers use this societal norm against their victims. A frequent social engineering ploy is to claim to be new to the organization to bypass normal security procedures. Another way this trait is exploited is during a *tailgating exploit*, i.e., an employee will hold a secured door open for someone who has their hands full or is on crutches.

Greed

Greed is one of the seven deadly sins and is frequently exploited by social engineers. The *Nigerian Prince* and *Lottery* scams are just two social engineering attacks that use greed to motivate victims. Other examples of social engineering attacks that involve greed are offers of free games or movies, discount coupons, and cash prizes.

Irritation

Irritation is the state of feeling impatient, annoyed, or a bit angry. It can used by a social engineering attack to get the victim to approve a prompt (MFA Prompt Bombing) just to get a continuous series of prompts to stop arriving on their phone. Another example of using irritation in a social engineering attack would be to send the same spam email repeatedly, hoping that the recipient will eventually open the attachment or click on a link in the body of it.

Urgency

Urgency, i.e., getting the victim to act quickly, is a factor in many social engineering attacks. If the bad actor can manipulate the victim into acting without thinking about what they are doing, then the attack is more likely to succeed. Convincing a user that his Facebook or Amazon account will be terminated if action is not taken immediately will very likely motivate them to click on a link they should know not to click.

Excitement

Excitement is an emotion that people relish. If the social engineer can induce a sense of excitement, perhaps by making the victim think he has won a valuable prize, then the target may not be as cautious or skeptical as usual. Another ploy is sending an email to the victim that claims to have tracking information for a package or gift.

THE HISTORY OF SOCIAL ENGINEERING

The concept of social engineering has a long history. It predates computers by hundreds (if not thousands) of years. Some early examples of this method of manipulating people include the following:

1. Genesis describes how the serpent in the Garden of Eden used social engineering on Eve to convince her to eat the fruit from the Tree of Good and Evil in the middle of the garden. It persuaded her that eating that fruit would give her knowledge.

2. During the mythical Trojan war, the Greek army pretended to give up and return home. They left behind a large wooden horse and a spy. The spy convinced the Trojans that the horse was an offering to the goddess Athena and would make Troy impregnable if it was brought inside the

city. Convinced that the horse was something useful they brought it into the city. Later that night, Odysseus and 30 other warriors climbed out of the horse and opened the city gates for the rest of the Greek army. The city was sacked and captured.

3. A Ponzi scheme is an investment fraud which promises investors abnormally high profits with little or no risk. No money is ever actually invested in anything. Early "investors" are paid their profits from later victims. Eventually, the scheme collapses when the number of new investors dries up. This type of social engineering scheme preys on victims' greed and fear of missing out on an opportunity. This form of investment scheme is named after Charles Ponzi, who devised his version of the scam in 1919, but similar scams predate him by decades.

4. During World War II, the Allies created an elaborate social engineering scheme to convince the Nazis where the upcoming invasion of continental Europe would take place. This deception included passing false information through double agents, bogus radio transmissions, body doubles of military leaders, and hundreds of dummy tanks and jeeps that could be seen by Nazi aircraft. The Allies tricked the Nazis into moving their forces away from the invasion site at Normandy.

Examples of Social Engineering Attacks

Some examples of modern social engineering attacks include the following:

Account Lockouts

An account lock attack is when a bad actor sends emails to potential victims claiming their account is either locked out or is about to be locked out. The account might be for a bank, PayPal, Facebook, Google, or other entity. The email will emphasize that action must be taken immediately. The email conveniently provides a link the victim can click on to get to the organization's login screen. Of course, the login Web page is fake and if the victim enters his account and password, they will be stolen by the cybercriminal.

Arrest Threats

In this social engineering attack, the bad actor calls, texts, or emails victims trying to convince them that a warrant has been issued for their arrest. The warrant might be for failure to appear for juror duty, unpaid taxes, numerous parking tickets, or missed a court date. If a fine is not paid immediately, then sheriff deputies or police officers will arrive and arrest the target. The source of the message is spoofed so it appears to have come from an official source. The keys to recognizing this scam are the urgency stressed in it and there will be an unusual method of paying the fine such as with gift cards or cryptocurrency.

Blackmail or Extortion Threats

A blackmail threat scam is when a social engineer contacts a victim and claims to possess sensitive or embarrassing information about them. If the victim does not make the demanded payment, frequently in a cryptocurrency, this information will be released to friends, family, or employer. The fear of embarrassment or loss of their job persuades people to pay the demanded money.

Business Email Compromise (BEC)

Business Email Compromise, also called *CEO fraud*, is when a social engineer attempts to trick employees in an organization into transferring money into an account he controls. Frequently, a BEC involves emails purportedly sent by the CEO or other executive asking the victim to make a payment to a new vendor or change the banking details for an existing vendor. Frequently, the payment has to be made immediately to get a contract or avoid a penalty. No matter the specific details of the scam, the intent is that money will be redirected to the cybercriminal's bank account.

Buyer Overpayment

This social engineering attack is initiated when a bad actor purchases an item online from an individual, maybe via Craig's List or Facebook Marketplace. The bad actor sends the seller a check for significantly more than the sale price. He asks the victim to refund him the difference via a digital route like Venmo. The victim ships out the item and refunds the overpayment to the bad actor. Within a short period of time, the victim's bank will inform him that the check bounced. The victim is out the item that was sold as well as the overpayment refund that was sent to the scammer.

Catphishing

Catphishing is when a scammer or social engineer creates a fake profile online on a social media site. The fake profile will usually be of a very attractive, talented person who is hoping to meet someone just like the potential victim. Typically, the intention is to use this profile to deceive victims in a romance scam. As the "relationship" advances, the bad actor will ask the victim for loans or monetary gifts. Once the criminal has determined that the victim can no longer provide funds, he will *ghost* (stop communicating suddenly with) the victim.

Celebrity Scams

There are several distinct kinds of celebrity-based social engineering scams, but all rely on the curiosity or excitement of potential victims. One form is based on emails that promise to provide celebrity gossip or risqué photographs. If the victim opens the attachment or clicks on the embedded link, they obtain malware.

In another version of this type of scam, the social engineer either sends out emails or creates online ads that use the likeness of celebrities to entice potential victims to buy products, make investments, or apply for contests. The victim loses whatever money was sent because there is no product, investment, or contest. Since there are always famous people, this form of social engineering attack will likely persist.

Donation Requests

Whenever tragedy strikes, there is always a burst of emails or pop-up ads soliciting donations for the victims of the disaster. Examples of the disaster might be a school shooting, tornado, hurricane, flooding, or a wildfire. Some of these pleas for assistance are legitimate, but unfortunately, many are created by social engineers who hope to take advantage of the public's generosity to enrich themselves. The best advice to potential donors is to ensure their donations reach the victims is to send money only to well-established charitable organizations.

Fraudulent Job Postings

In this social engineering scam, the cybercriminals create a Web site offering a number of well-paying job positions that need to be filled. To be considered for one of these jobs, an application must be completed and submitted. The application requires that confidential details like Social Security Number, address, date of birth, and email address be provided. Cybercriminals use scams like this to harvest and sell PII (Personal Identifiable Information) from desperate job seekers.

Great Deals

Social engineers will often advertise unbelievably good deals for consumer items on online auction sites or other Web sites. When the victim attempts to purchase the item, they will get nothing or an item of inferior quality. To avoid this type of social engineering hoax, the adage "if it seems too good to be true, it usually is" should be kept in mind.

IRS Refunds or Taxes Due

The victim receives an email claiming to be from the IRS stating that the recipient is entitled to a refund. A link is provided in the email where the refund can be claimed. Instead of getting money, the victim's Social Security Number, bank account number, and address will be stolen. *The IRS never sends unsolicited emails to taxpayers.* Anyone who receives an email claiming to be from the IRS should delete it immediately.

Lottery Scam

The victim is informed that he has won a lottery, but is told he needs to pay taxes, processing fees, or administrative costs up front. If the victim turns over the first payment, then there will be multiple requests for additional fees and payments. Eventually, the victim either runs out of money or realizes that he has been scammed. According to television station WINK in Fort Meyers, Florida, Americans lost about $227 million to lottery and related scams in 2020 [WIN21].

Nigerian Prince Scam

In this classic social engineering scheme, someone (usually, a "prince") with a fortune needs help to get it out of their country. All the person needs is a bank account into which the fortune can be moved. In return for his help, the victim is promised a percentage of the fortune. This scam seems so obvious that it should never work, but it has been working for decades. What makes this scam so successful for the cybercriminal is simple greed. Many people would love to receive a big payoff for almost no investment or effort.

The Grandparent Scam

In this scam, the cybercriminal calls the potential victim and tells him or her that one of their grandchildren needs money to get out of jail. The caller sometimes imitates the grandchild and other times pretends to be an authority figure like a lawyer or a sheriff. The story may be that the grandchild was in a car accident, was shoplifting, or has been accused of drug possession. The victim is coerced into paying money for the release of their loved one. The easiest way to avoid becoming a victim is to hang up and contact the "missing" grandchild. Unfortunately, fear for the safety of a loved one makes this a very successful social engineering scam.

Pig-Butchering Scams

A pig-butchering scam is a long-term swindle where the bad actor develops an online relationship with the victim and eventually convinces him or her to invest money in a "sure fire" investment opportunity, often involving crypto-currency. The initial contact with the victim often appears as mundane as a call or a text message being sent to the wrong number. Frequently the victim is deceived into believing that their investments are growing significantly to encourage additional "investments." *Time* magazine estimated that the global losses to this form of social engineering scam between January 2020 and February 2024 were more than $75 billion [TIM24].

Romance Scams

Romance scams are when cybercriminals strike up online romantic relation-ships with victims with the intent to steal from them. The "relationship" is conducted exclusively online because the bad actor always has reasonable sounding explanations why he or she cannot meet the victim in person or dur-ing an online video call. After the relationship deepens, the scammer will ask the victim for money. The claim will be that the money is needed to travel to visit the victim, pay for a health condition, make repairs after a car accident, help with living expenses after a job loss, or provide for a family member in need. If the first request for money is successful, it will be followed by addi-tional requests for larger amounts.

Tailgating

Also known as *piggybacking*, this technique is to follow another person through a secured door without the proper credentials, i.e., a card key. This is success-ful because most people are extremely reluctant to challenge someone who is following behind them. Often, the social engineer will be carrying something so it is obvious that he cannot open the door for himself. Someone carrying a box of doughnuts, a cake, or multiple bags of sandwiches does not seem very threatening, so people will frequently hold the door for him. Another ploy is for the criminal to use crutches or a cane to create sympathy and garner offers of assistance from legitimate employees.

Tech Support Scams

Phony tech support scams are when the potential victim is convinced by a pop-up message, cold call, or email that there is a problem with his phone or computer. The supposed problem is a virus, ransomware, or other kind of malware. The social engineer claims to be tech support and for a price will fix the problem. At best, the victim wastes money, but more likely will end up losing money and have some kind of malware installed on their device. Tech support scams were the most widely reported type of fraud affecting older adults in 2023, according to the FBI [FBI24].

Tech support teams from Microsoft, Google, Facebook, or any other legitimate organization will never call a user. If such a call is ever received, the best advice is to hang up.

Traveler in Trouble Request

In this scam, a social engineer takes over someone's email or social media account and sends out messages pretending to be that person. He claims that while on a trip overseas, his wallet, passport, and ticket were lost or stolen. He asks his "friends" to send him money digitally so he can make it home. This scam can be thwarted by contacting the "friend" by another channel to confirm the validity of the request. For example, if the request came via Facebook, then call or text the person making the request.

SOCIAL ENGINEERING TERMS

Baiting: This involves leaving malware infected USB drives at a site, hoping that people will insert them into their computers.

Brandjacking: Also known as brand impersonation, this is when a bad actor impersonates the brand or Web site of a legitimate organization to deceive current and potential customers.

Clickbait: This involves showing enticing images or links on a Web page to lure viewers to click on them. Once a victim clicks on the link, he is taken to a Web site controlled by a cybercriminal. At best, the victim will simply waste time on the Web site that probably contains fake news. At worst, his device will be infected with a keystroke logger, cryptojacking software, or another form of malware.

Clickjacking: This is an attack that tricks the victim into clicking on the link that appears to be for a trustworthy Web site but actually takes them somewhere else. The bad actor accomplishes this deception by overlaying a malicious Web page on top of a legitimate one.

Doxing: This involves publishing private or identifying information about someone in order to embarrass or humiliate the victim.

Dumpster diving: The practice of searching through the trash of a potential victim looking for passwords, account IDs, calendars, employee lists, organization charts, phone numbers, or any other information that will help the bad actor infiltrate the network.

Fullz: This is a term that means "full information," i.e., a comprehensive list of data about someone, e.g., name, address, Social Security Number, date of birth, and credit card number.

Open Source Intelligence (OSINT): This refers to information on an individual or organization that can be freely collected from public sources. Examples of OSINT sources include social media sites, newspaper articles, and Web sites hosted by organizations. OSINT is used by social engineers to perform reconnaissance on potential victims.

Pharming: This involves using malicious code to direct the victim into visiting a spoofed Web site. Once at that site, the victim may have personal information stolen or have his device infected with malware.

Phishing: This involves sending emails to potential victims that appear to be coming from a legitimate source. *Security* magazine estimates that over 1.76 billion phishing emails were sent in 2023 [SEC23]. The email is intended to trick the recipient into opening an attachment that has malware or click on a URL link that will take him to a Web site that will install malware on his device.

Pretexting: This refers to using a contrived story or pretext to gain the trust of a victim and manipulate them. An example of pretexting is when a criminal enters business premises while disguised as a technician, fire inspector, or phone repairman.

Pwn: Originating from mistyping the word "own," this term refers to compromising, controlling, or "owning" a person, computer, Web site, or application.

Scareware: This involves manipulating a victim by presenting a pop-up screen telling him that his computer is infected with a virus. The goal is to convince the victim to download questionable software to fix a non-existent problem. Sometimes, the cybercriminal will attempt to obtain remote control of the victim's computer. If this is accomplished, the cybercriminal may be able to install ransomware, a keystroke logger, or other virus. He may be able to obtain bank account details and withdraw funds from it.

Shoulder surfing: This involves spying, sometimes literally over the victim's shoulder, to obtain a PIN, password, or door entry code.

Smishing: This is SMS (text messaging) phishing, and tricking someone into downloading malware to their phone.

Spear phishing: This is a type of phishing attack that targets a specific individual. It is typically done after extensive reconnaissance is performed on the intended victim.

Spoofing: This involves deceiving the victim into thinking that a communication came from a legitimate source. Variations of spoofing are listed here:

a. *Caller ID spoofing*: The caller ID displayed has been altered.

b. *DNS spoofing*: Manipulating DNS (Domain Name Server) records so the victim is taken to a different, almost certainly malicious, Web site.

c. *Domain spoofing*: This is a technique used to fool an email recipient into believing it was sent by a legitimate organization. The spoofed domain name may be a deliberate misspelling of the actual domain, e.g., "g00gle.com" instead of "google.com."

d. *Email spoofing*: The email return address has been altered.

e. *Web spoofing*: This involves creating a fake Web site that mimics an actual site. The address may be off by a letter or digit. The spoofed site may be a login screen intended to capture the victim's account ID and password.

Typo squatting: This is also known as *URL hijacking*, and it takes advantage of spelling mistakes (typos) entered by Internet users. For example, a user might incorrectly type "Gooogle.com" instead of "Google.com" into their browser. When users make an error like this, they may end up at a Web site owned by a cybercriminal.

THE DANGERS OF SOCIAL ENGINEERING

Social engineering is extremely dangerous and such attacks account for 98% of all cyberattacks according to Splunk, a subsidiary of Cisco [SPL23]. According to IBM's 2023 *Cost of a Data Breach Report*, data breaches that began with a social engineering attack had an average cost of over $4.5 million [RES23].

There are no technology "solutions" that can prevent social engineering attacks. Tools like firewalls, antivirus software, network monitors, or having updated and patched software will not stop a well-designed social engineering attack. Technology cannot stop users from hurting themselves or the organizations they work for. The best defense against social engineering is for individuals and employees to become familiar with these tactics.

If a person has been scammed once, then there is a greater than average chance that he or she will be the victim of another scam attempt. In fact, some social engineers specialize in this type of scam. It is called a *follow-up scam*. The social engineers will call the victim and convince them that, for a price, they can help recover the money that was lost in the first social engineering attack.

THE EFFECTIVENESS OF SOCIAL ENGINEERING

Social engineering techniques are successful because they allow bad actors to bypass technology-oriented protections like firewalls, antivirus software, and spam filters. If a cybercriminal can convince a user or employee to help him, then he will be able to gain access to the building or office or computer that is his target. For example, if the cybercriminal can get an unwitting user to reveal his password, the cybercriminal will be able to log into the system or application without setting off any alarms.

Some of the reasons people succumb to social engineering attacks are included in this section.

Desire to Help

Most people want to help others whenever possible. In many attacks, the bad actor pretends to be new or not knowing how to do something. This plea for help may be underscored with the claim that he will get into trouble if he cannot complete a work assignment. The victim may have been in the same situation and wants to help someone they see as being like themselves.

Authority Figures

People tend to obey authority figures or someone perceived as an authority figure. They will do this even when being asked to skirt or outright break rules. If an email appears to be from the CEO or another high-ranking executive, people will likely respond to it quickly.

Scarcity

When potential victims are convinced that an item is scarce or otherwise difficult to obtain, they are more likely to act quickly. This method of manipulating consumers explains why Web sites frequently state that an offer is available for a "limited time only." Another example of emphasizing scarcity when booking hotel rooms, plane tickets, or concert tickets online is the Web site often claims that there are only one or two rooms or tickets left. The customer is urged to act immediately to avoid missing out.

Foot in the Door

A study by two Stanford University psychologists found that someone who has already agreed to a small request is more likely to agree to a larger request in the future [SCI16]. Social engineers use this technique to extract information from victims. Their first question will be something innocuous, like their email address. Later requests will be for more important or confidential information, such as details that the victim would not likely have provided if they had been asked for them initially.

Liking

People are more likely to be persuaded by someone that they like. Social engineers take advantage of this tendency by being polite and deferential toward their victims. Another human tendency is to like people that are similar to themselves. Social engineers often research potential victims to learn more about them. For example, the social engineer may try to learn where the victim went to college, what their hobbies are, and what sports teams they root for. This information is then used to convince their potential victims that they have much in common.

PREPARING FOR SOCIAL ENGINEERING ATTACKS

Bad actors know that the secret to a successful social engineering attack is preparation. They will learn all that they can about the target, whether it is an individual or an organization. The more a social engineer knows about the target, the better he is able to carry out his deception. Open source intelligence (OSINT), i.e., information that is freely available, can provide a social engineer with a wealth of information about potential targets. Potential OSINT sources include the following:

a. the organization's Web site

b. LinkedIn accounts belonging to the organization's employees

c. lists of employees at the organization

d. newspaper and magazine articles about the organization

e. published interviews with organization executives

f. social media accounts like Facebook, Twitter, TikTok, LinkedIn, Instagram, and YouTube created by employees or the organization itself

g. job posting Web sites like Monster, Indeed, ZipRecruiter, and GlassDoor. The skills mentioned on these sites tell the bad actors the hardware and software being used by the target.

h. photographs available online of the facility. Metadata associated with photographs can also be valuable to a social engineer.

i. maps of the target's property and surroundings

SOCIAL ENGINEERING ATTACKS ARE LIKELY TO WORSEN

Social engineering attacks are likely to worsen because they are extremely effective and relatively easy to execute. Using social engineering to penetrate an organization is much easier than searching for zero-day vulnerabilities. Bad actors prefer to take the path of least resistance.

Traditional phishing attacks have grammatical mistakes because the attackers are not always native speakers of the victim's language. This has been one of the best ways to spot a phishing email. Artificial intelligence (AI) will enable bad actors to create grammatically perfect emails and texts [FOR23]. AI will allow bad actors to create perfect phishing emails in virtually any language.

Deep fakes are images, videos, or audio clips created by AI software that appear to be realistic. This technology enables bad actors to create voice and video simulations capable of impersonating virtually anyone. In 2019, a UK energy firm fell victim to a whaling attack, e.g., a phishing attack, that used AI voice emulation software to impersonate the CEO of the parent company [PHO23]. The fake voice convinced the UK CEO to send 220,000 Euros to a new supplier. The new supplier was a front for the bad actors. The organization ended up losing all of the money.

A video deep fake hoax in February 2024 tricked a finance worker into paying $25 million to cybercriminals [INT24]. During a video conference call, the company CFO as well as other staff members who appeared to be participating in the call were all actually real-time deep fake creations. The impersonations of his coworkers were realistic enough to convince the victim that he should make the requested payment.

PROTECTION AGAINST SOCIAL ENGINEERING ATTACKS

There are a number of ways individuals and organizations can help avoid social engineering attacks. Some of the most important ones are as follows:

1. Recognize the red flags that indicate the situation is probably social engineering instead of a legitimate offer or deal.

    a. Any offer that sounds too good to be true is likely to be a scam. Examples are products being sold for much less than normal, great tickets to concerts at face value, or products that are extremely difficult to obtain.

    b. If the recipient feels he is being forced to make an immediate decision, then that is a strong indication that it is a social engineering situation.

    c. If the victim is warned not to talk to anyone about the offer or the situation, then it is very likely a scam. Social engineers who run lottery and grandparent scams tell the victims not to talk to anyone about it. This is done to prevent the victim from being talked out of sending the money to the scammer.

    d. If the call is making physical or emotional threats against the victim, then it is probably some kind of fraudulent situation.

    e. If the caller requires a non-standard payment method, e.g., gift cards instead of a check or credit card, then it is probably some kind of hoax.

2. Establish training for employees of an organization. According to Forbes, the percentage of employees who were victims of a phishing scam dropped from 32.4% to 5% after one year of training [FOR23]. Since new types of social engineering scams are constantly developed by bad actors, plan on updating and repeating training annually. If the organization does not have an internal group or department that can provide this, then engage a specialist organization to provide this invaluable training.

3. Always be skeptical of anything that seems odd or out of place.

4. Research claims of good deals and a vendor's reputation. If a vendor does not have a lengthy history, then the chances of the offer being fake is higher.

5. Be reluctant to provide information to an unknown person on the phone. In many instances, if the caller is who he claims to be, he should already have this information. For example, a representative of a bank would never call a bank customer and ask what their account number is.

6. Confirm requests or claims from friends or coworkers via a different channel, e.g., call them on the phone.

7. Be aware that email accounts can be hijacked. Email that appears to be from a friend or coworker can be spoofed or created by an account takeover situation.

8. Do not click on links in emails. Open a browser and go to the Web site by entering the URL address manually or use the URL saved in a Web browser's favorites list.

9. Don't give PII to a caller. Instead, get the phone number from a legitimate Web site and call them.

10. Do not open an email attachment unless it is expected and its legitimacy has been confirmed with the sender via a second channel.

11. Be extremely skeptical if someone calls claiming to be support tech from a vendor. Those organizations do *not* cold call customers. The customer must always initiate contact with a tech support call with a vendor.

12. Do not be tricked by "baiting" attacks, i.e., offers of free music, movie downloads, or free gaming software. It is very likely a scam intended to get credentials or download malware onto a victim's device.

13. Delete or ignore pop-ups on all computers and mobile phones. Enable a pop-up blocker in all browsers to prevent these from being a distraction and potential danger.

14. Never allow anyone to remotely take control of a computer. This is a very common ploy of cybercriminals to install malware on a device or to steal data from it.

15. The IRS, FBI, and sheriff's department will *never* initiate contact with a person by calling them on the phone. They will send a letter through the post office to establish initial contact.

16. If the caller is overwhelming someone with details, the best action is to ask them to send a letter explaining the details and hang up. If this is a scam, then the social engineer will most likely give up. The last thing he wants to do is put something down on paper and allow the potential victim to the time to review the details.

REFERENCES

[DEF24] "The Emotions of a Social Engineering Attack," available online at *https://www.defendify.com/wp-content/uploads/2022/10/The-Emotions-of-a-Social-Engineering-Attack.pdf*, 5/7/2024

[FBI24] "Elder Fraud, in Focus," available online at *https://www.fbi.gov/news/stories/elder-fraud-in-focus*, April 30, 2024.

[FOR23] Sjouwerman, Stu. "How AI is Changing Social Engineering Forever," available online at *https://www.forbes.com/sites/forbestechcouncil/2023/05/26/how-ai-is-changing-social-engineering-forever/?sh=1ce6e13321b0*, May 26, 2023

[INT24] Olney, Matthew. "How is AI changing Social Engineering attacks?", available online at *https://insights.integrity360.com/how-is-ai-changing-social-engineering-attacks*, March 5, 2024.

[PHO23]. Kostic, Nikola. "15 Examples of Social Engineering Attacks," available online at *https://phoenixnap.com/blog/social-engineering-examples*, July 26, 2023

[RES23] Aricioglu, Beyza. "Social Engineering Statistics to Know in 2024," available online at *https://www.resmo.com/blog/social-engineering-statistics*, October 31, 2023

[SCI16] Konnika, Maria. "The First 'Nigerian Prince' Scam," available online at *https://www.sciencefriday.com/articles/the-first-nigerian-prince-scam/*, January 15, 2016

[SEC23] "Report: Over 1.76 billion phishing emails were sent in 2023," available online at *https://www.securitymagazine.com/articles/100398-report-over-176-billion-phishing-emails-were-sent-in-2023*, February 13, 2024

[SPL23] Raza, Muhammad. "Social Engineering Attacks: The 4 Stage Lifecycle & Common Techniques," available online at *https://www.splunk.com/en_us/blog/learn/social-engineering-attacks.html*, Feb 13, 2023

[TEC21] Awati, Rahul. "ILOVEYOU virus," available online at *https://www.techtarget.com/searchsecurity/definition/ILOVEYOU-virus*, August 2021

[TIM24] Faux, Zeke. "New Study Estimates as Much as $75 Billion in Global Victims' Losses to Pig-Butchering Scam," available online at *https://time.com/6836703/pig-butchering-scam-victim-loss-money-study-crypto/*, February 29, 2024

[WIN21] CBS Staff. "Americans lost $227 million to fake sweepstakes, prize, and lottery scams in 2020, new report finds," available online at *https://winknews.com/2021/06/11/americans-lost-227-million-to-fake-sweepstakes-prize-and-lottery-scams-in-2020-new-report-finds/*, June 11, 2021

CHAPTER

5

PASSWORDS

BACKGROUND

Passwords are the most common protection for restricting access to computers, accounts, applications, and files. Users must remember and enter passwords or PINs (Personal Identification Number) to log into their computers, open up applications at work, access their bank accounts when using online banking or an ATM machine, and log into their social media accounts like Facebook and Twitter.

The number of passwords that each of us deals with on a regular basis is large. Studies by industry experts estimate that the average person has at least 80 [LOG24]. Some studies put that count as high as 240 passwords [DASH22].

Some examples of devices, accounts, or applications with passwords that the average user needs to remember are as follows:

1. network account at work

2. home computer

3. smart phone

4. tablet

5. HR system at work

6. Internet provider site

7. ATM PIN

8. bank account(s)

9. entertainment subscriptions like Netflix®, Hulu®, Prime®, or HBO Max®

10. retail sites like Amazon and Walmart

11. email account(s)

12. Microsoft Teams

13. Google accounts

14. Facebook

15. X (formerly Twitter)

16. LinkedIn

17. Ticketmaster

18. health provider portals

19. online newspaper or magazine subscriptions

20. public library accounts

21. consumer loyalty accounts like hotel, grocery stores, or restaurants

22. photo sharing applications

23. videoconferencing hubs like Zoom, GoToMeeting, or Cisco Webex

24. food delivery services like DoorDash or Grubhub

25. utility company Web sites

As the online aspects of our lives continue to grow, the number of accounts that we need to manage is likely to increase. This will certainly result in our having to create and remember additional passwords. For the majority of us, the list of passwords is already overwhelming.

One study found that the average Internet user was able to cope with four or five passwords at most [RACK22]. It is not surprising that people are using short, easy to remember passwords instead of long, complex ones.

HOW DO PASSWORDS WORK?

The way that passwords are implemented is more complicated than most users realize. Applications, networks, and Web sites keep a file or database of all user accounts and their passwords. The passwords in that file do not look like what the users enter. The passwords are encrypted by a piece of software called a *hash function*. Each password is converted or "hashed" into a unique, meaningless string of letters and numbers. Hashing is performed so that if the password file is accessed by cybercriminals, they will not see the actual passwords.

When a user creates a new account, he is required to create and type in his new password. The application converts the new password into a lengthy hashed password. For example, if "topsecret" was chosen as a password, the hashing algorithm will convert it into a random text string like "h2n7wm71qr0pm-vy5x3a2h7i0q1n6xl6f." The hashed version of this password will actually be much longer than the example shown above. The hashed password is associated with my account ID and stored in a password file or database.

Some important points to know about the hashing function are as follows:

1. The hashing function is a *one-way operation*: it cannot be reversed. Given a hashed password, it is impossible to determine what the original password was just by examining it.

2. If even a single letter in the original password is changed, then the hashed password will be completely different. There will be no similarity between the first and second hashed passwords.

3. There are many different hashing functions available for application developers to choose from. Some of the most secure ones are SHA256 and SHA512. A user will not know which hashing function was chosen by the developer, but that is irrelevant because their only concern is that the hashed password is secure.

4. The hashed passwords that are created by the hashing function or algorithm are always the same length. For example, SHA256 always creates a hashed password that is 256 characters long. SHA512 always creates a password that is 512 characters long. One of the benefits of a consistent length is that it prevents a hacker from guessing the length of the original password.

5. The chances of two different passwords having the same hashed password is possible, but is extremely unlikely.

Once an account, including the password, has been created, the application goes through the following steps to determine whether to grant or deny access to it the next time the user attempts to log in:

1. The user enters the account ID and password on the login screen.

2. The application or Web site reads both the ID and password.

3. If the account ID does not exist in the file or database, then the login account fails.

4. The application or Web site calls a function to convert the entered password into its corresponding hash value.

5. The application compares the calculated hash value with the hash value stored in the password file for that account ID.

6. If the two hash values match, then access to the application or Web site is granted.

7. If they do not match, then a message is displayed to the user that the entered information is incorrect.

8. It is considered a best practice not to identify whether the account ID, the password, or both were incorrect. If someone is trying to hack into the application, it is better to give them as little information as possible.

9. Many systems can be set up to limit the number of failed login attempts. If that threshold is exceeded, then the account is either locked or the user has to wait a predetermined amount of time to try again. This helps prevent a brute force attack, where humans or bots make repeated attempts to log into the application.

When passwords are thoughtfully chosen, they provide reasonable defense against intrusion. When chosen poorly, passwords provide virtually no defense against a skilled attacker. Unfortunately, in too many cases, users are not careful when choosing their passwords. The most significant errors that users make when choosing passwords are that they are too easily guessed and are reused across multiple accounts. Both types of mistakes make it easy for attackers to overcome this critical defense.

The passwords chosen can be considered either strong or weak. A weak password is one that can easily be guessed or cracked by an attacker. A strong password is one that cannot be guessed easily. With a little knowledge, it is possible to learn how to choose strong passwords for all accounts.

There are a limited number of keys on a computer keyboard:

- 26 lowercase letters
- 26 uppercase letters
- 10 digits
- 32 special characters, i.e., punctuation marks

This means that a one-character password has a maximum of 94 (26 + 26 + 10 + 32) combinations.

A two-character password has a maximum of 8,836 possible (94 * 94) combinations.

A three-character password has a maximum of 830,854 possible (94 * 94 * 94) combinations.

A four-character password has a maximum of 78,074,896 possible (94 * 94 * 94 * 94) combinations.

As can be seen, the possible number of combinations can be quite large.

The chart in Figure 5.1 shows how long it takes to crack a password using a brute force attack. This chart was compiled by Hive Systems in 2023 [HIVE23] and is available at *https://www.hivesystems.com/password-table*. As computers become faster, the time it takes to crack passwords will decrease.

TIME IT TAKES A HACKER TO BRUTE FORCE YOUR PASSWORD IN 2023

Number of Characters	Numbers Only	Lowercase Letters	Upper and Lowercase Letters	Numbers, Upper and Lowercase Letters	Numbers, Upper and Lowercase Letters, Symbols
4	Instantly	Instantly	Instantly	Instantly	Instantly
5	Instantly	Instantly	Instantly	Instantly	Instantly
6	Instantly	Instantly	Instantly	Instantly	Instantly
7	Instantly	Instantly	1 sec	2 secs	4 secs
8	Instantly	Instantly	28 secs	2 mins	5 mins
9	Instantly	3 secs	24 mins	2 hours	6 hours
10	Instantly	1 min	21 hours	5 days	2 weeks
11	Instantly	32 mins	1 month	10 months	3 years
12	1 sec	14 hours	6 years	53 years	226 years
13	5 secs	2 weeks	332 years	3k years	15k years
14	52 secs	1 year	17k years	202k years	1m years
15	9 mins	27 years	898k years	12m years	77m years
16	1 hour	713 years	46m years	779m years	5bn years
17	14 hours	18k years	2bn years	48bn years	380bn years
18	6 days	481k years	126bn years	2tn years	26tn years

HIVE SYSTEMS ❯ Learn how we made this table at **hivesystems.io/password**

FIGURE 5.1 Time to crack passwords of various lengths using a brute force attack

Even passwords that appear to be statistically strong can actually be weak if the password is not chosen carefully. Some of the traits of a weak password are as follows:

- using just lowercase letters instead of a combination of uppercase letters, lowercase letters, digits, and special characters
- always making the first character the only uppercase character
- choosing just letters followed by a single digit
- reusing the same password but only changing the final character, for example "secret1," "secret2," and "secret3"
- using a password that is a common, like "abcdef," "123456," "password," "secret," and "qwerty"
- passwords with obvious patterns like "123456," "abcdefg," "qwerty," and "asdfgh"
- using easily available personal information such as the following:

    i.   the user's name

    ii. another family member's name

    iii. the user's birthday

    iv. the user's anniversary

    v.   the user's alma mater

    vi. a pet's name

    vii. the user's address

    viii. the user's favorite sports team

Use of weak, short, repetitive, easily guessed, or reused passwords severely weakens the protection that passwords are supposed to provide. Attackers have seen similar, weak passwords and will crack them almost instantly. Such passwords can be determined through a sustained, dedicated attack.

Strong passwords provide significantly more protection for accounts. Some of the attributes of strong passwords are as follows:

- a minimum of 12 characters (Although longer passwords are more secure.). Given enough time, any password can be cracked by a dedicated attacker but the longer a password is the more time it will take to crack it.

- a mixture of lowercase letters, uppercase, digits, and special characters. Randomly arrange the characters. Do not always have the first letter of the password capitalized or the last character be a digit. Both of those patterns are predictable.
- Substitute some digits for similar looking letters, e.g., "3" for "E" or 0 (zero) for "O" ("oh"). This is worth doing, but do not assume this action by itself makes a password secure. Password cracking software will try zero as "O," three as "E," and one as "l."
- Avoid using any word found in a dictionary as a password. Password crackers use lists of dictionary words so anything from a dictionary provides significantly less protection.

Lists of the most commonly used passwords are published every year from data breaches. (Make sure you don't use any of them as a password) This is a recent list of the top passwords published by NordPass in 2023 [NOR23].

- 123456
- admin
- 12345678
- 1234
- 12345
- passwrd
- 123
- Aa123456
- 1234567890
- 1234567
- 123123
- 111111
- Password

REUSING PASSWORDS

Credentials for a Web site or application are composed of an account ID and a password. For some sites, the user can create their own account ID while on other sites it will be assigned to the user. When logging into a bank's Web site, the ID will probably be required to use the bank account number. For example, a Facebook account could be created with the ID like "KellyFromKillkenny." If possible, avoid reusing the account ID.

Never use the same password for multiple accounts. Account IDs and passwords that are used on multiple sites or applications can result in a security issue for the user, as can reusing passwords for personal accounts and work-related accounts. If a hacker is able to determine one of a victim's account IDs or passwords, then he now has access to multiple accounts. Unfortunately, too many of us are making it easy for cybercriminals to do this. A study done by Forbes found that, on average, people have at least four accounts with the same password [FORB24].

Cybercriminals frequently obtain user IDs and passwords from data breaches. The definition of a *personal data breach* according to the FBI is "a leak/spill of personal data which is released from a secure location to an untrusted environment. Also, a security incident in which an individual's sensitive, protected, or confidential data is copied, transmitted, viewed, stolen, or used by an unauthorized individual" [FBI23].

The number of data breach events and affected customer details is large. According to the FBI's 2023 *Internet Crime Report*, there were 55,851 reported data breaches that affected personal data. In the last five years, there were 250,087 breaches of this type [FBI23]. The exact number of breeches cannot be known because victims frequently do not report when their system is breached. Note that the previous numbers represent the number of complaints or known incidents, not the number of distinct individuals whose data was stolen.

Statista, a business intelligence platform, estimates that in 2023, there were 3,205 data compromises in the United States that affected over 353 million individuals [STA24]. In the previous statistic, some individuals must have been affected multiple times. NordLayer, a corporation that provides network access security services, estimates that over 16.5 billion accounts have been affected by data breaches since 2004 [NORD23]. Even if these statistics are not exact, it is undeniable that many accounts, likely ones belonging to the reader, were affected by data breaches.

Account data that is obtained from data breaches is regularly sold on the Dark Web. In July of 2024, a file was identified on a hacking site that contained almost 10 billion unique passwords [USA24]. This provides cybercriminals with a pool of credentials to work with. Their tactic will be to try logging into numerous Web sites using credentials acquired from data breaches. For example, assume a cybercriminal obtains credentials from the data breach of vendor "A." They will try using all of those credentials to see if any will give them access to a Netflix account, Amex account, or a Wells Fargo bank account. This only works when users reuse account IDs and passwords. According to the 2018 Verizon Data Breach report, 81% of data breaches were caused by stolen credentials [VER18].

Passphrases as Alternatives to Passwords

One alternative to a password is to use a passphrase. A *passphrase* (a portmanteau of "password" and "phrase") is a sequence of letters, words, and numbers that are related. The intention is for the passphrase to be complex enough to be secure but easier to remember than a list of random letters and numbers.

A passphrase can be based on a famous quote, a movie title, song lyrics, a motto, a book title, or something just made up. Making a slight modification to one of the words in the phrase will make it even more difficult for an attacker to guess. If the user is familiar with the original sequence of words, then a mnemonic passphrase based on it will be easier to remember than a random string of letters, digits, and special characters.

Some examples of passphrases are shown here:

- Itwasthebestoftimes or use the first letter of each word in this famous book opening Iwtbotiwtwot. Change of the letters into digits with this passphrase Iwtb0t1wtw0t
- TheBlizzardOfOz
- YoureTheOneThatILove or YoureTheOneThatIHate
- ShowMeThe$$$ or ShowMeTheMoneyHoney
- GoneWithTheWind
- TheseAreAFewOfMyFavoriteTings
- AFewG00dMens
- CallMeIshmael
- DoItToJulia
- HappyFamiliesUnhappyFamilies

The Efficacy of Passwords

The previous sections describe some of the shortcomings of using passwords as the primary method of protection has its flaws. With so many failings, why are passwords still being used? There are several explanations.

Passwords Are Easy to Implement

It is relatively easy to design and write code using a password as the gateway into an application or Web site. Too often security is not a high priority when applications are being developed so the designers use an approach that is well known and easy to implement.

Passwords Can Be Implemented Cheaply

Alternatives to passwords like fingerprints, facial recognition, multifactor authentication (MFA), and retinal scans are more complicated to put into practice than simply using a password. Frequently, they include a piece of hardware to implement and hardware costs money. It is cheaper to implement a basic login screen that requires an ID and a password.

Passwords are Familiar to Users

Entering a password to get access to a computer system has been common since the earliest days of computers. The concept is familiar to virtually everyone who uses a computer. Since everyone is so familiar with it, why change it?

Are Passwords Going Away?

Passwords will likely continue to be used for the foreseeable future.

WHY PASSWORDS NEED TO CHANGE

If passwords are relied on to protect application or data, then periodically, they need to be changed. Some of the reasons that passwords need to be changed are as follows:

- If a bad actor has cracked a password and has access to that application, then changing it will lock him out of that account. To regain access to it, they will have to start their password cracking efforts over again.
- Password attacks like a dictionary attack and a brute force attack are not instantaneous. Even using the fastest computers, it takes time to work through all the words in a dictionary file (and their variations) or all possible combinations of letters, digits, and special characters. If a strong

password is chosen, e.g., long, complex, not easily guessable, and a non-dictionary word, then it could take months or years to crack it. Periodically changing passwords will further hamper the efforts of password cracking attempts.

How Often to Change Passwords

Experts have different opinions regarding how often to change passwords. It might seem that changing passwords frequently would always be more secure, but that is not necessarily true. If users are forced to change their passwords too frequently, then it is likely that they will select passwords that are easily guessed or are simple variations of the current password. Another way users deal with having to change passwords too often is by writing them down. The strongest password in the world is worthless if it is written in a note under the keyboard. A good compromise seems to be to change passwords every 60 – 90 days.

There are circumstances that should always result in passwords being changed earlier than normal. They definitely need to be changed in the following scenarios:

- The password is associated with a Web site, social media platform or organization that has been hacked or had a data breach. When this happens, it is possible that the account information and password are now in the hands of cybercriminals. If a successful attack or breach at a vendor or site is in the news, then change any passwords to it as quickly as possible. Even if the organization states that very little or no PII (Personally Identifiable Information) was exposed, do not take a chance. In this situation, it is definitely better to be "safe than sorry."

- The account was accessed without authorization. Many sites will send a notification to an email address or phone number each time an account is accessed. For example, emails are sent out every time users log into their streaming services and other accounts. If a notification comes out and there was no authorized recent activity in the account then the user should log into it and change the password. (One word of warning: DO NOT click on a link included in such a notification. Sending out fake emails that an account has been accessed is a classic phishing technique. Type the URL into the browser or use the URL previously saved in the browser's favorites area.)

- If a device, e.g., smart phone, laptop, tablet, was lost or stolen, then change passwords immediately. Change the password of every account that was logged into from that device. If there is some question as to what accounts or Web sites were connected to from that device, then change all possible account passwords.

- If malware like ransomware, a virus, a Trojan horse, or a keylogger is found on the device, change the passwords of every account that might have connected to from the device. As in the previous situation, if in doubt, then change the password.

- An account was logged into from a public computer, e.g., at a hotel, a conference, or a public library or via a public Wi-Fi like in an airport or at a conference center. Using unsecured computers and Wi-Fi creates the scenario where a cybercriminal can capture any activity, including the account ID and password. If using public computers and Wi-Fis to access an account cannot be avoided, then remember to change the password of any account that was connected to from while using them.

- If someone who was once trusted is no longer reliable, then any account passwords they know should be changed. For example, a recent divorce, a breakup with a boyfriend / girlfriend, or a serious dispute with a family member would qualify for this situation. It would be advisable to change all passwords instead of just the ones that it is certain they knew.

- If there are any accounts that are no longer being used, then it is in prudent to close them. The danger of leaving such dormant accounts active is that if the site is breached then personal details might be captured and exposed by the attackers. Even if the same account ID or password are not being used on active accounts, it is always better to not have any PII in the hands of hackers or freely available on the Internet.

Properly Changing a Password

Changing a password means selecting a completely different one. Do not use a default word or phrase and simply append "1," "2," or "3" to it, like "Secret," "Secret1," and "Secret2." Do not alternate between two or three different passwords repeatedly. Do not reuse the same password for at least a year (preferably, never use it again).

HOW CYBERCRIMINALS CRACK PASSWORDS

There are many ways that attackers can figure out or crack passwords. Some of the most well-known ones are listed here. Lists like this will always be incomplete because bad actors are always devising new ways to access victim's accounts.

Password Cracking Tools

Password cracking is the process of determining the password to a potential victim's account or Web site. Cybercriminals have developed tools called *password crackers* to assist them in this process. Some of the techniques used by password crackers include the following:

- Dictionary attacks use all the words in one or more dictionary files.
- Brute force attacks attempt every possible combination of characters as the password.
- They can locate passwords that are cached, i.e., stored, in the memory of the computer being attacked.
- They can reveal the password behind the asterisks in password entry fields.
- They can monitor network traffic, a.k.a. "sniffing", to discover passwords sent across the network.
- They can perform attacks on multiple account passwords simultaneously.
- They can analyze Wi-Fi transmissions to identify and decrypt passwords being sent between devices.

If the existence of password cracking tools is not bad enough for the average user there is worse news. These tools are readily available on the Internet to be downloaded by anyone that wants them. This enables novice hackers to utilize tools that provide them with capabilities significantly above the skills they've developed personally.

Phishing

Phishing is a form of social engineering frequently used to trick victims into revealing their credentials like account ID and password. A typical phishing ploy is to send the victim an email stating that their bank account is about to be locked or closed due to suspicious activity, inactivity, or some other reason. The source of an email can be easily spoofed so it looks like it was sent by a bank or an organization that the victim deals with regularly. In reality, it was sent by a cybercriminal.

While the example above refers to a banking account being phished, it could just as easily be a credit card account, Amazon account, Netflix account, or an accountant's Web site. A phishing email can also appear to have been sent by a friend, doctor, the IRS, county assessor, department of motor vehicles, or insurance provider. Phishing emails can and do masquerade as any entity the attacker thinks will enable them to trick a victim into revealing information they want to obtain.

In some cases, the victim has no relationship with the organization mentioned in the email. The attackers frequently pick a large, well-known bank, credit card company or government agency and send out tens or hundreds of thousands of emails to email addresses they downloaded from a Dark Web site source. Since it costs them nothing to send out these emails, if only one recipient in a thousand or one in ten thousand falls for their scam, they are still making money. This phishing technique is called *spray and pray*.

The email contains a link that the victim is encouraged to click on to get easy access to their bank's Web site. The link, of course, does not really lead to the bank's Web site. It takes the victim to a Web site that is identical to the bank's login page but was created by and is controlled by the attackers.

Their objective is for the victim to enter their credentials, i.e., account ID and password, into the fake login page. While the victim is waiting for a response on the fake login page, their credentials are entered into the bank's actual Web site to confirm that what was entered is correct. Once the cybercriminals captured the ID and password, they will likely display an error screen advising the victim to try again later.

At this point, the victim has lost control of the account. The attacker is now able to log in and siphon off any funds in the account, change the password, uncover viewing history, or medical background information depending on what type of account they've broken into. Unless the victim is extremely fortunate, the cybercriminals will obtain their goals and be gone before anyone is aware that the account has been compromised.

The best protection against phishing attacks is to be extremely cautious when responding to unsolicited emails from what appear to be financial or other trusted institutions. Never click on a link provided in an email. Always use either a link saved in a browser's favorites or search for the vendor's Web site address online.

Looking closely at the URL link in the email may enable users to spot how it differs from the vendor's actual URL. Assume that the credit union is the Midwest Local Credit Union and their actual URL is *www.mlcu.com*. The link in the phishing email might be *www.rnlcu.com*. Examining the second

URL very closely, one can see that the "character" after the *www* is not actually an "m." It is actually the letter "r" immediately followed by the letter "n." When those two letters are next to each other, it is easy to be tricked into thinking that it is a single letter instead of two separate letters.

In other instances, a cybercriminal will subsite a "1" for an "l" or a "0" for an "o." They also might have a domain other than the normal ".com." The URL link in Figure 5.2 is an example of this kind of phishing email.

Dear Customer,

This is to inform you that we have seen suspicious activity on your account with Midwest Local Credit Union.
Due to this we will be suspending your account within the next 48 hours.
Please log into your account IMMEDIATELY to examine the recent activity and confirm whether it is valid or not.

For your convenience you can click on the following link to log into our website: www.rnlcu.com

Sincerely,

MLCU Customer Support

FIGURE 5.2 Phishing email with a fake URL link

Another red flag in phishing emails is a sense of urgency. Text in a phishing email is carefully crafted to make the recipient nervous or frightened. The victim is led to believe that if that link is not immediately clicked to validate the account, then something unfortunate will occur. The first instinct of most people is to pursue the recommended action without considering that it might be either fake or dangerous. Many types of social engineering are designed to get people to act without thinking. Slowing down and thinking carefully before taking any action is always the best response to a possible phishing email.

Other clues that an email may be a phishing attack include the following:

- The email is addressed to "Dear Customer" or a generic greeting instead of specifying the account holder's name.
- There are poor grammar, syntax, and spelling errors in the email. This is becoming less of an indicator as the bad actors improve their skills. This type of clue is almost certain to disappear as AI is used to create phishing emails instead of relying on them being written by hand.
- It asks for personal information, especially when the sender should already have that information. For example, banks already have the account numbers of all customers. There is no scenario in which they would ask someone to provide it to them.

▪ It includes a contact phone number that is not accurate. For example, a phishing email might list a support number that is not the same number as the one on the back of their credit card.

▪ The sender is using email when they would never do that. For example, the IRS will NEVER send an email stating that a taxpayer owes them money. All initial contact from the IRS will be via a letter through the USPO.

▪ If the email asks for funds in an unusual payment method the recipient should be very suspicious. No legitimate business or government entity will ask anyone to make a payment to them via Apple iTunes cards or VISA gift cards.

Dictionary Attack

This form of attack relies on an extremely large list of potential passwords (referred to as a *dictionary*) and the attack includes lists of words that were taken from an online dictionary. The attacker has software that will repeatedly try logging into the victims' accounts using every entry in the dictionary list.

This file is more than just a list of words found in the dictionary. It also includes passwords that have been commonly used in the past. The list can also include the names of sports teams, movies, books, universities, music groups, and place names. Dictionary lists exist for multiple languages, so this form of attack can be used against victims from every country in the world.

Password cracking software can be set up to try variations of each dictionary word. For example, as well as trying to use a basic word this attack will also try

▪ adding digits (1, 2, 3, etc.) to the end of the word

▪ capitalizing the first letter in the word

▪ switching letters like "o" with zero, "l" with the digit one, and "e" with the digit three

Guessing Passwords

Password attacks are automated to a large degree. If a potential victim is considered to be a high value target, then a hacker may take the time to learn as much as possible about them in order to guess possible passwords. Information about potential victims is readily available on the Internet, especially social media sites.

Details like the following can be found with minimal effort:

- date of birth
- maiden name
- mother's maiden name
- address
- college or university attended
- high school attended
- elementary school attended
- make or model of their first car
- pet names
- children's names
- nicknames
- sibling names
- sibling birthdates
- favorite sports team

The way to prevent a guessing attack is very simple. Do not use a password that can easily be guessed. Even if it does not seem possible that a hacker could possibly know the name of the junior high school a user attended, do not use that as a password. Learning the schools a victim attended or other personal details is not as challenging as most people think it is.

Installing Malware On A Computer

If the attacker can install certain types of software on a computer, then they do not have to guess the password because it will have already provided it to them. A *keystroke logger* is a piece of software that can be installed on a computer or smart phone that records all keyboard activity, i.e., every key that is pressed. A file with a record of keyboard activity will periodically be uploaded to a computer or server that the bad actor can access. Once this malware is on the device it is a simple matter for the bad actor to review keystroke activity and identify account IDs and passwords

Keystroke loggers can be embedded in an email attachment. If the attachment is clicked and opened, the malware will automatically be installed on the computer. Another way malware can be loaded onto a computer is by clicking on a link in a Web site that promises to download an image, cheat code, or a free game. No matter how it gets loaded onto the computer, it will silently be recording every keystroke, mouse click, and all the Web sites visited.

The best way to prevent becoming the victim of keystroke loggers and other malware is to be extremely careful about what gets installed on the device. This means not clicking on email attachments unless absolutely confident that the sender is trustworthy. It also means that software should only be downloaded from trustworthy sources.

A keystroke logger can also be a hardware device. For a hardware keystroke logger to be used, it must be physically attached to the computer. It might look like a dongle for a wireless mouse or keyboard that's plugged into a USB port. A physical keystroke logger can be spotted by periodically looking at the devices and cables that are plugged into the back of the computer. While this is a realistic security concern, it is not as big a problem as software that can be emailed to the victim from anywhere in the world.

Brute Force

A *brute force password attack* involves password cracking software written to repeatedly try password after password. This method might be employed by hackers if none of the previous forms of password attacks succeeded.

In most cases, brute force attacks are carried out by bots. A *bot* is a computer that has been infected with malware, e.g., a virus, leaving it under the control of a cybercriminal. The hacker can control a bot computer and make it send out phishing emails, participate in a DDoS (Distributed Denial of Service) attack, or participate in a brute force password attack. Coordinated efforts by a large number of bots allow the attacker to attempt up to millions of passwords per minute.

Factors on whether a brute force attack will be successful include the length of the password, password complexity, how frequently the user changes his password and the speed of the attacker's computer(s). The average user or organization cannot control the final factor, but can use stronger, specifically longer, more complex passwords to help prevent brute force attacks from succeeding.

Another way to help prevent or at least slow down a brute force attack is to configure accounts to be locked if more than a certain number of login attempts fail. Many applications and systems allow users to choose whether to lock the account if a certain number of login attempts occur. Three failed attempts is a common choice. This gives the user a reasonable chance to enter their password correctly, but still prevents a brute force attack from succeeding.

While it provides additional protection to accounts, there is a downside to this decision. If users lock themselves out of their account too frequently, then the Customer Service team supporting the application will be getting significantly more calls. A method of eliminating such calls is if the application allows users to unlock accounts on their own by having a new, temporary password sent to an email address associated with the account.

Credential Stuffing

Credential stuffing is a variation of the brute force attack. For this form of attack hackers use credentials, e.g., account IDs and passwords, that have been compromised, i.e., exposed, by a data breach attack on another company. According to Verizon's 2023 *Data Breach Investigations Report* (DBIR), 86% of data breaches involved the use of stolen credentials [VER23]. Frequently, the account ID of these exposed credentials are the victim's business or personal email address. Billions of compromised credentials have been exposed by data breaches over the years [DAR22]. Many of these compromised credentials can be purchased on the Dark Web.

Assume that a hacker wants to crack into the customer loyalty plan of a major chain of hotels named "Hotel X." To initiate this credential stuffing attack, the cybercriminal would download one of the many free password cracking tools from the Internet. He would then buy a list of compromised credentials off the Dark Web. He might start with a million sets of credentials. The cracking tool is set to run against the hotel chain's Web site (*www.hotelX.com*) and will try attempt to log in using all of the one million account IDs and passwords in his list one after the other.

If anyone in that list of one million data breach victims has a loyalty account at Hotel X and re-used the credentials exposed in the earlier data breach, then the attacker will be able to log into their Hotel X account. Once the attacker has access to the victim's loyalty account, he can access any data related to the victim stored by the loyalty card application. This could include credit card details, passport numbers, travel history, home and work addresses, and work and personal phone numbers. The attacker could also steal or redeem any points in the victim's rewards account.

The best defense against a credential stuffing attack is to use distinct passwords for each online account. It might not be practical to use distinct IDs for every account but avoiding password reuse is a good protection from this common type of attack.

Are Everyone's Credentials on the Dark Web?

If the estimate that over 24 billion credentials available on the Dark Web in 2022 is accurate then there is a good chance that the reader's credentials or the credentials of coworkers are among them. If one's credentials have been exposed, it would be an excellent idea to change those passwords.

How can it be determined whether any specific credential is out on the Dark Web? One way would be to delve into the Dark Web and search it personally for an individuals' email accounts or for the organization's domain name. The domain name is the part of the company's email address that comes after the "at" symbol (@). For example, email address *kelly.bourne@bourneco.com* has the domain name *bourneco.com*.

Most people do not have the knowledge, experience, or inclination to navigate the Dark Web. An alternative is to have an expert perform that search for them. Companies offer services that will monitor the Dark Web looking for the following information:

- credentials belonging to the requestor
- card numbers and driver license numbers belonging to the requestor
- sales of a company's products on illegal marketplaces
- confidential or proprietary data stolen from a company being offered for sale on the Dark Web

An individual can determine if his email address has been compromised by going to the Web site Have I Been Pwned at *https://haveibeenpawned.com*. The owners of this Web site have compiled a list of all credentials that have been compromised via data breaches. By entering an email address on this site, it is possible to search that list to determine whether those credentials, i.e., email address and a password, are on it. (The terms "pwn" and "pwned" mean that a victim has been controlled or compromised by another person.)

Once at that Web site, enter an email address into the text box and click the "pwned?" button. Figure 5.3 shows the results of an email address that does not exist in the list of compromised credentials. Figure 5.3 indicates the account has not been compromised.

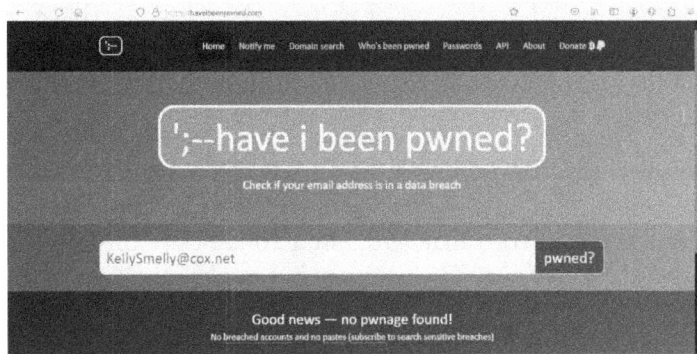

FIGURE 5.3 The results of an email address that does not exist in the list of compromised credentials

If the email account was found on this list, a screen like what's shown in Figure 5.4 will be displayed. Unfortunately, this Web site does not display the password associated with that email account in the data breach. If an account appears on this site, its passwords need to be changed. Its security would be heightened by implementing MFA to protect it.

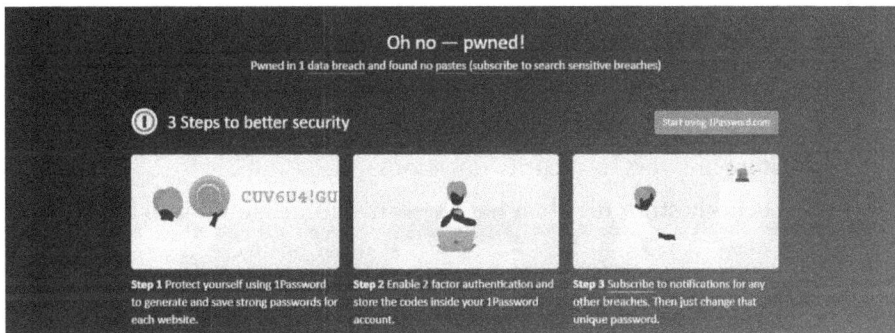

FIGURE 5.4 An account that has been compromised

This Web site provides a service that will notify the owner if their email account has been included in any future data breech. Simply click on the "Subscribe" link and enter an email address.

Password Managers

Users often receive challenging advice about passwords. They are told that they should be using lengthy, complex passwords. Using unique passwords for each of their dozens or scores of different applications is strongly advised.

Users are also advised to never write their passwords down. Finally, they are advised or required to change their passwords on a regular basis. Following all of these directives can make it difficult for a user to remember all of their passwords.

One solution is to install and use a password manager. It can store all a user's passwords in a single, secure location. When an application or a Web site is opened the password manager will automatically fill in the account ID and password for that site. The user just has to click the "log in" button.

Besides storing passwords, password managers can also generate passwords that are a random jumble of letters, digits, and special characters. This is ideally exactly what passwords should be, but rarely are since it is so difficult for the human mind to remember such passwords, especially when there are dozens of them.

A password manager works by encrypting all of the passwords in it and storing them in a single file. Even if a hacker were to gain access to the computer on which it is running, the password file in the manager would be indecipherable.

Other features that offered by some password managers include the ability to

- create new passwords that are extremely strong
- store PINs (Personal Identification Numbers)
- store credit card numbers, their expiration dates, and their CVV codes
- store answers to security questions
- securely store files that have sensitive information into them

Types of Password Managers

1. Browser-based password managers

Most browsers, including Chrome, Firefox, and Safari, offer a built-in password manager. Users may already be using a browser-based password manager without realizing it if they have ever clicked on the "Save" button on the popup message box when logging into a Web site. Figure 5.5 shows that message box asking whether to save the password in Firefox's internal password manager.

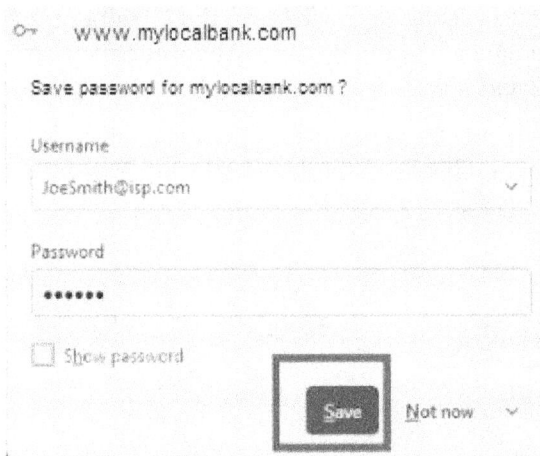

FIGURE 5.5 Saving a password in Firefox's internal password manager

The biggest advantage of using a browser's built-in password manager is the convenience. The user just navigates to the Web site and enters the account ID, and the password is auto-populated. Other advantages are that this type of password manager is already installed and it is free.

There are disadvantages to using browser-based password managers, including the following:

- Each browser has its own password manager. If a user saves his Netflix account in Firefox, then he will always have to use Firefox to log into Netflix. To log into Netflix using Chrome, then the password will have to be saved in Chrome's built-in password manager, too. Remembering which passwords have been saved in which browsers could become a major challenge when multiple browsers are being used.
- If a Netflix password is saved in both Firefox and Chrome and needs to updated, it will need to be updated in both browsers. It would be extremely easy for a user to forget to do this in all of their browsers.
- Not all browser password managers can generate passwords. The ability to create strong, random looking passwords is one of the major features of a password manager.
- The biggest disadvantage of browser-based password managers is that they are not secure. If someone is able to log into the browser, then they can see a list of all accounts and passwords that the browser has saved.

In Firefox, if the user clicks on the "hamburger button," i.e., the three horizontal bars in the upper right corner, they can select the "Passwords" option and see all of accounts, including the passwords, in plain text.

The account (JoeSmith@isp.com) and password (Secret1) for a hypothetical user and his bank, MyLocalBank, are shown in Figure 5.6.

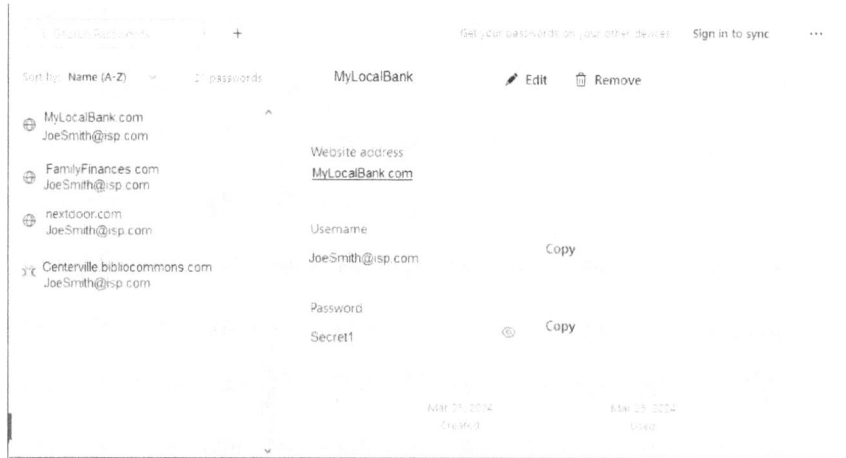

FIGURE 5.6 List of accounts and passwords in Firefox

If a home computer is not locked or the screen has not gone into sleep mode, it would take just a couple of seconds for a visitor to one's home to be able to learn enough to log into most of the account details and Web sites.

2. Local Password Managers

A local, or desktop-based, password manager is installed onto a desktop or laptop computer. The interface software and the encrypted password file will reside on that computer.

One of the greatest advantages of a local based password manager is that the encrypted file holding the passwords is stored on the local hard drive. Passwords will never be uploaded to another location or server.

Another point to consider when using a local password manager is that the owner is responsible for backing up the encrypted password file. If he fails to do this and the computer and password files are deleted, destroyed, or corrupted then those passwords are gone forever. It would be extremely easy for most of us to forget to back up that file regularly.

3. Cloud Password Managers

A *cloud-based password manager* stores its encrypted password file in the cloud, i.e., on a server provided by the password manager vendor. The location where passwords are stored is the primary difference between a local and a cloud-based password manager.

There are a number of advantages to a cloud-based password manager.

- The most significant advantage of a cloud password manager is that it is not limited to a single device. The same passwords can be accessed from any computer or smart phone and from anywhere in the world.
- Cloud-based password managers are as easy to use as local password managers.
- The vendor will ensure that the encrypted password file is backed up. If the user's computer crashed, burned in a house fire, or was stolen, then he can access his password file from another computer.
- Both local and cloud password managers are able to generate new passwords when the user is connecting to a Web site for the first time or when he needs to change an existing password. Passwords created by a password manager will be both long and complex. They will be strong enough that the user will not have to worry about passwords being breached by either a dictionary attack or a brute force attack.
- Many password vendors monitor Dark Web sites for information on credential breaches. If any of the user's credentials are exposed as a result of a breach, they will be notified.

Cloud-based password managers have the following disadvantages.

- This solution is Internet-dependent. If the user cannot access the vendor's server, then he will not have access to his passwords and cannot log into any of his applications or Web sites.
- Control over one's passwords' security has been given to a third party. The vendor almost certainly knows more about securing files than the average user does, but for some people, it is difficult to put this level of trust in another organization.

Downsides to Password Managers

There are downsides to using password managers, as well. Some of the most significant disadvantages include the following:

- There is a single point of failure. If hackers are ever able to break the defenses of the password manager being used, then they could gain access to all of the user's passwords. There have been incidents where password managers have been hacked.
- It is one password that cannot be forgotten or written down. If the master password is forgotten, then the ability to access all other passwords is lost. It would be extremely dangerous to write this password down since if someone else found it, they would be able to log into all of the user's applications and Web sites.
- Not all password managers support MFA (Multifactor Authentication). If using MFA is important to a user, then they will have to make sure the password manager chosen to use provides this capability.
- Compatibility issues with some Web sites. Not all Web sites are able to work with all password managers.
- In the event of the user's death or incapacitation, it would be extremely difficult or impossible for someone else to extract the passwords from the password manager. Possible solutions are to leave the master password with a trusted relative, include it in a will, or leave it in a safety deposit box to be opened only on the user's death or disability.

Free vs. Pay

Some password managers are available for free while others must be purchased. Some vendors offer free versions that do not provide all of the features available on their paid versions. Frequently, the free versions limit the number of devices that it can run on or the number of devices that connect to it or the number of passwords that can be stored.

Like many elements in life, there can be an element of "you get what you pay for" when choosing a free password manager. If the belief is that a password manager is needed to help protect passwords and other digital assets, then it is probably worth spending a relatively small amount of money on it every year.

Like most high-tech products, new password managers are being developed constantly and existing ones undergo regular change. By the time this book is in print, any recommendations will likely be outdated. Some of the most highly regarded password managers (in alphabetical order) when this book was being written are shown here:

- Bitwarden Free
- Bitwarden Premium
- Dashlane
- Dashlane Premium
- Keeper
- Keeper Free
- LastPass
- Password Boss
- Password Families

The screenshots below show the steps that are taken to log into a fictional app using Bitwarden.

Step 1: In the browser, bring up the app's login screen. This can be done by entering the URL into the browser or selecting the streaming site's address from the "Favorite" list. On the sign-in page, click on the "User ID" field. Figure 5.7 shows account name Bitwarden has associated with the Web site. Click on the user ID value presented by Bitwarden.

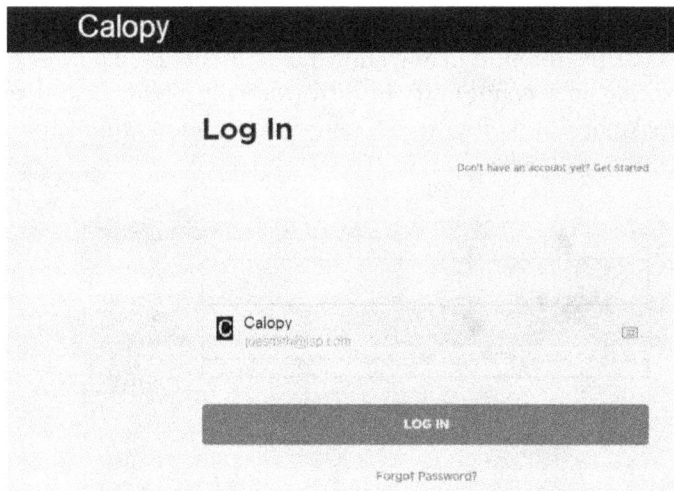

FIGURE 5.7 Step 1 using Bitwarden to log into a Web site

Step 2: Figure 5.8 shows that Bitwarden has auto-filled the password associated with this account and Web site Calopy. Click on the password field. The "LOG IN" button will be displayed. Click on it.

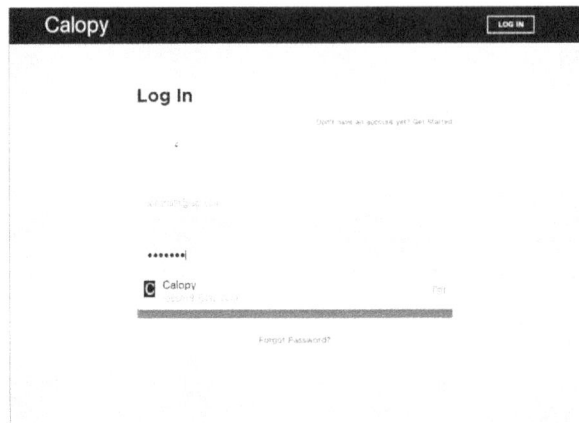

FIGURE 5.8 Second step of using Bitwarden to log into a Web site

Some password managers provide the option of using MFA to log into them. This provides an extra level of security for the application that figuratively holds the keys to the kingdom. Activating MFA for this important application is a wise choice.

One additional feature that Bitwarden offers is to determine whether a password has been found in any known data breaches. This option can be viewed by editing an account entry in Bitwarden and then clicking on the circle with a checkmark in it. Figure 5.9 shows the screen where the password for an account was checked.

FIGURE 5.9 Password checked against known data breaches

If the password was been found in a breach, the user will be warned with text like "This password has been exposed *X* time(s) in data breaches. You should change it." Checking all new passwords against known data breaches is excellent practice. Periodically checking all existing passwords is also a great precaution.

Social Engineering Password Scams

There will always be social engineering scams designed to get potential victims to reveal their passwords. It might be someone calling them claiming to be from his workplace, bank, a vendor like Microsoft or a social media organization. The deceptions used to trick the victim into revealing passwords are both creative and ever growing. Some examples are listed here:

- A caller may claim to be a systems engineer at an employer, bank, or ISP. They may say that they are doing testing and need to know a password to complete the test.

- A phishing email warns that an account is locked or is about to be locked. To avoid this, the recipient needs to click a link and unlock the account. The link actually leads to a fake Web site instead of the actual Web site of the bank, ISP, or CPA. The cybercriminals are hoping that victims will log onto their fake logon screen so credentials can be captured.

- A phishing email purportedly from the IRS claims the recipient owes back taxes. The recipient is urged to open the attachment to learn how to avoid additional penalties. If the email is opened, then spyware or a keylogger designed to steal passwords will be installed on the computer.

- Another IRS related scam is that the phishing email claims that a refund is set to be issued. All the recipient needs to do is to open the attachment and follow the directions on it.

- A phishing email claims that the recipient missed a court appearance or jury duty obligation. The attachment to the email supposedly provides details. If the attachment is opened then spyware designed to steal passwords will be installed on the computer.

- *Baiting* is a form of social engineering that relies on human curiosity to get people to open email attachments. The file attached to the email will have an interesting or provocative name like "Layoffs for Q1" or "Executive Compensation." If the recipient opens the file, then a form of malware will be installed on the computer.

No reputable vendor, corporation, or government agency will ever call or email anyone asking for their passwords. An email asking for it is almost certainly a scam. Delete it without clicking on any links in it. Getting a phone call that results in the caller asking for a password is also a scam and the call should be ended immediately.

Security Questions

Many Web sites, including banks and social media sites, have security questions or prompts that can be used to verify identity if the client forgets their password. Typically, the user is presented with a list of potential security questions. Examples of them include the following:

- City of birth?
- City where professional career started?
- Mother's maiden name?
- University graduated from?
- High school graduated from?
- Elementary school attended?
- Name of first pet?

The security questions (or *challenge questions*) chosen should have the following qualities:

- The answer cannot be researched or easily guessed. Examples of low-quality questions include "Mother's maiden name" or "High school graduated from." Answers to these can easily be researched. It is quite possible that a genealogy site lists details about the user's extended family. This is especially true if a family member is an avid amateur genealogist.
- Do not choose a question whose answer might have been revealed on a social media site. For example, the answer to city of first professional job may be listed on a LinkedIn page. Sports that the person participated in during high school may be listed on a Facebook account or on the high school's Web site.
- The question has many possible answers, but only the owner would know the correct answer.
- The ideal answer does not change over time. The name of a favorite movie can change over time, but the name of a first love will not. This will be easier to remember over a long period of time.

When creating an answer, one does not have to answer truthfully. The downside to this is that it is critical to remember the deception. For example, the name of a favorite movie actor can be used as the name of a first pet.

One last point is that just as it is a bad idea to reuse passwords on multiple sites, do not use the same security question on multiple Web sites. Doing that would enable a cybercriminal to gain control of multiple accounts if they were able to correctly guess the answer.

Final Tips For Protecting Passwords

- Do not write passwords down on a piece of paper and place it under a keyboard. Hiding passwords on the back of a photograph on the desk, under the mousepad, behind pictures on the wall, in a desk drawer, or any equally obvious place in the vicinity of the computer will not keep it secure.

- Ben Franklin said "Three can keep a secret, if two of them are dead." This sentiment applies to passwords just as much as to secrets. Unless there is a compelling reason for another person to know the password then do not tell anyone. One reasonable exception would be that a spouse needs to know the passwords of joint financial accounts.

- Do not let anyone watch as passwords or PINs are being entered. The phrase describing this is "shoulder surfing." If someone is lurking in the immediate area, then either ask them to leave, log in later, or make sure that the keys being pressed are shielded from their view.

REFERENCES

[DAR22] Chickowski, Ericak. "24+ Billion Credentials Circulating on the Dark Web in 2022," available online at *https://www.darkreading.com/vulnerabilities-threats/24-billion-credentials-circulate-dark-Web-2022*, June 15, 2022

[DASH22] Dashlane. "Report: A Global Look at Password Health" available online at *https://www.dashlane.com/global-password-health-score-report-2022*, January 2023

[FBI23] Langan, Timothy. "Federal Bureau of Investigation Internet Crime Report 2023," available online at *https://www.ic3.gov/Media/PDF/AnnualReport/2023_IC3Report.pdf*, December 2023

[FORB24] Haan, Katherine. "America's Password Habits: 46% Report Having their Password Stolen Over the Last Year," available online at *https://www.forbes.com/advisor/business/software/american-password-habits/*, June 3, 2024

[HIVE23] Hive Systems. "Are Your Passwords in the Green?," available online at *https://www.hivesystems.com/blog/are-your-passwords-in-the-green*, April 18, 2023

[LOG24] Kasyoki, Gloria. "How Many Passwords Does the Average Person Have," available online at *https://logmeonce.com/resources/how-many-passwords-does-the-average-person-have/*, March 28, 2024

[NOR23] NordPass. "Top 200 Most Common Passwords," available online at *https://nordpass.com/most-common-passwords-list/*, 2024

[NORD23] "Breakdown of the 12 most significant 2023 data breaches" available online at *https://nordlayer.com/blog/data-breaches-in-2023*, December 12, 2023

[RACK22], Rackspace Technology Staff. "World Password Day: Password Security Tips From a Cybersecurity Expert," available online at *https://www.rackspace.com/blog/world-password-day-security-tips-2022*, May 5, 2022

[SEC23] Security in Five. "Who Can Remember All This? How Our Brains Are Failing the Password Test of the Digital Age," available online at *https://securityinfive.com/who-can-remember-all-this-how-our-brains-are-failing-the-password-test-of-the-digital-age/*, March 28, 2024

[STA24] Petrosyan, Ani. "Number of data compromises and impacted individuals in US 2005-2023," available online at *https://www.statista.com/statistics/273550/data-breaches-recorded-in-the-united-states-by-number-of-breaches-and-records-exposed/*, Feb 12, 2024

[USA24] Lin-Fisher, Betty. "10 billion passwords have been leaked on a hacker site. Are you at risk?," available online at *https://www.usatoday.com/story/money/2024/07/11/10-billion-passwords-leaked-what-to-do/74366179007/*, July 11, 2024

[VER23] Verizon's "Data Breach Investigations Report" available online at *https://www.verizon.com/business/resources/reports/dbir/2023/*, Apr 2, 2024

6

MFA (MULTIFACTOR AUTHENTICATION)

MULTIFACTOR AUTHENTICATION (MFA)

MFA can be a valuable part of a layered security strategy referred as "defense in depth." The idea is to have multiple defensive layers so if a cybercriminal gets through one of them, he still will not have access to the files, data, or system. A real-world analogy of a multilayered security strategy could be the forms of security that a bank has in place. A bank might have some or all of the following security features:

1. clear lines of sight on the property so anyone approaching will be seen.

2. external security cameras

3. Access to the building is limited to strong, lockable external doors.

4. internal security cameras

5. armed guards inside the building

6. locked money drawers at each teller station

7. tellers who have undergone security training

8. panic or duress buttons that can be discreetly pushed by tellers

9. Customers are required to show identification to complete a transaction.

10. restricted areas protected by interior doors with keypad locks

11. a locked vault, which can be opened by a limited number of highly trusted employees

The concept behind MFA is that adding an additional layer to the authentication process makes it significantly harder for it to be breached. If an attacker has acquired a user's account ID and password, they would also need access to this additional security factor. MFA is not unbreakable, but when implemented correctly it provides substantially better security. According to Microsoft, there are over 300 million fraudulent access attempts every day on their cloud services. They estimate that 99.9% of these automated attacks can be blocked by MFA security [MIC23].

A cyber defense strategy that relies only on passwords can be defeated. The previous chapter described some of the main shortcomings of passwords, including the following:

- Users select weak passwords.
- Passwords are reused for multiple accounts.
- Attackers have powerful password cracking tools at their disposal.
- Social engineering can be extremely successful in tricking users into revealing their passwords.

WHAT ARE THE FACTORS?

The generally recognized factors in MFA are

- something you know, like a password, a Personal Identification Number (PIN) or the answer to a security question, sometimes called a challenge question. This factor is the one most likely to be compromised.
- something you have, like a card, a hardware token, a smart phone, or access to an email account
- something you are, like your fingerprints, your face, your voice, or your retinal pattern

Biometrics: "Something You Are"

The "something you know" and "something you have" factors are straightforward, but the "something you are" needs to be explained in greater detail. Biometric authentication is becoming a more common form of identification and access control. These systems use one of several physical characteristics of the user to prove that the person trying to gain access to the system truly is himself or herself.

Fingerprints and facial recognition are two of the most common forms of biometric authentication. Many smart phones have a fingerprint reader built into them which is used to unlock the phone. Other smart phones use the built-in camera and facial recognition software to unlock them. Fingerprint readers and dedicated cameras for facial scans can also be used to control access to computers and applications.

HOW MFA WORKS

MFA is a generic term. If two different components are required to gain access, it is referred to as *two-factor authentication* (2FA). If a third component is required, then it would be *three-factor authentication* (3FA). Most implementations are 2FA.

Logging onto an application on a computer or a Web site may require entering an account ID and a password. This is not considered MFA or 2FA because both factors (account ID and password) are something that you know. Since they are the same type of factor, it only qualifies as single factor authentication not multifactor.

Cards

A very common example of 2FA are the steps required when a bank account holder wants to withdraw money from an ATM machine. The two factors in this case are the bank card (something you have) and the PIN that must be entered (something you know). The account holder inserts his bank card into the slot (Factor 1) and when prompted types in the PIN (Factor 2). If the system confirms that the PIN is associated with the account, then access to the account is allowed.

Short Message Service (SMS)

Another common 2FA implementation is having a text message or code sent to a smart phone. After entering the account number and password, a new screen is displayed for the user. The user is required to enter a code into the text field that's now being displayed. The code will be sent as a text message to the user's smartphone. The user has a limited amount of time, 30 seconds to a minute is common, to correctly enter the code. Once it is been entered and authenticated by the system or application, then the user is granted access.

Security Keys

Physical "keys" can be the second factor in an MFA setup. In many cases, the key is a device that is similar to a USB drive or thumb drive. This type of device is also called a *token*. It is inserted into the USB drive of a desktop or laptop computer. If the user has the correct password and the correct security key, then access is granted.

A disadvantage of security keys is that they are not free. Each key can cost between $20 and $100. Respected vendors for these devices include Yubico, Thetis, SoloKeys, Google, and Nitrokey.

Examples of MFA Systems

2FA is frequently used by banks, online retailers, email providers, online gaming platforms, social media sites, and healthcare organizations. If MFA has not already activated MFA for all accounts, then seriously consider doing it. The organizations frequently have a link on the login page or the customization page to begin setting up MFA. If no such link exists, then click on links to the FAQ page or the Customer Service screen.

Health Provider Portal

Many health providers, e.g., hospital systems and doctors' groups, have an Internet portal that enables their patients to schedule appointments, view test results, see their account balance, and make a payment. Restricting access to just the patient is extremely important. In many cases, MFA is used to enforce security.

The steps to log into an account are described in the following sections.

Step 1 – After guiding the browser to the portal's Web site, the patient types in their name and password (Factor 1). Figure 6.1 shows the login screen with the name and password field in the upper right corner.

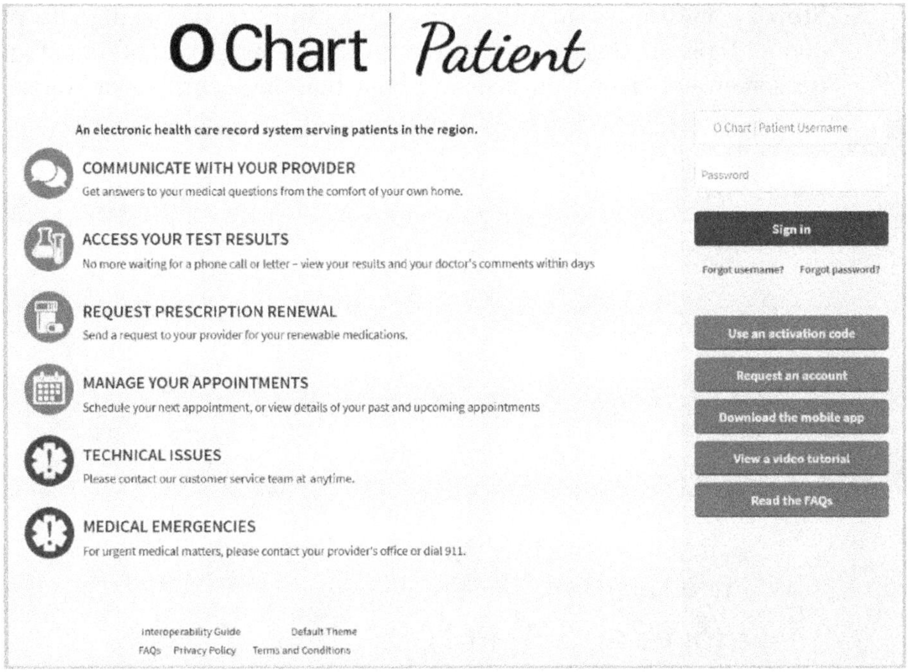

FIGURE 6.1 Health provider portal logon screen

Step 2 – The patient is given the choice of having a one-time security code sent to either their email address or their phone (Factor 2). Both the email address and phone number were set up when the patient originally created their account with the health care provider. Figure 6.2 shows this option screen.

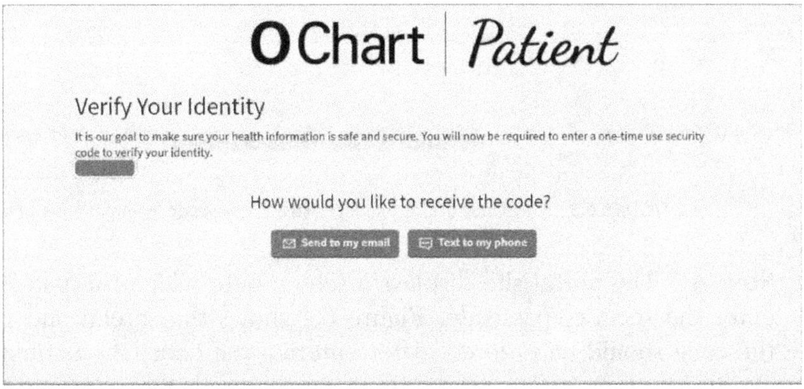

FIGURE 6.2 Choosing between having security code sent to an email address or texted to a phone

Step 3 – A text message with the one-time security code is sent to the patient's phone. Typically, this code will expire within a short period of time. Figure 6.3 is a screenshot taken from a smart phone that the security code was sent to.

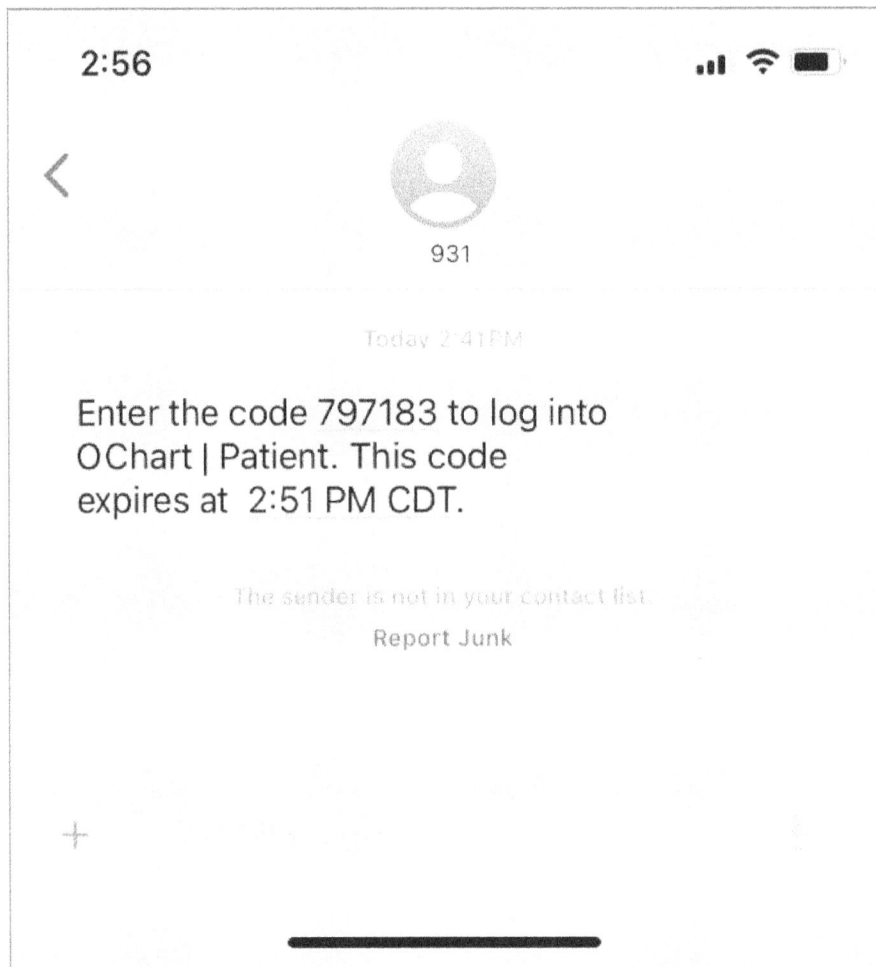

FIGURE 6.3 Screenshot of text message with security code from patient's phone

Step 4 – The portal site displays a screen onto which the patient needs to enter the security passcode. Figure 6.4 shows the screen and field where the code should be entered. After entering the code, the patient clicks the "Verify" button. If the correct code was entered, then the patient is given access to their health information.

O Chart | *Patient*

Verify Your Identity

Two-Step Verification

We've sent a security code to ***-***-2151.

Learn more

Enter your code below to continue.

> Enter Code

Verify

Didn't receive the code?
Resend code

Back

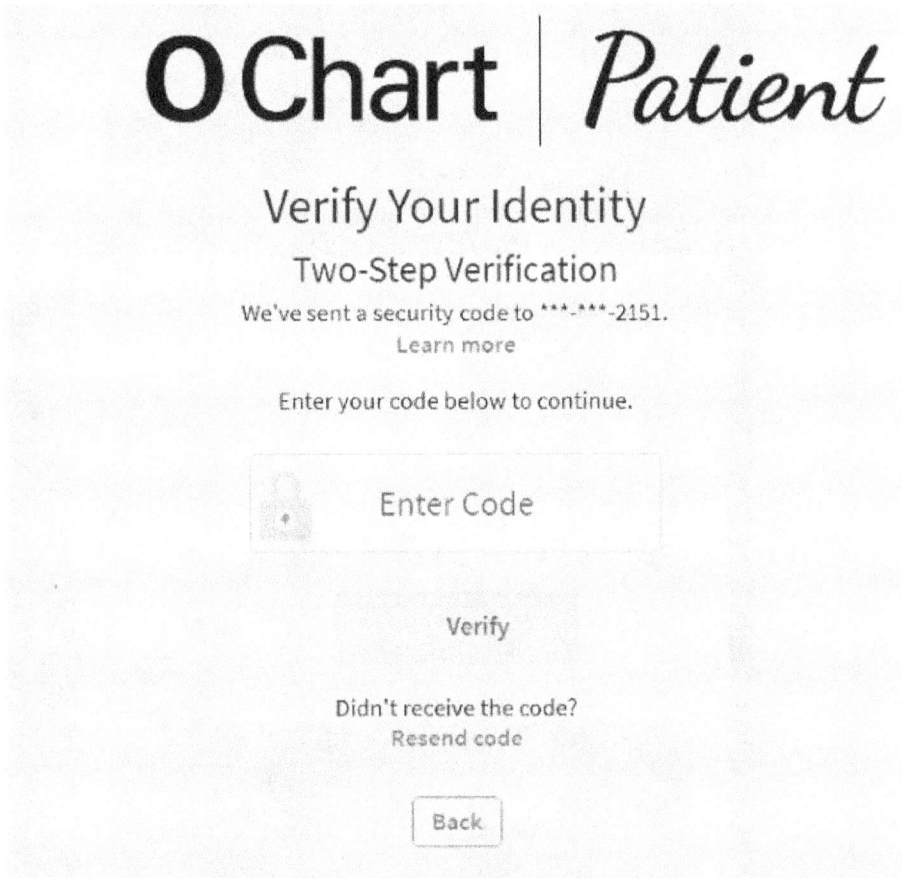

FIGURE 6.4 Portal screen where patient enters the security passcode

Financial Institution

Obviously, protecting access to investors' financial accounts and details is critical. If a cybercriminal was able to access an investor's account, he would be able to steal the client's assets. The 2FA logon steps for a retirement financial account are shown in the following sections.

Step 1 - After guiding the browser to the financial organization's Web site, the investor types in their name and password (Factor 1). Figure 6.5 shows the login screen with the name and password field.

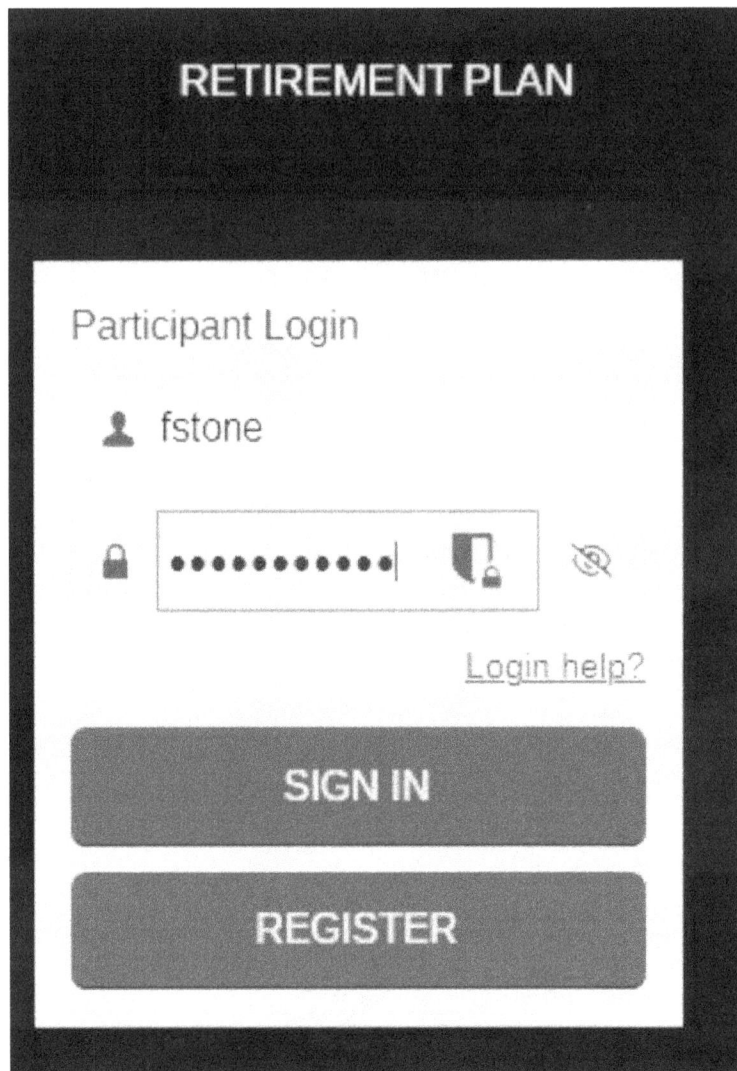

FIGURE 6.5 Financial organization's logon screen

Step 2 – The screen has a drop-down list box that provides the investor with choices where to have the one-time security code sent. In this example the code will be sent to a smart phone. Figure 6.6 shows this option screen.

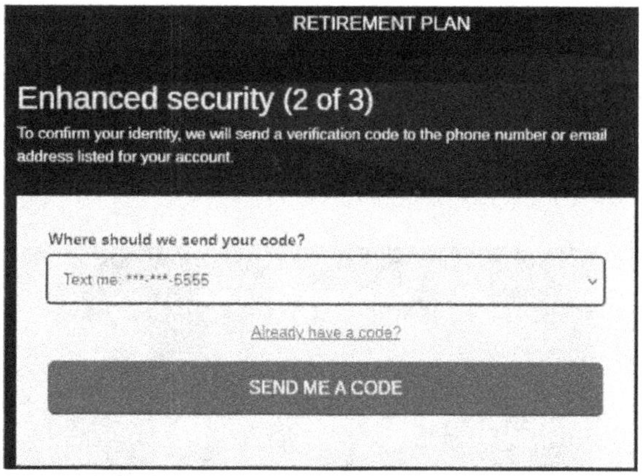

FIGURE 6.6 Choosing where to have the one-time security code sent

Step 3 – A text message with the code is sent to the investor's phone (Factor 2). In this example, the code will expire in 30 minutes. Figure 6.7 is a screenshot taken from the investor's phone showing the security code sent by the financial institution.

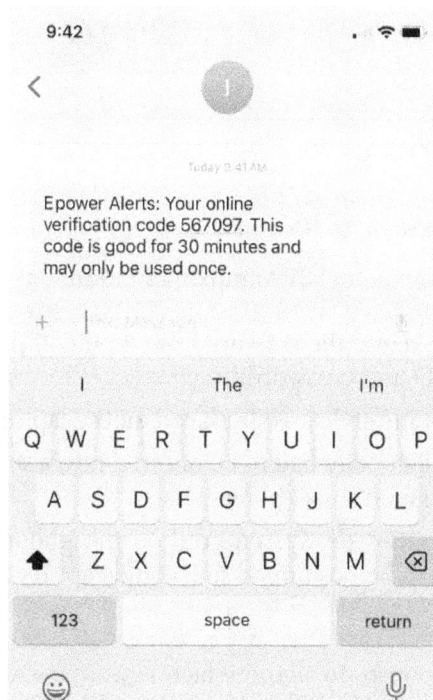

FIGURE 6.7 Screenshot of investor's phone showing text message with security code

Step 4 – The security code sent to the investor's phone needs to be entered into the final login field. Figure 6.8 shows the screen where the code should be entered. After entering the security code, the investor clicks the "Sign In" button. If the proper code was entered, the investor is given access to their financial account.

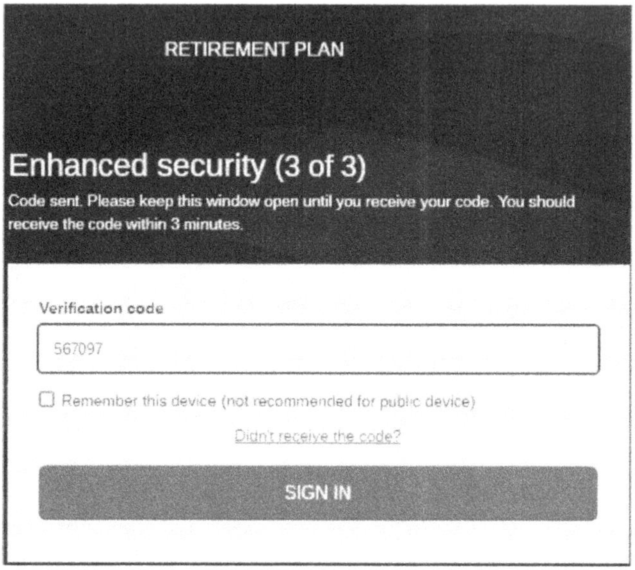

FIGURE 6.8 Portal screen where investor enters his security passcode

Anecdotal Experience with a 3FA

An example of an actual 3FA implementation is as follows:

- Users logged into the network from their company-issued laptop by entering their ID and password (Factor 1).
- A two-digit number was displayed on the laptop's login screen (Factor 2).
- That two-digit code had to be entered into a screen that came up on their company-issued smart phone (Factor 2).
- If the correct code was entered on the phone, then the camera on the phone had to be positioned so it could capture the image of the user's face (Factor 3).

Only if the responses to all three factors were correct would the user be given access to the network.

When to Use MFA

When should MFA be used to help secure accounts? The obvious answer is "whenever it is available," but the reality is that many users will not take the time or effort to set up MFA for every account and Web site. The list below shows examples of accounts and Web sites where this additional level of security should be set up.

- bank and credit union accounts
- brokerage accounts
- accountant and tax preparation professionals
- credit card accounts
- wealth management / retirement adviser
- lawyer
- doctor, dentist, pharmacist, and other health professionals
- insurance (life, health, and property) providers
- email provider
- social media accounts

PROS AND CONS OF MFA

There are advantages and disadvantages of MFA systems

Pros

- The additional layer of security provided by MFA is excellent protection against credential stuffing attacks.
- Sending a one-time password (OTP) or code to a user's phone is more secure than just a password.
- Setting up an MFA can be done by the user fairly easily.
- If a smart phone is chosen as the "something you have" factor, then MFA is affordable since most users already have a cell phone.

Cons

- If hardware tokens are chosen as the second factor, then they need to be acquired and distributed to the users.

- Hardware tokens and cell phones can be broken, lost, or stolen. The user's MFA authentication will not be possible until the device is repaired, found, or replaced.

- No matter how easy the MFA process is, some users will still resent having to perform the additional steps imposed by to get access to the computer, Web site, or application.

- If the network or Internet is down, then multifactor authentication cannot be completed and the user may be temporarily locked out of the application.

- No biometric scanner is 100% accurate. There will always be false positives (access is granted to someone who should not have it) and false negatives (access is denied to someone that should have it).

- All MFA implementations must be periodically reviewed and upgraded if they become outdated or have been compromised.

THE CHALLENGES TO MFA

While implementing MFA will provide additional security, it is not infallible. Some of the ways that MFA can be compromised are listed below. The point to the following sections is not that MFA is not worth doing (because it is), but that an implementation of MFA still requires users to be vigilant.

Biometric Authentication Security

Biometric authentication systems provide additional security but are not perfect. As new biometrics systems are developed and rolled out, attackers find ways to overcome them.

Hollywood movies include scenes of how biometric systems are defeated all the time. In reality, fooling a biometric system is not as it is portrayed in the movies. It can actually be a lot easier than the movies make it seem.

Fingerprint Readers

Fingerprint readers can be hacked. *PC Magazine* published an article claiming to have defeated fingerprint authentication with the following steps [PCMAG21]:

1. Take a photograph of the fingerprint.

2. Make a negative image using Photoshop®.

3. Print the negative image.

4. Layer a small amount of off-the-shelf wood glue on the printout.

The total effort cost the authors about $5 worth of supplies.

A 3D printer can be used to create a printed fingerprint that will deceive some fingerprint scanners [DEF20]. The process involves the use of a digital camera that has macro image functionality. You can then use an open-source Python tool to digitally optimize the fingerprint. Then, render the image into a 3D version with a 3D modeling tool, and print the image using a 3D printer. While this is not a simple process, a dedicated individual could follow it if the target was valuable enough.

Another method of hacking into a smart phone or touchscreen device like a tablet is called a *smudge attack* [BLA23]. The technique is based on the assumption that oily smudges of the device's owner always exist somewhere on the device, perhaps even on the fingerprint reader itself. The most basic version of this attack is to simply place a piece of adhesive tape over the owner's fingerprint scanner on the device and press on it. The tape will highlight the ridges of the owner's fingerprint, which may deceive the fingerprint reader. More complicated versions of this attack use cameras, special lighting, and a powder to highlight and capture clearer fingerprint images, which could be printed and used to defeat the fingerprint reader.

Voice Authentication

Voice authentication is another biometric authentication method. The system is trained by having the user repeat a specific phrase into a microphone multiple times. The user's unique vocal signature is saved in the authentication server's database. When the user wants to log in, they are prompted to repeat the authentication phrase. Voice analysis software compares the user's current voice with the stored sample. If they match, within allowable deviations, then access is granted.

To defeat this authentication method, malicious actors developed deep fake software that is capable of producing recordings of the target phrase based on recorded audio of the victim's voice. These voice samples were accurate enough to pass the voice authentication tests. Developers of the authentication software subsequently introduced "spoofing countermeasures" to detect the deep fakes. Researchers at the University of Waterloo claim to have been able to develop techniques that enable them to deceive the improved voice authentication systems [WAT23]. They claim a 99% success rate after only six attempts.

Facial Recognition

Facial recognition software is one of the most common biometric authentication measures. The majority of modern smart phones have built-in cameras that are used to capture an image of the user's face. Facial recognition software then compares the face just scanned with previously recorded facial images entered when the owner set the phone up. If the faces match, then access is granted.

Unfortunately, this security method is not foolproof. Every time a new smart phone or operating system is released, people can demonstrate that its facial recognition system can be beaten. Sometimes the hack is as simple as a photograph that has been printed out. Research done by Emma Woollacott at *Forbes* magazine tested 48 Android phones and found that 19 could be unlocked using a photograph of the owner printed on normal copier paper [FOR23]. In that study, however, none of the Apple phones tested were tricked by this attempted hack.

Researchers have tricked facial recognition systems by simply printing a photograph of the person [FAC23]. It is fairly easy to acquire a photo of just about anyone from social media sources like Facebook or LinkedIn. For facial recognition software that is not deceived by a two-dimensional photograph, then using the photo to create a mask of the person's face may be enough.

A more advanced technique, according to the same researchers, is to start with a digital photo and manipulate it using software to enhance it, resulting in a fake image that looks like the subject in 3D. The resulting image can deceive some MFA systems.

An even more complex method of tricking facial recognition systems would be to use deepfake technology. Artificial intelligence software can be used to create extremely realistic images and videos of the subject (*deepfakes*). This technology is widely available today and is becoming both more realistic and more readily available every day.

Social Engineering the Service Desk

A different method of defeating MFA authentication is to bypass the "what you have" factor altogether. There have been numerous incidents where a hacker has contacted an organization's help desk and impersonated an actual user, i.e., the victim. The hacker might have researched the user's background so he is able to successfully reply to challenge questions about the user.

Once the cybercriminal has misled the help desk into thinking that they are the user, they request that the phone number associated with the account be changed. From that point onward, the 2FA verification code will be sent to the hacker's phone instead of the user's phone.

Attacks of this nature can be prevented if the organization's help desk requires a very high level of proof before believing that a caller is actually the user and making any changes to the account. Attacks of this kind can be reduced if the user selects challenge questions that cannot be easily answered with a little searching of the Internet or social media.

SIM Swapping

A similar attack is to convince the user's mobile phone carrier to transfer the victim's phone number to a new SIM (Subscriber Identity Module) card. If the hacker can convince the phone carrier's support desk to transfer the account to a new SIM card, then he will receive all calls and messages sent to the victim's phone number. This enables him to receive and respond to 2FA authorization codes sent to the user's phone number.

SIM swapping attacks can be avoided if a higher level of proof is required by the carrier's support desk transferring a phone number to a new SIM card. Again, the user should select security questions that cannot be answered after a small investment of online snooping.

MFA Prompt Bombing

MFA prompt bombing, also called an *MFA fatigue attack*, relies on the carelessness or weariness of an inattentive user. For this attack to work, the attacker must already know the user's account ID and password. As explained earlier, credentials that are exposed during data breaches can be stolen or purchased off the Dark Web. The attacker then repeatedly attempts to log into the system using a user's valid credentials. Each login attempt generates a notification on the user's smart phone. For access to be granted the user must click a button indicating the access attempt is valid. The attacker is counting on the user either thinking that the prompt is legitimate or eventually approving the prompt just to make the notifications stop inundating their phone, especially if the calls are coming in at 1 a.m.

It might seem unlikely that this form of attack would work. In September 2022, an MFA prompt bombing attack was used to successfully compromise an account at a major ride sharing company [SPE2023]. In a separate incident in May 2022, hackers were able to infiltrate the corporate network of a major hardware provider using an MFA prompt bombing attack [STA22].

If an employee is on the receiving end of repetitive MFA requests that do not coincide with valid login attempts, they should immediately recognize that their credentials have been compromised. The steps that should be immediately taken are as follows:

1. Ignore this MFA request as well as any others that the user's actions did not initiate.

2. Change the password of the account related to this request. If any of the user's other accounts are using the same password, change all of them immediately.

3. The organization, e.g., employer, should advise all users to modify their passwords. If one user's credentials have been compromised by a data breach, then there is a good chance that others have been as well.

4. The organization should consider limiting the number of unsuccessful attempts that can occur before the account is locked.

5. Use this as a learning opportunity by providing security training for all users on MFA prompt bombing specifically and social engineering attacks in general.

STEALING BIOMETRIC DATA

One downside to using biometric data as an MFA factor is that it can be stolen. Researchers at NordVPN found 81,000 stolen digital fingerprints for sale on Dark Web forums [CYB23]. According to *The Washington Post*, a cybersecurity breach at the Office of Personnel Management resulted in 5.6 million sets of fingerprints being stolen [WASH15]. Federal experts believe the chances of the stolen fingerprints being misused is limited.

It seems obvious that as technology advances, stolen biometric data will be used to spoof MFA biometric authentication tests. Other forensic data such as voice recordings, facial scans, videos of people, and even iris scans could also be stolen and used to defeat MFA biometric security.

For users this represents a difficult choice. Biometric MFA security systems are convenient since they do not require users to memorize yet another password or to carry around a card, phone, or token. The challenge is when biometric data is stolen. Passwords can easily be changed, but it is not possible to change your fingerprints, face, or voice.

ADAPTIVE MFA

Adaptive MFA is a method of adapting or adjusting the level of authentication that is required based on a number of criteria. For example, if a user is on the company premises, then no additional factors beyond entering her account ID and password would be required. If that same user is logging into the system from another location, for example using the unsecured Wi-Fi in a coffee shop, then additional levels of authentication would be required.

Another example of what adaptive MFA might take into account is the timing of when the user is attempting to log into the application. If the user typically logs into the application during normal business hours, then no additional authentication might be required during the daytime. If the user attempts to log in at 3 a.m., then additional authentication, like sending a one-time security code to her phone, would be required to get access to the system.

An article on the Web site *Techtarget.com* lists factors that can be used to determine whether additional levels of MFA should be invoked [TEC23]. Some of the policy factors listed in this article include

- if geolocation information indicates the user has tried to log in from vastly separate locations within a short period of time.
- whether the antimalware software required by the organization's policies and guidelines is running on the user's device
- if this account has had numerous, consecutive login failures
- if the user is attempting to log into an application that he normally does not use
- if the user is attempting to access especially sensitive or valuable information

A significant advantage of adaptive MFA is that it provides additional security while minimizing impact on the user most of the time. When everything is "normal," i.e., the user is directly connected to the organization's network during normal business hours, then access will be granted. If something is unusual, e.g., the user is remote from a foreign country outside of normal business hours, then additional authentication factors will be required before access is granted. The result is a better experience for the user and greater security for the organization.

THE FUTURE OF MFA

The future of all MFA factors, but specifically biometric authentication, is clearly going to be an ongoing cycle of improved authentication versus more ingenious methods of hacking those methods. The availability of high-resolution cameras, 3D printers, and deepfake software will likely propel this challenging cycle for the foreseeable future. This conflict makes it essential that individuals and organizations implement the best conceivable MFA system that is reasonable for them. Any system put into production needs to be examined closely to ensure it was installed correctly; it also needs to be reviewed periodically to ensure it has not either been compromised or become outdated.

REFERENCES

[BLA23] Blackview Blog. "Can your fingerprints be stolen from a smartphone?," available online at *https://www.blackview.hk/blog/guides/can-fingerprint-be-stolen-from-phone*, Nov 09, 2023

[CYB23] "How to protect biometrics data from cybercriminals," available online at *https://www.industrialcybersecuritypulse.com/threats-vulnerabilities/hacking-off-your-finger-how-to-protect-biometric-data-from-cybercriminals/*, August 22, 2023

[DEF20] Kerner, Sean Michael. "#DEFCON: Bypassing Biometric Scanners with 3D Printed Fingerprints," available online at *https://www.infosecurity-magazine.com/news/defcon-bypassing-biometric-scanners/*, Apr 2, 2023

[FAC23] Admin. "Can Face Recognition Be Fooled By Photo?," available online at *https://faceonlive.com/can-face-recognition-be-fooled-by-photo/*, May 20, 2023

[FOR23] Woollacott, Emma. "Many Android Phones Can Be Unlocked with a Photo," available online at *https://www.forbes.com/sites/emmawoollacott/2023/05/19/many-android-phones-can-be-unlocked-with-a-photo/*, May 19, 2023

[MIC23]. Maynes, Melanie. "One simple action you can take to prevent 99.9 percent of attacks on your accounts," available online at *https://www.microsoft.com/en-us/security/blog/2019/08/20/one-simple-action-you-can-take-to-prevent-99-9-percent-of-account-attacks/*, August 20, 2019

[PCMAG23] Mott, Nathaniel. "Hacking Fingerprints is actually Pretty Easy – and Cheap," available online at *https://www.pcmag.com/news/hacking-fingerprints-is-actually-pretty-easy-and-cheap*, March 28, 2023

[SPE23] White, Marcus. "MFA prompt bombing: How it works and how to stop it," available online at *https://specopssoft.com/blog/mfa-prompt-bombing-how-it-works-and-how-to-stop-it/*, June 22, 2023

[STA22] Beer, Eliot. "Cisco hacked in latest social engineering breach," available online at *https://www.thestack.technology/cisco-network-hack-voice-phishing-mfa-fatigue/*, August 11, 2022

[TEC23] Bigelow, Stephen. "Adaptive multifactor authentication (adaptive MFA), available online at *https://www.techtarget.com/whatis/definition/adaptive-multifactor-authentication-adaptive-MFA*, December 2023

[WASH15] Peterson, Andrea. "OPM says 5.6 million fingerprints stolen in cyberattack, five times as many as previously thought," available online at *https://www.washingtonpost.com/news/the-switch/wp/2015/09/23/opm-now-says-more-than-five-million-fingerprints-compromised-in-breaches/*, September 23, 2015

[WAT23] University of Waterloo. "How secure are voice authentication systems really?," available online at *https://uwaterloo.ca/news/media/how-secure-are-voice-authentication-systems-really*, June 27, 2023

7

VIRUSES AND WORMS

WHAT IS A VIRUS?

A *virus* is a computer program created to do harm to any host computer or mobile device that it is able to install on. To be installed on a computer or mobile phone, however, a user must take action. This action might be to open an email attachment, download an executable file, or click on a pop-up ad displayed by a browser. If the user does not take the triggering action, then the virus cannot infect his device. Viruses also typically attempt to replicate themselves and get on other devices.

Once a virus has been installed on a device, then it will attempt to do several actions.

1. It can be programmed to do nothing at all immediately. Lying dormant is often an attempt to evade detection by antivirus software running on the device. After a preset period of time ranging from hours to days, it will begin executing.

2. It can begin by propagating itself. Techniques for spreading itself include

   a. attaching copies of itself to removable storage devices, e.g., USB drives, or network drives

   b. attaching copies of itself to email messages that are being sent

   c. attaching copies of itself to files that are frequently shared, for example music files (.MP3) or photograph files (.PNG, .JPEG, and .JPG)

3. It can begin damaging the computer that it is infected with.

VIRUSES VS. WORMS

The terms *worms* and *viruses* are often used interchangeably. Both viruses and worms are forms of malware. Worms are a type of virus. They are similar in that they are both computer programs and were written to infect computers, smart phones, and other electronic devices. Both can do enormous damage to systems, files, and data. The most significant difference between them is that a worm is a stand-alone program that can spread without the victim taking any action. A virus is a program that is attached to an executable file that already exists on a computer or other electronic device.

How Widespread Are Viruses?

Viruses are common on computers throughout the world. The five countries where computer viruses are most common are the United States, India, Japan, Taiwan, and Ukraine [WOR23]. It has been estimated that 32% of the world's computers are thought to have been infected with a virus at some point [WOR23]. WebFX estimates that 16 million US homes have been affected by a computer virus within the last two years [WEB24].

What Can a Virus Do?

Being a computer program, a virus can perform any actions that its creator has programmed it to perform. The damage a virus can cause is limited only to its creator's imagination and experience. WebFX estimates that viruses and spyware cost US households $4.5 billion and cost US businesses $55 billion every year [WEB24]. The following list of actions are just a few examples of what viruses can do:

a. install ransomware

b. install a keystroke logger

c. install spyware

d. locate and extract Personal Identifying Information (PII) data, banking information, credit card account numbers, and send it to the virus's creator

e. destroy or delete files, which may result in the device becoming inoperable

f. turn the device into a bot

g. install crypto mining malware

Devices a Virus Can Infect

Viruses can be written to infect any type of electronic device that runs software. Some examples include the following:

a.   computer servers

b.   desktop computers

c.   laptop computers

d.   tablets

e.   smart phones

f.   routers, including Wi-Fi routers

g.   smart TVs

h.   Internet of Things (IoT) devices like microwaves, refrigerators, lights, and washing machines

i.   security cameras

j.   printers and copy machines

A History of Viruses

An abbreviated list of some of the more infamous viruses and the year they affected the public is as follows:

2000 - ILOVEYOU victims received an email with "I Love You" in the subject line. If the email's attachment was opened, the virus would delete JPEG, MP3, and other files on the computer [CNN20]. It would then send an email with itself attached to every address in the victim's Outlook contact list. Considered the first truly global computer virus, it affected an estimated 45 million Windows computers in the first 24 hours. The damage caused is estimated at $10 billion.

2001 - Code Red exploited vulnerabilities in Microsoft's Internet Information Server (IIS). It defaced the affected Web site to indicate that the site had been hacked. From the 1st to the 19th of every month, it would spread to other vulnerable systems. This virus would participate in DDoS (Distributed Denial of Service) attacks from the 20th to the 27th of every month.

2003 - Sobig virus victims received an email that contained executable code. This code sent itself to all email addresses it found on the victim's computer. The Sobig virus was later modified to download a Trojan program that gave the virus writer control of the infected computer [COMP03]

2003 - Slammer, a.k.a. SQL Slammer – In 2003, this worm affected mostly computer servers that ran Microsoft's SQL Server, a relational database product. This code comes installed with many computers running Windows operating systems. The victim's computer did not actually have to be running the database software. Slammer spread itself by contacting other computers via UDP port 1434. This worm spread worldwide incredibly quickly. It is estimated that it propagated to about 75,000 computers within the first 10 minutes of its life [TWIN24].

2004 - Cabir was the first virus that infected mobile phones. It was able to infect the Symbian 60 OS [RET]. Cabir was able to infect its targets via Bluetooth.

2004 - MyDoom was a worm that was spread by emails. If the victim opened the email, then MyDoom would infect the computer and sent itself out to all of the victim's contacts via email. This virus spread to more than 500,000 in a single week [OKT23].

2004 - Sasser exploited computers with unpatched versions of Microsoft operating systems. This virus took advantage of a known flaw in the Windows operating system [WIR04]. It caused computers to crash and reboot continuously.

2007 - Zeus was a virus designed to steal banking credentials from victims. By 2010, the criminals behind Zeus had stolen over $70 million from their attacks [AVA22]. Some versions of the Zeus virus install ransomware on the victim's computer. This virus was spread via email that had a malicious link embedded in the email.

2008 - Conficker virus did not destroy or delete data, it just infected a device and then spread itself to other devices. The year it was first spotted it infected approximately 15 million computers [CYB17]. In 2009, a $250,000 reward was offered by Microsoft for information leading to the arrest of its author. That reward has not yet been claimed.

2016 – Mirai was a worm that infected IoT devices like baby monitors, routers, home appliances, and cameras that run a version of the Linux operating system. Infected devices are turned into zombies or bots. The resulting botnet or bot army was used to run DDoS attacks. It is estimated that Mirai had control over 200,000 to 300,000 devices [CYF22] in late 2016.

2017 - WannaCry was a ransomware virus that spread in May 2017. This virus impacted an estimated 230,000 computers and systems worldwide. This virus made use of a zero-day exploit in computers running legacy versions of the Microsoft Windows operating systems [UPG24].

How Viruses Spread

Some of the ways that a virus can infect a device are if the potential victim

a. opens infected email attachments

b. goes to an infected Web site

c. clicks on an infected pop-up screen

d. clicks on Web advertisements

e. connects to an infected Wi-Fi router

f. downloads an infected game, music, or video file

g. connects an infected removable storage device, e.g., a USB drive, to the computer

Signs of a Virus Infection

A virus-infected computer exhibits a range of symptoms. Some of the most common symptoms are as follows:

a. Performance will degrade.

b. The computer takes longer than normal to reboot.

c. Pop-up windows will appear.

d. The computer is more likely to crash. A Windows computer may display the Blue Screen of Death (BSoD).

e. The virus may generate and send out numerous emails from the computer.

f. The browser's normal home page has changed.

g. The browser toolbar is changed or a new toolbar may appear.

h. New or unexpected icons may appear on the Task Tray at the bottom of the monitor.

i. There are unexpected changes to passwords.

j. The free space on the computer's hard drive is reduced.

Signs of a Mobile Phone Infection

The signs that a mobile phone has been infected with a virus are slightly different from those on a desktop, laptop, or tablet computer. The most notable signs of a mobile phone infection are as follows:

a. Data usage is higher than normal.

b. Battery life is shorter than normal.

c. Performance is slower than normal.

d. The phone might feel warm or even hot to the touch.

e. Pop-up ads appear more frequently and in unexpected places.

f. Unfamiliar charges appear on your monthly phone bill.

g. Applications that are not familiar have been installed on the phone.

Ways to Avoid Catching Viruses

Some of the ways to avoid infecting a computer with a virus are as follows:

a. Install and regularly update an antivirus tool.

b. Keep all software, especially operating systems, and browsers, updated.

c. Install a firewall.

d. Do not click on unexpected pop-up windows or ads.

e. Be extremely cautious before opening email attachments, especially from unknown senders.

f. Disable the autorun feature on the computer.

g. Do not attach external storage devices, like USB drives, that haven't been scanned or proven trustworthy.

h. Download games, movies, and software tools only from authorized or well-known Web sites.

i. After downloading any files, scan them with an antivirus tool.

j. Back up files and data regularly. While this will not prevent catching a virus, it can make recovering from one much easier. (For more details on backups, refer to Chapter 11.)

Removing Viruses

The general steps to remove a virus from a computer are listed here. If the antivirus package installed on the device specifies different instructions, then follow them.

a. If an antivirus tool has not been installed on the computer already, then install one now. See the following section for more details about these tools.

b. Disconnect the computer from the Internet. This will help prevent the virus from spreading as well as prevent a reinfection from occurring while the original version of the virus is being removed.

c. Reboot the computer in safe mode. Doing this differs based on the type of computer and the version of the operating system being run, but typically requires that user press a certain key during the boot process.

d. Delete all temporary files from the computer. It is possible that the virus is hiding in one of these files. Deleting them may remove it.

e. Run a scan with the AV tool that was on the computer. If there is an option to run a partial or complete scan, then choose the complete scan.

f. The AV product may offer the option to delete or quarantine a file suspected of being malicious. If quarantine is chosen, the file will be isolated so it cannot do any harm. Later, if it is determined that the file is needed, it can be either deleted or restored.

g. Repeat scanning the computer until no viruses are detected.

h. Restore any missing or damaged files or applications from backup storage.

Antivirus (AV) Products

There is a subtle difference between antivirus and antimalware tools, even though the terms are frequently used interchangeably. Antivirus tools focus mainly on legacy threats like viruses, worms and Trojan Horses. Antimalware products are designed to protect against newer and more sophisticated threats like adware, keyloggers, phishing, ransomware and rootkits. Running both antivirus and antimalware tools can provide a greater level of protection than running either type of tool.

There are many AV tools on the market. Be sure to acquire a product from a reputable vendor. Some antivirus programs are free and others have a cost associated with them. Some of the most highly regarded tools are listed below. Of course, better tools might have become available after this book went to print, so please do some research before choosing an AV product.

- Microsoft Defender: This AV tool comes included with all versions of Microsoft's operating systems and will start running as soon as Windows is started.

- XProtect: Mac computers come preinstalled with XProtect to provide them with malware protection.

- McAfee Antivirus Plus: This software provides malware protection as well as a firewall, password manager, and multiple machine protection.

- Norton 360 Deluxe: This software provides malware protection, as well as additional features like backup software, a VPN, and a password manager.

- Bitdefender AntiVirus Plus: This company offers malware protection in addition to features like a password manager, a hardened browser, and a file shredder. This product works on the Linux operating system as well as Windows.

- Trend Micro Maximum Security: This company offers malware protection as well as features like a hardened browser, password manager, and parental controls.

- Sophos Home Premium: This company provides malware protection essentials at an economical price

AV For Mobile Phones

Mobile phones can succumb to viruses just like any other device that connects to the Internet. Mobile phone owners can minimize the chances of catching a virus by downloading apps only from trustworthy sites, not clicking on suspicious links, and not opening email attachments.

To provide additional protection, an AV product can be installed on the phone. The process of choosing the best AV product is the same as choosing the best AV for a desktop or laptop computer.

No AV Tool Is Perfect

No antivirus or antimalware product is perfect. None of them can provide an absolute guarantee that they will protect against every virus. The decision that a consumer must make is whether being protected from 80% or 90% of viruses is better than no protection at all. They may not provide absolute protection against every form of malware, but AV software is just one part of a multilayered defense (also referred to as *defense-in-depth*).

How AV Software Works

Antivirus and antimalware software is designed to detect and then either delete or quarantine malicious software on an electronic device. It is critical to have one of these tools running on all desktop computers, laptops, tablets, and smart phones. Not having this critical form of protection leaves these devices as easy targets for the myriad variations of malware in the world.

When installed on a device, AV tools will initially scan all existing files on it to determine whether they are viruses. New files will be scanned as they are loaded onto the device. External storage devices like USB drives and external hard drives will automatically be scanned when they are connected to the computer.

All legitimate vendors update their tools on a regular basis to identify new viruses and other malware. Most products will automatically be updated. If prompted about the automatic update setting during installation, be sure to agree to that. Not applying regular updates will leave the device less than fully protected.

One disadvantage is that AV programs running on the device will consume a percentage of the computer's processing power. This can make the device run a little more slowly than usual. Another flaw is that AV software can sometimes interfere with legitimate programs running on the computer. This is rare but can occur.

Most antivirus tools use one of the following techniques to detect malicious software.

Signature-Based Detection

In signature-based detection, the AV tool scans files looking for recognizable sequences of code from known viruses, i.e., signatures. If a file contains one of these signatures, it will be flagged as questionable. A robust AV tool can have hundreds of thousands or even millions of virus signatures that it scans for. A good AV tool will have its list of signatures updated regularly.

Signature-based detection has limitations. The most significant limitations are as follows:

- If the cybercriminals modify the code in their virus enough the recognizable signature is removed and thus can escape detection.
- Until a new virus has been identified by the maker of AV tools and its signature is added to the list, the AV tool will not recognize it. Viruses that have not been seen before are referred to as *zero-day* threats. Until these new threats are observed and added to the signature files, there is no protection against them.

Heuristic-Based Detection

One definition of the word *heuristic* is "enabling someone to discover or learn something for themselves." *Heuristic-based detection* attempts to learn what the code it is inspecting will do. It examines the code of files looking for patterns or tendencies that exist in known viruses. Then it tries to predict whether the new code is a virus or not. A primary goal of this type of detection is to be able to recognize viruses that have not been seen before.

A shortcoming is that heuristic-based tools can generate false positive alarms, i.e., declaring that a program is a virus when it actually is not and false negatives, i.e., not declaring that a program is a virus when it actually is a virus. Another shortcoming is that this method of detection requires significantly more CPU time than signature-based detection.

Behavior-Based Detection

Behavior-based analysis and detection is based on the actions that a program being examined takes rather than what its code looks like. If a program performs an action that is similar to actions performed by viruses, then it will be interpreted as a virus and be deleted or quarantined.

An advantage of a behavior-based detection method is that it can protect against new viruses by recognizing virus-like actions. A disadvantage of behavior-based detection is that if a virus takes a completely new approach, i.e., performs actions never seen before, then a behavior-based system will not identify it as a virus.

AV Qualities to Look For

There are a number of qualities that should be considered when choosing an AV package. Not all of them will be equally important to every consumer. The following sections describe qualities in AV tools that should be considered before making a purchase.

Compares Favorably to Other Tools

Perhaps the most important factor when comparing antivirus tools is how effective it is. A number of independent reviews of AV tools are published annually. Each of these reviews tend to rank the available AV tools in slightly different order. To be seriously considered, a tool should score in the top three or top five in most or all of the reviews.

Cost

The cost can be a significant consideration when acquiring an AV tool. There are many free tools available, but it is a reasonable assumption if a vendor earns money from the sale of its product it will have the funds to continually improve their product.

A factor in the cost of a particular tool can be the number of additional features it provides. If the extras are not needed then a basic, more economical product might be the best choice.

Operating Systems

Not all AV products can run on all operating systems. Most of them will work on some or all of the following environments:

- Windows
- Mac
- Linux
- Android
- iOS

If only a single device needs to be protected, then the decision will be relatively easy. If multiple operating systems need protection, then a product that covers all of them should be chosen. The alternative would be to have different AV products on each device. This can be done but will cost more in dollars and setup time.

Additional Features

Some AV production contains additional features like spam filters, file shredders, firewalls, ransomware protection, a VPN, password managers, and a hardened browser. These features can be considered but probably will not be the ultimate decision-maker. Most users do not typically utilize all of those extra features.

Multiple Devices

Devices like tablets and mobile phones also need to be protected. If the home or business has multiple devices, then an AV tool that can protect all of them becomes more useful. Some products' licenses cover only a single device, while others allow installation on multiple or unlimited devices. If multiple devices need protection, then this factor can become an important one.

Scheduling Options

Most AV tools can be initiated manually or at scheduled intervals. Running a scan during off hours is a great way to ensure scans are done regularly with minimal impact on users. Quick scans are also a useful option. Check the AV package being investigated to make sure that its scheduling options are sufficient.

Support

Most AV tool vendors provide support via both phone and chat. If the type and quality of support is important to a potential buyer, then keep this in mind before making the final decision.

Are Two Tools Better Than One?

If one AV tool is good, then would two AV tools be better? The reasoning behind this question is that if tool "A" does not catch a virus, then maybe tool

"B" will. Unfortunately, this is not necessarily true. The reasons for not running more than a single AV tool are as follows:

a. Different AV tools will likely view the other as a virus and try to delete or quarantine its rival.

b. It is possible that if two AV tools identify and attempt to quarantine or delete a suspicious file, then neither will do it properly.

c. There will be an increased usage of resources like the battery and CPU time.

d. Multiple notifications can be created for the same virus if each AV tool reports a suspicious file. At best, this will confuse the device owner and at worst may "train" him to ignore all notifications.

VIRUSES EVOLVE

Malware, including viruses, evolve constantly, and so must the antimalware protection on any device. Most vendors have automatic update options so new signatures and code are downloaded regularly. Be sure this is enabled on all devices. This will help ensure that protection is kept up with new viruses as they are found in the wild.

When the license for the current AV product expires, it would be very easy to simply renew the license. This might be a good time to review all available products. It is possible that the current choice is no longer the best option. A competitor may have improved their software and now provides better protection. Prices may have changed significantly. Regardless of whether the existing license is extended or a new AV product is chosen, it is important that the device not be left unprotected at any time.

The Future of Viruses

The future is certain to have as many or even more viruses than we currently have. Advances in AI and machine learning (ML) will enable cybercriminals to create viruses that are more intricate and adaptive than anything seen to date. Firms that specialize in antivirus tools and cybersecurity will also be using these new technologies to protect their clients against the next generation of viruses.

One area where an increase in the number of virus infections is almost certain to occur are IoT devices. These devices connect to the Internet through a local network. They can be simple or complex, and they can be found anywhere: in our homes, offices, manufacturing plants, and on our streets. There will be an estimated 75 billion IoT devices worldwide by 2025 [SDSU21]. Many of these devices have minimal security. If even a minuscule percentage of them were to be infected with viruses or other malware, the results could be catastrophic. (An entire chapter (18) of this book is devoted to IoT.)

REFERENCES

[AVA22] Belcic, Ivan. "What is the Zeus Trojan?," available online at *https://www.avast.com/c-zeus*, February 7, 2022

[CNN20] Griffiths, James. "I love you: How a badly-coded computer virus caused billions in damage and exposed vulnerabilities which remain 20 years on," available online at *https://www.cnn.com/2020/05/01/tech/iloveyou-virus-computer-security-intl-hnk/index.html*, May 3, 2020

[COMP03] Roberts, Paul. "Sobig worm getting bigger," available online at *https://www.computerworld.com/article/1333874/sobig-worm-getting-bigger.html*, January 15, 2003

[CYB17] O'Neill, Patrick Howell. "Conficker worm still spreading despite being nearly 10 years old," available online at *https://cyberscoop.com/conficker-trend-micro-2017/*, December 8, 2017

[CYF22] "Mirai – The Botnet that Made IoT Dangerous," available online at *https://www.cyfirma.com/blogs/mirai-the-botnet-that-made-iot-dangerous/*, September 15, 2022

[OKT23] "What is MyDoom Malware? History, How It Works & Defense," available online at *https://www.okta.com/identity-101/mydoom/*, Sept 15, 2023.

[RET] Clooke, Richard. "A brief history of mobile malware," available online at *https://www.retaildive.com/ex/mobilecommercedaily/a-brief-history-of-mobile-malware*, undated

[SDSU21] "What Does the Rise of IoT Devices Mean for Cybersecurity?," available online at *https://digitalskills.sdsu.edu/cybersecurity/what-does-the-rise-of-iot-devices-mean-for-cybersecurity/*, Sept 7, 2021

[TWIN24] Twingate Team. "What is SQL Slammer? How It Works & Examples," available online at *https://www.twingate.com/blog/glossary/sql%20slammer*, August 1, 2024

[UPG24]. Tunggal, Abi Tyas. "What is the Wannacry Ransomware Attack?," available online at *https://www.upguard.com/blog/wannacry*, April 25, 2024

[WEB24] "What is the Real Cost of Computer Viruses?," available online at *https://www.webfx.com/blog/Internet/cost-of-computer-viruses-infographic/*, May 13, 2024

[WIR04] "Sasser Worm Snakes into Windows," available online at *https://www.wired.com/2004/05/sasser-worm-snakes-into-windows/*, May 3, 2004

[WOR23] Craft, Darren. "Malware Statistics & Facts: Frequency, Impact & Cost," available online at *https://www.worthinsurance.com/post/malware-statistics*, October 24, 2023

PATCHES AND UPDATES

WHAT ARE PATCHES AND UPDATES?

All software has errors in it: the more lines of code in an application, the more errors it is likely to have in it. When the vendor that created the code finds and corrects an error, they release a *patch* to everyone who purchased their product. Patches may also address performance issues and security fixes.

Everyone needs to apply patches and update that become available for every piece of software that they own. From a household with a single desktop computer to the largest organization with tens of thousands of devices of all kinds, patching needs to be done regularly by everyone.

Patching is normally associated with software, but hardware can need patching as well. Firmware is a program that is written onto a chip's non-volatile memory. Non-volatile memory does not lose its contents when it is turned off or loses power. Firmware exists in devices like mobile phones, laptops, tablets, automobiles, appliances, routers, and Internet of Things (IoT) devices. A firmware update or patch overwrites existing code in the device. Ways to patch firmware can be extremely specific, so this book will not cover them. Instructions for firmware patches should be provided by the vendor that built the device.

Updates

An *update* is typically more extensive than a patch. It is likely to include new features for the software. The user interface for an application may have undergone a significant makeover. A major upgrade may actually be a complete rewrite of the code. Updates are released relatively infrequently, sometimes every few years.

Patches

Patches are released by vendors regularly, and many vendors release a collection of patches every month. A number of vendors, including Microsoft, Adobe, and Oracle, release a patch on the second Tuesday of every month. This day is typically referred to as "Patch Tuesday." Other vendors issue patches only when they accumulate multiple fixes that need to be corrected.

Cybercriminals closely watch the patches that vendors release on "Patch Tuesday" and other days, looking for a way to exploit vulnerabilities that are being fixed. Unfortunately, many individuals and organizations do not apply patches quickly or regularly. If they do not install these patches, then cybercriminals can take advantage of their vulnerabilities.

If a serious vulnerability is discovered in a product and the fix needs to be distributed immediately, the vendor probably will not wait for the next regularly scheduled patch release. They will release this patch immediately. This is referred to as an *out-of-band* patch.

It is the responsibility of the user or an organization's IT group to keep track of their software and whether it has been patched. Some resources to help keep software up to date are as follows:

a. Regularly check the vendor's release calendar.

b. Sign up for vendor emails or alerts.

c. Monitor security bulletins published by the vendor.

d. Perform an Internet search for patch information.

e. Join or be aware of user groups associated with the organization's most important applications. User groups or forums can be a great way to see if other sites have experienced problems with the latest patch.

PATCH AND UPGRADE TERMS

a. *Build*: a collection of software that has been released as a unit

b. *Coldfix*: an update that requires the application or entire computer to be taken down for the fix to go into effect

c. *Hot patch*: a method of installing operating system changes without having to reboot the device

d. *Hotfix*: a method of applying a patch, frequently one that addresses a single critical bug or vulnerability, that does not require the computer to be rebooted

e. *Live patch*: similar to a hotfix, a live patch can be applied without requiring the system to be rebooted

f. *Point release*: another name for a patch or patch release. The implication of the word "patch" is that the release deals with small changes rather than significant ones.

g. *Release notes*: the documentation that accompanies a patch or upgrade. These notes explain what the changes do and how to apply the patch or upgrade.

h. *Service pack*: a cumulative set of patches and updates that can be installed at one time

i. *Security patch*: a patch that focuses on fixing security vulnerabilities rather than feature changes.

j. *Unofficial patch*: patches that are developed by a third-party rather than the vendor that originally released the software. Unofficial patches are usually associated with gaming software rather than operating systems and business applications. Before installing an unofficial patch, the trustworthiness of the patch's source should be carefully evaluated.

VERSION NUMBERS

Commercial software distributed to customers or clients has a version or release number associated with it. It is used by the vendor to identify it; the version number can be tracked back to identify all of the software modules that created that specific version.

Most software has a screen that displays the version that is currently installed and running. The version number is frequently presented as three values separated by decimal points, for example 17.3.5. In this example, "17" is the major version, "3" is the minor version, and "5" is the patch level. Different vendors may handle this information in a variety of ways. For example, a vendor might have four numbers instead of three. Figure 8.1 shows the version number of a computer running Windows.

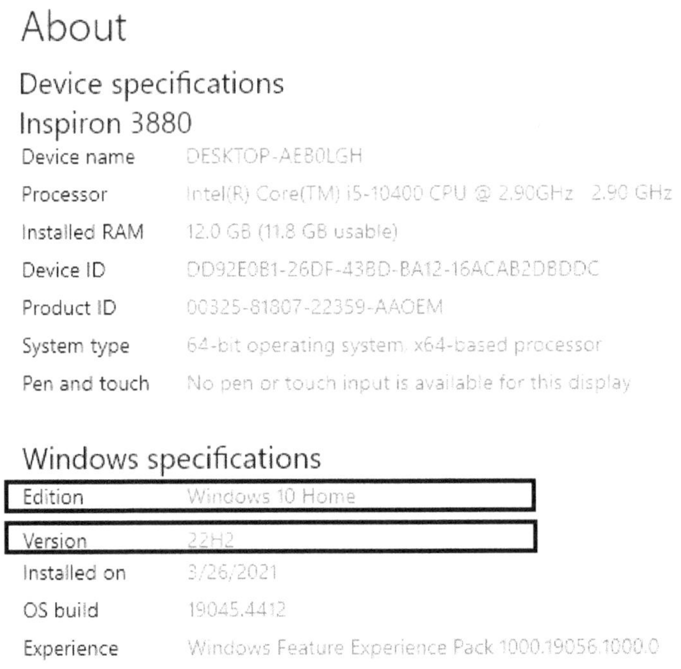

About

Device specifications
Inspiron 3880

Device name	DESKTOP-AEB0LGH
Processor	Intel(R) Core(TM) i5-10400 CPU @ 2.90GHz 2.90 GHz
Installed RAM	12.0 GB (11.8 GB usable)
Device ID	DD92E0B1-26DF-438D-BA12-16ACAB2DBDDC
Product ID	00325-81807-22359-AAOEM
System type	64-bit operating system, x64-based processor
Pen and touch	No pen or touch input is available for this display

Windows specifications

Edition	Windows 10 Home
Version	22H2
Installed on	3/26/2021
OS build	19045.4412
Experience	Windows Feature Experience Pack 1000.19056.1000.0

FIGURE 8.1 Version number of Windows

When contacting a vendor to resolve a problem, provide the version information of the software to them. If a ticket is being filled out, be sure to include it. This will help their support team investigate and correct the issue more quickly.

Figure 8.2 shows the version number of the application Notepad++® installed on a computer. For this application, the version number, v8.5.4, is displayed toward the top of the screen.

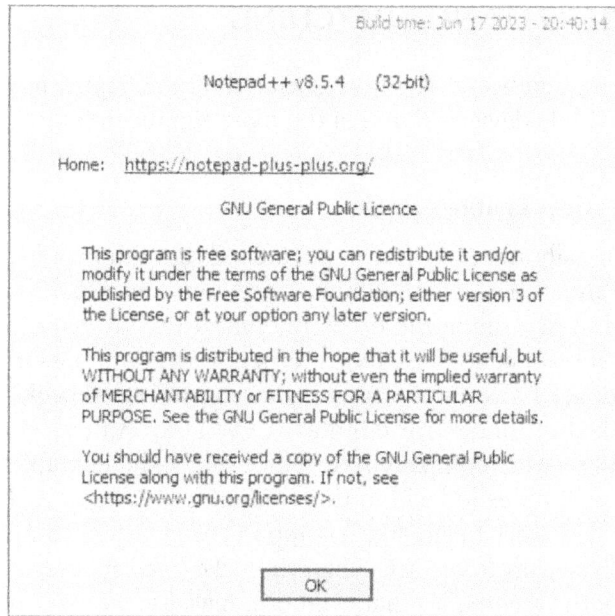

FIGURE 8.2 Version number of an application

The version of iOS® on an iPhone® is shown in Figure 8.3. This phone is running version 17.4.1. (The screen is available by selecting Settings > General > About.)

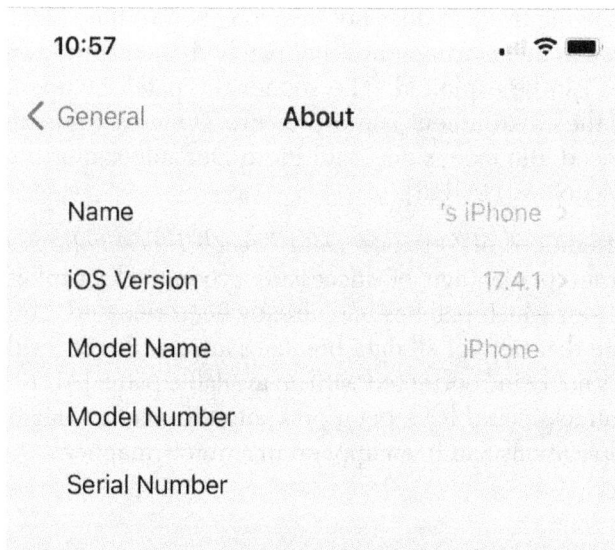

FIGURE 8.3 Version number on an iPhone

THE DANGERS OF NOT PATCHING

There are significant dangers associated with not applying patches to computers or mobile devices. Some of the more significant ones are described here.

Unpatched Devices Enable Attacks

It is generally accepted that an unpatched computer connected to the Internet will be attacked quickly and regularly. Numerous experiments have been performed to determine the exact amount of time it takes. SANS's (SysAdmin, Audit, Network and Security) Internet Storm Center estimated that the "survival" time of a computer running an unpatched version of Windows would be hacked in under five minutes [COMP08]. An experiment performed in 2021 by security company Axis found that a "honeytrap" they set up had its first exploit uploaded within three minutes [AXIS21]. A "honeypot" or "honeytrap" is a mechanism, like a computer, or a virtual computer, that has been specially set up to attract cybercriminals. Security researchers use them to monitor the techniques that cybercriminals use to attack computers.

Patching is critical to removing vulnerabilities. According to a survey of nearly 3,000 IT professionals by the Ponemon Institute, 60% of respondents whose organizations had a data breach said the breaches could have occurred because a patch was available for a known vulnerability but not applied [PON24].

Cybercriminals scrutinize patch release announcements closely to understand what is being fixed. It does not take long before they identify a way to exploit the flaws. If an environment is not patched, then these newly exposed vulnerabilities can be exploited. The sooner the patch or upgrade is in place, the sooner the environment is more secure. "Once a vulnerability and patch are announced, the race is on," said Piero DePaoli, senior director of marketing at ServiceNow [DAR18].

Recent editions of Verizon's *Data Breach Investigations Report* state that a significant percentage of successful cyberattacks exploited known vulnerabilities for which patches had already been released. Some industry experts estimate that 60% of all data breaches are the direct result of known vulnerabilities not being corrected with an available patch [AUT19]. This means that many attacks could have been prevented if readily available patches to OSes and applications had been applied in a timely manner.

Here are some examples of data breaches that could have been prevented by applying available patches:

Equifax

The personal data of 147 million people was exposed in this 2017 data breach. Attackers entered Equifax's system in mid-May via a widely known Web application vulnerability for which a patch was available in March 2017 [CSO20]. Equifax agreed to a settlement that included paying up to $425 million to help victims of the data breach [FTC20].

Heartland Payment Systems

In January 2008, Heartland Payment Systems announced that it had been the victim of a data breach. The attackers had used an SQL inject exploit to gain access to Heartland's network [RES19]. The stolen data would enable the bad actors to create tens of millions of counterfeit credit cards identical to cards held by consumers. Heartland paid about $140 million in fines and penalties [FOR15].

SingHealth

One-and-a-half million patients of the Singapore Health System had their PII stolen in July of 2018. Hackers were able to do so because a workstation was running a version of Microsoft Outlook that was not updated with a patch to address the problem. According to the organization's CIO, that server had not been updated in over a year [STR18]. Normally, patches are applied to it several times a month.

WannaCry

The WannaCry ransomware attack was directed against computers running the Windows operating system. This malware was launched in May of 2017. A patch that corrected the vulnerability exploited by WannaCry had been released by Microsoft two months before the attack took place [CSO22]. If that patch had been universally installed, the 200,000+ computers impacted by WannaCry would not have been infected.

Potential Costs of Not Patching

Insufficient or nonexistent patching practically invites cyberattacks. Data breaches, ransomware, and other cyber-attacks are expensive. According to an IBM survey, the average global cost of a data breach in 2023 was $4.45 million [IBM24]. Sopho, a cybersecurity firm, estimates that the average cost to recover from a ransomware attack in 2021 was $1.85 million [SOP22].

Some of the costs associated with a data breach might be covered by cyber insurance, but it is unlikely that all costs will be covered. Some examples of costs associated with a data breach incident include the following:

- cost of hiring outside consultants to correct the problem
- loss of business revenue during the attack and recovery period
- permanent loss of customers in the event of a data breach
- cost of sending out breach notifications
- fines levied by a federal or local regulatory agency can be substantial
- legal fees to defend the organization and its employees
- potential civil lawsuit and class action suit
- additional stress on employees as well as potential departure of valuable employees
- cost of credit monitoring services frequently required or offered to customers' whose PII was exposed
- increase of cyber insurance premiums

DOWNSIDE OF PATCHING

While keeping all software updated by applying patches on a regular basis is optimal, there are arguments for not applying them. Some of the justifications for not patching have merit, but overall, the patching advantages heavily outweigh the disadvantages. Some of the possible downsides of patching are described in the points below.

- It is possible for a patch to break parts of the computer system. The changes introduced by a patch may be incompatible with other hardware or software. This is a legitimate argument, but the risks of it happening are low. Breaking parts of the computer system can be avoided by testing patches and installing them in limited, pilot phase initially.
- It takes time and effort to keep up with all the patches that are issued by various vendors. The organization may not have personnel available to

handle all of them. This is another valid issue. The reality is that not applying patches could be incredibly costly so the manpower to apply them needs to be found.

- Online systems may have to be taken down to apply patches. This is true but does not justify not patching them. The time to install them needs to be worked out with the operations team.

- Patches need to be tested. This requires additional time and possibly a test environment. Virtual machines can be created to simulate most computing environments. If the organization does not have or cannot afford a testing environment, then it is possible that virtual machines can be used to create a suitable testing environment.

- It is possible that patches will introduce new errors or vulnerabilities. This is a valid concern, but the chances of it happening are almost certainly lower than not patching. Thorough testing prior to installing patches on the production environment can alleviate this concern.

SOFTWARE THAT NEEDS PATCHING

Categories and specific types of software that need to be patched are listed below. All of them need to be patched regularly.

Operating Systems

Operating systems oversee all of the programs and applications that run on a computing device. A modern operating system can have 60 million lines of code. With that much code, it should not be a surprise that vulnerabilities or bugs will be found that require patching.

Examples of operating systems are as follows:

- Windows®
- UNIX / Linux
- Mac OS
- iOS®
- Android

Browsers

Browsers are programs that enable users to display and navigate the World Wide Web. Modern browsers also contain millions of lines of code. With such a large code base, patches for Web browsers are distributed regularly. Examples of popular Web browsers include the following:

- Apple Safari®
- Google Chrome
- Microsoft Edge
- Mozilla Firefox®
- Opera

User-Oriented Applications

The list of applications designed to be used in the home and office is long and incredibly varied. What might surprise the reader is how complex these programs can be. Word processors like Microsoft Word® can have over 50 million lines of code. Video games can have 50 or 60 million lines of code. Examples of user applications that need to be patched include the following:

- word processing applications, e.g., Microsoft Word®
- spreadsheet applications, e.g., Microsoft Excel®
- presentation software, e.g., Microsoft PowerPoint®
- personal finance applications
- photo album software
- instant messaging packages
- video chat software, e.g., Skype®
- media player software, e.g., videos and music
- .gaming software

Business-Oriented Applications

Cybercriminals know that business applications hold confidential information so they are frequently targeted. Keeping these applications patched is extremely important. Examples of these applications include the following:

- CRM (Customer Resource Management) applications, e.g., Salesforce® and Pipedrive®

- accounting applications, e.g., QuickBooks® and Workday®
- billing software, e.g., Salesforce®
- database software, e.g., Oracle® and Microsoft SQL Server®
- payroll software, e.g., ADP® and Paychex®
- email packages, e.g., ProtonMail® and Zoho Mail®
- asset management software, e.g., Rippling® and Freshservice®

Software that is running in the cloud or on a vendor's platform cannot be patched by the user so it does not need to be included in the inventory. Examples of applications like this are Microsoft 365®, Google Tools®, Salesforce®, Slack®, and Tableau®.

Development Platforms and Support Software

Software developers use many tools, and some components of those tools exist only on the developers' workstations; others, however, get installed on end user's devices. Cybercriminals know that if they can penetrate a developer's tools, that may lead to infiltrating every user and organization that uses the software. Examples of this type of software includes the following:

- Platforms like Microsoft .NET®, Eclipse®, and GitHub®
- Programming languages, like C#, Perl, Python, Java
- Drivers for devices like graphics cards, hard drives, monitors, printers, speakers, and cameras

PATCH MANAGEMENT

Patch management means having a well-defined, documented process of applying patches to software on a consistent basis. Having a process in place for this task makes it more likely that it will be done correctly, regularly, and to all computers that require it. If patching is done in an ad hoc manner, then it is much less likely that it will be done properly.

The larger the organization is, the greater the need for a well-organized patch management process. An individual user or a very small organization may have a very simple patch management system.

There are no "perfect" steps in a patch management process. Different organizations have different steps in their list. The following steps are the basics and can be enhanced to fit the specific needs of any organization.

1. Take an inventory of all the software that exists in the organization and what exactly needs to be kept updated. For a household or a small business, this can be quick and easy. The larger an organization is the greater the effort it will take to create an accurate inventory.

   An inventory can be put together manually or by one of many tools available for this can be used. For a large organization, an automated tool can be very effective. Two examples of tools that inventory hardware and software are Network Inventory Advisor® and ManageEngine's AssetExplorer®.

To see the list of applications on a Windows computer, right-click the Windows key and select "Apps." Figure 8.4 shows the list of applications on a Windows computer.

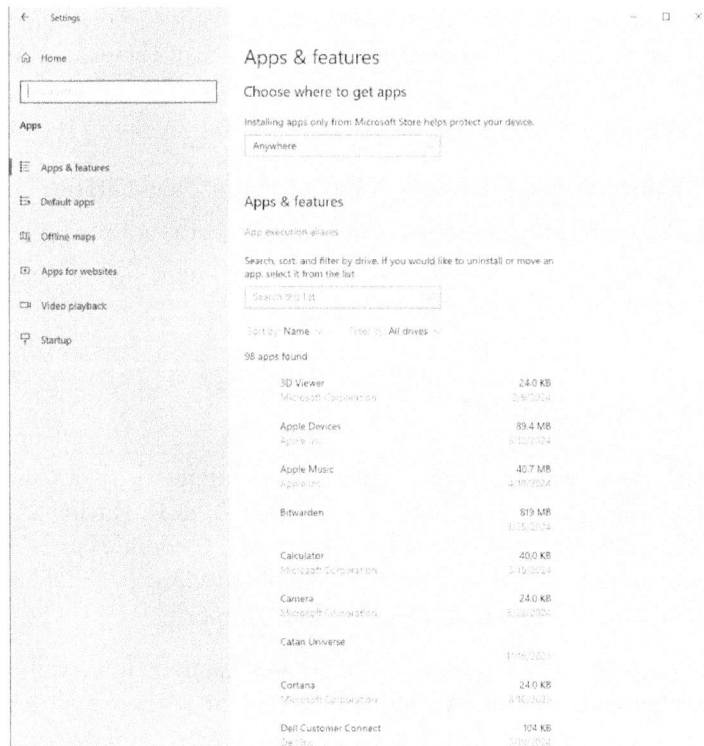

FIGURE 8.4 List of applications on a Windows computer

In a large organization, some users may have installed hardware or software without the knowledge of the IT group. This is referred to as "shadow IT." Like any other software, it needs to be patched. It is difficult for the IT group to patch these applications if they do not know about them. A tool that creates a software inventory may reveal this "unseen" software. Another option would be for the IT group to communicate with everyone in the organization explaining the dangers of unpatched shadow IT and request that it be disclosed.

2. Prioritize software into which should be patched first and which can wait. For example, operating systems are more critical than gaming software and Web browsers are more critical than media player software.

3. Monitor vendor Web sites for patch release details. Once information on a new patch is available, then review the release notes for details on what is being changed and how to apply the changes.

4. If the organization has a test environment, then patches should be applied to it first. Once it has been updated, the applications and systems should be thoroughly tested to determine whether the patches were effective. Confirming that the patch has not created new problems is also very important. Once all testing has been completed, then patching the production environment can be done.

5. If production systems need to be taken down to apply the patches, coordinate with the user community in advance. Nothing will enrage users quicker than the system going down just before an event that cannot be postponed. For example, it is poor planning to patch a production accounting system the day that the monthly or quarterly books are being closed.

6. Document all changes that are going to be made to the production environment. If the organization has a Configuration Management tool, then enter details for this patch into it.

7. Create backups of the production environment before making any changes to it. These backups might be needed if a patch needs to be rolled back.

8. Deploy the patch(es) on a limited number of production devices. Monitor those systems to ensure that the changes had no adverse effects.

9. Deploy the patch(es) on the remaining production systems.

10. Monitor all production systems after the patches have been applied. The user community should be told that changes were made so they can be looking for problems as well.

REBOOTING AFTER A PATCH

Depending on the software involved, the computer may or may not need to be rebooted after a patch has been installed. UNIX systems do not typically need to be restarted after a patch, although there are exceptions. Windows system tend to require a reboot after patching. Apple Macs should be rebooted. If an application has been patched, then there is a good chance no reboot will be needed. To be absolutely sure whether a reboot is required, refer to the release notes provided by the vendor for the patch.

ROLLBACK PLANS

Unfortunately, a very small percentage of patches will encounter problems when they are applied. If problems occur, then the patch might need to be removed. Removing a patch is called a *rollback*. Some situations that might require a rollback include the following:

a. The patch installation might encounter problems and fail.

b. The patch might introduce new problems like instability or severe performance issues.

c. The patch might be incompatible with hardware or other software.

To be prepared for this unlikely event, a rollback plan should be created prior to applying patches. Possible resources for writing the rollback plan are as follows:

a. Release notes for the patch may have instructions for backing it out. For example, the patch might be changing a specific executable or library file. The notes might advise that this file be copied in advance. If instructions for a rollback are provided in the release notes, then they should be followed.

b. The patch installation process might have a rollback or uninstall option that can be selected.

c. Some patching tools provide a rollback wizard to simplify this process.

d. Restore the software components that were changed from backup file.

e. Restore the computer from a checkpoint or snapshot that was taken just prior to applying the patch.

f. If the software being patched is an application, then it might need to be reinstalled from scratch.

AUTOMATIC UPDATES

Some devices and software can be set to update automatically. Enabling this option can save time. Additionally, it is an excellent way to ensure that patches are loaded as soon as they become available. One example is the Microsoft Windows operating system. It can be set up to update on a computer whenever a new patch or release becomes available. Figure 8.5 shows how to enable this on a PC.

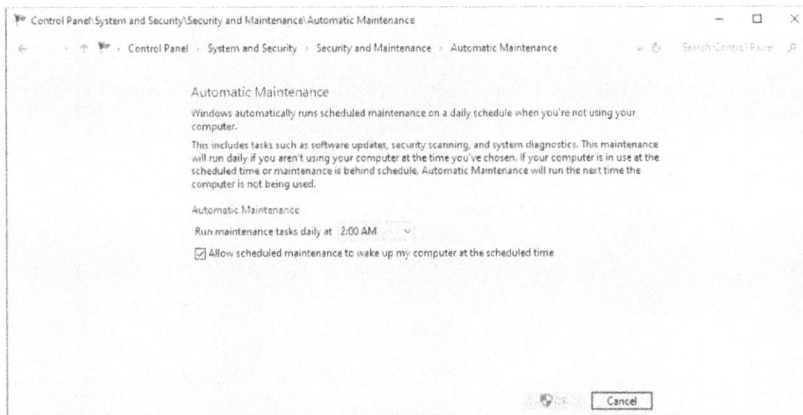

FIGURE 8.5 Setting Windows to update automatically

Browsers can also be set to update automatically. Figure 8.6 shows the setting on Mozilla Firefox to allow automatic updating.

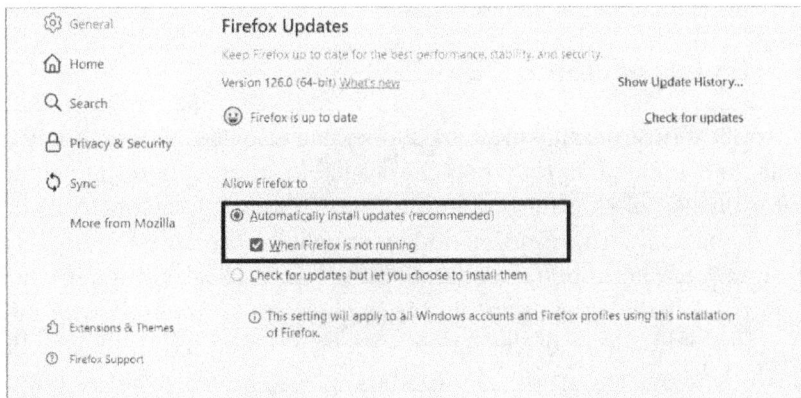

FIGURE 8.6 Setting Firefox to update automatically

Mobile phones can also be set to have their operating systems updated automatically. Figure 8.7 shows the setting so iOS on an iPhone will be updated automatically.

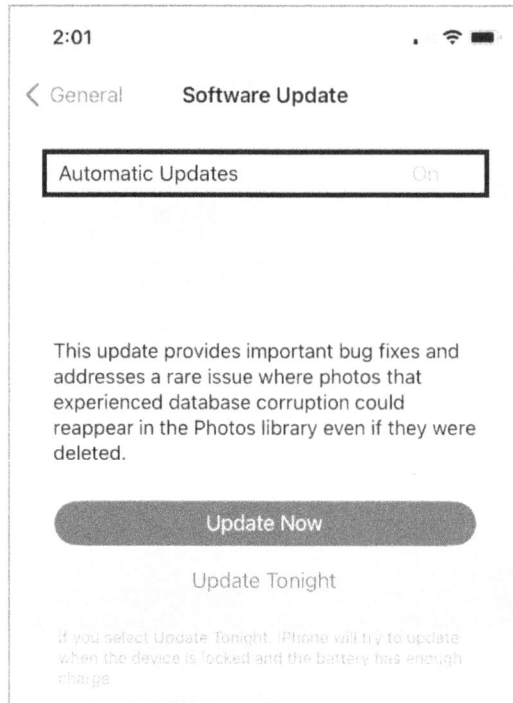

FIGURE 8.7 Updating an iPhone's operating system automatically

UPDATES ON MOBILE DEVICES

Applications running on smart phones can also have vulnerabilities. If patches are not applied as they become available, then cybercriminals have a better chance of causing problems. Smart phone applications are not updated automatically. This must be done manually by the user. Figure 8.8 shows how an app on an iPhone is updated. Step 1 is to click on the "Apple apps" icon in the left-most screen. Step 2 is to click the small circle with initials in the upper right corner of the center screenshot. Step 3 is to click on the "Update All" icon or the "Update" button on the apps to be updated on the right-most screenshot.

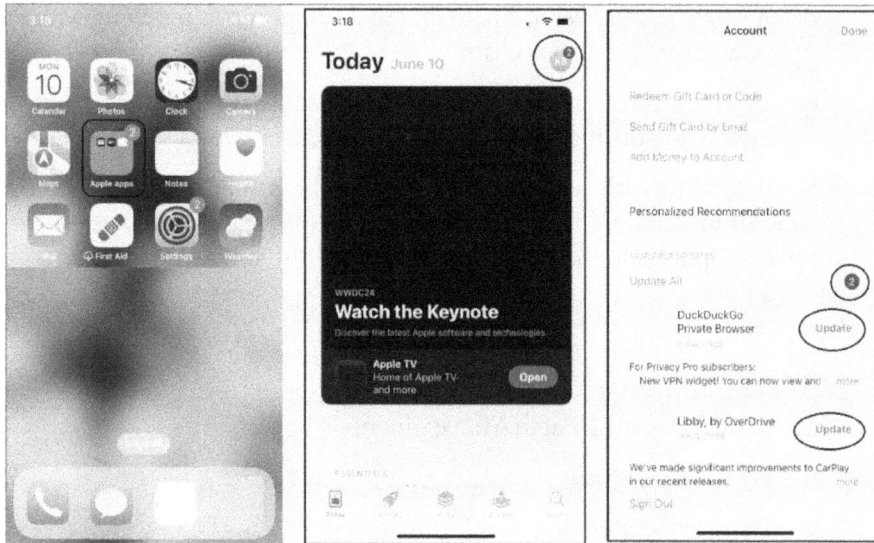

FIGURE 8.8 Updating applications on an iPhone

PATCHING TOOLS

If an organization has a large number of desktops, laptops, or servers, applying patches to them individually can be time-consuming. Having to perform numerous updates manually can also lead to making the occasional mistake or inadvertently skipping one or more machines.

There are tools available which can automate the process of applying patches. Some tools are able to apply patches to multiple different operating systems as well as many different applications. The ability to scan a computer or network to identify software that potentially needs to be updated is a feature available on most patching tools.

Some of the advantages of utilizing an automated patching tool include the following:

a. It will be faster than applying patches by hand, especially if the organization has a large number of computers.

b. The human error factor is eliminated.

c. It can complete the job more consistently than a person can do it.

d. A single person using a patching tool can perform patching with less man-power, i.e., less labor costs.

e. Patching tools can be scheduled to install patches during non-business hours, i.e., during the middle of the night or over a weekend.

Some tools provide a free version that can be used to evaluate whether it is a good fit for an organization. Examples of tools that can be used to patch multiple computers for an organization include the following:

a. Atera®

b. Avira®

c. Avast® Business Patch Management

d. GFI® LanGuard

e. Heimdal® Patch and Asset Management

f. Ivanti® Patch

g. ManageEngine® Patch Manager Plus

h. NinjaOne®

i. SolarWinds® Patch Manager

j. Microsoft Windows Server® Update Services (WSUS)

There are some situations where applying patches should not be automated. Some examples of when it is best to apply patches manually are as follows:

a. The patch needs to be installed in a critical production environment.

b. The patch is particularly complex. One that might require choosing from numerous options or settings.

c. It is custom written software that relies on a specific version of the operating system that needs to be patched.

d. They are extremely old applications that have caused issues when patches were applied in the past.

e. They are licensed applications that have been heavily customized for the organization.

BEWARE OF FAKE PATCHES

Cybercriminals are known to send out emails notifying the recipient that a patch of their software needs to be applied. These emails can be extremely convincing. They will include icons, email addresses, and names that were copied from the vendor's Web site or emails in them. The email's return address will appear to be from the vendor. If the recipient clicks on the link or opens the attachment, they will install malware instead of a patch. Always be skeptical of unsolicited emails with software update files attached to them. The best protection against this scam is to go directly to the vendor's Web site and download patch files from it.

Another method of delivering fake patches used by bad actors is via pop-up ads in a browser session. The pop-up ad will state that the browser is outdated and needs to be updated. It will also emphasize the dangers of not keeping browsers updated, which ironically is true. The best defense against this type of attack is to have a pop-up ad blocker set up on all browsers.

NOT ALL SOFTWARE CAN BE PATCHED

As important as patches are to keeping a system secure, they are not available for every piece of software. Patches are only released for products that the vendor is still supporting. If users are relying on older, unsupported versions of applications or operating systems, there may not be any patches for them. Most vendors provide customers with months or years of warning when a particular product will stop being supported. It is the responsibility of the consumer to make plans to migrate to a supported version of the software.

Microsoft provides end of support information for its products that reach their end of support in 2025. This information is available at the following URL: *https://learn.microsoft.com/en-us/lifecycle/end-of-support/end-of-support-2025*. Examples of Microsoft products that have defined "End of Support" dates are shown in the following table.

TABLE 8.1 Microsoft products with "End of Support" dates

Product	End of Support
Microsoft SQL Server, Extended Security Update Year 3	July 8, 2025
Visual Studio 2022, Version 17.8 (LTSC channel)	July 8, 2025
Access 2016	October 14, 2025

(Continued)

Product	End of Support
Access 2019	October 14, 2025
Excel 2016	October 14, 2025
Excel 2019	October 14, 2025
Microsoft Office 2016	October 14, 2025
Microsoft Office 2019	October 14, 2025
Skype for Business Server 2016	October 14, 2025
Skype for Business Server 2019	October 14, 2025
Windows 10 2015 LTSB	October 14, 2025
Windows Server 2012, Extended Security Update Year 2	October 14, 2025
Word 2016	October 14, 2025
Word 2019	October 14, 2025

It is uncommon, but some users continue to rely on software from a vendor that has gone out of business. Obviously, they will not receive patches for these products. Their best option is to migrate to another software package as quickly as possible.

REFERENCES

[AUT19] Levenson, Jon. "Bad Cyber Hygiene: 60 Percent of Breaches Tied to Unpatched Vulnerabilities," available online at *https://www.automox.com/blog/bad-cyber-hygiene-breaches-tied-to-unpatched-vulnerabilities*, June 18, 2019

[AXIS21] "How do Hackers Hack—An Experiment in Open Portal Attacks," available online at *https://www.linkedin.com/pulse/how-do-hackers-hack-experiment-open-portal-attacks-axis-security/*, September 3, 2021

[COMP08] Keizer, Gregg. "Unpatched Windows PCs fall to hacker in under 5 minutes, says ISC," available online at *https://www.computerworld.com/article/1568973/unpatched-windows-pcs-fall-to-hackers-in-under-5-minutes-says-isc.html*, July 14, 2008

[CSO20] Fruhlinger, Josh. "Equifax data breach FAQ: What happened, who was affected, what was the impact?," available online at *https://www.csoonline.com/article/567833/equifax-data-breach-faq-what-happened-who-was-affected-what-was-the-impact.html*, February 12, 2020

[CSO22] Fruhlinger, Josh. "WannCry explained: A perfect ransomware storm," available online at *https://www.csoonline.com/article/563017/wannacry-explained-a-perfect-ransomware-storm.html*, August 24, 2022

[DAR18] Higgins, Kelly Jackson. "Unpatched Vulnerabilities the Source of Most Data Breaches," available online at *https://www.darkreading.com/ vulnerabilities-threats/unpatched-vulnerabilities-the-source-of-most- data-breaches*, April 5, 2018

[FOR15] Lewis, Dave. "Heartland Payment Systems Suffers Data Breach," available online at *https://www.forbes.com/sites/davelewis/2015/05/31/ heartland-payment-systems-suffers-data-breach/?sh=57486d30744a*, May 31, 2015

[FTC19] "Equifax to Pay $575 Million as Part of Settlement with FTC, CFPB, and States Related to 2017 Data Breach," available online at *https:// www.ftc.gov/news-events/news/press-releases/2019/07/equifax-pay-575- million-part-settlement-ftc-cfpb-states-related-2017-data-breach*, July 22, 2019

[FTC20] "Equifax Data Breach Settlement," available online at *https://www.ftc. gov/enforcement/refunds/equifax-data-breach-settlement*, December 2022

[IBM24] "Cost of Data Breach Report," available online at *https://www.ibm. com/reports/data-breach*, January 2024

[PON24] "Costs and Consequences of gaps in Vulnerability Response," available online at *https://www.servicenow.com/content/dam/servicenow- assets/public/en-us/doc-type/resource-center/analyst-report/ponemon- state-of-vulnerability-response.pdf*, May 21, 2024

[RES19] Cingolani, Alessandro. "Heartland Data Breach Analysis," available online at *https://www.researchgate.net/publication/346975125_Heartland_ Data_Breach_Analysis*, February 19, 2019

[SOP22] "Ransomware Recovery Cost Reaches Nearly $2 Million, More Than Doubling in a Year, Sophos Survey Shows," available online at *https:// www.sophos.com/en-us/press/press-releases/2021/04/ransomware- recovery-cost-reaches-nearly-dollar-2-million-more-than-doubling-in-a- year*, April 27, 2021

[STR18] Tham, Irene. "Exploited server in SingHealth cyber attack did not get security updates for 14 months, CIO finds," available online at *https:// www.straitstimes.com/singapore/hacked-singhealth-server-had-not-had- security-update-for-14-months-cyber-attack-coi-finds*, September 27, 2018

9

EMAIL

Email is used worldwide on a regular basis for both personal and business communication. Use of other forms of communication like collaborative platforms, video conference calls, instant messaging, and social media for business are becoming popular, but email is likely to continue to be a useful form of communication for the foreseeable future.

Worldwide, approximately 347 billion emails were sent in 2023 [VENN23]. It is estimated that in 2023, the average person received 121 emails every day [VENN23]. It is used at work, home, and on mobile devices, but because of its ubiquitousness, people tend to overlook the downsides of using email.

UNDERSTANDING EMAIL

While email is a large part of daily communication on the Web, not everyone understands how it works. A very simplified overview of how email works is provided in the following sections.

Parts of an Email Address

Every email address has three parts to it.

1. username
2. the "at" symbol @
3. domain name

Figure 9.1 shows an example of an email address. In this example the user-name is "kelly.bourne" and the domain name is "computers.net."

New Message

To   kelly.bourne@computers.net ×

FIGURE 9.1 Three parts of an email address

Email Providers

An *email provider* is a company that moves emails from one user to another. Users interact with email clients, but email providers are how the messages get moved.

Examples of some of the largest email providers are as follows:

- Gmail
- Google
- Proton Mail
- Yahoo Mail
- Zoho Mail

Email Clients

When users send or receive an email, they are interfacing with an application called an *email client*. The email client relies on an email provider to send the emails to the intended recipients.

One way to clarify the difference between an email provider and an email client is to think about how physical mail is moved by the United States Postal Service (USPS). Local grocery stores like Kroger's®, Hy-Vee®, or Publix® may allow people to drop off letters there. They will even weigh and stamp packages, but they don't actually move letters to their destinations. A USPS employee comes to the store to pick up letters so the Post Office can move the mail to its destination. In this regard, the local grocery store is like an email client because it "collects" letters from the customer. The USPS is like an email provider because it actually moves the mail to its destination.

An email provider might also offer an email client to users. For example, you might have the Outlook email client on your desktop and Microsoft Outlook might also be your email provider. You might be using a Gmail account with a Google email client.

Email Client Functions

Email clients provide functions like the following to users:

- Enable users to create email.
- Allow users to specify the recipient(s) of the email.
- Allow users to send or transmit emails.
- Enable users to receive and read email messages.
- Allow users to create folders where email messages can be stored.
- Enable users to create a list of contacts that emails can be sent to.
- Filter incoming emails to eliminate spam messages.

Examples of Email Clients

Examples of email clients are as follows:

- Microsoft Outlook®
- Gmail®
- Mozilla Thunderbird®
- Apple Mail
- Proton Mail
- Samsung Mail

Types of Email Clients

The fundamental types of email client are as follows:

- Web-based email clients are accessed via a Web browser. Since these do not require that software be installed on a device, they allow a user to access email from any device with a browser anywhere in the world. Gmail is one of the most widely used Web-based email clients in the world.
- Desktop-based email clients are applications that are installed on a desktop or laptop computer. They allow emails to be stored locally on the

device so emails can be accessed even if there is no access to the Internet. Microsoft's Outlook is an example of this type of email client.

* Mobile email clients are specifically designed to work on mobile phones and tablets. These enable users to work with their emails anywhere and anytime. The Apple Mail app is available to all iPhone users.

* Groupware email clients emphasize features like collaboration and teamwork that are imported to organizations. Some features included in groupware email clients are shared calendars, task management, and document sharing.

SMTP Server

Whenever an email is sent, the email client sends it to an SMTP (Simple Mail Transfer Protocol) server. The SMTP server is like the local post office for a physical piece of mail. It receives the letter and forwards it on the next step toward its destination.

The SMTP server will not initially know where the destination email server is located. To get the destination's details, it asks the Domain Name System (DNS) for this information. The DNS can be thought of as a giant address book that knows the address of every computer on the Internet. DNS translates the destination domain, *computers.net* in this example, to an IP address. IP addresses are a set of four numbers that are the address of an electronic device connected to the Internet. The IP address of *computers.net* might be 255.255.255.255.

Establishing a Connection

Using the IP address that was just received from the DNS server, the sending SMTP server will establish a connection to the destination SMTP server across the Internet. The connection between them is channeled through multiple intermediate servers called *routers*. The email is sent from router to router until it reaches the destination SMTP server used by the recipient. The recipient can now open the email from their SMTP server.

The email's sender has no control over the path that it will travel across the Internet. The path may even include foreign countries. If a second email is sent moments later to the same destination, there is no guarantee that it will be sent along the same path.

Two important points to understand from the brief description of how email works is to recognize that a sender has no control of the path it takes and that every router along that path has access to the email's metadata, including its text.

Metadata

In addition to the text in the body, every email has additional information called *metadata*, which is the information about the email. Email metadata include details about the message being sent, and the most important metadata details are as follows:

a. the sender's email address, including the username, and domain name

b. the destination email address, including the username and domain name

c. details on any attachments. If an image is attached, it has its own metadata.

d. subject line contents

e. email addresses of anyone being copied on the email (CC or BCC)

f. the date and time the email was sent

g. message body, i.e., the text in the email

h. message-ID, a unique message ID associated with this email

EMAIL DANGERS

Email is inherently an insecure method of communication. Security was not built into the email system when it was originally created in 1969, which is when the earliest version of the Internet was created; email was limited to four universities. In an environment where there were so few sites and many of the users on the network knew each other, security was not seen as important. The concept of how much the Internet and email would flourish in the next 50 years would have been unthinkable to the original designers.

Some of email's risks are due to actions of the users. Others are caused by the actions of others. Descriptions of some potential risks are provided here.

Blind Copy

If additional recipients are carbon copied (CC) on an email, then everyone on the chain is aware of their inclusion. If a recipient is added as a blind copy (BCC), this addition is only known to the person who added the BCC recipient. "Reply All" responses to the original email will also be sent to the "hidden" recipients. The results can range from professional embarrassment to disclosure of confidential information.

Business Email Compromise (BEC)

BEC is a form of social engineering attack where a cybercriminal convinces an email recipient that the email was sent by a superior or higher up in the organization. The intent of the attack is usually to send money or information to the wrong party. FBI statistics show that in 2022, BEC attacks were responsible for over $83 million in reported losses [FBI23]. Actual losses are probably higher, since many organizations are reluctant to publicly announce that they have been the victim of a scam.

Another variation of a BEC scam is when the cybercriminal, acting as an executive, requests that the victim send him copies of all employee W-2 tax forms. If the victim emails out those forms, the cybercriminal will have a wealth of personally identifiable information for the organization's employees, contractors, and interns.

Email Account Takeover Attacks

If a cybercriminal is able to take over a victim's email account, then the contents of every email received or sent by the victim is available to the attacker. The kind of details potentially in emails could be extremely damaging if they became public or were sold on the Dark Web. Some of the information that could be exposed includes the following:

a. Social Security numbers

b. salary details

c. bank account numbers

d. credit card numbers

e. health related information

f. travel plans

g. login credentials

h. details of business deals

i. ongoing negotiation details

j. details on upcoming mergers or acquisitions

k. personal information

Another major problem of an email account takeover is that the cybercriminal can send out emails that appear to be coming from the victim. This can lead to social engineering attacks directed at all of the victim's contacts. If any of them respond to these bogus emails, it will lead to yet more victims.

Emails at Work

If an employee sends personal email on a computer owned by their employer, there is no legal expectation of privacy. The employer has the right to monitor and read any emails sent or received on that computer. If the employee is not aware of this, they could end up inadvertently revealing a great deal of personal information.

EMAIL SECURITY

Unless it has been encrypted, an email has no privacy. Its contents can be viewed at any of the servers it bounces to along the path from the sender to the receiver. Email contents have often been compared to the back of a post-card—anyone that wants to read it can do so. To ensure privacy an email has to be encrypted. Tools that are available to encrypt emails are discussed later in this chapter.

Email Forwarding

If a cybercriminal is able to get access to an email account, he may set it to automatically forward all or some emails to another account. With this alteration in place, he has access to everything the user does in his email account. With this information, the cybercriminal can access any accounts whose credentials are discussed in emails. He could also use this access to set up a Business Email Compromise (BEC) scam.

The best defense against this form of attack is to disable email forwarding. It is also wise to regularly check to make sure that rules to do this have not been created. Encrypting the contents of emails can also prevent anyone from reading them.

Phishing

Phishing, spear phishing, and whaling attacks and how to avoid them are described in Chapter 2. *Security Magazine* reports that over 90% of data breaches began with a phishing attack [SEC24]. The same source estimates that over 1.76 billion phishing emails were sent in 2023. If even a tiny fraction of them is successful, that is a large number of victims. The FBI Internet Crime Complaint Center (IC3) received more complaints about phishing than any other type of cybercrime [FBI24].

Ransomware

Ransomware is discussed in Chapter 3. The Verizon 2023 *Data Breach Investigations Report* found that approximately 33% of all ransomware attacks began with an email [VER23]. Even if that statistic changes by the time this page is read, it is guaranteed that phishing emails will still be the cause of a large percentage of ransomware attacks.

Reply All

When responding to an email, it is very easy to click on the "Reply All" icon instead of "Reply." This mistake is not caused by cybercriminals, but by the user. Even a self-inflicted situation like this can be either embarrassing or reveal confidential information.

Spam

As long as people will be using email, there will be spam. One source claims that over 160 billion spam emails are sent every day [EMAIL23]. Estimates of the percentage of all emails sent that are spam or otherwise malicious range from 46% [EMAIL23] to 85% [YAHOO23]. Common topics pitched by spam emails include prizes/giveaways, job opportunities, password updates, fake invoices, gambling, and romance scams.

The best steps an individual can take to avoid spam-related scams are as follows:

a. If an email is obviously questionable, then mark it as spam and block the sender. Blocking or reporting spam can have the additional effect of training a spam filter so it can prevent similar spam emails in the future.

b. Delete obvious spam emails without opening them. Some emails can inform the sender that they have been opened. This lets the sender know that the receiver's email account is active and will result in additional email being sent to it.

c. Never open an email attachment on a questionable email.

d. Never click on an embedded link in a questionable email.

e. Create a temporary email account to use for online shopping, signing up for services or other instances in which a valid mail address needs to be provided but the user does not want to provide his "real" email address. Doing this can help protect the reader's "real" email address from being inundated with spam.

f. Tighten up privacy settings on social media sites to reduce the number of people that can see one's email address.

g. Unsubscribe from email lists. The fewer spammers and mass marketers that have an email address on their lists, the fewer span emails will be sent to it.

Spam Filters

Spam filters are designed to detect and reject email that is unsolicited, unwanted, and potentially dangerous from reaching the inboxes of consumers. Ideally, a spam filter would block almost all phishing emails. A spam filter can be considered the outermost line of defense for email. Some unwanted emails may be able to sneak past a spam filter, but the overwhelming majority of them will be turned back by a good filter. Major email providers like Gmail, Proton Mail, Outlook, and Yahoo! mail include spam filters to protect their clients from unwanted malware.

The algorithms that drive spam filters look for certain attributes in emails being scanned. If an email exhibits too many of them, it will be marked as spam and either not delivered or sent to a "Spam" folder. Some of the attributes used to identify spam are as follows:

a. numerous spelling or grammar errors in the subject line or body of the email

b. using all caps in the subject line

c. multiple exclamation marks

d. trigger words like "free," "win $$," "make money," "discount," "limited time", "free" and "risk free"

e. generic greetings

f. numerous links in the body of the email

g. an email that was sent out in a large bulk with similar emails

h. an email that includes a form asking for the recipient's personal information

i. attachments that could contain an executable or a macro

j. emails from a public domain like *@gmail.com* or *@yahoo.com*

k. emails from an invalid domain like *@macrosoft.com* or *@micr0soft.com*

l. emails that convey a sense of great urgency

Spam filters also block senders that are known to send out numerous or dangerous emails. This is referred to as a *blacklist filter*. Known spammers will change their domains to avoid being blocked, but their new domain will eventually be blocked as well.

No filter will catch 100% of spam emails. A small percentage of them will slip through no matter how good the spam filter is. This means that all users need to be aware of the dangers of spam and how to spot it.

When the inevitable spam email gets past the filter, users can identify it as spam so the filter will catch similar emails in the future. For most email applications, marking an email as spam is as simple as right-clicking on it and selecting "Spam" or "Junk." This should prevent similar emails from slipping past the filter but if the sender's email address or the subject line changes the filter might not block it. Trying to block all spam is very challenging, as when one source of spam is blocked, it simply comes from other sources.

It is possible that legitimate emails will be identified as spam by a spam filter. If an expected email has not arrived, then checking for it in the spam folder of the email application is a good idea. Occasionally checking that folder, even if no emails are missing, is also recommended.

Spoofing

Spoofing an email address is an attack technique used to trick users into opening an email because it appears to have been sent by someone they know and trust. Once they open an email from a spoofed sender, they are encouraged to click on an embedded URL in the body of the email or open an attachment that has malware in it. Chapter 2 of this book covers email spoofing and phishing in great detail.

Spy Pixels

Spy pixels (also called email trackers, Web bugs, and Web beacons) are a method of tracking when a recipient has opened an email. They are usually an image, GIF, or PNG file in an email. This image can be unnoticeable since it can be as small as a single pixel. When the recipient opens the email, a message is returned to the sender so he knows that the email was opened. There are legitimate uses for spy pixels, but it would be impossible to argue that they do not have problems.

Some, but not all, users have legal protection against spy pixels. Email trackers are prohibited by the EU's General Data Protection Regulation (GDPR) unless the recipient has unambiguously consented to this monitoring [GDPR06]. Tracking pixels are prohibited by HIPAA rules if they disclose PHI (Personal Health Information) to third parties without authorization [HHS24]. The California Privacy Rights Act of 2020 (CCPA) also requires that the consumer provide explicit consent before spy pixels can be used to track them [XYZ21]. Unfortunately, some organizations do not follow those regulations. In Arizona, a class action suit against violators has been lodged [BEN24] over their usage.

Users can take the following actions to help ensure that their emails are not being tracked. Some steps that can be taken include the following:

- Never agree to being tracked by email trackers.
- Enabling ad blocking in a browser will eliminate pop-up ads and avoid any spy pixels in them from being displayed on a browser.
- Use a security-oriented email provider that protects users against spy pixels.
- Some browsers have a setting that will block tracking pixels. In Firefox changing the "Enhanced Tracking Protection" setting to "Strict" will block tracking pixels.
- Use a browser extension that blocks email tracking. PixelBlock® and Trocker® are examples of extensions that will protect users from being tracked.
- Using a Virtual Private Network (VPN) can disguise the user's actual location. VPNs are discussed in Chapter 13.

Wrong Addresses

When email addresses are entered manually, it is quite possible to enter it incorrectly. The best outcome of a mistake like this is that the email does not go anywhere, i.e., the email is sent to a non-existent address. The worst case is it gets sent to someone that will take advantage of this mistake. The best option is to select email addresses from the contacts list or click the "Reply" button on a previous email with the intended recipient. If an address must be entered manually, then be sure to double-check it before clicking the "Send" button.

PROTECTING AGAINST EMAIL RISKS

The following steps can be taken to help protect users against email dangers. Some of them are similar to steps protecting users from other cyber dangers like account takeover, phishing, and ransomware.

Strong Passwords

Use a strong password for the email account. It should be at least twelve characters long and include non-alphabetic characters. Just as important, this password should not be used for any other account.

Two Factor Authentication

Set up two factor authentication for all email accounts. Most email providers offer this extra level of authentication. The time it takes to log in using MFA is well worth it to protect something as important as this frequently used method of communications.

Confirm Via Another Channel

If an email is unexpected, unusual, or asks the recipient to do something out of the ordinary, then it is sensible to confirm that it is legitimate before performing the requested action. If an email is questionable, then replying via email is not safe. Another channel, like a phone call or text message, should be used to validate the message.

Do Not Open Phishing Emails

Chapter 4 on social engineering has an entire section on the dangers of phishing emails and how to avoid them. The best advice is to simply not open email that is likely to be a scam or phishing email. When in doubt, do not open it.

Encrypting Email

To be certain that an email remains confidential, it should be encrypted. There are a number of ways to encrypt email.

a. A very simple way to encrypt email attachments is to password protect the files before sending them. For example, if a PDF or .xlsx file is being sent via email, then protect it with a password before attaching it to the email. The password should not be included in the body of the email. It needs to be sent via a separate channel, for example, by a text message or a phone call. The drawbacks of this method are that it takes extra effort and the body of the email itself is not encrypted.

b. Email services that are privacy conscious provide end-to-end-encrypt for all emails sent using them. Examples include Proton Mail®, Hushmail®, and Tuta®.

c. Some email services provide an option that allows the user to encrypt an email. Gmail® allows the user to turn on "confidential mode" to protect email. Microsoft Office® and Apple's iOS® devices also provide ways to encrypt email.

d. Email services that do not directly provide this option allow for a third-party service to encrypt emails.

Use a Secure Email Service

Email security can be enhanced by choosing an email service that focuses on providing security. Features that a security conscious email product has includes the following:

a. end-to-end encryption (E2EE) to ensure that an email is encrypted when it is created and can only read by the recipient

b. the ability to use an alias when sending email

c. strict policies on not sharing client data with any third parties

d. two factor authentication to help prevent a bad actor from taking over the account

e. the ability to sign-up and pay for the service anonymously. This significantly enhances the user's privacy.

f. servers that are physically located in countries that have strong privacy laws

g. many experts feel that the transparency of an open-source email provider allows an extra degree of confidence in the quality of its code.

Unattended Computers

Leaving a computer unattended is extremely dangerous, as the device itself can be stolen. This possibility may seem unlikely, especially in an office environment, but it happens frequently. According to Gitnux, over two million laptops are stolen in the United States every year, and 97% of stolen laptops are never recovered [GITN24].

It would take only seconds for a coworker, stranger, or intruder to read, copy, or send emails from the device. Even if the email application has not been left open, it would not be difficult for a thief or intruder to open it up quickly.

Obtaining passwords from an unlocked, unattended computer can take just a few seconds. If they are saved in a browser's password manager, all the cybercriminal needs to do it click the *Application Menu*, click *Passwords*, and click the "eye" icon to display the password in clear text. Figure 9.2 shows how this can be done. Once a cybercriminal knows the application or Web site, username, and password, there is nothing to stop him from taking over an account.

FIGURE 9.2 Viewing passwords in Firefox's password vault

Never leave a computer unattended, even if it is only for a few seconds. Take the time to lock the screen or, if it is a laptop, take it with you. This will prevent outright theft of the device.

Delete Old/Unneeded Email

Periodically review accumulated emails. If old emails are no longer needed, then delete them. This is especially important if the emails contain confidential or proprietary information. Do not forget to review and clean out emails in the *Sent* and *Draft* folders.

Simply deleting an email might not mean that it is really gone. Some vendors preserve deleted emails in a *Deleted* folder for a certain amount of time or until they are specifically deleted from that folder. Be sure to understand how the email service works. If emails are moved to a *Deleted* folder, then deleting them from it gets rid of them. If emails are kept for 30 days or another time period, then perhaps cleaning out old emails more frequently will minimize this issue.

EMAIL ACCOUNTS GET HACKED

Breaking into email accounts is a priority for cybercriminals. Access to a corporate email account can lead to additional access within the organization's network. Hacking into a personal email account can yield information on the victim's other accounts because so many accounts use an email address as the account name. This includes social media, bank accounts, online shopping accounts, and credit card information. In 2022, Norton reported that 14% of all consumers detected unauthorized access to an email account [NOR21]. In 2023, Forbes magazine reported that 15% of users had a breach of their email accounts [FOR24]. The possibility of having an email account getting hacked is significant.

Signs of a Hacked Email Account

Password Has Been Changed

The most obvious sign that an email account has been hacked is if the password to it no longer works. If the owner of the account did not make this change, then it is certain that a cybercriminal has taken over the account.

The owner needs to change the password to something new, but this will be complicated because he does not have the current password. The victim needs to contact the email provider and explain what happened. This should enable him to change the password.

Comments from Contacts

If friends or coworkers have received unusual or unexpected emails from the victim, this is another sign that the account has been compromised. The victim should reach out to all of his contacts via another channel like a phone call or text to explain what has happened and warn them that any recent emails from him might contain malware and should be deleted.

Once he has regained control of the existing account or created a new account, he will need to inform his contacts a second time, again via another channel. This is a time-consuming task but must be done to regain the trust of people that received spam from the account.

Unexpected Emails

Seeing unexpected emails in the *Sent* folder is also indicative that the account was hijacked. This might not apply because an experienced cybercriminal is likely to cover his trail by deleting emails from the *Sent* folder.

Log File

Some email services allow the user to see a list of the dates, times, and IP addresses of every time the account was logged into. If the victim still has access to the account, then looking at this log might help determine whether someone else has been logging into it.

Recovering from a Hacked Email Account

The steps to recover a hacked email account are similar to other account takeover situations. The steps to take include the following:

1. Log out of all accounts and Web sites. Then log off the computer and power it down. Restart the computer.

2. Run an antivirus tool on the computer. If the option exists, choose the deepest or most thorough scan available.

3. Change the passwords of all accounts. If the cybercriminal has penetrated an email account, he might have gained access to other information. It is better to change all the passwords of all accounts.

4. Enable Multiple Factor Authentication to help prevent another takeover of this email account.

5. Alert friends and coworkers that the email account was taken over but is back in the user's control.

EMAIL PROVIDERS

Choosing an email provider may not seem like a big decision, but it actually is an extremely important choice. Points that need to be considered when making this choice include security, efficiency, and continuity.

Employer's Account

One possible choice is to use an email account provided by an employer for personal usage. This is not usually a useful choice, though. First, many, if not most, employers prohibit employees from using their business email account for personal use. Doing this could potentially be grounds for dismissal. Other employees may be doing it, but that is also not wise.

Second, employers have the right to monitor and read any email sent on the company's account. It is possible that email administrators at the organization will either look for personal emails or stumble across them at some point. The average user may think that they are not sending confidential information in their emails, but it happens more often than they think. Some examples of information they may not want an employer or coworkers to know about include Social Security Numbers, credit card account numbers, bank account numbers, financial status, investment details, health related information, travel plans, relationships that are meant to be hidden, comments made about the organization or coworkers, and resumes sent out to potential future employers.

A third reason not to use an employer's email account is continuity. When the employee leaves the organization, they will no longer have access to that email account. They will also lose access to any email history and will be forced to reach out to all of their contacts and let them know about their new email address. It is so much better to avoid these issues by getting an email address that is not employer-related.

ISP-Provided Email Accounts

One of the most common choices for an email account is to use the email service that is provided by the user's ISP (Internet Service Provider). Most ISPs provide this capability. Many allow multiple emails accounts to be created. It is convenient and it is usually included in the Internet access package for no additional charge.

One compelling reason for not using the ISP provided email is the lack of portability. If the decision is made to switch to a new ISP, then the current email address will no longer be available. (Of course, the user can let all of his contacts know that his email address has changed, but that is an inconvenience.)

Another problem with using an ISP's email service is that the email address is frequently used as the account name or ID on a Web site or application. Changing ISPs means those accounts may need to be changed. New accounts may have to be created with the new email address. This could be even more time-consuming than alerting all email contacts about the new address.

Free vs. Paid Providers

One of the factors in choosing an email provider is whether to use one of the many free emails providers or pay a provider for email. There is a saying in the IT industry: "If you're not paying for the product, then you are the product." This saying means that all vendors have to make money to stay in business. If users are not paying for the product, then the vendor has to earn money some other way. One way that vendors can potentially monetize the product is to scan their client's emails to gather information about them. These personal details are either sold to a data broker or used to customize advertisements shown to the client.

Free Accounts

Some of the major free email services are as follows:

a. Gmail®

b. Outlook®

c. Yahoo Mail

d. iCloud Mail

e. AOL Mail®

Paid Accounts

Email services that require payment include the following:

a. Proton Mail®—free plans are available

b. Tuta®—free plans are available

c. Neo—limited-time free plans are available

d. Zoho—15-day free trial plan is available

e. Mailbox.org—30-day free trial plan is available

Tools that Provide Protection

Third-Party Spam Filters

Most email services provide spam filtering, but an additional filtering capability is available from third parties. These providers analyze email and eliminate spam before it is delivered to the client's email server. This additional check could be especially useful to an organization that uses an internal email server. Third-party spam filters can also be set up for commercial email providers like Gmail and Outlook.

Phishing Awareness Training

If users receive training emails that simulate an email phishing attack, they can learn to recognize phishing attempts. Simulated phishing emails can be sent out by an internal group or by a security vendor that specializes in this type of training. Organizations like KnowB4 can send out simulated phishing emails and provide statistics showing how many employees did not recognize a phishing email when they received one.

THE FUTURE OF EMAIL THREATS

Like many areas in cybersecurity, the competition between spammers and spam filters never ends. Vendors that provide spam filters adjust their tools to catch all current versions of spam emails. The spammers develop new ways to get their junk email through the filters. Vendors update their logic to catch the new examples of spam. This cycle is likely to continue.

Artificial Intelligence

The advent of powerful and readily available artificial intelligence (AI) tools will certainly increase the number and quality of spam emails. Some ways in which AI could escalate email attacks include the following:

Fewer Errors

Spelling errors and grammar errors are a common way to identify spam or malicious emails. AI will undoubtedly help bad actors improve the quality of their emails.

Automated Attacks

AI might be used to devise and carry out email attacks without the cybercriminal participating. This could lead to attacks occurring all the time. It could also allow cybercriminals to tailor every phishing email to the intended recipient, i.e., spear phishing attempts instead of generic phishing.

Deepfakes

Deepfake technology could be included in email attacks. Audio or video clips could perfectly impersonate coworkers or executives. Victims would likely comply with a request if a voice or video message from their superior or a high-level executive directing them to take that action.

Evading Detection

Machine learning might be used to help email attacks evade detection by current spam filters. They could learn which emails are recognized as spam and alter them enough to improve the chances of getting past spam filters and antivirus tools.

REFERENCES

[BEN24] Eisen, Mark. "Beware of the Spy Pixel: Arizona Faces New Class Action Trend Under Privacy Law," available online at https://www.beneschlaw.com/resources/beware-*of-the-spy-pixel-arizona-faces-new-class-action-trend-under-privacy-law.html*, May 28, 2024

[EMAIL23] Ellis, Cai & Brandl, Robert. "Spam Statistics (2024): New Data on Junk Email, AI Scams, & Phishing," available online at *https://www.emailtooltester.com/en/blog/spam-statistics/*, October 16, 2024

[FBI23] "Internet Crime Complaint Center Releases 2022 Statistics," available online at *https://www.fbi.gov/contact-us/field-offices/sanfrancisco/news/fbi-releases-Internet-crime-report*, March 22, 2023

[FBI24] "FBI Releases Internet Crime Report," available online at https://*www.fbi.gov/contact-us/field-offices/sanfrancisco/news/fbi-releases-Internet-crime-report*, April 4, 2024

[FOR24] Haan, Katherine. "America's Password Habits: 46% Report Having their Password Stolen Over the Last Year," available online at *https://www.forbes.com/advisor/business/software/american-password-habits/*, June 3, 2024

[GDPR06] "Email Tracking," available online at *https://www.gdpreu.org/gdpr-compliance/email-tracking/*, February 2006

[GITN24] "Must-Know Laptop Theft Statistics," available online at *https://gitnux.org/laptop-theft-statistics/*, May 27, 2024

[HHS24] "Use of Online Tracking Technologies by HIPA Covered Entities and Business Associates," available online at *https://www.hhs.gov/hipaa/for-professionals/privacy/guidance/hipaa-online-tracking/index.html*, March 18, 2024

[NOR21] "2021 Norton Cyber Safety Insights Report Global Results," available online at *https://now.symassets.com/content/dam/norton/campaign/NortonReport/2021/2021_NortonLifeLock_Cyber_Safety_Insights_Report_Global_Results.pdf*, May 2021

[SEC24] Daughterty, Taelor. "Credential phishing accounted for 91% of active threat reports," available online at *https://www.securitymagazine.com/articles/100569-credential-phishing-accounted-for-91-of-active-threat-reports*, April 10, 2024

[VENN23] Ramuthi, Danesh. "25 Key Email Statistics Defining Modern Email Landscape," available online at *https://venngage.com/blog/email-stats/*, November 28, 2023

[VER23] Verizon's "Data Breach Investigations Report" available online at *https://www.verizon.com/business/resources/reports/dbir/2023/*, Apr 2, 2024

[XYZ21] "Spy Pixels in Emails: Why You Should Be Worried," available online at *https://www.thexyz.com/blog/spy-pixels-in-emails-why-you-should-be-worried/*, June 28, 2021

[YAHOO23] "Mimecast: Spam Email Statistics," available online at *https://finance.yahoo.com/news/mimecast-spam-email-statistics-130000494.html*, March 31, 2023

CHAPTER **10**

SOCIAL MEDIA

Social media has become very popular over the last 10 or 20 years. It is estimated that over five billion people around the world use some form of social media [SMART24], which is about 62% of everyone on Earth. Almost two and a half hours per day is spent on social media by the typical user [DATA24]. Typically, younger people spend more time online than their elders, and women are online longer than men.

Cybercriminals view social media as a place to find potential victims. It is estimated that two out of every five Americans has had at least one account compromised [STAX24]. In January of 2024, a leak of 26 billion records from social media sites was revealed [INFO24]. The records came from popular social media sites including LinkedIn, Snapchat, Venmo, Adobe, and X [NEW24]. The breach was informally called MOAB—the "Mother of All Breaches." As enormous as this breach was, some experts predict that even larger breaches will come to light in the future.

SOCIAL MEDIA PLATFORMS

Estimates of which social media platforms are the most popular abound but vary widely. Rankings can be based on the number of accounts, number of visits per month, unique visitors per month, or other metrics. One survey ranked them, along with their estimated number of monthly active users (MAUs) [SEA24].

1. Facebook®   3 billion
2. YouTube®   2.5 billion
3. Instagram®   2 billion
4. Tik Tok   1.2 billion
5. Snapchat   750 million
6. X (Twitter)   540 million
7. Pinterest   465 million
8. Reddit   430 million
9. LinkedIn   350 million
10. Threads   100 million

THE DANGERS OF SOCIAL MEDIA

Social media sites can be entertaining, educational, a means of socializing, and a way of transacting business, but they are not without risk. Some of the risks associated with social media are described here.

a. Bots on social media are accounts controlled by a computer program that is designed to mimic human behavior. One intent of bots is to make it appear that a political position is widely supported when it actually has limited support. Bots can also scrape data from legitimate accounts, click on ads, and send messages to legitimate accounts. The estimated number of social media accounts that are actually bots varies widely. For X (Twitter), the estimated percentage of bots ranges from 25 to 68% [WUSL22]. Some experts estimate that 4-5% of Instagram accounts are bots [FRAU24]. Other social media sites likely have a significant percentage of bots, as well.

b. *Catphishing* is when a bad actor creates a fake identity with the intention of tricking a victim into believing they are in an online friendship or romance. The intent is to harm the victim by embarrassing, scamming, blackmailing, or stealing their identity. Always be cautious when engaging in a new relationship. If it feels like the relationship is moving too fast or the other person is trying to manipulate you, then end or slow the speed of the relationship.

c. *Cyberbullying* is when a cybercriminal uses technology like social media to threaten, harass, embarrass, or otherwise target a victim. The effects of cyberbullying can be devastating on the victim, especially when the target is a child. There have been numerous cases of cyberbullying victims committing suicide.

d. Fake giveaways on social media are often used by the bad actors to increase their number of followers or to collect personal information about potential victims. If an offer requires significant personal information or seems too good to be true then it may be a fraud.

e. Identity theft can occur when cybercriminals use social media sites to steal personally identifiable information (PII). Once they have this information, they will attempt to take over email accounts, social media accounts, or investment accounts. If a cybercriminal is able to get control of a victim's social media account, they may run phishing attacks directed at the victim's followers.

f. *Likejacking* is a scam on Facebook that gets the victim to click the "Like" button on the cybercriminal's video, image, or offer. The purpose is to either gather information about potential victims or install malware on their smart phone or computer.

g. The loss of privacy is a problem on social media sites. The sites track almost everything users do in order to harvest details about individual's activities, interests, personal characteristics, political views, purchasing habits, and online behaviors [EPIC24]. That data is then either sold to a data broker or used to drive further user engagement on the social media site.

h. *Misinformation* (fake news) can spread quickly on social media sites. One recent example involves a faked video on TikTok that supposedly had the final moments of a tourist submersible that imploded while diving to the Titanic wreck. The fake video had 4.9 million views in just 10 days [USPI24]. Misinformation tends to spread faster than accurate information because it generates a stronger reaction from viewers. Bots also play a significant factor in the dissemination of fake news.

i. Phishing scams direct users to fake login pages that mimic the login pages of actual social media sites. When the unknowing user logs into the fake site, it allows the cybercriminal to harvest his account credentials. The user is then seamlessly redirected to the real login page. Once the cybercriminal has the credentials, he can log into the victim's account to steal personal data, monitor activity, or send phishing messages to the victim's contacts.

j. Cyberstalking is online harassment in the form of bullying, threats or intimidation that is perpetrated via an electronic medium including social media [SMVLC24]. It can escalate into danger in the real world. Actions considered to be cyberstalking include abusive or threatening texts. Children are especially vulnerable to cyberbullying.

k. *Trolls* on social media are people who deliberately circulate inflammatory content. When a troll responds to another user's post, their comments go far beyond constructive criticism. Their intent is to get a reaction from everyone. The best advice for dealing with trolls is to ignore them, block them, and report them to the site's moderator.

BAD ADVICE

The Internet and social media sites can be sources of bad advice. Anyone can portray themselves as an expert and dispense worthless, even dangerous, information. Some examples of advice from social media sites that should be avoided are as follows:

Tax Advice

The IRS warns that social media sources routinely circulate inaccurate or misleading tax information [IRS24]. One scheme encourages taxpayers to fill out their W-2 forms with inflated income and withholding figures to get an unwarranted return. When the inaccurate information is uncovered, the taxpayer will be held legally responsible for tax fraud.

Legal Advice

Taking legal advice from a person that may or may not be qualified to give that advice is not wise. Even if the contributor has a legal background, they could be from a different country or jurisdiction so their advice could be inaccurate. If their advice causes problems, the victim will have little or no chance of obtaining legal help.

Health Advice

Social media sites like TikTok, Instagram, and YouTube have advice on health, wellness, and self-care. Taking health advice from a social media source could put your life at risk. There is no way to confirm the credentials, experience, or intent of someone who posts medical advice on a social media account.

Following medical advice from an unknown person on the Internet is foolish at best and life threatening at worst.

Investment Advice

Anyone can offer investment advice, but all opinions are not equally valuable. Consider the following story: In late September of 1929, Joe Kennedy, the father of President John F. Kennedy, was offered investment advice by a young elevator operator. The young man told Kennedy how much money he had made in the stock market by buying stocks on the margin, i.e., by borrowing the money to buy them. Understanding how overextended the market must be if everyone was doing the same as this young man, Kennedy sold all of his stock market holdings that day. Within weeks the market crashed. That decision helped Kennedy avoid going bankrupt as thousands of other investors did. The anonymous advisers on social media may be as unqualified as the young man who offered investment advice to Kennedy just before the Wall Street crash of 1929.

FRAUD INITIATED ON SOCIAL MEDIA SITES

The FTC (Federal Trade Commission) reported that between January 2021 and June 2023, $2.7 billion was lost to fraud originating on social media [FTC23]. One in four people who reported losing money to fraud since 2021 said it started on social media according to the FTC. The breakdown of losses was as follows:

- Investment related   53%
- Romance scams   14%
- Other   27%
- Online shopping   8%

NOTE   *The percentage total exceeds 100% due to rounding.*

Investment Scams

Social media is used by many people to learn about investment opportunities. Unfortunately, frauds and scam artists are there to take advantage of potential investors. It is trivial for a scam artist to create a Web site showing his expertise. That Web site might look very similar to a legitimate firm's site. It is also easy for scam artists to create other social media accounts which claim the scam artist is helpful and showed them how make "a fortune" with their investing advice.

Pig Butchering Scams

Pig butchering scams begin when a crook creates a fake online identity, usually with an image that is of a person living a rich and successful lifestyle. The scam artist then tries to connect to people on dating or other social media sites. The pretense is frequently that a text was for someone else, i.e., a wrong number. The crook initiates a relationship with the potential victim by pretending to be interested in his or her life. To ingratiate themselves, the cybercriminal will fabricate a life that is very similar to the victim's. At some point, the cybercriminal will confide to the victim that he made a great deal of money by investing and advise that the victim make similar investments, frequently in cryptocurrency. In the end, of course, the victim loses all of their money on worthless investments.

Ponzi Schemes

A Ponzi scheme is when a cybercriminal pays out high returns to early investors by using money from later investors. There are no actual financial investments supporting the scheme. For a while, it will appear that investors are all making money. The scheme can continue for years or even decades. It eventually ends when no additional investors can be found or the cybercriminal can no longer keep paying out returns. One recent Ponzi scheme was perpetrated by Bernie Madoff.

Cryptocurrency

Many investment scams take advantage of peoples' fear of missing out on an opportunity. This is especially true if they do not really understand the investment that is being proposed. Investing in cryptocurrency is an example of this. When the word "cryptocurrency" is mentioned, most people think of Bitcoin, but there are thousands of virtual currencies or digital assets. As of March 12, 2024, there were 13,217 different cryptocurrencies [EXPL24]. Many financial scams encourage potential investors to buy into some of the more obscure or less well traded cryptocurrencies. There is an extremely high chance that the victim will lose most or all of his money on an investment like this.

Pump and Dump

A pump and dump scam involves the shares of infrequently traded, low priced stocks. Sometimes these are called "penny stocks" because their current value is less than a dollar. The cybercriminal will encourage his victims to purchase a particular stock. If enough people buy the stock, the price will be "pumped up," or inflated. As soon as the value rises, the cybercriminal will sell, or "dump," shares that he purchased earlier at a low price. At some point, the share values will decline significantly and the victims will lose most or all of their investment.

Celebrity Testimonials

Scam artists frequently include fraudulent testimonials from regular people as well as celebrities [SEC22]. In July 2020, a cyberattack was able to hijack the Twitter accounts of 130 celebrities, including Barrack Obama, Joe Biden, and Bill Gates [AURA23]. The attackers sent out tweets from the hijacked accounts, claiming that if the recipient sent the account holder $1,000 in Bitcoin, they would receive $2,000 back. Getting double their money back sounded like a great investment to some gullible victims. Of course, none of them received the promised $2,000 in Bitcoin. It was estimated that the cybercriminals absconded with over $100,000 in Bitcoin.

Romance Scams

The basics of romance scams is that a scam artist uses social media to convince the victim that he or she is in love with the victim. The relationship will always be long-distance and conducted entirely online. The cybercriminal will have a succession of vaguely believable explanations for why they cannot meet in person. Once the victim is emotionally committed to the relationship, the cybercriminal will start making requests for loans or gifts or offer investment suggestions. Eventually the victim will run out of money or patience, and the cybercriminal will disappear.

Money Mules

A dangerous new version of the romance scam is for the victim to become a money laundering accomplice. In this variation, after the cybercriminal has convinced the victim that they are in love, the cybercriminal asks the victim to move money from the criminal's bank account to an account that the victim opened. The victim was led to believe that they were helping their romantic partner with a new, legitimate business. They are, however, helping to launder or hide illegally gained money. At this point, the victim has become a criminal even if he or she does not realize it. When the illegal activity is uncovered, the victim may find themself in the unenviable position of having no money, being abandoned by his romantic interest, and under arrest.

Investment Red Flags

Some red flags that investment opportunities might be scams include the following:

a. the promise of unrealistically high returns with little or no risk

b. If the investment is not made immediately, the opportunity will be unavailable (sense of urgency).

c. The company behind the investment is in a foreign country.

d. The investment is not a normal stock or bond.

e. The victim in encouraged to get their friends and family to invest, as well.

f. The method of payment may involve cryptocurrency or other unconventional means.

g. No matter how much the victim invests, he is encouraged to invest even more.

h. The investment involves a secret method or strategy that is not available to everyone.

Online Shopping Scams

Global sales related to social media are projected to reach $1.2 trillion in 2025 [ACC22]. Unfortunately, the rate of online shopping scams is climbing just as rapidly. US consumers lost almost $1.2 billion dollars between January 2021 and June 2023 to social media related shopping scams, according to the FTC [FTC23].

In most cases the consumer pays, but never gets the product. In other cases, the product is received but is of lower quality than promised and may be outright dangerous. Some of the most common online shipping scams are as follows:

a. products that claim to support a charity

b. free trial offers of services that end up being difficult or impossible to terminate

c. counterfeit products

d. poor or non-existent customer service

e. return policies that prevent returns or have unexpectedly high return fees

Avoiding Social Media Scams

Avoiding a social media-based scam does not require a technical solution. Most of the steps for avoiding all forms of social media scams include common sense and practicing some caution. Some examples are as follows:

a. Limit the personal information about yourself that is posted on social media.

b. If a friendship seems to be turning into romance too quickly, be very cautious. This could well be a romance scam.

c. Never send money to someone you have not met yet, no matter how pitiful or convincing a story they tell.

d. If a deal with an unknown company seems too good to be true, spend some time researching the company before making any purchases. Search online for the company's name and "scam" or "complaint." The company may turn out to be fraudulent.

e. Messages from social media friends asking for money or promoting an investment opportunity may be an indication that their social media account has been hacked. Before responding, try to contact them via a phone call or a text message.

f. Any request for payment in cryptocurrency, gift cards, or a wire transfer should be met with skepticism. It is common for cybercriminals to want to be paid in unusual ways to avoid normal financial channels.

g. Do not link social media accounts. This may make it easier to log into them, but it also makes it easier for bad actors to access all social media accounts if they're able to break into any of the victim's accounts.

h. Only deal with secure Web sites. To determine whether a Web site is secure, look at its URL. Secure sites begin with *https://*. Avoid dealing with sites that begin with *http://*.

i. Read the reviews posted on the company's Web site but realize they can be faked. If all of the reviews are positive or if they all seem extremely similar, they could have been posted by the cybercriminal who runs the business.

BEING TRACKED BY SOCIAL MEDIA APPS

Social media sites typically collect data about their clients' activity. Platforms like Instagram, Facebook, YouTube, X, Snapchat, and TikTok collect large amounts of data on their users [TAHO22]. This data is analyzed and either sold to a data broker or used to customize the ads and content that users will see. When users see advertisements on a social media site, it is safe to assume that the site was paid to show that ad to the user.

Personally Identifiable Information Collected

Most people do not think their social media accounts discloses much PII online, but these accounts actually reveal a significant amount of information. With so much information being collected on users, it is extremely likely that it is available to be purchased. It is also possible for it to be stolen by cyber-criminals. Even if a user is careful to limit the PII they reveal about themselves, social media sites are likely to acquire the following information from that site or from other online sources [IDEN24].

a. full name

b. date of birth

c. city of birth

d. city and state of current and past residences

e. race

f. email address

g. phone number

h. nicknames

i. relationship status, i.e., married, divorced, single

j. religious beliefs.

k. high school and colleges attended

l. hobbies

m. profession and job title

n. current and past employers.

o. recent vacation destinations

p. favorite restaurants

q. photos of them, family, friends, coworkers, and neighbors

r. previous purchases

s. content shared or uploaded to social media sites.

People share too much on their social media accounts. Do not overshare, especially confidential information. That information can easily become OSINT (Open-Source Intelligence) used by cybercriminals to facilitate many kinds of cyberattacks including phishing, spearfishing, account takeover, and identity theft.

Web Scraping

It is possible for people or entities not associated with social media sites to acquire a significant amount of data on social media users. The technique to do this is called *Web scraping* or *screen scraping*. Web scrapers are software applications (a.k.a. bots) that visit thousands of Web sites and copy information from their pages. The data that is "scraped" is then stored in a database where it can be organized for later retrieval.

Web scrapers are not looking for information on a specific individual. They are programmed to access virtually any social media site that is on the Internet. They run constantly and capture every personal detail that they can find. This information is then merged with other data on individuals and sold to marketers or data brokers. In late 2021, an attempt was made to sell personal data on 1.5 billion accounts scraped from Facebook [STAX24].

The range of data that is collected by Web scraping bots is astonishing. Some examples of that data include the following:

a. complete name

b. email addresses

c. current and past residences

d. photographs posted on social media. These can be used to feed facial recognition systems. They can also be used to identify friendships and family relationships.

e. Photographs posted online can yield metadata like exactly where the photograph was taken, when it was taken, and the kind of camera used.

f. health issues

g. food allergies

h. medicines being taken

i. comments that people have posted on social media sites

j. customer reviews posted on social media, including Yelp, and other sites

k. video clips showing family, friends, recreational activities, and vacations

l. automobiles owned

m. political affiliations and leanings

n. professional details like job history, salary, names of coworkers, and experience

o. professional organization membership and certifications earned

p. conferences attended or presented at

q. educational details

r. achievements and awards

s. hobbies

t. travel itineraries

u. dining and entertainment preferences

v. consumer preferences between products and vendors

w. favorite sports and sports teams

x. dating habits

Hack Yourself

You can learn much about yourself within just a few minutes of online searching. When performing this exercise, start with a blank sheet of paper. Write down everything that is found. Start by searching for your name using a search engine. Then search in some of the major social media sites to find information. Check on a "white pages" Web site to see if it has your address and living companions. Read some of your posts on Twitter or another site to see what a cybercriminal might be able to learn about your politics or social views. Write it all down. If you are like the average person, the list of personal information that can be found in a short period of time will be extensive and surprising.

SOCIAL MEDIA AND HACKING

Social media sites have a tremendous amount of personally identifiable information (PII). Cybercriminals are interested in gaining access to both individual accounts and entire Web sites. There have been numerous examples of both types of attacks.

Social Media Site Attacks

The following describe just a small number of social media sites that have been hacked in the last few years:

X, which was Twitter at that time, was hacked in July of 2022 [TECH24]. An estimated 200 million user accounts were compromised. Details about them were later posted on the Dark Web. PII that was exposed included names, email addresses, social media profiles, and usernames [TWIN24].

In June of 2021, the data of approximately 700 million accounts from professional networking site LinkedIn were posted for sale on the Dark Web [FDM23]. The type of information exposed were full names, addresses, email addresses, phone numbers, geolocation records, genders, and related names used on other social media accounts [SCRUB24].

Facebook, the largest social media site, has had a number of data breaches over the years. In April of 2019, a security firm determined that 540 million records had been exposed [WIRE21].

Data exposed in this breach included Facebook IDs, phone number, and other personal details.

Consequences of a Site Being Breached

Whenever a social media site is breached, a large amount of user-related information can be leaked. This information can be used by cybercriminals to attack the victims. One form of attack is to use the compromised addresses and other personal details to send out phishing emails to owners of the breached accounts.

Another frequent type of attack is a credential stuffing attack. Knowing that users frequently reuse passwords for multiple accounts, the cybercriminals attempt to log into other social media accounts using account names and passwords obtained from the breached site. Since the average person reuses their passwords on four different accounts, this attack is frequently successful [FORB24].

Social Media Accounts Get Hacked

It is not just the regular people who have their social media accounts hacked. Numerous celebrities have also been hacked. *Friends'* actress Lisa Kudrow had her Twitter account hacked in an unusual way. She had posted a photograph to her account, and a cybercriminal noticed that included in the photo was a sticky note that had her password written on it [DIG23].

Facebook founder Mark Zukerberg's account on Twitter was broken into when cybercriminals guessed his password [NBC16]. They found out that he had reused that password on multiple other social media accounts and caused him additional problems [INFO16].

How are Social Media Accounts Hacked?

Password attacks using dictionary attacks have been successful because sites did not restrict the number of failed login attempts that could be made. Attackers used a program to guess every word in a dictionary until the correct password was identified.

Guessing passwords based on personal details is another way to hack an account. One celebrity's social media account was broken into when a cybercriminal guessed that her password was the name of her dog—Tinkerbell.

Phishing emails are another method of breaking into a victim's social media account. If the victim is subject to this type of attack, they can lose control of their accounts.

Recognizing That an Account Has Been Hacked

Some of the indications that a social media account has been hacked or taken over include the following:

a. Emails come from the social media site warning about unauthorized access. These need to be examined to ensure they are not actually phishing emails.

b. The password no longer works.

c. Friends on that site have seen unusual messages posted on the victim's account.

d. The login history for that site indicates the account was accessed at unusual times.

e. The site's login history indicates the account has been logged into from other locations or countries.

f. There has been a significant number of new friends added to the friend list.

g. Privacy settings on the account have been modified.

Recovering from a Hacked Account

Different social media sites can have unique recommended steps for recovering an account on their site. If the site has specific advice, then that should be followed. If the site does not provide recommendations the following steps can be taken.

a. Change the account's password. Be sure the new password is a strong one.

b. If it is not possible to change the password, for example if the cybercriminal has already changed it, then contact the site's customer support and let them know the account has been taken over. Request that control of it be returned to you.

c. Sign out of all devices. This will ensure that anyone logged into the account is also logged out of the site.

d. Enable two factor authentication. This will help prevent another account takeover situation.

e. Check the account's setting or preferences to ensure they have not been modified. Make sure that the correct email address and phone number are listed for account recovery situations.

f. Report the takeover event with the social media site.

g. Alert friends and followers about the incident and advise them to ignore or delete recent messages from the affected account

h. Confirm that no other social media accounts have been taken over. This is especially likely to have happened if different accounts have the same password.

i. Remove any harmful or offensive posts or content that the cybercriminal added.

SOCIAL MEDIA ALGORITHMS

What users see on social media sites is not random. Algorithms developed by social media site programmers exert enormous influence over what users see on their sites. Algorithms are processes or rules used by a computer program to achieve an objective. One of the primary goals of these algorithms is to keep the user engaged on the site as long as possible [MED23]. The reason for this is that the longer a user stays online, the more ads they are exposed to and the more money the site makes.

A downside of these algorithms is that they show the user content similar to what they have seen in the past, a situation known as a *filter bubble* [OPB23]. Filter bubbles tend to isolate users by reinforcing what they already are viewing. A conservative user will only see conservative news or opinions and a liberal user will only see liberal material. This can have an impact on how they live their lives in relation to others with different viewpoints.

USING SOCIAL MEDIA SAFELY

Many activities in life, like driving, flying, exercising, and going to the mall, include a level of risk. Using social media is no different. The best that one can do is to take sensible precautions to ensure a reasonable level of security. The following steps can help provide a reasonable level of care when using social media.

Account Profile

When a social media account is opened, the user will be prompted to set up a profile describing themselves. A long list of questions about their interests, education, expertise, professional and social affiliations, activities, and locations will be asked. The user will also be asked to add a photograph to the profile. All of the profile information is available to just about everyone.

The user is under no obligation to provide all of these details. It would be best to be very cautious regarding what is added to the profile. The user can always add more information to their profile at a later time.

Ad Blocker

Popup ads are a common method used to attack users. The best defense against them is to install an ad blocker on all browsers. If a new browser is installed, then make sure that it has an ad blocker, too.

Antivirus Software

All computers that are connected to the Internet should have antivirus software installed on them. This software should be from a reputable vendor and should be kept current.

Be Skeptical

Always be skeptical of people you have not dealt with before and the offers they make. If a deal or an offer seems too good to be true, it might be a scam or attempt to break into an account.

Face Recognition

Some social media platforms have the ability to collect and recognize people's faces. If a user adds a photograph of himself to his profile, then the platform will recognize and tag him in photos posted by anyone using that social media platform. This feature can be viewed as an invasion of privacy and makes many people uncomfortable.

Everyone needs to decide for themselves whether they are comfortable with this type of exposure. If they are not, the user should not add a photograph to their profile. Another option is to disable the facial recognition option if it is available on the platform.

Multifactor Authentication

If the social media site allows multifactor authentication to be implemented, then do that. According to an article on PC Magazine's Web site many of the major sites including Facebook, Instagram, LinkedIn, Nextdoor, Pinterest, Reddit, Snapchat, TikTok, Weibo, X, and Yelp allow MFA [PCMAG23]. Adding MFA will significantly enhance an account's security.

Passwords

A strong password is a first step to safely using social media. Password tips include the following:

a. Create a strong password, at least 12 characters, including numbers and non-alphabetic characters.

b. Never use a dictionary word as a password.

c. Never base passwords on something a cybercriminal could guess, such as a mother's maiden name or the high school attended.

d. Change passwords periodically.

e. Do not use any password for multiple accounts

f. Never share passwords with anyone.

g. Use a password manager.

Privacy Settings

Adjust privacy settings to limit what the general public can see about the account. Only some relatives and close friends should be able to see everything. Do not allow social media applications to access the phone's microphone, camera, or GPS data.

Shut Down Unused Accounts

If a social media account is no longer being used, then seriously consider closing it. One danger associated with an unused account is that if a cybercriminal takes it over, the owner might not be aware of it for a long time. Once a cybercriminal has control of an account, they can post misinformation or operate a scam from it. The blame would be attributed to the account's owner instead of the cybercriminal [LOOM23].

Updates and Patches

Apply upgrades and patches to operating system, Internet browsers, and all other apps. Apply patches as quickly as possible once they are released.

REFERENCES

[ACC22] "Shopping on Social Media Platforms Expected to Reach $1.2 Trillion Globally by 2025, New Accenture Study Finds," available online at *https://newsroom.accenture.com/news/2022/shopping-on-social-media-platforms-expected-to-reach-1-2-trillion-globally-by-2025-new-accenture-study-finds*, January 04, 2022

[ADD24] Miller, Jessica. "Social Media Addiction Statistics," available online at *https://www.addictionhelp.com/social-media-addiction/statistics/*, March 28, 2024

[AURA23] DiNardi, Gaetano. "80+ of the Worst Hacked Celebrities from the Last Decade," available online at *https://www.aura.com/learn/hacked-celebrities*, March 16, 2023

[DATA24] Kemp, Simon. "The Time We Spend on Social Media," available online at *https://datareportal.com/reports/digital-2024-deep-dive-the-time-we-spend-on-social-media*, January 31, 2024

[DIG23] Agomuoh, Fionna. "These embarrassing passwords got celebrities hacked," available online at *https://www.digitaltrends.com/computing/embarrassing-password-got-celebrities-hacked/*, May 19, 2023

[EPIC24] Electronic Privacy Information Center. "Social Media Privacy," available online at *https://epic.org/issues/consumer-privacy/social-media-privacy/*, undated

[EXPL24] Howarth, Josh. "How Many Cryptocurrencies are There in 2024," available online at *https://explodingtopics.com/blog/number-of-cryptocurrencies*, March 12, 2024

[FDM23] Brown, Paul. "Top 5 Social Media Heists of the Last Decade," available online at *https://www.fdmgroup.com/news-insights/top-social-media-heists/*, March 05, 2023

[FORB24] Haan, Katherine. "America's Password Habits: 46% Report Having their Password Stolen Over the Last Year," available online at *https://www.forbes.com/advisor/business/software/american-password-habits/*, June 3, 2024

[FRAU24] "Instagram Spam Bots: Here's How to Stop the Madness," available online at *https://fraudblocker.com/articles/instagram-spam-bots-how-to-stop-the-madness*, March 18, 2024

[FTC23] Fletcher, Emma. "Social Media: A Golden Goose for Scammers," available online at *https://www.ftc.gov/news-events/data-visualizations/data-spotlight/2023/10/social-media-golden-goose-scammers*, October 6, 2023

[IDEN24] MacKay, Jory. "How to Avoid Social Media Identity Theft," available online at *https://www.identityguard.com/news/social-media-identity-theft*, February 14, 2024

[INFO16] Kawamoto, Dawn. "Mark Zuckerberg's LinkedIn, Other Social Media Accounts Hacked," available online at *https://www.informationweek.com/cyber-resilience/mark-zuckerberg-s-linkedin-other-social-media-accounts-hacked#close-modal*, June 6, 2016

[INFO24] Pallardy, Carrie. "What Security Leaders Need to Know About the 'Mother of All Breaches'," available online at *https://www.informationweek.com/cybersecurity/what-security-leaders-need-to-know-about-the-mother-of-all-breaches-#close-modal*, February 1, 2024

[IRS24] "Dirty Dozen: Taking tax advice on social media can be bad news for taxpayers," available online at *https://www.irs.gov/newsroom/dirty-dozen-taking-tax-advice-on-social-media-can-be-bad-news-for-taxpayers-inaccurate-or-misleading-tax-information-circulating*, April 8, 2024

[LOOM23] "How to Protect Yourself Against These 23 Social Media Risks," available online at *https://www.loomly.com/blog/social-media-risks*, August 4, 2023

[MED23] Gordon, M. "The Dark Side of Social Media Algorithms: What You Need to Know," available online at *https://medium.com/digital-empowerment-online-safety-navigating/the-dark-side-of-social-media-algorithms-what-you-need-to-know-43fe3963b5a6*, September 10, 2023

[NBC16] Ellyat, Holly. "Zuckerberg's Social Media Accounts Hacked, Password Revealed as 'Dadada'," available online at *https://www.nbcnews.com/tech/tech-news/zuckerberg-s-social-media-accounts-hacked-password-revealed-dadada-n586286*, June 6, 2016

[NEW24] Kato, Brooke. " 'Mother of all breaches' data lead reveals 26 billion account records stolen from Twitter, LinkedIn, more," available online at *https://nypost.com/2024/01/23/lifestyle/extremely-dangerous-leak-reveals-26-billion-account-records-stolen-from-twitter-linkedin-more-mother-of-all-breaches/*, January 23, 2024

[OPB23] Jingnan, Huo. "New study shows just how Facebook's algorithm shapes conservative and liberal bubbles," available online at *https://www.opb.org/article/2023/07/27/new-study-shows-just-how-facebook-s-algorithm-shapes-conservative-and-liberal-bubbles/*, Jul 27, 2023

[PCMAG23] Griffith, Eric. "Multi-Factor Authentication: Who Has It and How to Set It Up," available online at *https://www.pcmag.com/how-to/multi-factor-authentication-2fa-who-has-it-and-how-to-set-it-up*, March 8, 2023

[SCRUB24] "LinkedIn Data Leak—What We Can Do About It," available online at *https://scrubbed.net/blog/linkedin-data-leak-what-we-can-do-about-it/*, June 9, 2024

[SEA24] Walsh, Shelley. "The Top 10 Social Media Sites & Platforms," available online at *https://www.searchenginejournal.com/social-media/social-media-platforms/*, April 3, 2024

[SEC22] "Social Media and Investment Fraud—Investor Alert," available online at *https://www.sec.gov/oiea/investor-alerts-and-bulletins/social-media-and-investment-fraud-investor-alert*, August 29, 2022

[SMAR24] Chaffey, Dave. "Global social media statistics research summary May 2024," available online at *https://www.smartinsights.com/social-media-marketing/social-media-strategy/new-global-social-media-research/*, May 01, 2024

[SMVLC24] "What is Cyberstalking?," available online at *https://socialmediavictims.org/what-is-cyberstalking/*, February 26, 2024

[STAX24] Abel, Spencer. "Top Social Media Hacking Statistics & Trends for 2024," available online at *https://www.stationx.net/social-media-hacking-statistics/*, February 7, 2024

[TAHO22] Dager, Jack. "The Reality of Social Media Data Tracking," available online at *https://www.tahzoo.com/insights/the_reality_of_social_media_data_tracking/*, September 2022

[TECH24] Hetler, Amanda. "6 common social media privacy concerns," available online at *https://www.techtarget.com/whatis/feature/6-common-social-media-privacy-issues*, April 23, 2024

[TWIN24] Twingate Team. "What happened in the Twitter data breach?," available online at *https://www.twingate.com/blog/tips/twitter-data-breach*, February 8, 2024

[USPI24] Micich, Anastasia. "How misinformation on social media has changed news," available online at *https://pirg.org/edfund/articles/misinformation-on-social-media/*, November 22, 2023

[WIRE21] Newman, Lily Hay. "What Really Caused Facebook's 500M-User Data Leak?," available online at *https://www.wired.com/story/facebook-data-leak-500-million-users-phone-numbers/*, April 6, 2021

[WUSL22] Ballard, Shawn. "Are bots winning the war to control social media?," available online at *https://artsci.wustl.edu/ampersand/are-bots-winning-war-control-social-media*, November 1, 2022

CHAPTER 11

BACKUPS

WHAT IS A BACKUP?

A *backup* is the process of copying all or the most important files and applications from an electronic device to a storage device. Its primary purpose is to help restore the computer if the disk crashes, a ransomware attack occurs, files are accidentally deleted, or the computer is damaged by a natural disaster.

Backups Are Critical

Backups are important because businesses and consumers rely on their electronic devices for a range of purposes. For most businesses and organizations, if anything were to happen to their computers, it would be extremely difficult or even impossible to conduct routine operations without them. Backups are one of the primary resources that enable a business to recover after a failure of their computer systems.

It is possible for a business to recover from a significant computer failure without having backups but it would not be easy. Without backups it will certainly take much longer to recreate the IT environment. Rebuilding the data that was lost would almost certainly take even longer. The cost of computers being down is high: According to Unity Communications, the cost of IT downtime can range from $5,600 and $9,000 per minute, depending on company size and industry [UNI24]. Not many businesses can afford to have their computer systems down for an extended period of time without heavily damaging their financial situation or their ability to continue to do business.

When a Backup Might be Needed

Computer systems, even ones in homes and small businesses, can be complicated. There are many occasions when a backup is necessary. Some of the more common situations when backups might be called upon to help rebuild systems are described in the following sections.

Cyberattacks

Any individual or entity that has one or more computers connected to the Internet is at risk of a cybercriminal attacking them. Cyberattacks against large corporations certainly happen, but small and medium businesses are actually a more frequent target. Research by the National Cyber Security Alliance states that almost 50% of all small businesses have been the target of a cyberattack [INC2017]. As many as 60% of small and medium sized businesses that are attacked go out of business within six months [INC2017].

Examples of cyberattacks that affect individuals and organizations of all sizes occur daily. Any of them could require that the computer system be restored from backup files. Variations of cyberattacks include the following:

a. ransomware

b. viruses and other malware

c. social engineering

d. phishing

e. cryptojacking

f. spoofing

All forms of cyberattacks are dangerous, but recently, ransomware has been the most prominent. If an individual or organization is hit with a ransomware attack, there are essentially two choices: pay the ransom or restore the system from backups. If backups do not exist, then paying the ransom may be the only option. It might be possible to rebuild the system, but without backups, valuable data may be difficult or impossible to recreate.

If a ransomware attack occurs,

a. verify that the backup files themselves have not been encrypted or corrupted. If the backups are offline, they are more likely to be unaffected (but you should still check them).

b. Do not connect the backup device to the computer or network until all traces of the ransomware have been removed.

Human Error

Cyberattacks are not the only thing that can cause computer systems to fail. The Uptime Institute estimates that almost 40% of organizations had a major outage that can be traced back to human error in the past three years [UPT22]. The overwhelming majority of these incidents occur because people fail to follow established procedures or the procedures were poorly designed. Human error can result in data being deleted, applications being misconfigured, or systems crashing. Each of these scenarios can require that a backup be used to rebuild the system.

Hardware Failure

Hardware does need to be periodically replaced, as every hardware device will eventually fail. Disk drives, for example, are complicated mechanical devices that revolve at extremely high speeds. Some high-end models spin at 10,000 or higher rpm. Backblaze conducted a detailed study of 25,000 disk drives over about four years and found that a reasonable life expectancy is six years and nine months [BACK21]. (Do you have any hard drives older than six years?)

 Solid-state drives do not have any moving parts and do last longer, but even they will not last forever. Numerous studies have stated that SSDs can be expected to last for up to ten years [RECOV22]. That is an improvement over a traditional hard drive, but they will eventually need to be replaced.

Other electronic devices also have limited lifetimes. Laptops and servers can be expected to last three to five years. Random Access Memory (RAM) can last for ten or more years. Routers can last five years but are likely to be replaced more frequently than that to take advantage of performance improvements.

As the saying goes "your mileage may vary," so the above estimates can vary depending on the environment in which the devices are operating and usage rates.

Disasters: Natural and Otherwise

If you read the newspaper, watch the TV news, or scan the headlines on your favorite Web site, you will certainly have noticed that the frequency of natural disasters appears to have accelerated. It seems like a week or month does not pass without a major disaster occurring. In addition to the human toll, those disasters also impact computers systems. Regardless of whether the affected systems are in homes, small offices, or data centers, there is a good chance that a computer will need to be rebuilt using backup files. Examples of disasters that have the potential to affect computers include the following:

a. earthquakes

b. fires, both home fires and wildfires

c. floods

d. hurricanes and the storm surges that accompany them

e. landslides

f. power outages

g. power surges

h. riots or other civil disturbances

i. storms

j. terrorist attacks

k. tornadoes

l. volcanic activity

m. war

Devices That Need to Be Backed Up

A general guideline is that any device capable of storing new data needs to be backed up. Devices that need to be backed up and the types of files that should be focused on are listed here.

a. desktop and laptop computers—specifically business documents, financial records, personal letters, photographs, music library, videos, emails, databases, and passwords

b. tablets—If a tablet is used to create or update documents, then it should be backed up. If it is only used for browsing the Internet, watching movies, or playing online games, then it does not need to be backed up.

c. smart phones—photographs, emails, messages, books, calendar entries, and purchased applications

Devices That Do Not Need Backing Up

a. tablets—when used only for browsing, watching movies, and playing games

b. IoT (Internet of Things) devices

Data That Should Be Backed Up

The list of what needs to be backed up is highly dependent on the company. For most individuals and organizations, the following types of files are likely candidates for being included in the backup list:

a. documents created using a word processor

b. spreadsheet files

c. photos

d. videos

e. music

f. games

g. browser favorites

For businesses data, the following information needs to be backed up:

- credit card transactions
- receipts
- client information
- invoicing data
- billing data
- receivables data
- personal and payroll data
- project management data

Applications

The decision whether to back up application software can be complicated. The first point to consider is whether the application is running locally or not. If the application is running on the vendor's platform, e.g., SaaS (Software as a Service), then it cannot be backed up. If a customer's site crashes, it does not affect the application running on the vendor's servers.

If the application software is running locally, i.e., on a server located at the organization's facility, then a method of backing it up needs to be established. Any applications that are considered critical should be backed up.

Applications that are not critical can be reloaded from the original media or downloaded from the vendor's Web site once the computer or system has been restored. A non-critical application is anything that the teams can function without for a short period of time without impacting productivity. Examples of this would include utilities or reports that are used infrequently.

Excluding non-critical applications from being included in the backups has the following advantages:

a. Backups will be created more quickly.

b. Backups will take up less space.

c. Backup files that are smaller can be restored more quickly.

OPERATING SYSTEMS (OSs)

The operating system (OS) is what allows a computer to function, and so it needs to be backed up. The problem with backing up OSs is that they are very large and have a great number of files. The average computer user would not know which files need to be included in a backup to ensure all operating system components are included. The best choices for the average user to back up the OS would be to use one of the following methods. Each of them is described later in this chapter.

a. Disk Image

b. Windows Restore Point

c. Third-Party Backup Tool

Different Backups

Not all backups are intended to capture the same collection of data. The three major types of backups are as follows.

Full

A *full backup* is exactly what it sounds like: everything is copied to the backup device. The advantage of a full backup is that it creates a complete, stand-alone snapshot of the computer at one moment in time. Using a full backup, it is possible to restore the computer to the exact state when the backup was taken.

Unfortunately, full backups have drawbacks. They take the longest to create and they require the most space. If a full backup is made every day, it would require a significant amount of storage space and a lot of time each day for the backup process to run.

Incremental

An *incremental backup* captures everything that has changed since the last backup of any type was done. It is a common practice common to create a full backup once a week and then incremental backups on the other six days of the week.

For example, if a full backup was made on Sunday at 12:01 a.m., then an incremental backup made on Monday at 12:01 a.m. would capture files that were created or modified on Sunday. An incremental backup made on Tuesday at 12:01 a.m. would capture files that were created or modified on Monday. Wednesday's incremental backup would capture files created or modified on Tuesday, and so on.

One advantage of incremental backups is that they take less storage space than multiple full backups because only files that have changed are captured. Creating an incremental backup is faster than creating a full backup for the same reason.

A disadvantage of using incremental backups is that when restoring the system, the full backup needs to be restored first and then all of the incremental backups after that. If the system needs to be restored on Wednesday, the Sunday's full backup would be restored then Monday's incremental would be restored and then Tuesday's incremental would be restored. This multi-step process is more complicated and takes longer than it takes to just restore a full backup.

Differential

A *differential backup* captures everything that has changed since a specific point in time. It is a common practice common to take a full backup once a week and then create differential backups the other 6 days of the week.

For example, if a full backup was made on Sunday at 12:01 a.m. then a differential backup made on Monday at 12:01 a.m. would capture files that were created or modified since Sunday. A differential backup made on Tuesday at 12:01 a.m. would capture files that were created or modified on Sunday or Monday. Wednesday's differential backup would capture files created or modified on Sunday, Monday, or Tuesday.

A differential backup takes less storage space than multiple full backups, but more space than incremental backups because files that were changed on any given day since the full backup will be included in all of the differential backups for the rest of the week. A file changed on Sunday will be included in differential backups created on Monday through Saturday. A file changed on Wednesday will be included in differential backups created on Thursday through Saturday.

To restore the computer, a full backup would be applied and then only the most recent differential file would be applied. This is significantly faster and easier than having to apply multiple incremental backup files.

Combining Different Types of Backups

Combining full backups with daily incremental or differential backups is a very common practice. For example, companies often create a full backup every Sunday and then incremental or differential backups on the other six days. Deciding whether to use either incremental or differential backups is up to the staff at the company. Either method can provide an effective method of creating backups that can be used to restore the computer or system in the aftermath of a cyberattack or natural disaster.

How Often Should Backups Be Created?

How often a backup should be performed depends on several issues. The first is the type of data. In situations where new data is not coming in or being created and changes are infrequent, then creating a backup once a week is probably sufficient. If the organization is one where the data is more dynamic, then daily backups are necessary. An organization that has a constant stream of data might choose to back up data multiple times a day.

Creating a full backup once a week and then incremental or differential backups on the other days is sufficient for more individuals and organizations. The bottom line is how much data is the organization willing to lose.

Backup Media

There are several types of media that backups can be made on. Each of them has advantages and disadvantages. The following sections briefly describe some of the more common media used for storing backups.

Network Attached Storage (NAS)

A network attached storage device is a dedicated storage device, like a disk drive, that is available on a network. It can be used by employees of the organization to store files. It can also be used as a location for storing backup files.

The advantages of NAS devices are that they are fast and large, up to hundreds of terabytes. NAS devices are also reasonably affordable if a large amount of storage is necessary. It is also relatively easy to expand the storage capacity of a NAS.

External Hard Drives

An external hard drive can easily be used for backup purposes. They range in size from one terabyte to multiple terabytes. One can be found that can satisfy the backup requirements for most individuals and small to medium sized organizations. Larger corporations would likely need to use another type of media for their backups.

The advantages of external hard drives are that they are reasonably priced, available in many sizes, and can connect to about any computer. They can be easily plugged into a computer and used. Then after the backup is complete, they can be unplugged and stored safely.

External hard drives have some disadvantages associated with them.

a. Being relatively small, they can be lost or stolen. When not in use, they should be placed in a safe place, preferably a locked storage cabinet or safe.

b. Being a mechanical device, they will eventually fail. It is reasonable to expect them to last for three to five years. Failures are more likely if they are not handled carefully.

c. An external hard drive cannot just be unplugged from a computer. It needs to be "ejected" properly before being unplugged. If this is not done correctly then files on the drive can be corrupted and unusable. The drive will have to be reformatted before it can be used again. To eject an external device from a Windows computer, perform the following steps:

1. Click the "Show Hidden Icons" icon on the system tray. It looks like an up arrow.

2. Click on the icon that looks like a flash drive or USB connector.

3. Click the "Eject" line for the device.

The screenshot in Figure 11.1 shows where to perform the above steps.

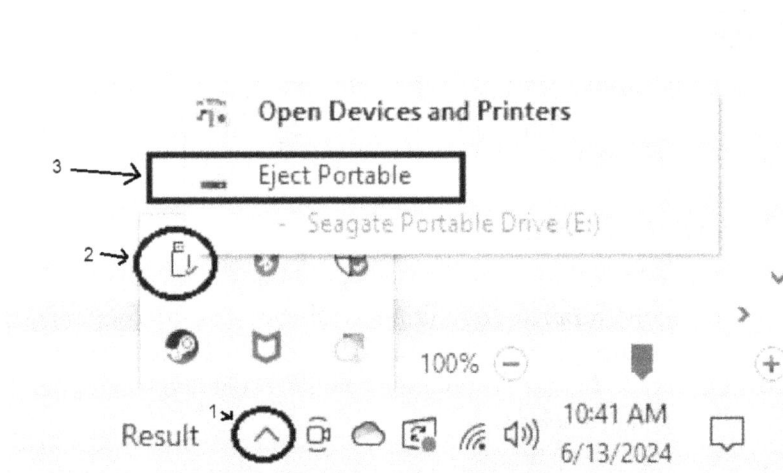

FIGURE 11.1   Steps to eject an external storage device

USB Drives

USB drives, a.k.a. memory sticks or thumb drives, have the same advantages and disadvantages that external hard drives have. Since they are smaller than an external hard drive, they are susceptible to getting lost or stolen.

The Cloud

Storing backup files in "the cloud" is extremely common. Like other storage options it has both pros and cons.

Pros

a. Using storage in the cloud for large backup files is likely to be cheaper than if the organization or individual purchased hard drives or NAS for themselves.

b. Cloud vendors typically have more redundancies than most organizations have in place. For example, there will be RAID (Redundant Arrays of Inexpensive Disks) drives, redundant power supplies, and redundant network connections.

c. Cloud storage is *scalable*, i.e., if an organization grows and requires additional storage, the cloud vendor will be able to provide it without much difficulty.

d. A cloud vendor can store a client's data in multiple, widely separated locations. This lessens the chances that natural disasters or human errors will wipe it out.

e. Large tech companies like Microsoft, Apple, and Google offer cloud storage that is embedded in widely used operating systems and applications. These can be used to create backups automatically. For example, Microsoft's storage product is called OneDrive® and Apple's product is iCloud®. Google has a cloud storage option called Google Cloud®.

f. Numerous companies offer generous amounts of free cloud storage. Dropbox lets user store 2 GB free. Nordlocker has 3 GB of free cloud storage. Apple's iCloud and Microsoft's OneDrive both offer 5 GB for free. Google gives the first 15 GB of online storage away free.

Cons

a. To access cloud storage, an Internet connection is required. If the client does not have a connection with sufficient bandwidth, then creating backups or restoring from them will be slow.

b. Clients give up a great deal of control when they move their data to a cloud vendor's site. This is not necessarily a negative, but it might create some challenges for employees or organizations.

c. Cloud vendors hold significant amounts of data for numerous clients. Large amounts of data can be a tempting target for cybercriminals. Clients must be willing to trust that vendors have adequate protection from cyber intrusions.

d. If the client becomes dissatisfied with a cloud vendor's performance, migrating from that vendor to another can be difficult, expensive, and time consuming. It can be expensive especially if it means leaving before the contracted time period has not been reached yet.

CDs or DVDs

CDs or DVDs can be used to store backups for an individual or a small business. They have advantages, but also have some very distinct shortcomings. Each is described below.

Pros

a. CDs and DVDs are relatively inexpensive, although they are not as widely available as they have been in the past.

b. They are relatively small and easy to store

c. DVDs and CDs are relatively stable. It is projected that a DVD can still be usable after 50 to 100 years [CAN20]. A CD-RW can be usable for 20-50 years [CAN20].

d. Drives for CDs and DVDs are available and inexpensive.

Cons

a. Their storage capacity is relatively small. A CD holds up to 700 MB and a DVD about 4.7 GB.

b. They are significantly slower than a hard drive.

c. Supplies of blank CDs and DVDs are not as available as they were in the past.

d. If they are damaged, e.g., scratched, they may not be readable.

e. New laptops and desktops do not have internal CD/DVD drives, so an external drive will need to be acquired.

Tape

Using tape drives as backup media is not as popular as in the past, but that does not mean tape is not worth considering by an organization. The pros and cons are listed here:

Pros

a. Tape can be cheaper per TB (Terabyte) than a hard drive.

b. Tape drives experience lower rates of mechanical failure than a hard drive since they are not constantly spinning.

c. Tape drives are very scalable, since storing additional data simply requires that additional tape cartridges be purchased.

Cons

a. A tape drive must be purchased.

b. Tapes cannot be reused indefinitely. Eventually they will start experiencing high error rates.

c. They are slower than disk drives and USB drives.

BACKUP MEDIA AND STORAGE CONCERNS

Part of the process of setting up a backup system is deciding where to store the backup media. Regardless of the physical site chosen, the media must be stored in a secure place like a locked cabinet. When making the decision on where to store the backup files two versions of an on/off concept need to be decided. The two pairs of choices are online vs. offline and on-site vs. off-site.

Online vs. Offline

The first on/off pairing is online vs. offline. *Online* refers to a media that is constantly available. A SAN drive is typically always online, i.e., available, at all times. An *offline* media is not available until an action is performed. For example, an external hard drive is not online until it is physically connected to a computer or server. A tape cartridge is not available until it is inserted into the tape drive.

The advantage of online storage is that the resource and any files on it are available at all times. This means that a backup can be created or read at any time. Backups can be scheduled to run anytime, day or night, without physical intervention to make the storage resource available.

The disadvantage of online storage is that being available on the network at all times, it can be corrupted or deleted by a cybercriminal, virus, ransomware attack, or as the result of an accident. In September of 2023, Johnson Controls experienced a ransomware attack with a note that said "Files are encrypted. Backups are deleted." [CON24] An organization expecting to recover from a ransomware attack by rebuilding their system from online backup files would have problems when they discover that those have been encrypted, too.

Offline storage media is not constantly available. This means that it takes physical action to make it ready for a backup job. It also means that if the files are not online, they cannot be corrupted or deleted by a cybercriminal, virus, ransomware attack, or accidentally.

On-site vs. Off-site

The second on/off pair is on-site vs. off-site. *On-site* means at the same location where the production data normally resides. *Off-site* means at another, typically distant, location.

The advantage of backups being located on-site is that they can be stored or retrieved very quickly. The location might be in the server room or in a nearby storage closet. The disadvantage of storing backup files on-site is that if the site experiences a disaster like a fire, flood, tornado, or hurricane, then both the production data and the backup files could be lost. If the plan is to rebuild the system after a disaster from backup files, then it might not be possible if they were destroyed in the disaster.

Storing backup media in an off-site location means that someone will have to physically transport the media to and from the off-site location. If a file or entire computer needs to be restored, then the process cannot begin until the necessary media has been retrieved from the off-site facility. The upside of off-site storage is that a natural disaster that impacts the production site probably will not affect the off-site storage location.

There is an entire industry devoted to providing customers with off-site storage. These vendors will pick up media at the customer's site and transport it to a safe storage location. If the customer needs to perform a recovery, the vendor will transport the correct media back to the customer's location.

Examples of off-site storage vendors include the following:

- Access
- Iron Mountain
- Meyer
- Corodata

3-2-1 Rule

In the world of backups, there is a rule known as the "3-2-1- Rule." The essence of this rule is to have the following:

3 copies of the data—Each of the three copies of the data needs to be physically distinct from the others. For example, if two copies of the data are on the same external hard drive, that does not qualify for the "three copies" rule. The production copy of the data qualifies as one of the three copies.

2 different media types—For example, one backup could be on an external hard drive hard drive and the second could be on a thumb drive.

1 copy must be off-site, i.e., stored at a different location.

Immutability

Immutability, the quality that something cannot be changed, is recommended for data storage media. If backups are immutable, then the organization does not have to worry about them being encrypted by ransomware, deleted by a virus, overwritten by a subsequent backup, or deliberately modified by a cybercriminal or a malicious insider.

Methods of making backups immutable include the following:

a. Write Once, Read Many (WORM) media: Immutable media includes CDs, DVDs and magnetic tape that can only be written to once.

b. Cloud-based backup services: Some cloud-based services offer immutable backups.

c. Air-Gapped Backups: Air-gapping completely disconnects the media from the network. Offline storage like this cannot be affected by ransomware or other viruses. Caution must be exercised when air-gapped backups are brought online to facilitate a restore process. If the virus has not been eradicated, its remnants could access the backups when they come online.

d. Linux Immutability: The Linux file system offers an immutable attribute for files. Any files with that setting enabled cannot be modified. Once a file has that attribute no one, not even the root user, can modify it.

CREATING A BACKUP

There are a number of ways to actually back up files or an entire computer. The more common methods are listed here.

Cloning

Cloning the entire hard drive in a computer or server is one option for backing up a system. The advantages and disadvantages of using clones for backups are described in the following sections.

Advantages of Clones

a. Creating a clone ensures that all data on the system has been backed up and a snapshot of it can be restored.

b. If third-party software is used to create the clones, then it is a relatively easy task and can be scheduled to run regularly, e.g., daily, at the same time.

Disadvantages of Clones

a. A clone provides a snapshot of the computer or drive at the time it was created. If the disaster occurs twelve hours after the clone was created, then any data added or system changes performed in the last twelve hours will be lost.

b. Creating clones consumes a significant amount of storage space. Fortunately, storage space is relatively inexpensive and is likely to get cheaper in the future.

c. If multiple clones are created, each of them must be on a separate storage device. If all clones are on a single device, the failure or corruption of that device would leave the user or organization without any backups.

Creating a Windows Clone

On a Windows computer, a clone (a *full image*) can be created using an internal function called "Backup and Restore (Windows 7)." Note that this function also works on Windows 10 and 11 despite the name. To reach this screen, bring up the Control Panel screen by right-clicking the Windows icon on the lower left part of the screen and selecting the "Run" option. Enter "Control Panel" in the text field for the name of the program to run. When the Under "System and Security," select the "Backup and Restore (Windows 7)" option. Click the "Set up a backup" option. Figure 11.2 shows the screen that will be displayed.

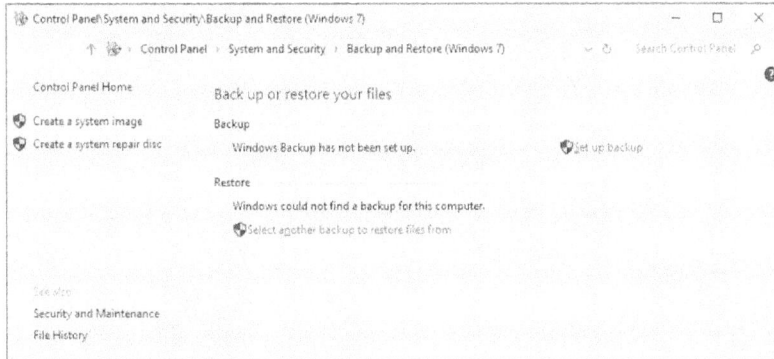

FIGURE 11.2 Creating a Windows system image

Ensure that the external hard drive to be used is connected to the computer being backed up. Select the correct drive from the list of possible destination drives. Click the "Next" button. Figure 11.3 shows the "Set up backup" window.

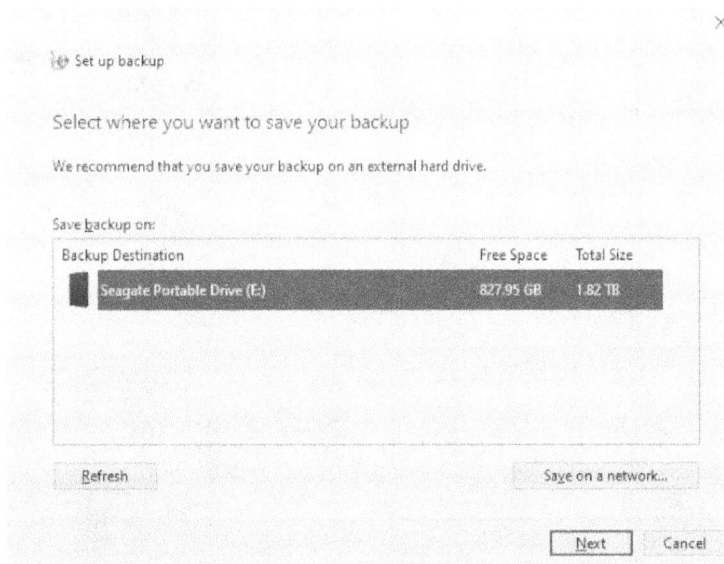

FIGURE 11.3 Selecting the backup destination

The next step is to determine what should be written on the image being created. The safest option is "Let Windows choose (recommended)." Click the "Next" button. Figure 11.4 has this screen.

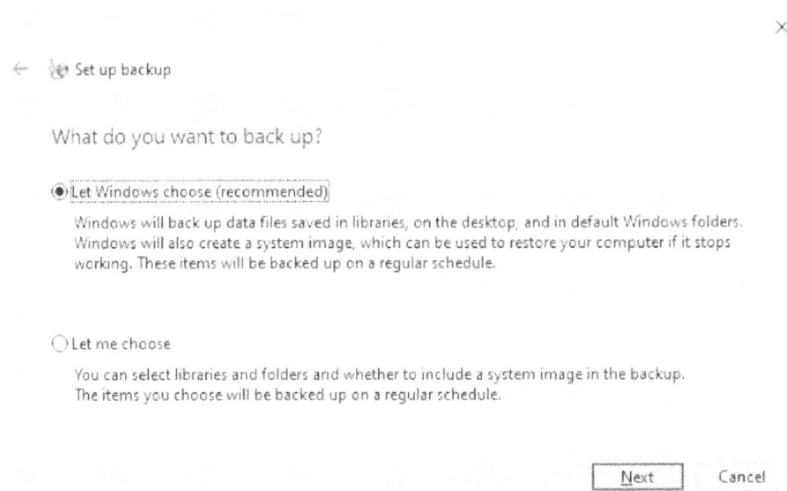

FIGURE 11.4 Backup options

Windows provides a chance to review the settings before the imaging process is started. Figure 11.5 shows the settings that have been chosen. If everything is correct, click on the "Save settings and exit" button.

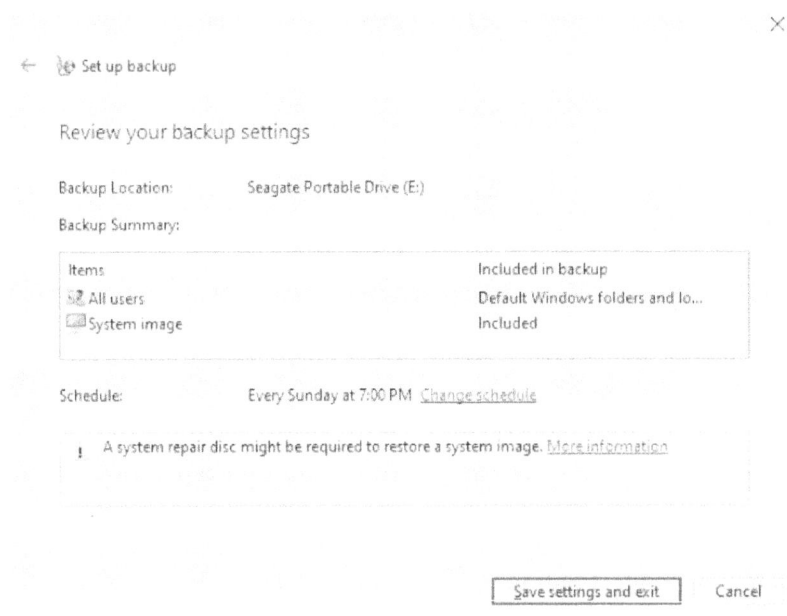

FIGURE 11.5 Save settings and exit screen

The final step is to begin image creation. Figure 11.6 shows that you need to click the "Back up now" button. Exactly how long it will take to create the image will depend on the size of the image and the speed of both disk drives involved. It is likely that it will take several hours. Minimizing activity on the computer while it is being imaged is recommended.

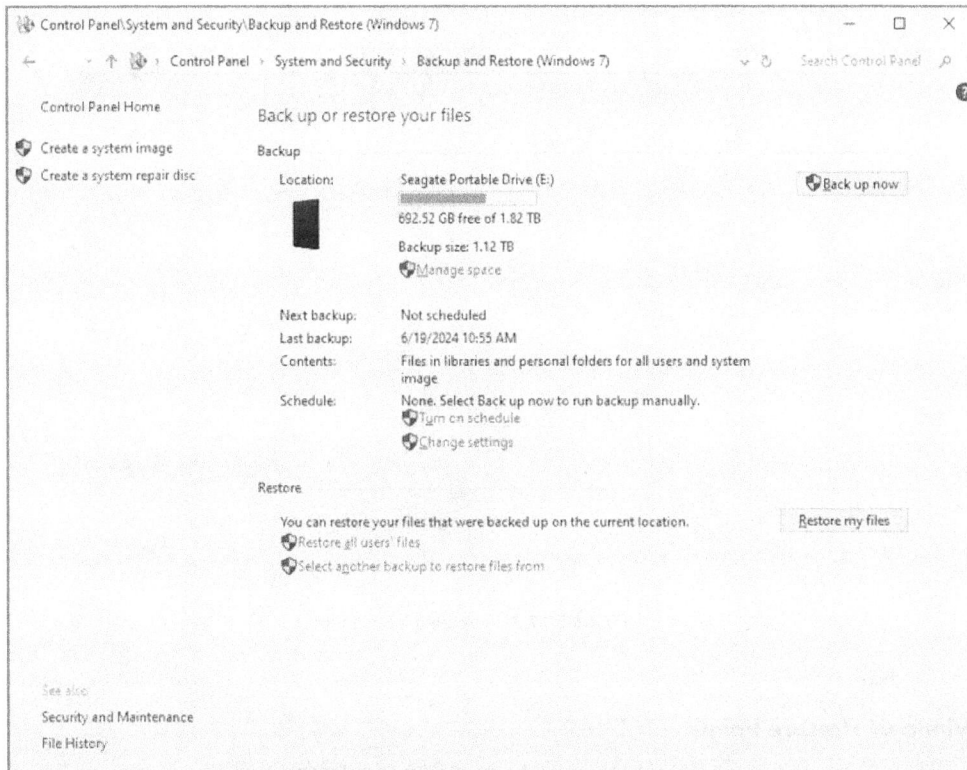

FIGURE 11.6 Launching the "Create Image Process"

To restore the system from an image, click the "Restore my files" button or the link "Restore all users' files" shown on Figure 11.6. The screen shown in Figure 11.7 will be displayed. If multiple backups are displayed, choose the one that the restore should be created from.

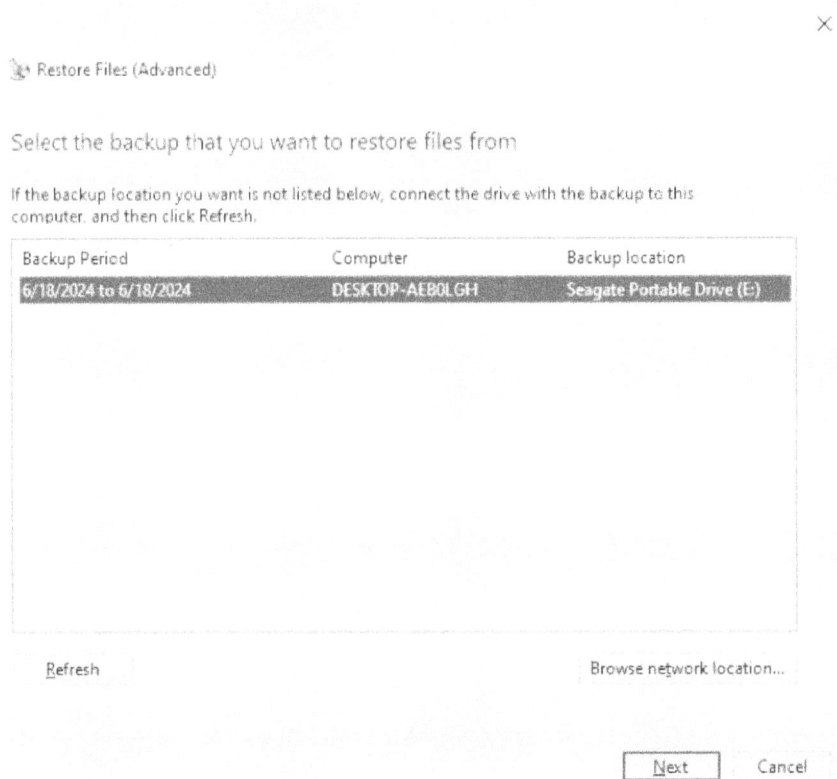

FIGURE 11.7 Restoring from an image

Windows Restore Points

A *restore point* creates a snapshot of essential Windows operating system components and supporting files. Creating a restore point is a way for someone who is not familiar with the Windows operating system to back it up. Examples of files that are saved by a restore point include the following:

a. Windows operating system files

b. drivers

c. system registry

d. system configuration settings

e. executable files

Almost as important as what a restore point saves is what it does not save. It does not save any of the user's data. Specifically, it does not save the following types of files:

a. documents

b. photographs

c. music files

d. video files

e. account passwords

f. emails

One common use for a restore point is to take a snapshot of the computer's environment before an update is applied to the operating system. It can also be used to make a copy before an application is loaded or before a significant piece of hardware is attached to the computer. If the upgrade does not succeed, then the computer can be reverted back to a working state.

Creating a Restore Point

Windows defaults to creating restore points automatically. One is created weekly, typically during non-working hours like early on Sunday mornings. Restore point files are not retained indefinitely. After about 90 days, they will be deleted. If a large number of them exist, then the oldest one will be deleted to make space for a new one.

A restore point is also created automatically before Windows is updated or patched. If the update or patch is not successful, then the most recent restore point will automatically be used to back out any changes that were made. The system should be in its original state after the restore point is completed.

It is possible to manually create a restore point. To create one bring up the System Properties window and click the "Create" button. Figure 11.8 shows that screen and button. Creating a restore point should only take a few minutes.

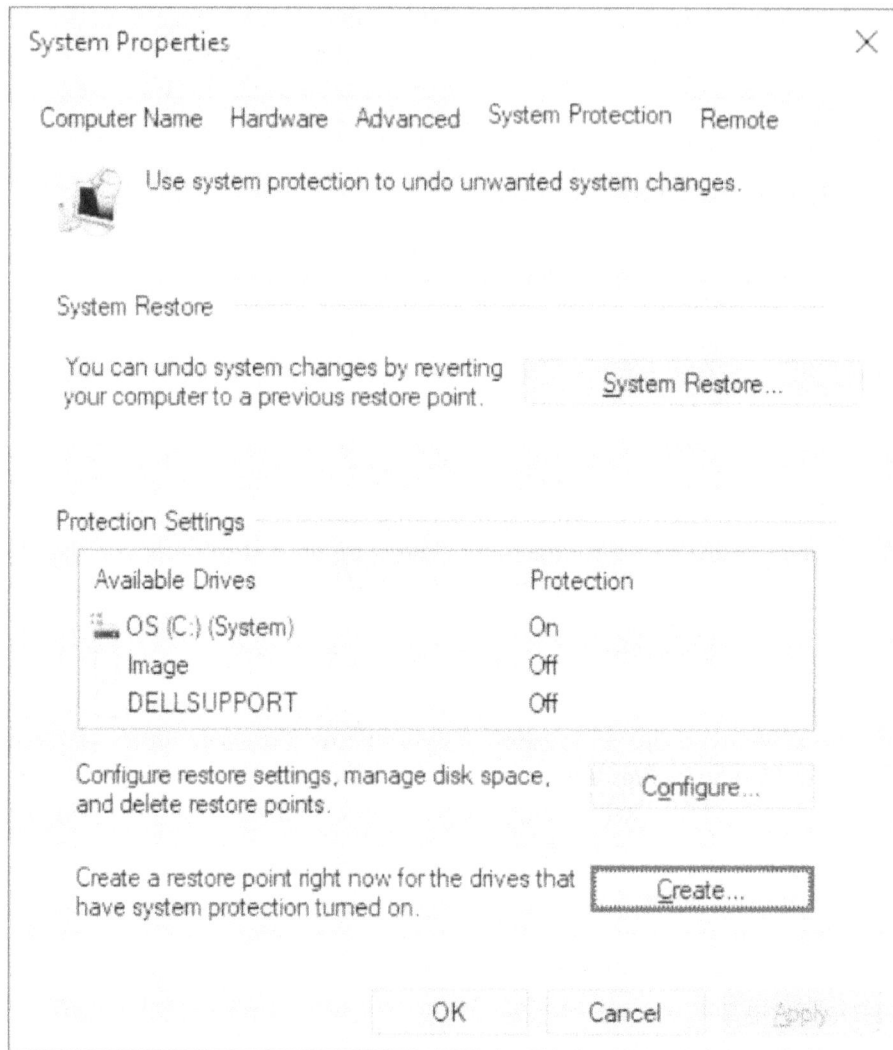

FIGURE 11.8 Button to create a restore point

To view the list of all existing restore points click on the "System Restore" button on the System Properties window. Then click on radio button option "Choose a different restore point." Figure 11.9 shows the "System Restore" button.

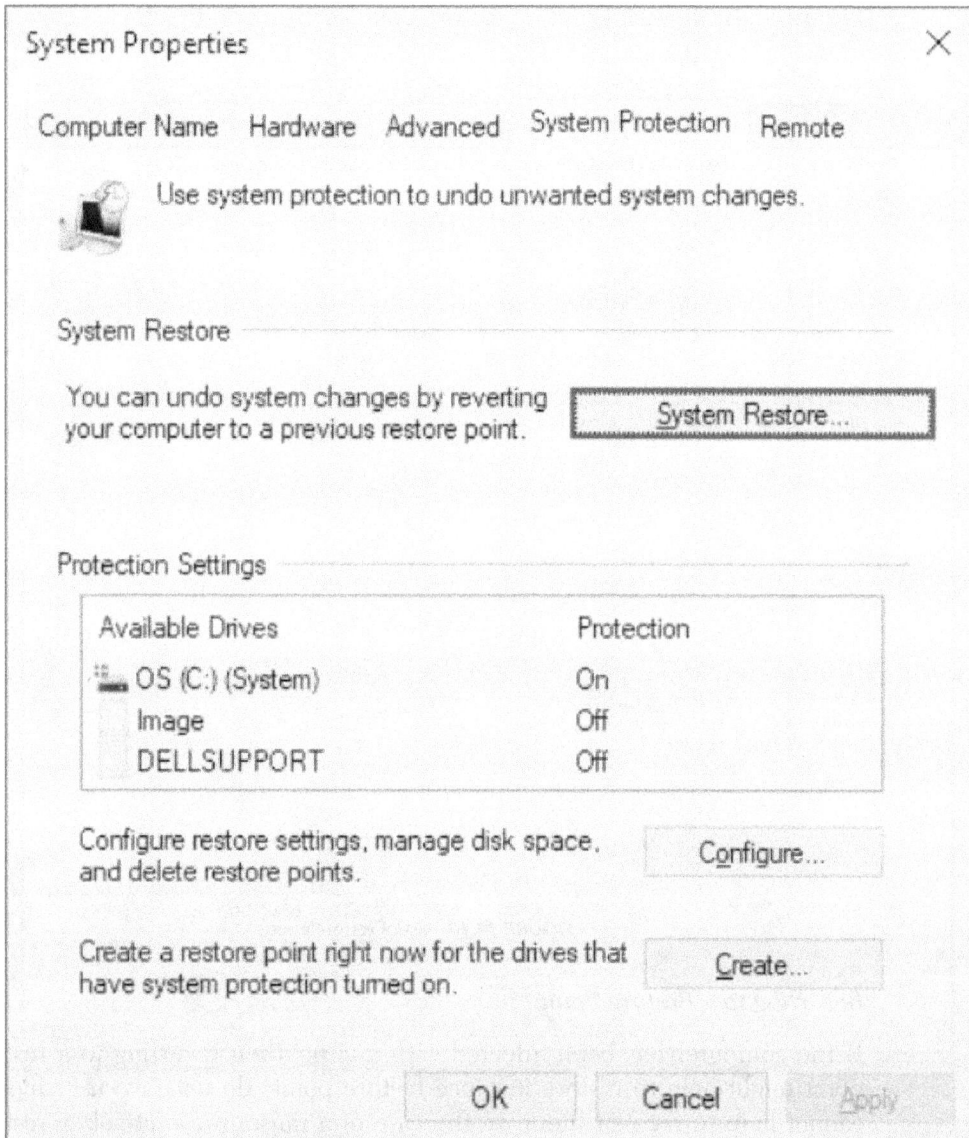

System Properties   ✕

Computer Name   Hardware   Advanced   System Protection   Remote

Use system protection to undo unwanted system changes.

System Restore

You can undo system changes by reverting   System Restore...
your computer to a previous restore point.

Protection Settings

Available Drives	Protection
OS (C:) (System)	On
Image	Off
DELLSUPPORT	Off

Configure restore settings, manage disk space,   Configure...
and delete restore points.

Create a restore point right now for the drives that   Create...
have system protection turned on.

OK   Cancel   Apply

FIGURE 11.9 Viewing a list of restore points

Figure 11.10 shows a list of all restore points existing on the device currently.

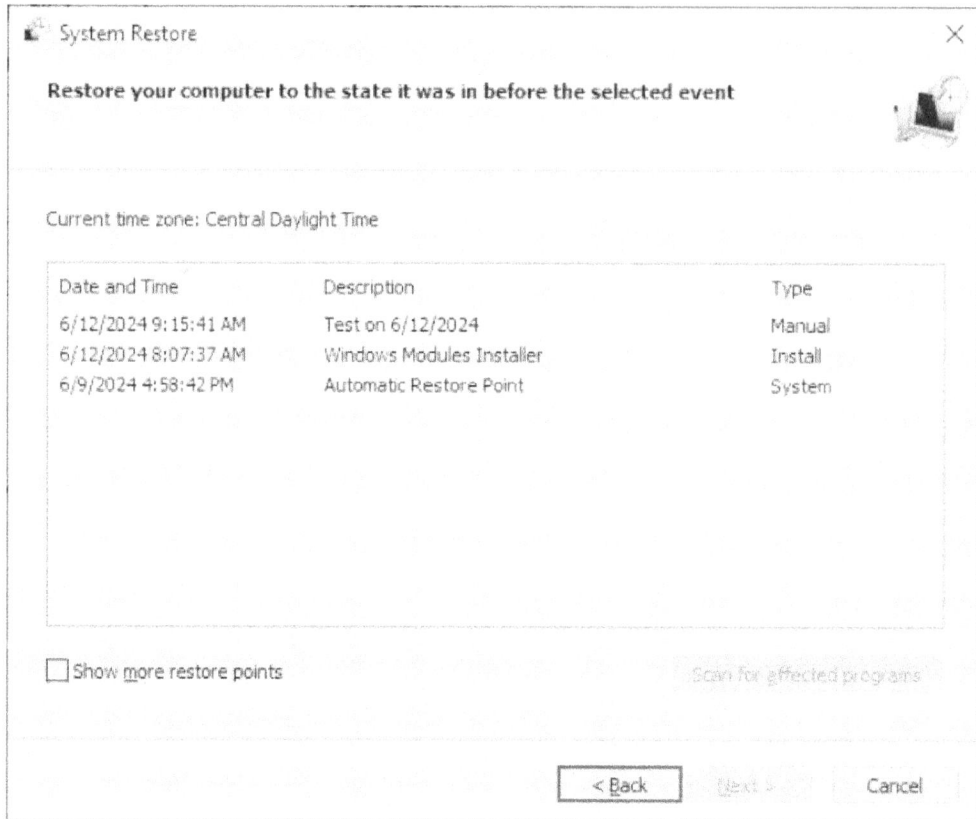

FIGURE 11.10 List of restore points

Reverting to a Restore Point

If the computer has been infected with a virus, then reverting to a restore point might help to restore it. Since restore points do not save user files, it cannot help to recover them. In the case of a ransomware attack, a restore point could help recover the Windows operating system, but nothing else. Backup files would be needed to recover user data.

It is very easy to launch a system restore. On the System Properties screen, click the "System Restore" button. Figure 11.10 shows this screen and button. On the "System Restore" screen, choose between the default option "Recommended restore" and "Choose a different restore point" option. Then click the "Next" button. Figure 11.11 shows where to choose that option.

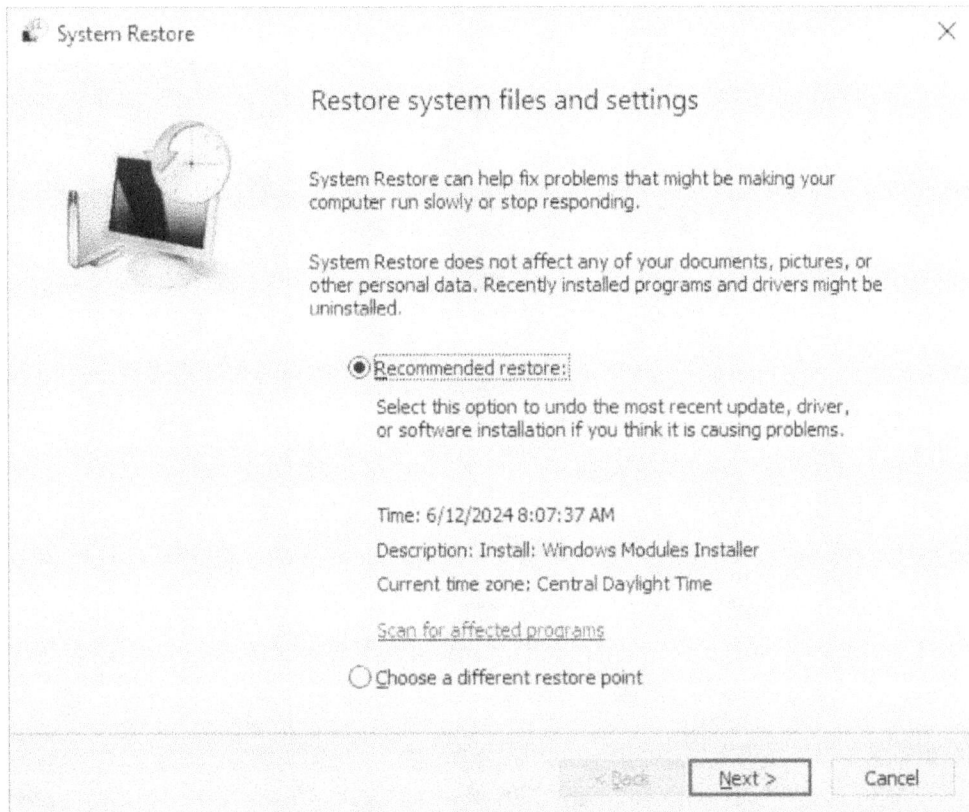

System Restore ✕

Restore system files and settings

System Restore can help fix problems that might be making your computer run slowly or stop responding.

System Restore does not affect any of your documents, pictures, or other personal data. Recently installed programs and drivers might be uninstalled.

⦿ Recommended restore:

   Select this option to undo the most recent update, driver, or software installation if you think it is causing problems.

   Time: 6/12/2024 8:07:37 AM

   Description: Install: Windows Modules Installer

   Current time zone: Central Daylight Time

   Scan for affected programs

○ Choose a different restore point

< Back   Next >   Cancel

FIGURE 11.11 Launching a restore

The next screen displayed allows the user to confirm that a restore should be done. It recommends that all programs and files be saved and closed. Click the "Finish" button to initiate the restore. Figure 11.12 shows this screen.

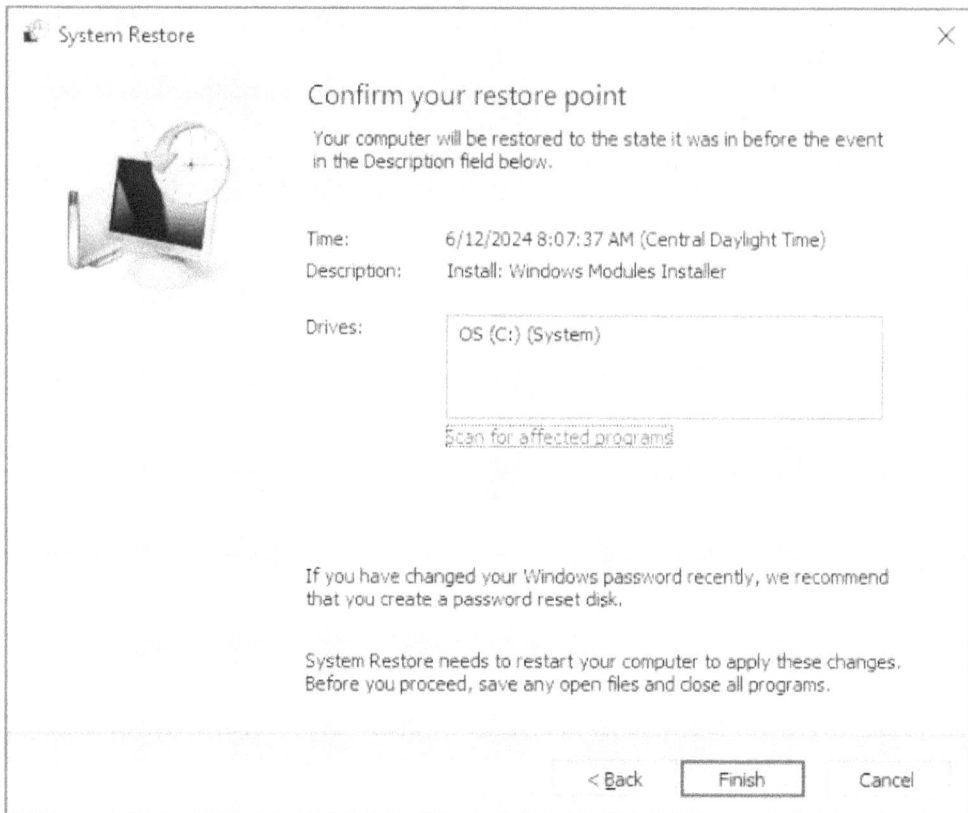

System Restore   ×

Confirm your restore point

Your computer will be restored to the state it was in before the event
in the Description field below.

Time: 6/12/2024 8:07:37 AM (Central Daylight Time)
Description: Install: Windows Modules Installer

Drives: OS (C:) (System)

Scan for affected programs

If you have changed your Windows password recently, we recommend
that you create a password reset disk.

System Restore needs to restart your computer to apply these changes.
Before you proceed, save any open files and close all programs.

< Back   Finish   Cancel

FIGURE 11.12 Launching a restore

Windows File History

Windows file history is a capability that allows the user to back up selected
subdirectories to an external drive. This backup process allows the user to
select what will be backed up and how frequently this will be done.

Creating Backups in the File History

Bring up the "Settings" screen by left-clicking the Windows icon on the lower
left part of the screen and clicking on the "Run" option. Click on the "Update &
Security" link. On the "Update & Security" window, select the "Files backup"

link. Figure 11.13 shows the screen that will be displayed. To define the destination drive, click on the plus sign next to the "Add a drive" label. On the "Select a drive" window, select the drive where the backup should be created.

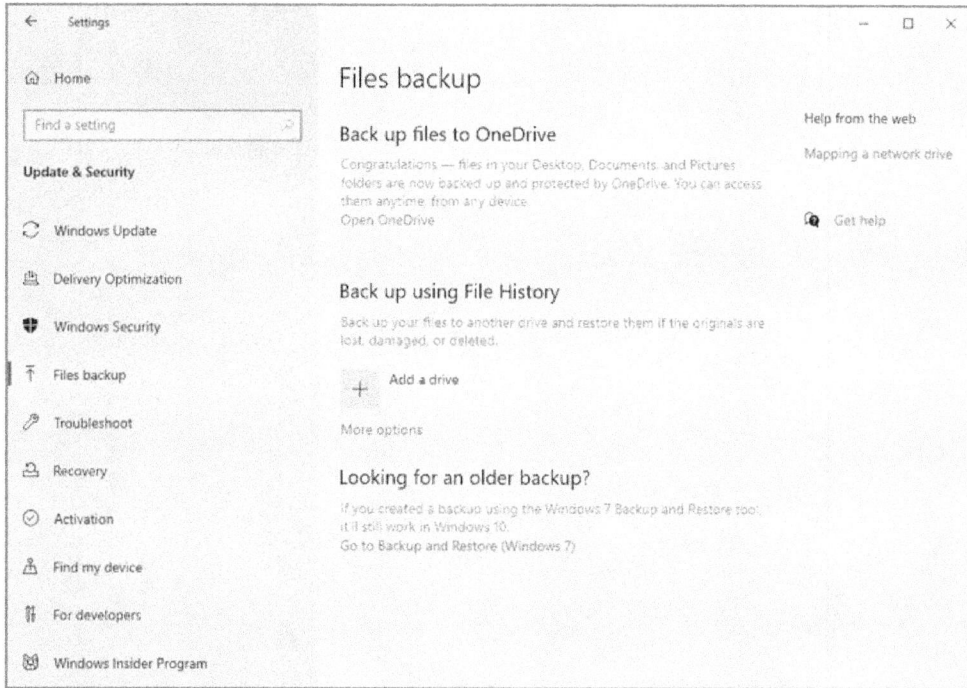

FIGURE 11.13 Setting file history options

On the "Files backup" screen, click the "More options" link. The "Backup options" window shown in Figure 11.14 gives the user a great deal of control over the file history back up process.

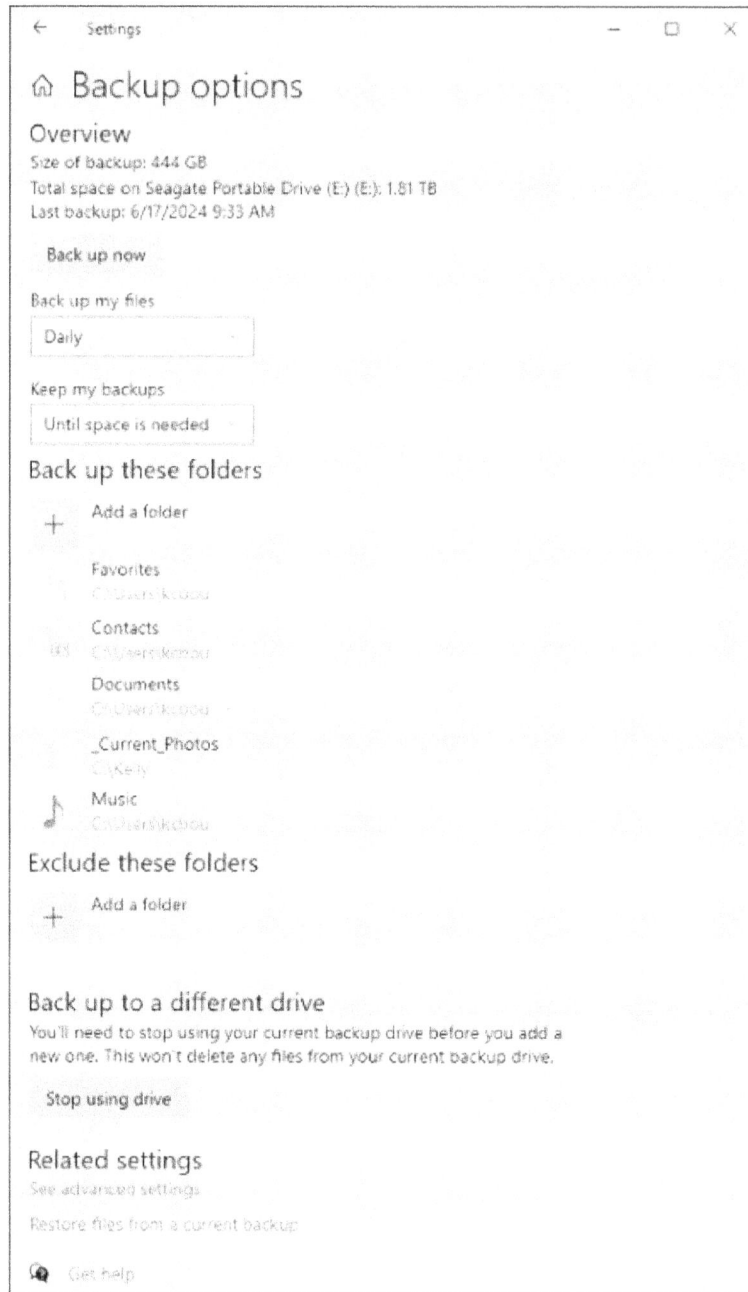

FIGURE 11.14 Setting up Windows file history

The following list describes setup options available on this page.

a.   The ability to begin the backup process now

b.   The ability to set the frequency of how often backups are created: The options range from every 10 minutes to daily.

c.   The ability to set how long the backups will be retained: The options range from "Until space is needed," 1/3/6/9 months, 1 or 2 years, and forever.

d.   The ability to select which folders will be backed up: To remove a folder from the default list, click on it and click the "Remove" button. To add a folder to the list, click on the "+" icon that is labeled "Add a folder." Drill down to the folder, select it, and click the "Choose this folder" button.

e.   The ability to exclude folders from the back up. To specify that a folder should not be backed up, click the "+" icon labeled "Add a folder." Drill down to the folder, select it, and click the "Choose this folder" button.

Once the specifications are set, click the "Save Changes" button.

Restoring from the File History

Follow these steps to restore files and directories from a file history backup to the computer:

1.   On the "Backup options" screen, click the "Restore files from a current backup" link.

2.   The window shown in Figure 11.15 will be displayed. Select the subdirectories that should be restored.

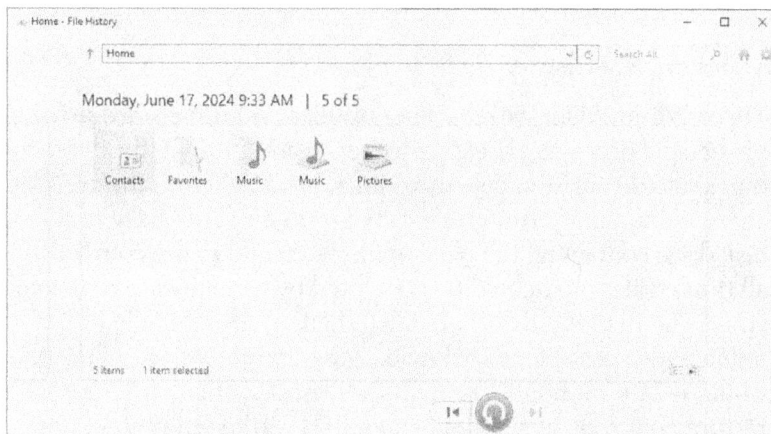

FIGURE 11.15 Restoring subdirectories from a file history backup

3. Click the "Action" icon (it is a green circle with a counterclockwise arrow in it).

4. If there are files with the same name in both the original subdirectory and the backup, a window like the one shown in Figure 11.16 appears. Click the option to either replace the files, skip the files, or decide for each file.

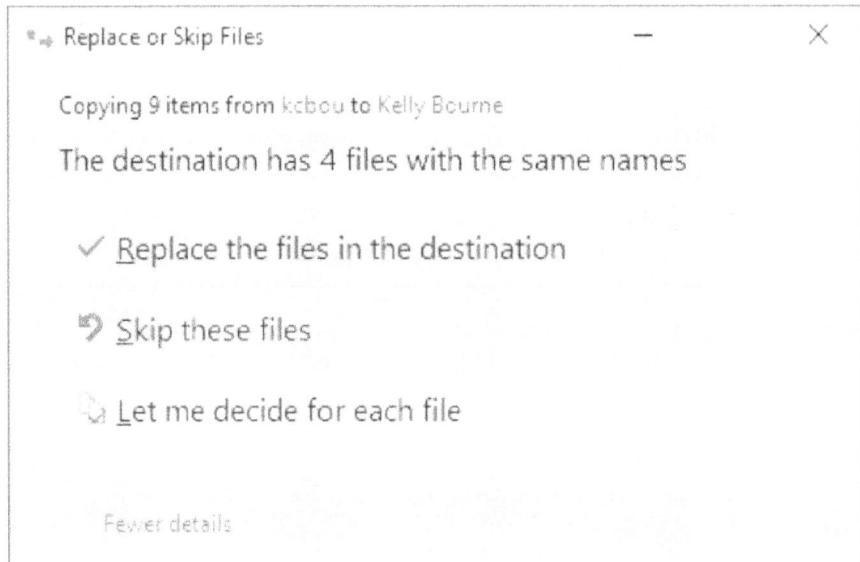

FIGURE 11.16 Replace or skip files

5. When the restore is complete, a window with the File Explorer showing the subdirectory that was just restored will be displayed.

Security and the File History

There is a problem with backing up files and directories using Windows file history: In order for backups to be created automatically at the scheduled times, the destination disk drive must be attached to the computer. This creates a vulnerability from a security viewpoint. It is risky to have the external disk drive containing the backup files attached to the computer or network at all times. Files on it could be encrypted by ransomware or deleted by another virus. The files could also be deleted either accidentally or intentionally. It is unlikely, but possible, that the disk drive could fail. Any of the above scenarios would delete invaluable backup files. Backup files, whether they be images, restore points, or selected files should be offline to protect them.

One solution would be to rotate through multiple external drives. Create a file history backup on disk "A." Detach it from the network and attach disk "B." At the scheduled time, a file history backup will be created on disk "B." Repeat the process for the other drives.

Apple Time Machine

The Apple Mac has an excellent backup utility called "Time Machine." This built-in tool can back up files to USB or Thunderbolt drives. Like so many tools created by Apple, it is intuitive to use and works as advertised. If an individual or organization has Mac computers, then using Time Machine is a good choice for backing up data.

BACKUP TOOLS

There are many third-party tools that can back up Windows computers. Some manufacturers of external hard drives include backup utilities with their hardware that are useful for the average user or small to medium sized organization.

Some of the features that should be included in tools that are being considered are as follows:

a. User interface: The user interface should be easy to use and understand.

b. Scheduling: Any backup software being considered should be able to run backups at set times and configurable intervals, e.g., daily and weekly.

c. Clones or directory backups: The ability to create a clone of a disk drive or back up just specific directories is extremely valuable.

d. Destination devices: The tool should be able to create backups on external hard disk drives, USB drives, DVDs, NAS (Network Area Storage) devices, and cloud storage services like Google Drive, Dropbox, and OneDrive.

e. Multiple computers: If the user or organization has multiple computers, then the third-party utility should be able to create backups for all of them.

f. Restoring: The process of restoring from a backup should be intuitive. This is especially important because if a restore becomes necessary, making mistakes during the process could be disastrous.

g. Boot media: If the system experienced an extreme failure, then it might not be able to boot on its own. To assist in the recovery process, a bootable DVD or USB drive might be needed. Some back up tools can create boot media. Of course, the user needs to create the boot media in advance.

h. Continuous backups: Critical files or data, especially those that change frequently, might need to be backed up constantly. If the user or organization has data that fits this description, then a third-party tool that is capable of real-time or continuous backups should be chosen.

ENCRYPT BACKUPS

Backup files need to be encrypted. It does not matter whether they are created with a function available in the operating system or via a third-party tool, are images or the contents of directories, are stored on-site or off-site, or are online or offline. Any data at rest or in motion needs to be encrypted. This includes data included in a backup.

If backups are not encrypted, then the data within them is vulnerable to exposure. Encrypted backup files can still be affected by ransomware or other viruses, but their data cannot be exfiltrated and used to extort a payment to avoid it being revealed publicly.

For organizations, encryption is required by data privacy regulations including the GDPR, CCPA, HIPAA, and Sarbanes-Oxley Act. Those regulations apply equally to production data as well as backups. If backups are not encrypted and become part of a data breach, then rebuilding computers might just be the beginning of the organization's problems.

RECOVERY PLAN

Having a recovery plan that shows in detail how to restore entire computers and subdirectories on individual computers is critical. It should be developed and reviewed regularly to ensure that it is complete and accurate.

Any recovery plan should include prioritizations, i.e., what should be restored first. For example, if multiple applications are dependent on a database existing, then the database application should be restored before the applications.

Everyone who has any responsibility for recovering data should have access to this plan. A current hard copy of the plan should always be available because the computer might be unavailable when it needs to be executed.

MANUAL OR AUTOMATED?

The question of whether creating backups should be a manual or an automated process is a decision every company needs to make. An automated process is "easier" once it is set up to create backups on a preset schedule. If backups rely on someone starting them, it is possible that they will be forgotten. Overall, an automated process is better.

One caveat is that if the backup process is launched automatically, then someone needs to confirm that each backup was created successfully and without errors. It is very easy to forget about an automated process once it has run successfully a few times. It could be problematic if an automated backup process failed repeatedly, and this is not discovered until a backup was needed.

TESTING BACKUPS

If ransomware or another disaster occurs, then the backups needed to restore the computer(s) or entire network must be valid. Unfortunately, a backup process that has not been tested cannot be trusted. Some examples of problems that testing might uncover include the following:

a. Errors occurred on the destination media that no one noticed.

b. Critical directories and files were not being backed up.

c. New computers or servers recently added to the environment are not being backed up.

d. The encryption/decryption keys being used are incorrect.

e. An insider has deliberately sabotaged the backup process.

A formal test plan should be written and adhered to when the backup process is being tested. The testing required will be different for every site, but some examples of the testing that should be done include the following:

a. Testing the backup process and output should be performed regularly, at least annually.

b. Confirm that the written recovery plan is complete and accurate.

c. Confirm that the backup media can be read. If backups are written to multiple types of media, e.g., external hard drives and tape, or multiple locations, then testing of each media type and from each location should be performed.

d. Confirm that the encryption/decryption keys are correct.

e. Confirm that all devices, especially new computers and servers, are included in the backup process.

f. Restore an image or clone to a test computer. Obviously, the test machine should be similar (if not identical) to the production device that the image was created from.

g. Spot-check a reasonable number of directories and individual files to confirm that the backup data is identical to the production data.

h. If the testing process can be automated, it will be more efficient and could enable more frequent testing.

i. As new applications, devices, and databases are included in the environment, they should be included in the testing process.

REFERENCES

[BACK21] Klein, Andy. "How Long Do Disk Drives Last?," available online at *https://www.backblaze.com/blog/how-long-do-disk-drives-last/*, December 17, 2021

[CAN20] "Longevity of Recordable CDs, DVDs and Blu-rays," available online at *https://www.canada.ca/en/conservation-institute/services/conservation-preservation-publications/canadian-conservation-institute-notes/longevity-recordable-cds-dvds.html*, January 7, 2020

[CON24] Youngerwood, Doron. "Storage & Backups Under Attack. This Is What To Do About It," available online *at https://www.continuitysoftware.com/blog/storage-backups-under-attack-this-is-what-to-do-about-it/*, February 28, 2024

[INC2017] Kouloulos, Thomas. "60 Percent of Companies Fail in 6 Months Because of This (It's Not What You Think)," available online at *https://www.inc.com/thomas-koulopoulos/the-biggest-risk-to-your-business-cant-be-eliminated-heres-how-you-can-survive-i.html*, May 11, 2017

[RECOV22] Etezadi, Daniel. "SSD Lifespan: How Long Can A Solid-State Drive Last?," available online at *https://recoverysquad.com.au/ssd-lifespan-how-long-can-a-solid-state-drive-last/*, May 14, 2022

[UNI24] Santos, Allie Delos. "The True Cost of IT Downtime," available online at *https://unity-connect.com/our-resources/blog/it-downtime/*, May 25, 2024

[UPT22] "Uptime Institute's 2022 Outage Analysis Finds Downtime Costs and Consequences Worsening as Industry Efforts to Curb Outage Frequency Falls Short," available online at *https://uptimeinstitute.com/about-ui/press-releases/2022-outage-analysis-finds-downtime-costs-and-consequences-worsening*, June 8, 2022

CHAPTER 12

BROWSING SAFELY

People spend a considerable amount of time on the Internet. An article in Fortune magazine reported that Internet users between 16 and 64 spend an average of 6 hours and 40 every day online [FORT24]. That adds up to more than 17 years of their adult lives. The numbers are averages, which means that some people spend less time online while others spend even more time on the Internet.

Unfortunately, the Internet is not a safe place. Browser-based attacks are increasing, according to a report by Menlo Security. Phishing attacks increased 198% during the second half of 2023 [TECH24]. Other examples of attacks that can affect users of browsers are as follows:

a. Typo-squatting: Cybercriminals create a Web site with a URL similar to a legitimate one. If a user enters the fake URL, they see a login screen and enter their credentials. Cybercriminals can use this information to take over the accounts.

b. Cross-site scripting (XSS): This form of attack takes advantage of flaws in Web sites to inject malicious code into the site. When a user visits the site, his browser will execute the script on it. This technique is frequently used to install malware on the user's computer or exfiltrate personal data from it. In 2019, the online video game Fortnite was a victim of an XSS attack. The accounts of 200 million users were exposed to the perpetrators [COMP23].

c. Man-in-the-Middle (MitM) Attacks: These attacks intercept communications between a browser session and the Web site it is connected with. This attack allows the cybercriminal to listen in on or modify the data being exchanged. It might enable them to acquire the user's login IDs and passwords. MitM attacks are frequently associated with public Wi-Fi sites.

BROWSING FUNDAMENTALS

In order to understand the dangers of browsing on the Web, it is necessary to understand all of the aspects involved. The following sections will explain each of these components.

Internet vs. World Wide Web

The terms "Internet" and "Word Wide Web" are frequently used interchangeably, but they are not the same. The Internet is a network of connected computers. The World Wide Web, frequently referred to as just "the Web," is a collection of Web sites or pages that reside on Internet servers. The two pieces can be thought of as hardware (the Internet) and software (the Web).

Browsers

An Internet browser is an application that runs on a computer or smartphone to display text, images, and video from the World Wide Web. Web pages include both data and Hypertext Markup Language (HTML). Web browsers read HTML, which tells them how to format and display the data, e.g., text, images, and video.

Browsers run on desktop computers, laptops, tables, and smart phones. Some of the most widely used Web browsers are as follows:

a. Chrome®

b. Safari®

c. Edge®

d. Firefox®

e. Opera®

Search Engine

A search engine is an application that allows users to enter terms they want to know more about. The search engine has a database of known Web pages along with metadata about each of them. The Web sites are ranked by the search engine and it presents the ones most likely to contain the data that the user is seeking.

The primary source of income for search engines is charging businesses to display advertisements of their products on pages shown to users. Search engine vendors also receive payments when users click on links and are taken to the business' Web site.

Some of the most frequently used search engines are as follows:

- Google
- Bing
- Yahoo!
- DuckDuckGo
- Baidu

Internet Service Providers (ISP)

To connect with the Internet users, both individuals and organizations need to go through an Internet Service Provider (ISP). As well as access to the Internet, an ISP can provide its customers with hardware like modems and routers. Users can acquire additional services like email, customer support, domain registration, and Web hosting from their ISP.

Examples of US-based ISPs include the following:

- AT&T Internet
- CenturyLink
- Comcast
- Cox Communications
- Sprint
- Verizon

Extensions and Plug-ins

Extensions and plug-ins ins (a.k.a. add-ons) are pieces of software that can be downloaded and installed in a browser to add additional features to it. They allow users to customize browsers to meet their needs. Examples of features that can be added to a browser include the following:

- ad blocking
- cookie management
- automatically silence videos that play on Web sites

- language translation
- read email from within the browser without having to explicitly open Gmail
- create notifications in the browser when new email is received
- synchronize passwords for multiple Web sites
- correct grammar and spelling errors
- view multimedia content like videos and animation

Extension Dangers

Like any other software extensions, plug-ins can be risky if they were written by cybercriminals. A study by Spin.AI found that 51% of the 300,000 browser extensions studied could exhibit potentially malicious behaviors [DARK23]. The best way to avoid security risks when using extensions and plug-ins is to research any extension or plug-in before downloading it. It is also safer, but not an absolute guarantee, to only download extensions from reputable sites like those hosted by browser vendors.

Examples of malicious activity that extensions and plug-ins have executed include the following:

- hijack online game accounts and steal in-game assets
- hijack Facebook accounts
- install malware on the victim's computer
- read the victim's email
- bypass two-factor authentication and steal cryptocurrency
- insert advertisements into search results

Loading and Removing Extensions

Every browser provides the user with the ability to maintain, i.e., install and remove, extensions and plug-ins. To get to this screen in Chrome, click on the three vertical lines in the upper right-hand corner and click on "Settings." Then, in the left margin, click on "Extensions and Themes."

Figure 12.1 shows the list of extensions currently installed in Chrome. An extension can be removed by clicking on the "Remove" button under it. Click the link titled "Chrome Web Store" to search for new extensions available for download. The steps in other browsers are similar.

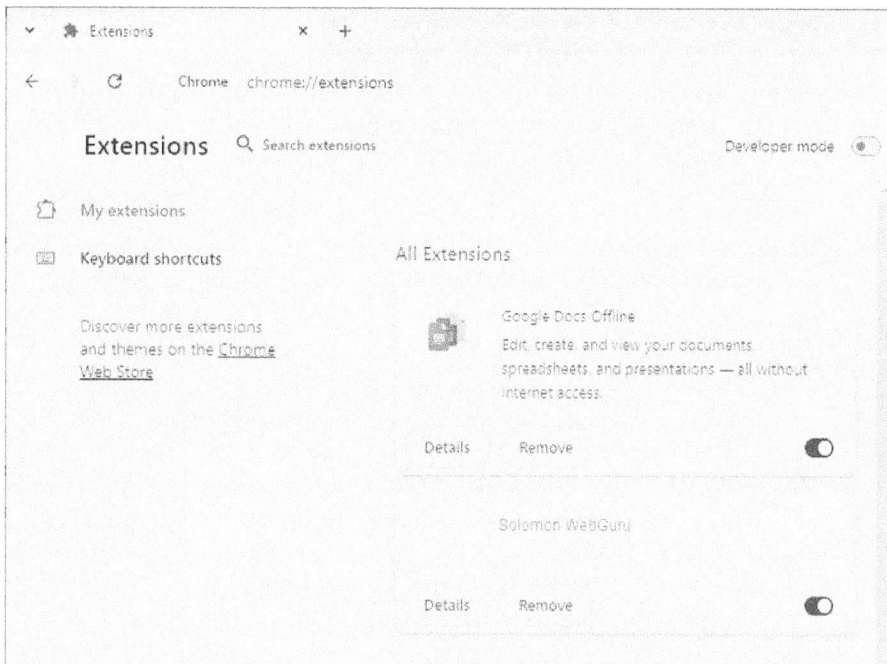

FIGURE 12.1 Chrome's extension management window

Scripts

A script is a series of instructions that a computer performs. There are two types of scripts related to browsers and the Internet: client-side scripts and server-side scripts. In the context of browsing the Internet, the individual's computer or smart phone is the client. Client-side scripts run on them. The computers that support Web sites are the servers. Server-side scripts run on them. The two types of scripts act together to provide features like better graphics, dynamic content, faster loading, and the ability for the user to interact with the Web site.

Wi-Fi

When users are away from their homes or offices and want to browse the Internet, they have two choices. They can use their smart phone's data plan or they can connect to a nearby Wi-Fi network. One danger associated with connecting to a public W-Fi is that it might have been set up by a malicious actor instead of the coffee shop or restaurant being patronized. If it is the former, then there is a good chance that the cybercriminal is eavesdropping on communications between the smart phone and the Web site. This can allow him to capture login credentials, read email, or install malware on the device.

If a public Wi-Fi must be relied on, then you should use a Virtual Private Network (VPN). A VPN encrypts all communications between the smart phone and destination Web site to prevent anyone from listening to or interfering with communications. Chapter 13 covers VPNs in detail.

BROWSING DANGERS

Ads

Most Web sites display ads to users. Ads are a source of revenue for the Web site owner. Ads, even ones on trusted Web sites, can contain malicious scripts that will attempt to hurt or deceive the viewer. Pop-up ads can claim the computer is infected with a virus trying to trick the user into clicking a link that actually will install a virus. An ad can also be intriguing enough that the viewer will click on it and the Web page brought up installs malware on the user's device.

The best defense against pop-up ads is to set the browser so it will not display them. Most, if not all, browsers have a setting to block ads. Figures 12.2, 12.3, and 12.4 show how to change this setting in Chrome. The steps in other browsers are similar.

In Chrome, click on the three vertical dots in the upper right corner of the screen and click on the "Settings" option. On the "You and Chrome" screen that is displayed, click on the three vertical lines next to "Settings" in the upper left corner. Figure 12.2 shows the list of options that will be displayed. Click on the "Privacy and security" link.

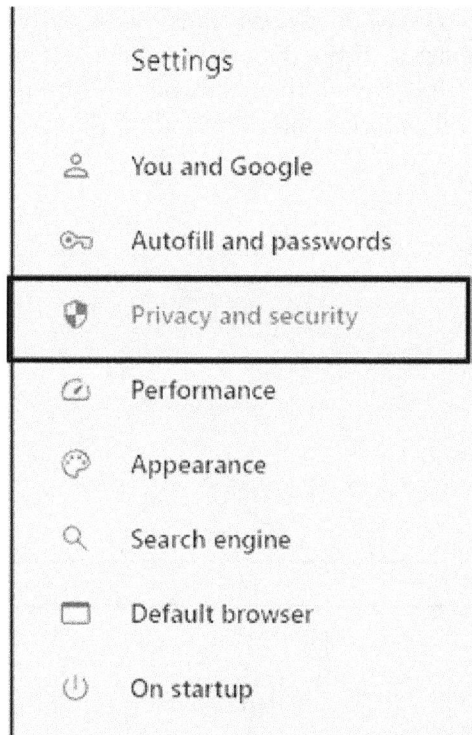

FIGURE 12.2 First step to block pop-up ads in Chrome

Figure 12.3 shows the options that will be displayed after clicking "Privacy and security" on the previous figure. Click on the "Site settings" area.

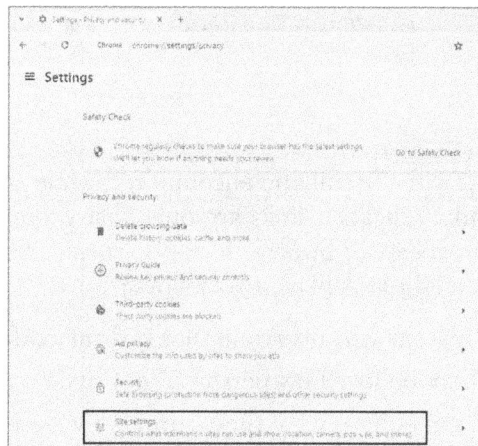

FIGURE 12.3 Second step to block pop-up ads in Chrome

Figure 12.4 shows the third step in the process. Scroll down until the "Content" section is displayed. If the option for "Do not allow sites to send pop-ups or use redirects" is selected, then click on it. Close the "Settings" window and any changes will automatically be saved.

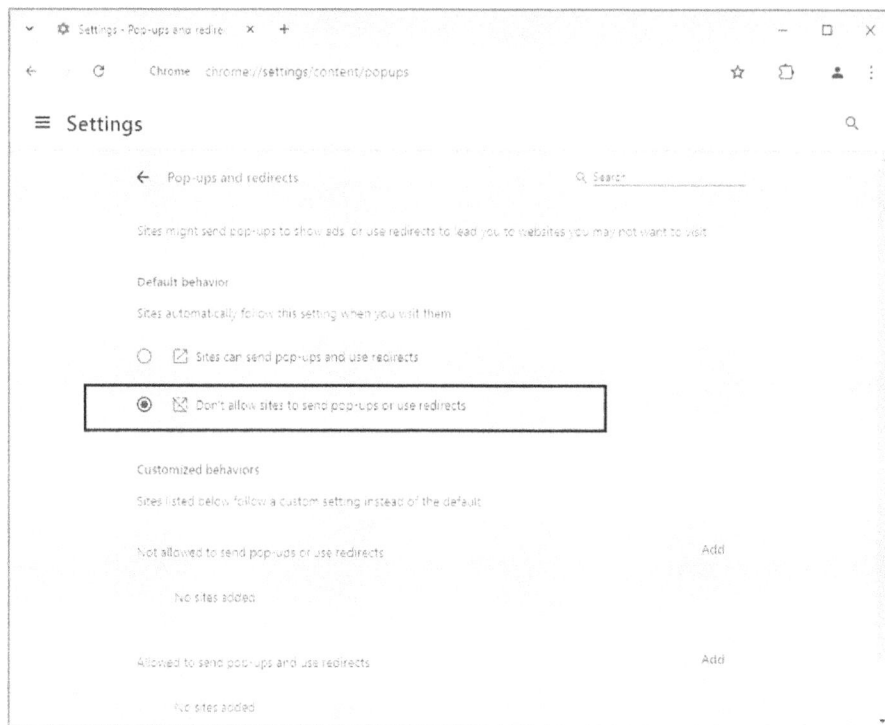

FIGURE 12.4 Third step to block pop-up ads in Chrome

Clickbait

A danger that will certainly be encountered while browsing the Internet are "clickbait" links. Clickbait links are ones that promise to lead the viewer to something provocative, bizarre, lurid, or risqué. Some examples of what a clickbait link might look like are as follows:

- "The 10 reasons why everyone should drink coffee."
- "You will not believe how person 'Y' got rich."
- "You will not believe what these former TV stars look like now."

- "Experts say these 10 phrases should never be said to children!"
- "The 10 best resolutions to make this New Year's Day."
- "What is your cat's Zodiac sign?"
- "Which *Friends* cast member are you?"

The intention of clickbait is to keep the user online and view additional Web pages. More time online and more Web pages viewed means more money for those Web sites.

The least danger associated with these links is that the viewer will waste time on fake news or an endless cycle of additional clickbait ads. The worst scenario is that the Web site it leads to will attempt to infect the viewer's computer with malware.

Some browser extensions can provide partial protection against clickbait. They accomplish this by blocking articles that have titles which include a specific list of words. The flaw in this approach is that if new or different titles are developed by the Web site owners, they will be able to get past the list of blocked words.

The only real protection against clickbait links is self-restraint. Be aware that sensationalist headlines are just a lure. Avoid wasting time and a possible malware infection by avoiding these enticements.

Cookies

Cookies are small text files created on the viewer's computer when he visits a Web site. Other names for them are "HTTP cookies," "browser cookies," "Internet cookies," and "Web cookies." The intent of cookies is to make the viewer's interaction with the Web site better. Some ways this is done include the following:

- If the user entered text into a form, those details can automatically be filled in the next time the Web site is visited.
- If the user has items in a shopping cart and leaves the Web site, the next time he returns to the Web site the cart will still have those items in it.
- If the user has a preference for the type of material he likes, that can be stored. For example, when viewing an online newspaper, it will automatically display his favorite section.
- The user can automatically be logged into a Web site: for example, his email account credentials can be entered for him.

Cookie Contents

Each cookie has a unique ID that is associated with the viewer's computer. Examples of data about the viewer that is frequently captured and saved in cookies includes the following:

- any data entered on a form on the Web site including username, email address, and phone number
- IP address of the computer or smart phone
- location, i.e., county or city
- login credentials
- preferences like language, time zone, and format
- specific Web pages that have been visited
- search history
- products that have been clicked on to see additional details
- previous purchases

Different Types of Cookies

There are several different types of cookies used by Web sites. An explanation of why each type is needed and what it does is described here.

a. Session cookies: These are temporary cookies created for each browsing session. They are used to hold information about the current session or interaction with the Web site. Session cookies are deleted when the Web site session ends.

b. Persistent cookies: These exist or persist across multiple sessions with a Web site. They are used to hold data that is useful for a future session. Examples of the data they hold include login credentials, preferences, and shopping cart contents. Persistent cookies have an expiration date set by the Web site and will be deleted once that date has been reached. The GDPR requires that persistent cookies last no more than a year. After that, the user must consent to another one being created.

c. First-party cookies: A cookie that contains information restricted to the Web site that created it. For example, the Web site *www.cabelas.com* might create a cookie that contains only data related to that Web site. In general, first-party cookies do not represent a threat to a user's privacy or security.

d. Third-party cookies: A third-party cookie is created by someone other than a Web site owner when a Web site is visited. They are used by advertisers to track all of the Web sites that users visit. This type of cookie poses a significant security and privacy risk for consumers. Most Web browsers block third-party cookies by default. If the browser does not block third-party cookies by default, the users should set it to block them.

e. Supercookies: These are also called "Flash cookies" or "Local Shared Objects (LSOs)," and are not technically cookies. They do behave like cookies, so they are included in this list. They are not associated with any specific Web site. ISPs or other technology companies secretly use them to track user's online habits to customize the ads that users see. Supercookies are not stored in the browser cache so they cannot be deleted by simply clearing the cache like other cookies. Some forms of supercookies, called zombie cookies, can even resurrect themselves after being deleted by the users. Third-party tools like CCleaner® or Click&Clean® can delete supercookies. This form of cookie definitely has the potential to threaten users' privacy and security.

Identifying Cookies Created by Website

Free Web sites exist that will identify the types of cookies created by any Web site. One example of these sites is "Cookieserve" at *https://www.cookieserve. com*. At Cookieserve, the user can enter a Web site's URL and receive the following information:

- overall count of cookies created by the Web site
- framework used to drive the Web site, e.g., HTML, Joomla, and WordPress
- domain that is creating the cookie
- description of what the cookie does
- duration of cookie, e.g., session, 15 minutes, 1 month, or 1 year
- type of cookie, e.g., as necessary, analytics, functional, performance, advertising, or other

You should gather the details on the number of cookies created by frequently visited Web sites. Very few Web sites do not create any cookies. Many of them create substantially more cookies than you might expect.

Cookies and Privacy

The more controversial aspect of cookies is that they are used to track users' activities on the Internet. First-party cookies are relatively safe but can be abused. Third-party and supercookies almost always participate in tracking that most users would consider abusive.

Permission to Create Cookies

Web sites are now legally required to request permission before creating cookies on a viewer's computer due to laws like the EU's General Data Protection Regulation (GDPR) and the California Consumer Privacy Act (CCPA). This is why Internet users are prompted to give permission to create cookies when visiting Web sites.

When presented with the option to agree to cookies being created for a Web site, what is the correct response? Ideally cookies exist to provide the user with a better experience on the Web site. If the Web site is not one that is visited often, then does a "better experience" really matter? If the Web site is one that is visited frequently and belongs to an established, reputable organization, then it is probably safe to agree.

Some downsides of declining cookies are that the user might have to re-enter information or the Web site will not be customized for him. Cookies should definitely be rejected in the following circumstances:

- If the Web site is not encrypted, i.e., does not have a URL that begins with HTTPS. It would be reckless to enter any data on a Web site that does not use encryption.
- If the Web site requires that PII data like a Social Security Number, credit card numbers, or driver's license ID
- If the browser displays a warning that the current Web site is known to be dangerous or risky, then the user should not agree to allow cookies.
- If the Web site is requesting permission to create third-party cookies, then it should be denied. Third-party cookies are only used to track the user's Internet activity.

Purging Cookies

All browsers provide a way for users to purge cookies that have been created. Click on the icon with three horizontal lines (this is also called the "hamburger button" or the "menu button") in the upper right corner of a Firefox browser.

Then click the "Settings" option. On the "Settings" page, click "Privacy & Security" in the left margin. Scroll down to the "Cookies and Site Data" section. Figure 12.5 shows this part of the settings window.

FIGURE 12.5 Managing cookies

Clicking the "Clear Data" button will bring up the window shown in Figure 12.6. The options to clear cookies and clear cached Web content are available to the user. Check the appropriate box(es) and click the "Clear" button.

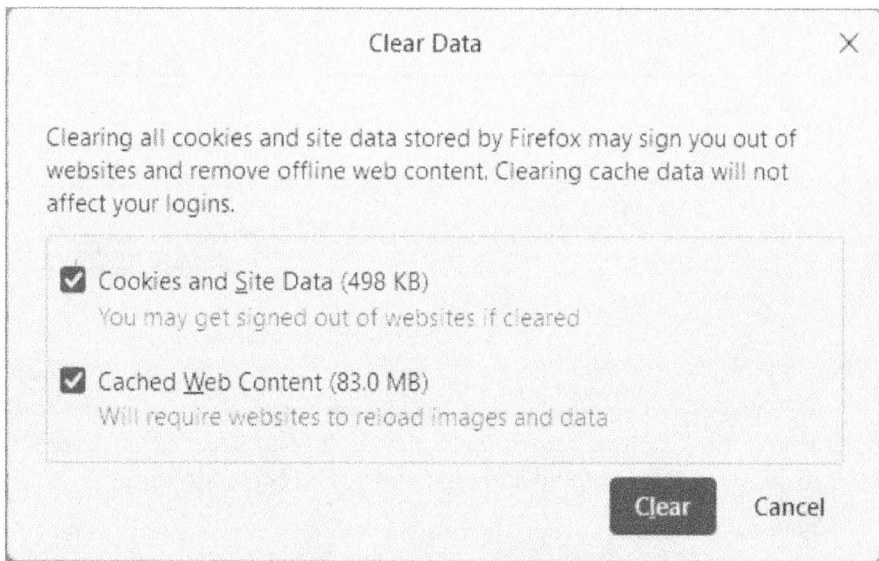

FIGURE 12.6 Managing cookies, clearing data

To see a list of all Web sites that currently have cookies stored in the browser, click the "Manage Data" button shown in figure 12.5. The "Manage Cookies and Site Data" window shown in Figure 12.7 will be displayed. On this screen, every site that currently has a cookie is listed. To delete a specific cookie, select it and click the "Remove Selected" button. To remove all cookies, click the "Remove All" button.

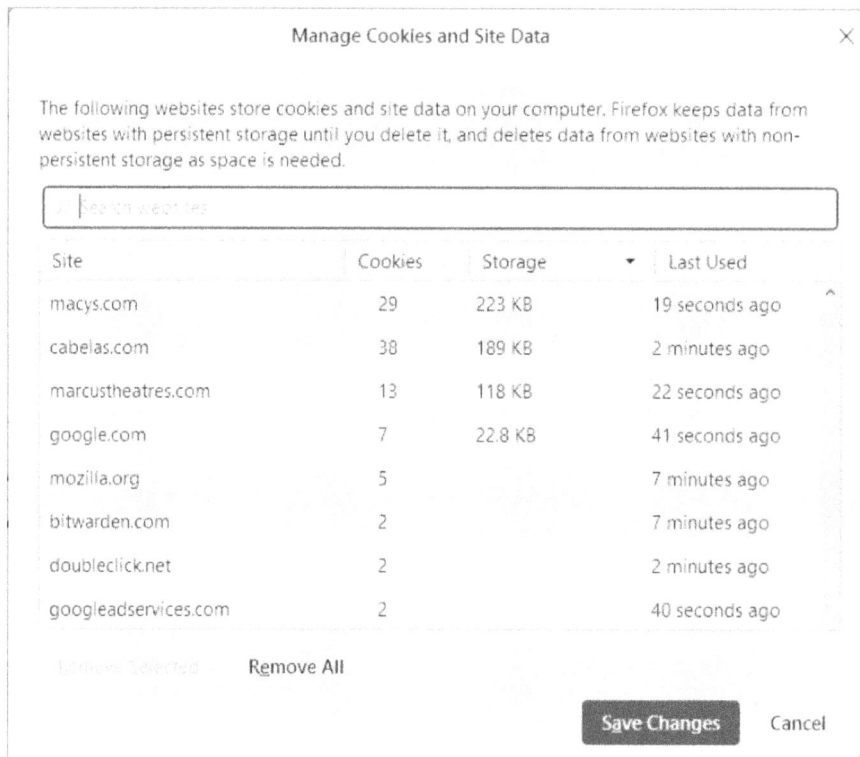

Site	Cookies	Storage ▾	Last Used
macys.com	29	223 KB	19 seconds ago
cabelas.com	38	189 KB	2 minutes ago
marcustheatres.com	13	118 KB	22 seconds ago
google.com	7	22.8 KB	41 seconds ago
mozilla.org	5		7 minutes ago
bitwarden.com	2		7 minutes ago
doubleclick.net	2		2 minutes ago
googleadservices.com	2		40 seconds ago

Manage Cookies and Site Data

The following websites store cookies and site data on your computer. Firefox keeps data from websites with persistent storage until you delete it, and deletes data from websites with non-persistent storage as space is needed.

Remove All

Save Changes   Cancel

FIGURE 12.7 Managing specific cookies

To always block or always allow cookies from specific sites, click the "Manage Exceptions" button shown in Figure 12.5. The "Exceptions" screen that is displayed allows users to add or remove Web site addresses.

Deleting all cookies when the browser closes is a wise precaution. In Firefox, this setting can be chosen by checking the box labeled "Delete cookies and site data when Firefox is closed" field shown on Figure 12.5. Other browsers have similar options.

Downloads

A significant danger while browsing the Web is downloading files from dangerous sources. It is extremely common for cybercriminals to try to trick the viewer into downloading a file that contains malware. If the victim does that, they can end up with ransomware, virus, or keystroke logging software on their device. Downloads should only be done from legitimate sources.

Fingerprinting

Fingerprinting is a form of tracking users' activity on the Internet. A digital fingerprint is a list of characteristics gathered by cybercriminals to identify and track people. Each individual piece of data seems harmless, but if enough small details are collected, it can create a profile that is detailed enough to identify individuals. This technique can allow individual users to be identified with a 90% accuracy rate [FING24].

Types of data that are collected by fingerprinting processes include the following:

a. type of device, i.e., computer or smart phone being used

b. IP address

c. browser type being used, e.g., Chrome, Firefox, Edge, or Safari

d. browser version

e. extensions and plug-ins installed in the browser

f. operating system running on the computer or smartphone

g. time zone that the user lives in

h. default language of the user

i. default font selected by the user

j. keyboard layout

k. Websites visited and the amount of time spent at each one

The goal of digital fingerprinting is to learn more about the users so that customized marketing can be done. The more that marketers know about individual consumers, the better they choose ads that consumers are more likely to respond to. The problem is that most consumers are not aware that they are being monitored this way. They have not been given the option of allowing it or prohibiting this level of tracking.

Phishing Attacks

Phishing attacks are frequently associated with emails, but they come in different forms. A phishing site will appear to be one for a legitimate organization. It may request that the visitor provide personal information to enter it. The intent of these sites is to acquire personal data of the viewers that can later be used for identity theft or other forms or fraud. There are an estimated 13.5 million Web sites that are phishing sites [META24]. (There are probably many more than that estimation.)

Privacy

Surfing the Web, i.e., what Web sites an individual visits, is not usually completely private. The list of people or organizations capable of knowing which Web sites an individual has visited is considerable. The list includes the following:

a. Individuals: Anyone with access to the computer or smartphone can review previous activity

b. ISP: The Internet Service Provider has records of Web sites visited.

c. Cell phone provider: Cellular providers have records of the Internet activity for all of their clients.

d. Search Engines: Search engines like Google or Bing are aware of search results and likely Web sites visited.

e. Advertisers: Advertisers use cookies to track Web sites visited.

f. Wi-Fi Network Administrators: These admins have access to logs of traffic across their network.

g. Website Administrators: Admins have access to logs listing visitors to their Web site.

h. Applications: Applications have records listing accounts that have logged in.

i. Employers: For most employees, there is no expectation of privacy regarding Web sites visited while using company owned devices.

j. Government agencies: Government agencies can serve subpoenas on cellular providers and ISPs to obtain records of Internet activities of consumers.

k. Cybercriminals: Cybercriminals can obtain the Internet activity of individuals by either hacking into computers or performing social engineering attacks.

Steps to maintain a higher level of Internet privacy are included in the section "Steps to Surf Securely" later in this chapter.

Tracking

Each of us is being tracked every time we open a browser and visit Web sites on the World Wide Web. Advertisers want to know which Web sites each of us visit, how often we visit them, and how much time we spend there. They analyze this data to build profiles on everyone. With this information, they can display ads selected specifically for each of us. They want us to click on the ads that generate income for them.

WI-FI

Using public Wi-Fi can be dangerous. According to a 2023 article in Forbes Adviser, 43% of those participating in the survey said their online security was compromised while using public Wi-Fi [FORB23]. The locations with the highest percentage of responders reporting compromises were at airports.

Even if they are safer than in the past, it is probably better not to conduct confidential activities on public Wi-Fi. Casually surfing and playing games should be fine, but banking transactions should not be undertaken at the local coffee shop.

Some tips for safely connecting to the Internet using a public Wi-Fi include the following:

- Verify that the Web site uses encryption. Secure Web sites begin with the letters "https://." Another way of recognizing this is the locked padlock icon to the left of the URL.
- Use a VPN when you are connected to a public Wi-Fi.
- Avoid visiting sites that require the entry of an account ID, password, or credit card number while using public Wi-Fi.
- Use multi-factor authentication when connecting to a Web site via Wi-Fi.

> ▪ If connecting to a sensitive site like a bank is absolutely necessary, then seriously consider changing the account's passwords as soon as a secure network is available.

STEPS TO SURF SECURELY

There are several steps that an individual can take to keep their Web browsing safe and retain a high degree of privacy. Some are easy and some are a little more complicated, but none of them are too challenging for most users.

Antivirus Software

Install antivirus software from a reputable vendor on all computers and smart phones. Once it has been installed, make sure that it is updated regularly.

Autofill

Most browsers offer the option to autofill, i.e., automatically complete, fields like names, addresses, and credit card numbers. Activating this option makes it easier and faster to complete Web site forms. The downside is that the browser maintains this data internally. If a cybercriminal or insider has access to the browser, they could see your credit card number along with its expiration date. Is this option worth the risk? Everyone must weigh the benefits and dangers of this convenience for themselves.

Be Cautious

Exercise caution when browsing on the Internet. Do not assume that Web sites are safe or that files being downloaded are always benign. Exercise a good degree of caution. If something seems too good to be true, then it is probably not true.

Browser Cache

A browser cache is a relatively small area in memory where the browser stores data, specifically details about Web pages from sites that have been visited recently. Using a cache can significantly increase the browser's performance.

If a user revisits a Web site, then the browser can retrieve its pages from the cache instead of having them sent across the Internet.

One danger of caching Web pages is that if a cybercriminal can access the cache, then he will be able to see what Web sites the user has visited recently. Clearing the cache, i.e., deleting its contents, prevents anyone else from accessing this data.

There are other reasons for emptying out this cache. Clearing it can speed up the browser by removing references to Web sites that have not been visited recently. It can also prevent problems accessing new versions of previously visited Web site pages.

To clear the cache on a Firefox browser, follow the steps listed here. Click on the icon with three horizontal lines in the upper right corner of a Firefox browser. This is also called the "hamburger button" or the "menu button." Select the "Settings" link. Click on the "Privacy & Security" option. Figure 12.8 shows the "Privacy & Security" screen.

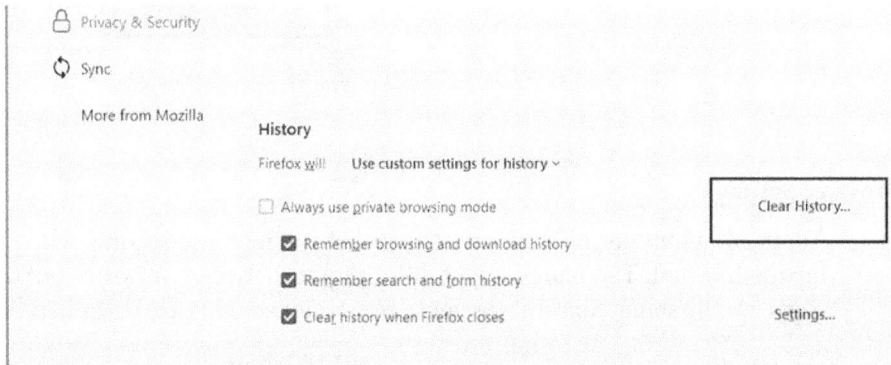

FIGURE 12.8 First step to clear the cache in Firefox

Scroll down to the "History" section and the "Privacy & Security" screen. Click the "Clear History" button. Figure 12.9 shows the window that will be displayed. Make sure the "Cache" box is checked. If other historical data, like cookies, browsing history, and logins, should be deleted, then ensure the corresponding boxes are checked. Click the "Clear Now" button.

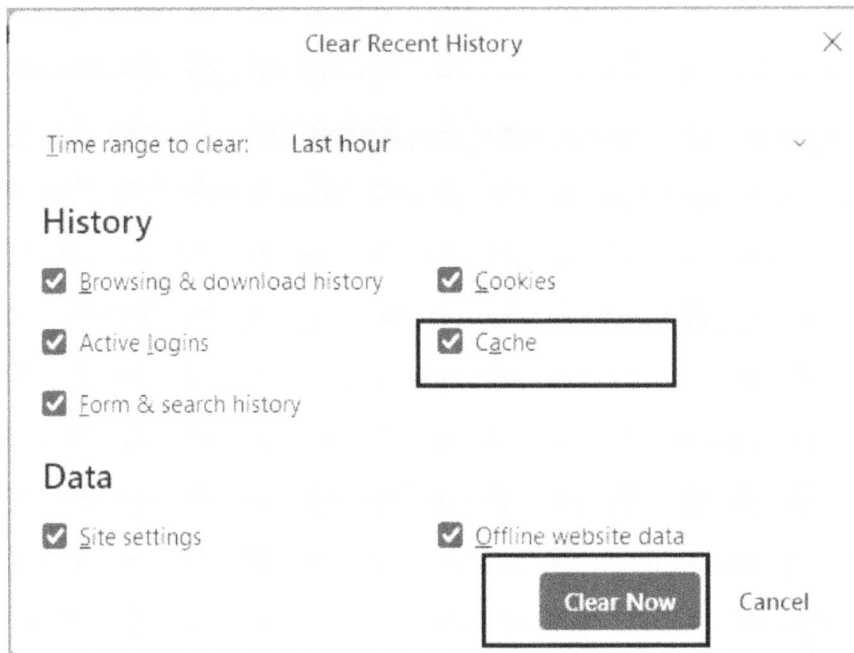

FIGURE 12.9 Second step to clear the cache in Firefox

Browser Settings

There are a number of browser settings that can increase security when accessing the Internet. The names might differ slightly between browsers, but the concepts are the same. Some of the more important settings are described below.

- Disable stored passwords: Browsers can autofill passwords when logging into Web sites. This is convenient but means that the password is being stored in the browser. Anyone that can access the browser will be able to view them.

- Autofill: When enabled, autofill will automatically file fields like addresses and payment methods. This is convenient, but the disadvantage is that personal information is stored in the browser. If anyone else can access the browser, they can see this information.

- Block pop-up windows: This browser setting will block pop-up ads from being displayed to the user. Preventing potentially dangerous ads from being displayed is an excellent way to avoid accidentally clicking on them.

- Warnings when a Web site tries to install an add-on: Giving the user the choice of whether an add-on should be installed can prevent dangerous add-ons from being installed.

- Reject third-party cookies: Rejecting third-party cookies can significantly improve the user's level of privacy when browsing the Internet.

- Delete cookies when the browser is closed: This setting does exactly what it sounds like.

- Do not sell or share data: Some browsers have a setting that tells Web sites not to sell or share the user's data. In jurisdictions like California, Colorado, and Connecticut, this can be legally enforceable. In other jurisdictions, it is more of a request than a mandate.

- Block Web Tracking: Some browsers have an option to send Web sites a "Do Not Track" request. Unfortunately, this is a request rather than a demand, but it is worth enabling.

- Limit access to location, camera, and microphone: Many Web sites will request access to location data access, camera access, and microphone access. Unless there is a legitimate reason for them to have this access it is better to block that access.

- Block dangerous downloads: When this setting is enabled, the browser will block the download of any content that is suspected of being dangerous.

Click-To-Play

Click-to-play is feature that requires the user to decide whether or not third-party code, e.g., a plug-in, should display the content on a Web site. Enabling click-to-play lets the user decide whether to avoid ads that play automatically when a Web site is visited. It can also protect the user from malicious software being automatically installed on his computer.

Most browsers allow the user to enable the click-to-play by taking a couple of steps. In Firefox, the steps to change that setting are shown in Figures 12.10 and 12.11. Other browsers will have similar steps to make this change.

Click on the icon with three horizontal lines in the upper right corner of a Firefox browser. This is sometimes called the "hamburger button" or "menu button." Select the "Settings" link. Click on the "Privacy & Security" option. Then scroll down to the "Permissions" section. Figure 12.10 shows the Permissions options.

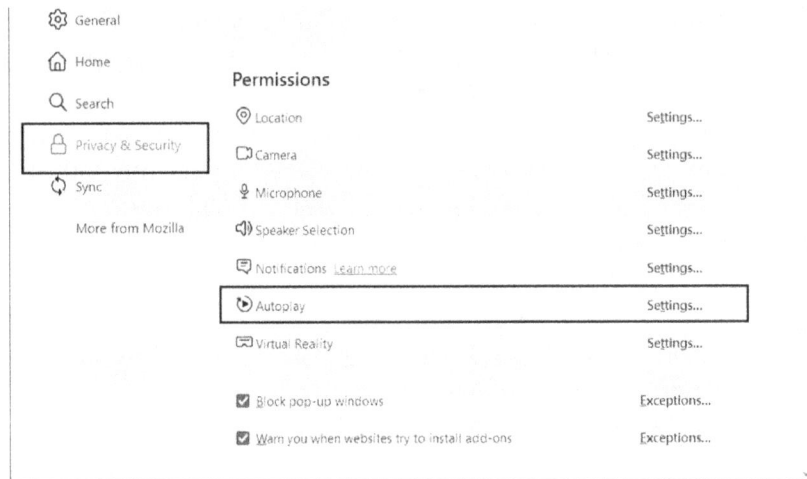

FIGURE 12.10 Steps to set the Click-To-Play or Autoplay option

On the screen shown in Figure 12.10, click the "Settings" button next to the "Autoplay" option. Figure 12.11 shows the available settings for autoplay. The default options are "Allow Audio and Video," "Block Audio," and "Block Audio and Video." If a change to this setting is made, click the "Save Changes" button. There is also the option to specify Web sites that the default setting does not apply to.

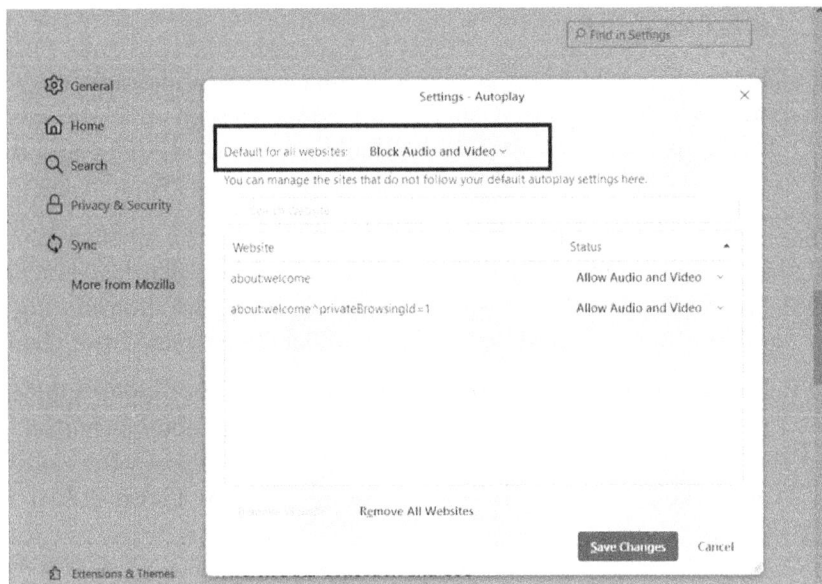

FIGURE 12.11 Choosing Click-To-Play setting values

Delete Web Browsing History

Most browsers allow the user to delete Web browsing history whenever the browser application is exited, i.e., closed. Everyone should have their browsers set to do this. Retaining the browser history is an invitation to cybercriminals and advertisers to build a profile on the user's history and interests. This may seem like a minor point, but it is a good step in taking back privacy.

Incognito Browsing

Most browsers have a privacy, a.k.a. incognito, mode, that hides browsing history. This may prevent other users of the computer or browser from seeing which Web sites the browser has been at, but the degree of privacy is not absolute.

The ISP (Internet Service Provider) still knows all of the Web sites that have been visited, even if Incognito mode has been enabled. It is also possible that the Web sites visited created cookies on the device so advertisers can see which Web sites have been visited.

Privacy Tools

A class of tools and utilities exist that promise to enhance security and privacy by deleting files and data on computers and smartphones that users are unaware of. Examples of the data that these tools erase include the following:

- temporary files created by applications and Web browsers
- lists of Web sites recently visited
- browser search history
- lists of documents that were recently opened
- browser cookies
- passwords saved by browsers
- data used to autofill forms; examples of this data include credit card numbers, addresses, and phone numbers

Some of these tools are browser extensions while others are stand-alone applications. A partial listing of tools like this is as follows:

- CCleaner®
- Cleaner One®

- Clear Master®
- Privacy Cleaner®
- SlimCleaner®

SECURE BROWSERS

When browsing the Internet, there are numerous groups that want to track users. Using a secure browser can help prevent them from accumulating data about the user. Examples of browsers that emphasize safety include the following:

- Brave®
- DuckDuckGo®
- Epic®
- Firefox®
- Ghostery®
- Tor browser®

VPN

A Virtual Private Network (VPN) is an intermediary service between a user's computer and the Web site being visited that provides a high level of security and anonymity. It has been described as a tunnel between the user's computer and Web site that no one else can access. Chapter 13 in this book is devoted to VPNs.

Transport Layer Security (TLS) vs. Secure Socket Layer (SSL)

TLS and SSL are protocols that provide security between Web browsers and Web sites. TLS is the more recent and more secure of the two protocols and should be used. Browser settings should be updated to disable using the SSL protocol and enable the TLS protocol.

The steps to disable SSL and enable TLS are more complicated than most browser settings. The steps can also vary significantly in different browsers. Rather than providing instructions here, which might become outdated, it would be better for the reader to search for them on the Internet. The phrase for this type of search would be "How to set SSL or TLS on my XXX browser," where XXX is the browser being used.

UPDATE THE BROWSER

Keeping browsers as well as operating systems, antivirus, and other software updated is an extremely important step toward online safety. All users should set their browsers and operating systems to be updated automatically. This will help ensure the browser and computer are as protected as possible.

The steps to keep specific browsers updated are described in the following sections.

Firefox

To reach the browser update settings in Firefox, click on the three vertical lines (the "hamburger button") in the upper right corner. On the "General" screen, scroll down to the section titled "Firefox Updates." Figure 12.12 shows this screen.

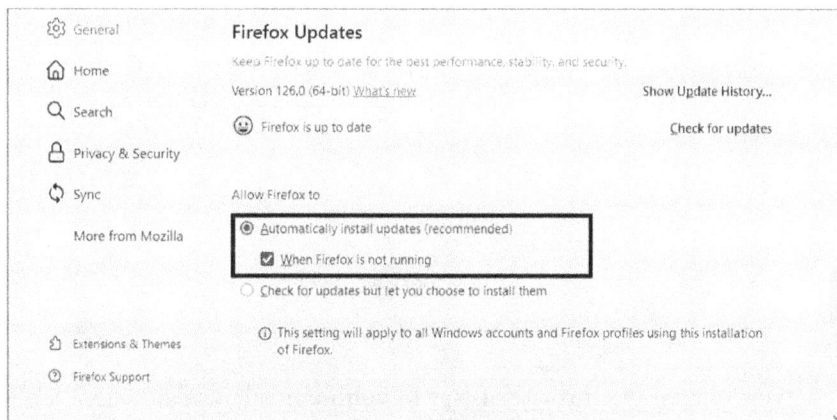

FIGURE 12.12 Firefox update screen

Firefox's choices for updates are to allow them to be installed automatically or to give the user a choice of whether or not to install them. The better choice is to have them automatically installed.

The user can verify that Firefox is currently up to date by clicking the "Check for updates" button. If an update is available, the user will be given the option of installing it.

Chrome

Chrome defaults to automatically installing updates whenever one is available. To confirm that it is on the latest version, click on the three vertical dots (referred to as an ellipses) in the upper right corner of Chrome. Select the "Help" option and then sub-option "About Google Chrome." The screen that will be displayed is shown in Figure 12.13.

If the version of Chrome is current, the phrase "Chrome is up to date" will be displayed just below the Google Chrome logo. This is shown in Figure 12.13. If this installation is not current, then a button labeled "Update Google Chrome" will be displayed. Click that button to update Chrome to the most current version.

FIGURE 12.13 Chrome update screen

Edge

Microsoft's Edge browser is set to automatically update when a new version is available. To confirm that it is on the most recent version, click the three vertical dots in the upper right corner of Edge. Select the option "Help and Feedback," and then the sub-option "About Microsoft Edge." This screen is shown in Figure 12.14.

If the latest version of Edge is installed on this computer, the phrase "Microsoft Edge is up to date" will be displayed below the Microsoft Edge logo. If Edge is not on the latest version, then it will be updated automatically. Once the update has been completed, Edge has to be closed and restarted for the changes to take effect.

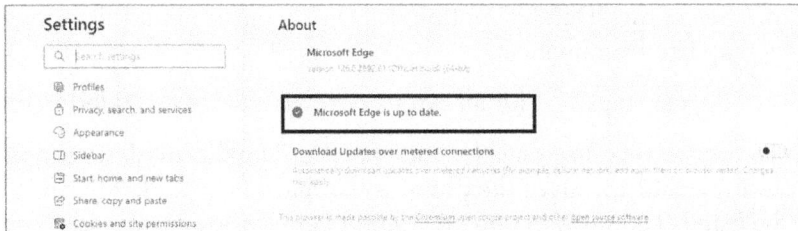

FIGURE 12.14 Edge update screen

Updating Extensions and Plug-Ins

Extensions and plug-ins (a.k.a. add-ons) need to be updated. The steps to keep them current differ slightly between browsers.

The steps to update extension in Firefox are listed here:

1. Click the three horizontal lines (a.k.a. the menu button), click on "Add-ons and themes."

2. In the left margin, click on "Extensions."

3. Under section "Manage Your Extensions," click the horizontal ellipses next to the desired extension and click on "Manage." Figure 12.15 shows the update options for the extension.

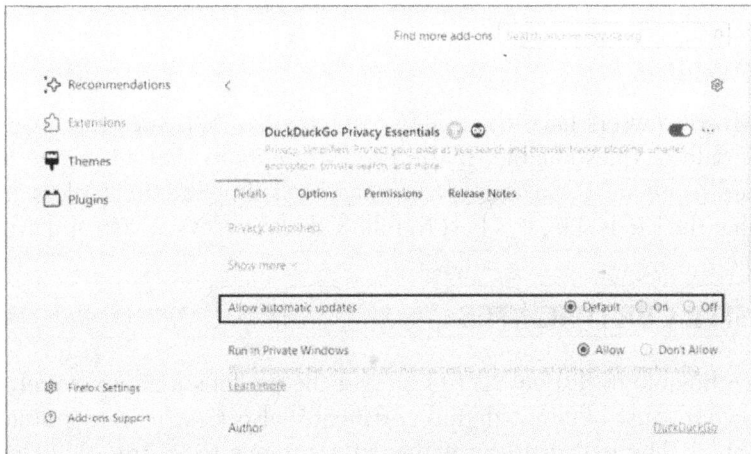

FIGURE 12.15 Firefox extension update screen

4. Select the "Default" option or "On" to ensure that this extension will be updated automatically.

5. Repeat steps 1- 4 for all extensions that have been added to the browser.

To update plug-ins, click on the "plug-ins" link in the left margin, as shown in Figure 12.15. All of the plug-ins that have been added to this browser will be listed. The steps to update a plug-in are the same as those for extensions.

Secure Web Sites

Secure Web sites have "https://" at the beginning of their address, i.e., their URL. HTTPS stands for "Hypertext Transfer Protocol Secure." A secure Web site also has a padlock icon to the left of the URL. Figure 12.16 shows a Web site URL that has the HTTPS and padlock icon. A Web site that does not begin with HTTPS may be safe to browse but should not be considered safe enough to share personal information with or make purchases at.

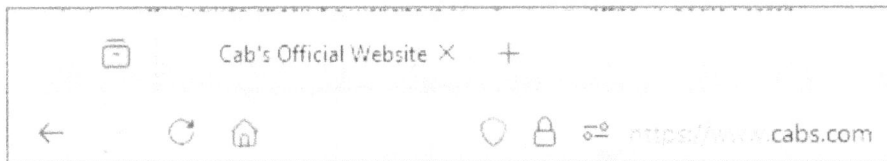

FIGURE 12.16 A secure HTTPS Web site

Unsafe Websites

Most browsers have the ability to recognize Web sites that are known to be unsafe or questionable. If the user attempts to visit an unsafe Web site, the browser issues a warning advising against visiting the site. Unless the user knows that the site is safe, it is best to follow the browser's advice and avoid the site.

WEB SITE CERTIFICATES

To be able to display "HTTPS" and the padlock icon on a Web site, the site owner must obtain a digital certificate, also known as a "public key certificate." The certificate provides an assurance to visitors that the Web site is authentic and can be trusted. The certificate includes a public key that is used by browsers to encrypt data going to and from the Web site. The encryption process ensures that these communications are secure and cannot be eavesdropped on by anyone.

Certificates are issued by a certificate authority (CA). Examples of CAs are DigiCert, SSL Corp, Thawte, and Comodo SSL. To obtain one, the Web site owner must provide details such as the name of the certificate holder, contact info, and the requestor's public key to the CA. Once the Web site owner obtains a certificate, they install it on their Web server. From that point onwards, whenever a browser connects to the Web site, it will use the TLS or SSL protocol to communicate with the Web site.

If the user wants to learn more about the Web site's certificate details, they can left click on the padlock icon and select "Connection Secure" and then "More Information." A window similar to the one shown in Figure 12.17 will be displayed that includes details about the Web site and its certificate. The screen also provides information on how many times the user has been to that Web site.

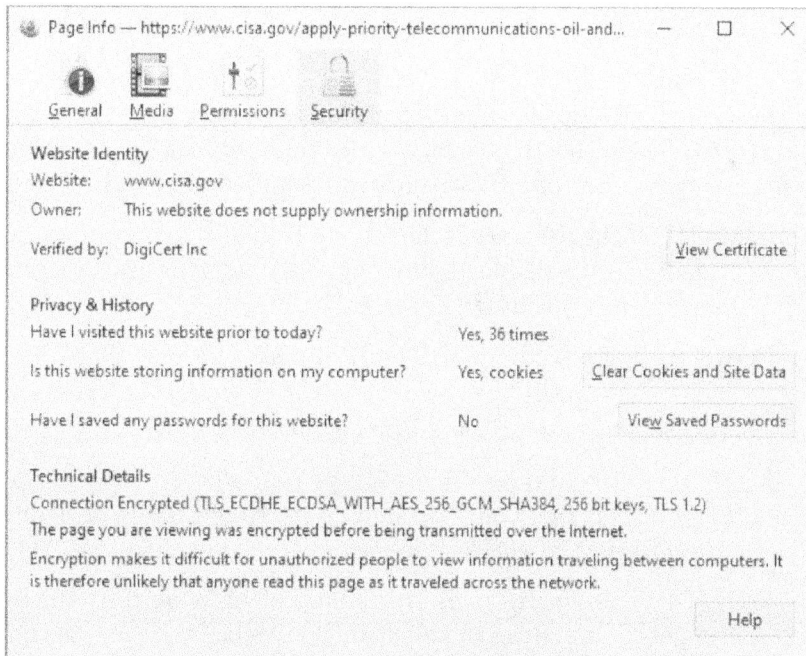

FIGURE 12.17 Website certificate details

BROWSER SECURITY MAINTENANCE STEPS

Some preventive maintenance steps that should be performed on all browsers regularly are listed here. While nothing can guarantee absolute safety on the world wide Web, these steps will help:

a. Purge your browsers' cache and cookies regularly.

b. Set the browser to purge each time it closes.

c. Periodically delete all cookies and browser history manually.

d. Set your browser to block dangerous downloads and provide a warning about unwanted downloads.

e. Review what extensions plug-ins are installed and enabled regularly. Uninstall any that are no longer needed or were not intentionally installed.

REFERENCES

[COMP23] Dahan, Marc. "Top 6 Web browser attacks and how to avoid them," available online at *https://www.comparitech.com/blog/information-security/web-browser-attacks/*, October 19, 2023

[DARK23] Vijayan, Jai. "More Than Half of Browser Extensions Pose Security Risks," available online at *https://www.darkreading.com/cloud-security/more-than-half-of-browser-extensions-pose-security-risks*, August 22, 2023

[FING24] "The Beginner's Guide to Browser Fingerprinting for Fraud Detection," available online at *https://fingerprint.com/blog/what-is-browser-fingerprinting/*, February 22, 2024

[FORB23] Haan, Katherine. "The Real Risks of Public Wi-Fi: Key Statistics and Usage Data," available online at *https://www.forbes.com/advisor/business/public-wifi-risks/*, February 9, 2023

[FORT24] Leake, Lindsey. "17 years of your adult life may be spent online. These expert tips may help curb your screen time," available online at *https://fortune.com/well/article/screen-time-over-lifespan/*, March 6, 2024

[META24] "10 Examples of Technological Risks on the Internet: Abuses, Dangers, and Relevant Statistics," available online at *https://www.metabaseq.com/10-examples-of-technological-risks-on-the-internet-abuses-dangers-and-relevant-statistics/*, June 25, 2024

[TECH24] Mello, John. "Browser-Based Phishing Attacks Jump 198% in Second Half of 2023," available online at *https://www.technewsworld.com/story/browser-based-phishing-attacks-jump-198-in-second-half-of-2023-178980.html*, January 24, 2024

CHAPTER 13

VIRTUAL PRIVATE NETWORKS

WHAT IS A VIRTUAL PRIVATE NETWORK?

A Virtual Private Network (VPN) provides secure communications between a user's device and Web sites being visited. It is often described as a tunnel between the two points. Instead of the communications going to the user's ISP (Internet Service Provider), it goes through a server provided by the VPN vendor. The only IP address that the ISP and Web site can see is that of the VPN server. Essentially no one other than the VPN vendor knows who the user is or what Web sites they are visiting.

Another advantage of using a VPN is that all of the communications between the user and the Web site being visited are encrypted. This prevents anyone from eavesdropping on those communications.

WHY USE A VPN?

The primary reason for using a VPN is to protect personal privacy. VPNs provide privacy when the user is browsing the Internet from a desktop or laptop device, as well as from a smartphone. Privacy and anonymity are needed any time anyone connects to the Internet.

Privacy is not guaranteed to consumers. The US Congress passed legislation that allows an ISP to collect data on its clients and sell it [PCMAG24]. ISPs claim that all of the data has been anonymized and users have nothing to worry about. They claim that anonymized data has been stripped of all personally identifiable information (PII). This sounds useful, but that practice does not guarantee anonymity.

Studies have repeatedly shown that anonymizing data by removing names and IDs does not prevent it from being traced back to individuals [EFF23]. A paper presented by John Sullivan of Princeton University at the 2017 World Wide Web Conference in Perth, Australia showed that browsing histories could be linked to their owner's social media profiles [PRIN17]. For that paper, the researchers compared the Web browsing data of 374 volunteers against hundreds of millions of public social media feeds. They were able to identify 70% of the volunteers.

Until laws are passed that prevent personal data, even after being anonymized, from being sold, our online activities are not private or anonymous. Individuals must take steps to achieve any level of privacy. One important step is to use a VPN whenever connecting to the Internet.

HOW A VPN WORKS

One part of installing VPN software on a computer or smart phone is to load a browser extension specific to the user's browser(s). From that point on, the browser will communicate with the destination Web site via the VPN service. The steps to connect with a Web site are as follows:

1. The connection process is initiated when the user opens a browser to connect to a Web site. VPN software running on the user's phone or computer is called the *VPN client*.

2. The user's data is encrypted by the VPN client on the user's device. This encryption prevents the ISP or anyone else from listening to or modifying the data.

3. The encrypted data is transmitted by the VPN client across the Internet to a computer owned by the VPN service called a *VPN server*. All communications flow through the ISP that the user normally connects to.

4. The VPN server establishes a connection with the Web site specified by the user. Data encrypted by the VPN client is now decrypted by the VPN server and sent across the Internet to the destination Web site.

5. The Web site handles the page request and responds to the VPN server without knowing the user's identity or location.

6. The VPN server encrypts the message sent by the Web site and forwards it to the VPN client.

7. The VPN client decrypts the message and displays it in the user's browser.

The user is not aware of the VPN software involved in this process, other than perhaps to notice a slightly slower response time. Once the VPN software has been installed, the user does not need to take any further actions.

VPN Strengths

The strengths of a good VPN are significant. Some of the most important ones are as follows:

- allows the user to view Web sites without revealing his or her IP address or geographic location

- prevents anyone from eavesdropping on Internet activity including Internet searches, emails, online purchases, browsing history, or data entered into Web site forms

- can help to bypass restrictions imposed by an employer, ISP, or government on which Web sites can be accessed

- allows public Wi-Fi to be used safely

- protects confidential information like passwords, bank account, and credit card numbers

- allows the user to stream video without having what is being streamed tracked by the ISP or government

- Most VPN services have servers in multiple countries. Users can alternate between them to further obfuscate their geographic location.

VPN Limitations

As effective as they are, VPNs are not without limitations. Some of their weaknesses are as follows:

- Using a VPN may slow Web browsing performance. Sending communications to another server, i.e., the VPN server, takes additional time. It also takes time to encrypt communications between the user and destination Web site.

- VPNs do not provide protection from malware, viruses, phishing attacks, or ransomware. The user still needs antivirus software running on his computer and must exercise caution when opening email attachments or clicking on links.

- A VPN does not prevent the Web site from creating cookies. The user must set his browser to block third-party cookies and reject first-party cookies when browsing.

- Applications and Web sites that a user logs into using an account ID will still have a record of the user's activity. Of course, if a fake, or dummy account ID is being used that can protect the user's identity.

- Some streaming services are able to recognize when a VPN is being used by a user because the IP address of the VPN server is used by multiple users. They may require that the user disable the VPN before viewing streamed material.

WHEN TO USE A VPN

The default should be to always use a VPN. If that is not viable, then one should be used whenever the user is as follows:

- using a public Wi-Fi
- conducting online business transactions
- sending email
- accessing applications that require a password
- doing anything that the user would like to be kept private

VPNS DO NOT GUARANTEE 100% ANONYMITY

VPNs greatly improve user privacy and anonymity but unfortunately, they do not guarantee 100% anonymity. The two ways in which the user can still be tracked are described here.

Digital Fingerprinting

Digital fingerprinting is a process of collecting and analyzing specific details about a consumer's device and browser [SPLUNK23]. Some of the data points used by digital fingerprinting are as follows:

- device details like the device's make and model, operating system, and screen resolution
- default browser type and version
- browser settings like default language, local time zone, default zoom value selected

- fonts installed
- browser plug-ins that exist
- hardware details of the computer's graphic card and driver
- cookies that exist on the device
- install an ad blocker on the browser

Digital fingerprinting can be employed to track individuals even when a VPN is being used by capturing data about the user's session and platform. To reduce the chances of being fingerprinted this way, the user should try to make his environment as commonplace as possible. Appearing to be a common user makes the user look just like everyone else on the Internet. Some steps to make it more challenging to identify a user via his online fingerprint are as follows:

- Set the browser to block cookies from being installed on the device.
- Keep the operating system updated. An OS that is noticeably outdated makes the digital fingerprint more distinctive.
- Using an unusual browser is conspicuous, so use one of the more popular browsers.
- Disable JavaScript on the browser. This prevents the Web site from detecting extensions and plug-ins. The downside to this is some Web sites will not function correctly if JavaScript is not enabled.
- Remove any browser plug-ins that are not being used.

Discreet VPN Services

If the VPN service retains log entries of client activities, those logs can be used to identify clients and their online activity. Log entries could be revealed by either a cybercriminal, an insider, or a government subpoena. The safest VPN services do not maintain any logs of client activity. If data that could be used to identify the client is not being retained, then it cannot be stolen or subpoenaed.

TOOLS USED IN CONJUNCTION WITH A VPN

The ability of a VPN to preserve anonymity is enhanced if the user takes additional steps, such as the following:

- Secure browser: Any browser used should be one that emphasizes security.
- Ad blocker: A pop-up ad blocking should be enabled in the browser.
- MFA: Using multifactor authentication is always good practice.

CHOOSING A VPN SERVICE

It is important to realize that a VPN service sees everything that the user wants to keep hidden from everyone. It knows the user's identity, IP address, and Web sites visited. This makes it crucial to choose a trustworthy VPN service. Before selecting a VPN service, the user needs to research them to make sure that a trustworthy VPN service is selected.

A second factor when choosing a VPN service is the country where it is located, or more importantly, the privacy laws in that country. An oppressive or authoritarian government might require that VPN client activities be given to the authorities. Countries that have strong privacy laws include Iceland, Norway, Japan, and Switzerland [PRIV22].

A third factor to consider is how much hardware the VPN service provides. Part of what the VPN service provides is an actual server, i.e., a computer. If a great deal of activity is running through a limited number of servers, then performance can degrade. The VPN service chosen should have enough servers and other hardware to avoid performance bottlenecks.

A fourth factor is whether the VPN service is compatible with the environment(s) of the user. A user might have both Windows and MacOS computers. The user's phones might be iOS, Android, or both. Browsers being used might include Chrome, Edge, Firefox, or Safari. Any VPN service being considered should support all the user's needs.

A final factor in the decision is the encryption protocol that is used by the VPN service. If the service has a weak or outdated protocol in place, then the user's data will not be secure. Any VPN service being considered should employ a secure protocol. Advanced Encryption Standard (AES) is currently considered the most secure encryption algorithm.

FREE VPN VS. PAID VPN

There are many VPN services available, including free and paid options. Free VPNs may provide adequate functionality, but the old saying "you get what you pay for" should be kept in mind. The reality is that running a VPN service is expensive. It needs computer servers, utilities, network bandwidth, software, and staff to support it. It is difficult to fund an operation with those requirements without a regular income stream.

Potential shortcomings of free VPN services include the following:

- Some free VPN tools track the user's online activity. A study by the ICSI Networking and Security Group found that 72% of free VPN services embedded third-party tracking tools in their software [FORT24].
- Some free VPNs being offered are not actually VPNs at all. They are malware that cybercriminals are hoping unsuspecting consumers will download.
- Bandwidth might be limited.
- The number of physical VPN servers might be limited.
- Ads may be displayed to the user.
- They might offer fewer countries through which connections can be made.
- Logs of user activity might be kept, which could result in user activity being revealed.
- Without the income generated by paid fees, a free VPN service might not survive.

One example of a free VPN app that was shown to be problematic was SuperVPN. In June of 2023, the details on 360 million user records associated with the free VPN service SuperVPN were found by researcher Jeremiah Fowler [CPO23]. The records included details like IP addresses, email addresses, and geolocations that identified individual users. SuperVPN has been downloaded over 100 million times from Google Play Store, Apple Store, and other sites.

SECURE VPN PRODUCTS

There are many VPN companies that provide excellent service for the price. Some of the more popular VPNs are listed below. Before selecting a service, the reader should perform his own research since there may be new ones and the current service providers may no longer be offered or not be as highly regarded as they are now.

- CyberGhost®
- ExpressVPN®
- NordVPN®
- Norton Secure VPN®
- ProtonVPN®
- Surfshark®

SETTING UP A VPN

The steps for setting up and using a VPN will differ for each vendor. Installing Surfshark was not any different from installing other applications. The following instructions were followed to install and start using Surfshark:

1. Log into Surfshark's Web site: *httsp://surfshark.com.*

2. Select the desired plan to purchase. Surfshark, like most other VPNs, offers a 30-day money back guarantee.

3. When prompted, enter an email address and password. Make sure the password is strong!

4. Click the "Download Windows app" button.

5. In the *Downloads* folder, double-click on SurfsharkSetup.exe.

6. Click "Yes" to allow Surfshark to make changes on the PC.

7. Click the "Install" button on the setup window.

8. Click the "Finish" button.

9. On the "It's time to connect!" screen, click the login button. When prompted, enter the email address and password entered in Step 3.

10. A list of countries will be displayed. These are the locations where Surfshark has servers positioned. Here, you can choose the initial server location. This can be changed later.

Surfshark can be opened like any other application. On a Windows computer, Surfshark can be launched by left-clicking the "Windows" icon, scrolling down the list of applications, and clicking its icon. The main screen provides a list of VPN server locations that are available.

After installing Surfshark, there are many options that can be set. Some of the more important ones are described here:

- Surfshark defaults to being launched when the computer starts up. This can be disabled on the "Settings" screen.

- The VPN server being used can be changed at any time. Simply click on one of the countries listed on the main page.

- Countries with servers in multiple cities have a down arrow next to them. Click on the down arrow and the complete list of cities will be displayed.

For example, Canada has multiple cities where VPN servers are located. Any of them can be selected.

▪ To be extra cautious, the VPN can be instructed to pass through multiple hops. Click on the "Multihop" option shown on the main page. This provides an extra layer of security, but performance is likely to suffer since all communications are now passing through two VPN servers.

▪ VPN functionality can be paused by clicking the "Pause" button on the main page. It can be paused for 5 minutes, 30 minutes, or 2 hours.

▪ VPN functionality can be stopped by clicking the "Disconnect" button on the main page.

Confirming That VPN is Working

Confirming that the user's IP address is being obscured is easily done. With the VPN disabled, go to Web site *https://showmyip.com*. That site will display a screen that lists the user's actual IP address, country, city, zip code, and time zone. For example, some initial details for a user in Chicago might show the "United States" as the country, "Chicago" as the city, and "60006" as the ZIP code.

Let's consider another example of the Surfshark VPN, with Canada chosen as the location of the VPN server to be used. We can open the ShowMyIP Web site again and check the displayed values. The values in the same fields now show "Canada" as the country, "Montreal" as the city and "H3H" as the ZIP code. The values for the IPv4 address, time zone, and ISP have all changed, as well.

Another way to verify that the VPN is working is to bring up Google's main page and select the "News" option. The top stories for the country where the VPN server is located will be listed. Instead of seeing news items for the United States, you should see news from Canada since the VPN server the computer is connected through is located in Montreal, Canada.

Surfshark on iPhone

Installing Surfshark on an iPhone is similar to installing other mobile applications. You can install it, activate it, and choose a VPN server location just like we did for the desktop computer example. After installation, open the Web site *https://showmyip.com* on your iPhone. It should show an IP address that is associated with the VPN server location you chose instead of your actual physical location or service provider. Details like the IP address, country, region, city, zip code, time zone, and ISP are all associated with the VPN server instead of your iPhone.

Experience with Surfshark

The author's personal experience is that performance when using Surfshark was not any different than when not using a VPN. Some reviews of VPNs state that users can expect performance to be 10-20% slower. If the response time is unacceptably slow, choose a VPN server in a different location. A server in the user's own country or a neighboring country may provide better performance.

Another issue that can arise when using a VPN is the higher number of CAPTCHA (Completely Automated Test to tell Computers and Humans Apart) screens appearing than did previously. One reason is that the IP address of the VPN server is also used by other VPN customers. If the Web site identifies many simultaneous connections with the same IP address, it may suspect they are from bots instead of from humans [PRI23]. CAPTCHA screens are the Web site's method of verifying that the connections are human originated.

Some of the ways to reduce the number of CAPTCHA screens when using a VPN are as follows:

- Select a VPN server in your own country.
- Disable the VPN service and then reconnect. This may change the IP address assigned. The Web site may not be able to identify the new IP address.
- Clear the browser history. Steps for clearing history are on the "Settings" screen. Then examine the "Privacy and Security" option (or a similar option, depending on the browser).
- Use a different browser. If the initial browser was Chrome, then try using Firefox.
- If the VPN service allows the choice between a dedicated or static IP address, choose the dedicated address. No one else will be assigned this IP address so the Web site will not identify the connection request as part of a bot attack.

REFERENCES

[CPO23] Hope Alicia. "Free VPN Data Leak Exposed Over 360 Million User Records," available online at *https://www.cpomagazine.com/cyber-security/ free-vpn-data-leak-exposed-over-360-million-user-records/*, June 5, 2023

[EFF23] Collings, Paige. "Debunking the Myth of 'Anonymous' Data," available online at *https://www.eff.org/deeplinks/2023/11/debunking-myth- anonymous-data*, November 10, 2023

[FORT24] "VPN Security: How Secure Is It & Do You Need One," available online at *https://www.fortinet.com/resources/cyberglossary/are-vpns-safe*, July 1, 2024

[PCMAG24] Stobing, Chris. "The Best VPN Services for 2024," available online at *https://www.pcmag.com/picks/the-best-vpn-services*, June 21, 2024

[PRI23] Hassel, Kristin. "Tired of Getting CAPTCHAs with a VPN? Here's How to Avoid Them," available online at *https://www.privateinternetaccess.com/blog/how-to-avoid-captchas-vpn/*, October 6, 2023

[PRIN17] Sullivan, John. "Your 'anonymized' Web browsing history may not be anonymous," available online at *https://www.princeton.edu/news/2017/01/23/your-anonymized-web-browsing-history-may-not-be-anonymous*, January 23, 2017

[PRIV22] Mash, Stephen. "Data Privacy Rankings—Top 5 and Bottom 5 Countries," available online at *https://privacyhq.com/news/world-data-privacy-rankings-countries/*, 2022

[SPLUNK23] Lange, Kayly. "How Digital Fingerprinting Tracks, Identifies & Affects Us," available online at *https://www.splunk.com/en_us/blog/learn/digital-fingerprints.html*, June 09, 2023

14

FIREWALLS

A *firewall* is a hardware device or software program that protects a network or computer from dangerous Internet traffic. It is a filter between the Internet and a network or a computer. It does this by recognizing and rejecting communication requests that are potentially dangerous.

The original definition of a "firewall" was a barrier of material between two buildings that would slow the spread of fire. If one building was burning, the firewall would help prevent the fire from spreading to other buildings. In the computer security context, a firewall serves much the same purpose, it helps prevent the spread of malware infection from the Internet to a computer or from computer to computer.

Firewall Breach Examples

The costs of a firewall breach can be enormous. Two examples of significant data breaches that involved firewalls are described below.

Retail company Target had data affecting over 40 million customers exposed in 2013 [RED21]. The attack was actually directed toward a third-party vendor's network. A misconfigured firewall allowed the culprits access to Target's Web site. The incident cost Target an estimated $200 million.

In March 2017, a consumer complaint Web portal at Equifax was hacked using a known vulnerability that had not been patched. Personally identifiable information (PII) impacting hundreds of millions of individuals was stolen.

A Web application firewall (WAF) vulnerability played a part in this massive data breach. Equifax eventually settled a class action suit against it for $1.38 billion [SEC20].

CONCEPTS NEEDED TO UNDERSTAND FIREWALLS

To grasp how a firewall works, there are several concepts that need to be understood. These concepts are described in the following sections.

IP Addresses

An IP address is the equivalent of a computer's mailing address. Every device that is connected to the Internet has a unique IP address. These addresses are expressed as four sets of numbers divided by periods. For example, 142.250.190.68 is the address of a Google server. The lowest IP address is 0.0.0.0 and the highest is 255.255.255.255.

NOTE   *The above explanation is for IPv4, which is the most common form of Internet addressing. IPv6 exists but is not as widely used as IPv4.*

Packets

Communications between computers across the Internet are broken down into packets. Each packet contains source and destination addresses, data being sent, and header information. A message traveling between computers may be composed of a single packet or many packets depending on its size. Once all of the packets have been received by the destination computer, the message is assembled and acted upon.

A firewall on the source computer inspects each packet as it is being sent off. Another firewall on the destination computer inspects each packet as it is being received. Either firewall can reject or ignore a packet that it inspects.

Ports

Network ports identify endpoints that allow data to be exchanged between two computers. They are not physical entities like USB ports in the side of a computer are. They are managed by the computer's operating system. Port numbers range from 0 to 65536.

Network ports can be compared to extension numbers in a telephone system. For example, Sally and her coworker Mike are both in the same office and have the same phone number, but they have different extensions. Sally might have extension 123, and Mike might have extension 456.

Ports are associated with services, i.e., programs, or protocols running on the computer. A few examples of ports and the protocols they are commonly assigned to are shown here.

Port	Service or Protocol That Commonly Uses It
21	FTP (File Transfer Protocol) is a protocol used to transfer files between computers.
22	SSH (Secure Shell) is a method of executing commands on a remote computer.
23	Telnet is an interactive connection between two computers.
25	SMTP (Simple Mail Transfer Protocol) is a protocol for sending email between two computers.
80	HTTP (Hyper Text Transfer Protocol) is the protocol used by the World Wide Web to display Web pages on a user's computer.
443	HTTPS (HTTP Secure) is an encrypted version of HTTP.

Closed, Filtered, and Open Ports

A *closed port* ignores any communication attempts made to it. If a person or program from another computer attempts to communicate through a closed port, it will be ignored.

A *filtered port* is one that is open, but communications on it are being monitored by the firewall. Firewall rules determine whether attempts to establish communications through the port will be allowed or ignored.

An *open port* is set up to accept all incoming connections. No monitoring or filtering is performed by the firewall on an open port.

Ports that are used to accept email, browse the World Wide Web, perform file transfers, stream video, and enable online gaming needs to be either open or filtered.

Leaving a port open can be dangerous if the service using that port has a weakness or vulnerability that can be exploited by cybercriminals or malicious software. For example, port 21 is typically used by FTP (File Transfer Protocol) to move files between computers. FTP is an outdated protocol and has the following vulnerabilities:

- Passwords can be discovered by brute force attacks.

- Historically, the username and password were both set to "anonymous." If this account has not been disabled, cybercriminals can log in using it.

- A *directory traversal attack* can be attempted. In this attack, if a cybercriminal is able to log in with valid credentials, he will try to move or traverse to other directory(s) that he normally should not be able to access.

- FTP does not have a built-in mechanism to log user activity. If a cybercriminal is able to log onto an FTP account, there will be no way to document what files he might have uploaded, downloaded, or deleted.

WHAT A FIREWALL DOES

A firewall monitors or filters traffic into and out of a computer. Monitoring outbound traffic might seem unnecessary, but it is actually very important. Some instances in which outbound traffic can be dangerous and should be prevented include the following:

- If a virus, Trojan horse, or other malware has been installed on a computer, it will likely try to infect other computers.

- An infected computer may try to communicate with a command computer.

- Outbound traffic might be an attempt to exfiltrate stolen data to another computer.

- An outbound filter can also stop traffic if the computer has become a bot and is trying to participate in a DOS (Denial of Service) attack on other computers.

Without a firewall, there is no control over the traffic that can enter or leave a network or computer. It is inevitable that some of this traffic will be unauthorized and dangerous. Firewall rules can prevent traffic from reaching closed ports. Rules can also deny communication attempts from known malicious IP addresses, called *blacklisting*. Rules can also *whitelist* an IP address, i.e., specify sites that can always connect.

A firewall can stop unauthorized access by cybercriminals onto a computer or network. It can prevent users from visiting unauthorized sites and downloading malware. A firewall can block confidential data from being moved off a computer. If one computer in an organization is infected with a virus, a software firewall can help prevent the virus from spreading to other computers within the organization.

A firewall protects the user from annoyances as well as danger. By blocking messages for online advertising, gaming, and gambling, a firewall reduces distractions as well as situations where a user can click on potentially dangerous links.

HOW A FIREWALL WORKS

A firewall examines connection attempts and data packets that are trying to communicate with the computer. Packets from IP addresses that are known to host dangerous activity are blocked. Data in packets is analyzed, and if the contents are harmful, the packet will be denied. Emails with executable attachments, e.g., having an ".exe" extension, can be blocked by a firewall. Packets that are part of a session that was initiated by the computer, for example a Web site responding to a user request, will typically be allowed through the firewall.

Hardware vs. Software

Firewalls can be either a hardware device or a software application. Typically, a hardware firewall is positioned between an organization's network and the Internet. It is able to protect the entire network including every device connected to it. A software firewall is installed on a computer and protects just that device. The two different forms of firewall can be used together, i.e., a hardware firewall on the network and software firewalls on every individual computer.

Each form of firewall has its strengths and weaknesses. Some examples are as follows:

- A hardware firewall requires more expertise to set up and maintain. Software firewalls can be deployed and maintained by individuals that do not have security related training.
- Hardware firewalls are the more expensive of the two. Frequently, software firewalls are built into operating systems (including Windows and Mac). They are also included in some antivirus packages. McAfee, Bitdefender, and Norton all have antivirus packages that include software firewalls.
- Hardware firewalls can typically handle more traffic because the device includes its own processing power. A software firewall consumes CPU cycles that would otherwise be dedicated to user applications.

- Upgrading a software firewall is much easier than upgrading a hardware version. This software can be set to update automatically. Updating a hardware version requires new hardware and manual intervention.

- One hardware firewall installed at the right location can protect every device on the network. A software firewall only protects the computer it is been loaded on.

FIREWALL RULES

In the simplest terms, a firewall blocks unwanted traffic, both inbound and outbound traffic. Rules can be written that specify exactly what gets blocked and what is allowed through. Each data packet coming across the network is examined by the firewall to determine whether any of the rules should be applied to it. Rules should be written to enforce a policy of "least privilege" to minimize access to what is absolutely necessary. This reduces the risk of unauthorized intrusions.

Each rule can either permit or deny access. For example, a rule might specify that any inbound communications from IP address 10.10.10.2 should be denied. Another rule might be that any inbound communication from IP address 20.20.20.20 on port 8080 be allowed.

Default Rules

Firewalls typically block all inbound traffic unless the port needs to be open. Outbound traffic is generally allowed.

Firewall rules are applied starting at the top of the list and working down the list. Once a rule is applied against a packet, no further rule checking is performed for the packet. Because of the way they are applied, more specific rules should appear higher in the list than more generalized rules.

Who Creates the Rules?

In a large organization, an IT security specialist or security team would likely create and maintain firewall rules. The rules could also be handled by a network administrator. The average computer user is typically unaware of the existence of these rules and would not have the access to create or modify them.

Preset rules for software firewalls are created by the vendor when their product is installed. Most users should accept them as a baseline. Additional rules can be created as needed if the computer owner is willing and able to learn about firewalls and rules.

A user interface exists so the user does not have to actually "write" rules. The interface is more like having a wizard present the user with a series of screens asking for details on the rule. The steps to create a rule in Windows Defender are shown below.

1. Right-click on the Windows icon at the bottom left corner of the monitor.

2. Click on "Run," enter "Control Panel," and press the Enter key.

3. On the "Control Panel" window click on the "System and Security" link.

4. On the "System and Security" window, click on "Windows Defender Firewall" link.

5. Click on the "Advanced Settings" link shown in Figure 14.1.

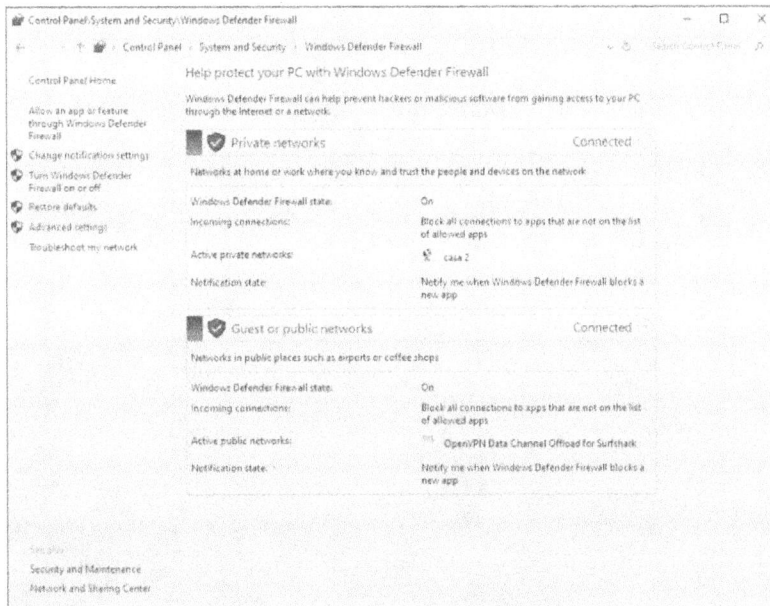

FIGURE 14.1 Microsoft Windows Defender firewall

6. Click on "Inbound Rules" or "Outbound Rules." In this example, "Inbound" will be selected.

7. In the upper right corner, click on "New Rule" as shown in Figure 14.2

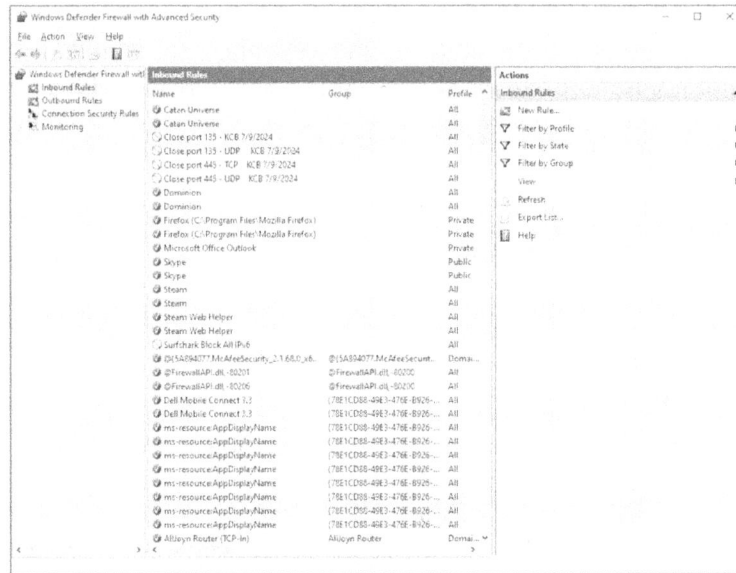

FIGURE 14.2 Creating a new Inbound Rule

8. On the "New Inbound Rule Wizard," select the appropriate rule type option. In this example, we are creating a port-based rule. Figure 14.3 shows the rule type selection screen.

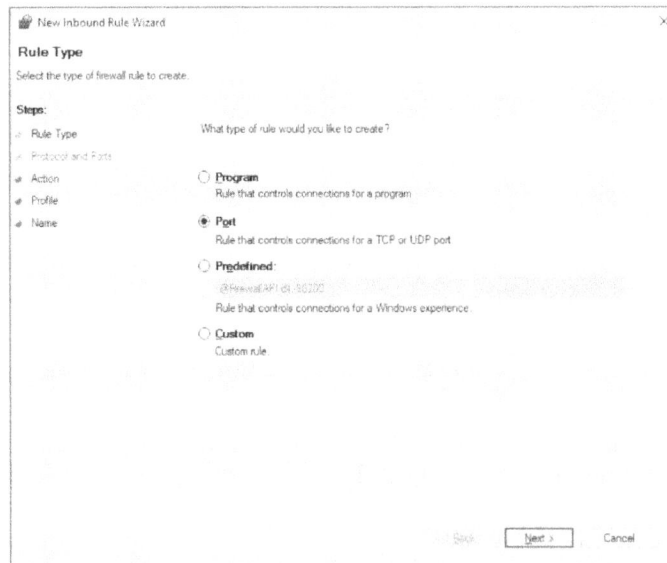

FIGURE 14.3 The new Inbound Rule is based on the port number.

9. The "Protocol and Ports" screen of the wizard lets the user specify the protocol and port number. In simplest terms, the difference between TCP (Transmission Control Protocol) and UDP (User Datagram Protocol) is that TCP is slower but more reliable. UDP is faster, but not as reliable. Figure 14.4 shows that the rule being created applies to protocol TCP and port 80.

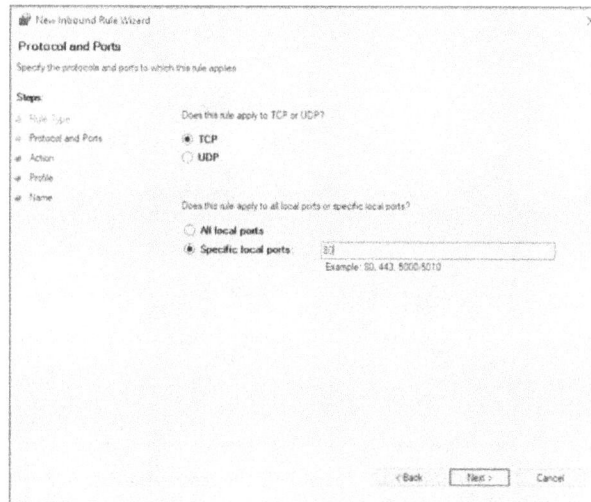

FIGURE 14.4 The new Inbound Rule is based on the port number.

10. The next specification is how the rule will respond to communications requests. The choices are to allow them, allow them only when it is secure, or to block them. Figure 14.5 shows the block choice has been selected.

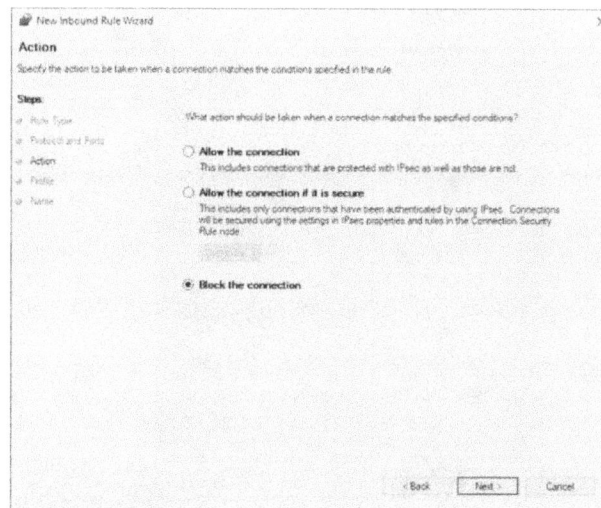

FIGURE 14.5 Determines the actions the new rule will take

11. The final specification is when the rule is applied. The options are when the computer is connected to a domain, private network, or a public network. Figure 14.6 shows that the public option was selected.

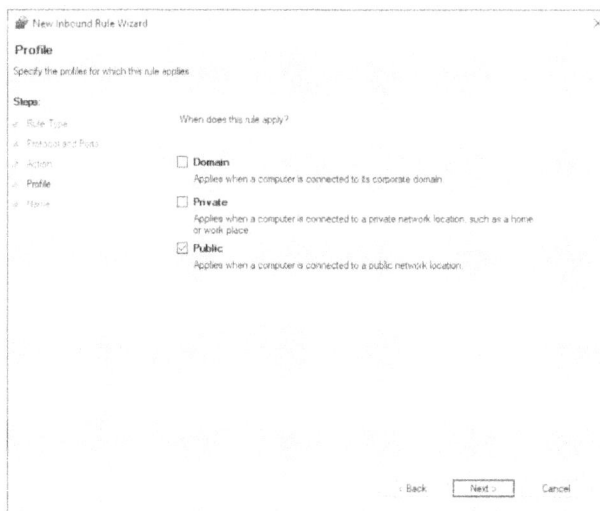

FIGURE 14.6 Determines the actions the new rule will take

12. Rules need to be named. This might seem like a trivial decision, but if there are many rules in the firewall an appropriate name can make it significantly easier to find later. Figure 14.7 shows the naming screen. After entering a name, click the "Finish" button.

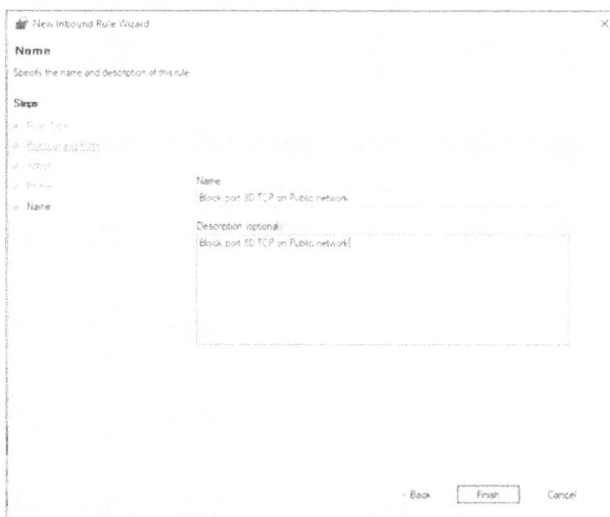

FIGURE 14.7 Naming the new rule

13. After saving the new rule, the screen will list all rules on the server. The pane on the left allows Inbound or Outbound rules to be displayed. Rules can be ordered by any fields in the window. Figure 14.8 shows the listing of all existing rules.

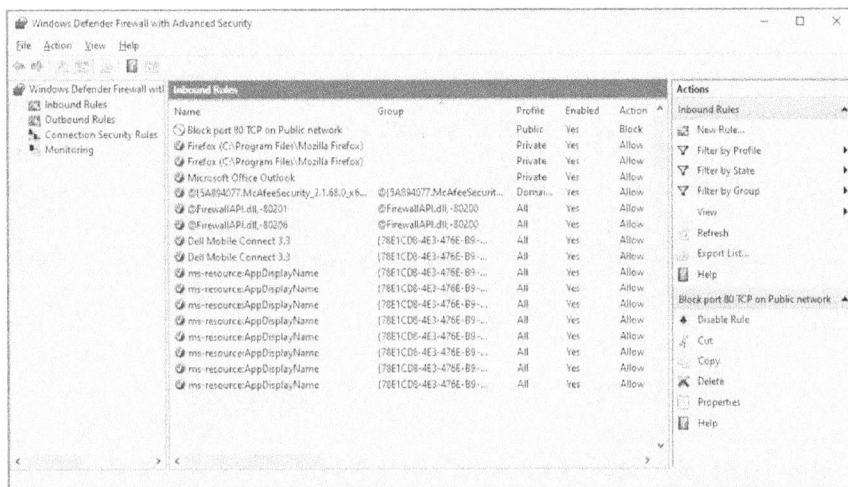

FIGURE 14.8 List of all Inbound Rules

Logs

Firewalls create logs showing the details of how packets were handled, i.e., whether they were accepted or rejected. These logs can be reviewed to detect anomalies or trends. Tools like Splunk®, ELK Stack®, and Graylog® are available to help analyze log entries. Examples of unusual activity could include the following:

- Numerous unsuccessful access attempts from a single IP address or a group of IP addresses. This could indicate an attack. A new firewall rule denying all inbound and outbound traffic from that site(s) should be created.

- A high number of connection attempts to one port from many different IP addresses could indicate another type of attack. Cybercriminals could be probing that port. A new firewall rule denying inbound traffic to it should be created.

▪ Outbound activity at times when no one is using the computer. If this is not related to an automated process like an update, then it could indicate a virus or other malware is exfiltrating data from the computer. It could also be that the computer is part of a DOS (Denial of Service) or DDOS (Distributed Denial of Service) attack.

FIREWALLS DO NOT PROTECT AGAINST ALL THREATS

Firewalls cannot protect computers from all threats. Malware that invades a computer when an email attachment is opened, a dangerous link is clicked, or a password is guessed are examples of threats that firewalls will not protect against. Other threats that firewalls are not designed to foil include the following:

▪ insider attacks
▪ malware loaded from a USB drive
▪ phishing
▪ physical attacks or thefts
▪ social engineering
▪ zero-day threats

FIREWALLS ARE PREINSTALLED ON MOST OPERATING SYSTEMS

Most operating systems include a basic firewall. Some of them are adequate and some are good. The computer user should decide whether the current one should be replaced with a third-party package. A description of operating systems and their preinstalled firewalls are listed here.

Linux

There are many different distributions of Linux, e.g., Debian, Fedora, Red Hat Enterprise, SUSE, and Ubuntu. By default, Linux has an internal firewall, but it needs to be activated for it to protect the site. Linus has good protection because most ports default as closed, but activating the firewall is still recommended.

Mac

MacOS includes a built-in firewall, but the default is for it to be disabled. The MacOS does not have many services listening on ports for connection attempts, so the firewall is not as critical as it is on other computers. Even if a computer is thought to be extremely secure, activating the firewall is always advisable.

Windows

The Windows Defender firewall comes preinstalled on all computers with Windows 10 and 11 operating systems. It's officially called the Windows Defender Firewall with Advanced Security (WFAS). From a user viewpoint, it is important to ensure that it is activated if the user chooses to utilize it. If a third-party firewall is installed on a Windows computer, then Windows Defender Firewall will turn itself off.

DO SMART PHONES NEED FIREWALLS?

A smart phone is just a computer that allows the user to make calls to other phones. Any device, including smart phones, that connect to the Internet need to be protected from cyberattacks. Firewalls can protect smart phones in the same way that they protect other types of computers.

Android

Android phones do not have a built-in firewall. Third-party firewall applications can be purchased and downloaded from the Google Play Store.

iPhones

iPhones are designed to have limited listening ports to minimize the danger of being impacted by attacks. Unnecessary network utilities have been removed to further minimize their "attack surface." Most experts feel that an iPhone does not need to have a third-party firewall installed on them. Users who are extremely concerned about security can improve the protection of their iPhones with Apple's "Lockdown Mode."

Smart Phone Third-party Firewalls

Some examples of vendors that provide firewalls for both Android and iOS phones are listed below. The reader, of course, should do his own research before choosing a firewall application.

- Avast
- Bitdefender
- McAfee
- Norton
- TotalAV

ROUTER FIREWALLS

A router is an electronic device that connects two or more networks and manages the flow of data between them. In a home environment, the router is likely to be positioned between the ISP cable coming into the home and devices like desktop computers. A large percentage of homes routers can be wired to a desktop computer as well as being capable of handling wireless communications with tablets, smart phones, smart TVs, printers, etc.

Most modern routers include a firewall. It will block communications from the Internet that were not initiated from the computer. If the router includes a firewall, it is best to make sure it is active. Details on routers, including how to activate a firewall, are included in Chapter 16 (Home Networks).

THIRD-PARTY FIREWALL PRODUCTS

There are many vendors that sell both hardware and software firewall products. Each individual needs to do their own research before buying and installing any firewall.

Hardware Firewalls

Hardware firewalls for large corporations will not be covered here. The only ones we discuss are those for small to medium businesses and home offices.

- Barracuda Cisco Meraki MX64®
- Fortinet FortiGate 30E®
- Netgate 2100®
- Netgear ProSafe Firewall®
- Palo Alto K2-Series®

Software Firewalls

Some of the most highly rated software firewalls at the time of this writing were as follows:

- Avast Premium Security®
- Bitdefender Total Security®
- Fortinet: Next Generation Firewall (NGFW)®
- Norton 360 Deluxe®
- Sophos Firewall®
- Windows Defender®

FINAL FIREWALL ADVICE

Here are some final tips for maintaining and strengthening firewall protection.

- Change the default passwords for hardware and software firewall accounts. If possible, rename the account so it is not obvious that it has access to the firewall's administration.
- If a third-party firewall is installed, make sure that it is updated regularly. Most software firewalls can be set to receive and automatically install updates.
- A firewall is not a substitute for antivirus (AV) software. Even with a firewall installed, antivirus software is still needed.
- Opening questionable email attachments or clicking on links in email can still allow a virus to be downloaded, even if a firewall has been installed.
- When in doubt, access to a port should be denied.

REFERENCES

[RED21] Jones, Corrin. "Warnings (& Lessons) of the 2013 Target Data Breach," available online at *https://redriver.com/security/target-data-breach*, October 2021

[SEC20] "Equifax Settles 2017 Data Breach for $1.38 Billion," available online at *https://www.securitymagazine.com/articles/91573-equifax-settles-2017-data-breach-for-138-billion*, January 20, 2020

15

MOBILE DEVICES

Mobile devices are generally considered to be smart phones and tablets. They are basically any electronic device that can be easily carried and is able to connect to the Internet.

THE RISKS FOR MOBILE DEVICES

Mobile devices have additional risks beyond the ones associated with laptops and desktop computers. Some of these risks are as follows:

- There are an enormous number of mobile devices. Almost every adult in the US has one: An article by the Pew Research Center found that 97% of Americans owned a smart phone as of 2023 [PEW24]. Since these devices are so prevalent, they are potential targets for cybercriminals.

- Mobile devices, particularly smart phones, are almost always turned on. People very seldom turn them off. Being active all the time enables cybercriminals to threaten them constantly.

- Smart phones contain an enormous amount of personal information about their owners. Examples include photographs, credit card numbers, bank account numbers, passwords, driver's license data, passport data, contacts, text messages, history of Internet searches, airline ticket details, and the locations and times of where the owner has travelled. This list does not include the data collected about users by the applications loaded onto the phone.

- Unlike desktop computers, mobile devices are used in multiple locations. At every coffee shop, hotel lobby, and airport gate, there is a chance that the device will be stolen or eavesdropped on, either visually or electronically.

- Many users do not understand that their smart phone is fundamentally a computer that can make calls and send text messages. Without this understanding, they are more careless than they should be with what is essentially an extremely powerful and very personal computer.

- Users often load applications onto their phones without knowing how much personal data those apps can access and accumulate.

- Users conduct a great deal of business on devices that are not necessarily secure. They log into financial Web sites, send and receive emails with confidential information, and make purchases online. All of these activities could be exposing private data to cybercriminals in the area.

- Mobile phones are frequently connected to Wi-Fi networks, and many of these Wi-Fi networks are not what they purport to be. More information on the dangers of Wi-Fi appears later in this chapter.

- Because they are so small, mobile devices are more likely to get lost, misplaced, or stolen than a desktop or laptop. If a device is lost, then all of the personal information on it could become available to others.

METHODS OF WIRELESS COMMUNICATION

There are many forms of wireless communication systems that a mobile device is capable of using. The most common of them are described here.

- Wi-Fi (Wireless Fidelity) is a wireless networking technology that is frequently used to connect laptops, desktops, smart phones, and tablets to the Internet. Wi-Fi allows people to access the Internet using their smartphones without needing to resort to the data plan provided by their cellular provider.

  Depending on the protocol and frequency being used, the range for a typical home Wi-Fi router is 120 to 400 feet. Signals weaken when traveling through walls and other obstructions. This range can be both useful and challenging. The upside is that it enables the owner to access the Internet from anywhere in the house. The downside is that anyone within range can potentially access it, too.

Dangers associated with public Wi-Fi can be avoided if the user takes the following steps:

- Confirm that the correct network is being accessed. Cybercriminals set up Wi-Fi networks so they can eavesdrop on victims.
- Use a VPN when connecting to a public Wi-Fi.
- Turn off the auto-connect feature on smartphones and tablets.
- Use MFA (Multi-Factor Authentication) when connecting to Web sites that contain personal information.
- Avoid conducting financial transactions over a public Wi-Fi.

- Bluetooth is a wireless technology that is frequently used to pair devices like keyboards, mouse, headphones, ear buds, fitness trackers, and speakers to smartphones. The range for a Bluetooth signal varies, but it is typically limited to about 33 feet or 10 meters.

Some of the dangers associated with Bluetooth communications are as follows:

- Information can be stolen from user devices via Bluetooth.
- Bluetooth connections can be used to secretly listen to conversations.
- Denial of Service (DoS) attacks can be launched using Bluetooth communications.
- If a car is equipped with Bluetooth, it is possible to eavesdrop on conversations taking place in it.

Steps that can be taken to avoid Bluetooth risks include the following:

- Update the device's operating system frequently.
- Make sure that the device's Bluetooth "discoverable" setting is disabled unless it is actually in the process of pairing with a new Bluetooth device.
- Do not pair with a new device in public. When pairing with a new device, like headphones, do this somewhere that cannot be electronically overheard.
- Delete Bluetooth connections for devices that are no longer being used.

- Avoid discussing sensitive information over a Bluetooth connection. While it is not likely that someone may overhear or monitor your conversation, it is still a possibility.

- NFC (Near Field Communication) is a short-range wireless communications technique that works when two devices are brought within a few centimeters of each other. Most modern smart phones support NFC. It is frequently used to make payments, and can also be used for accessing buildings, renting scooters, opening car doors, and navigating municipal transit systems.

  There are dangers of using NFC for transactions, but they are limited. If a cybercriminal positioned their own device next to a consumer's smartphone, it could be possible for him to eavesdrop on this form of communication. It would be theoretically possible for a cybercriminal to have an NFC capable device and brush up against a consumer to steal data or trigger a transaction, but the odds of it happening to any one individual is extremely low.

SMART PHONE ATTACKS

Mobile devices have many of the same cybersecurity risks as traditional computers with a few additional ones unique to the mobile environment. Some of these risks are described here.

Bluetooth

Bluetooth technology was described in an earlier section. It can be abused to gain access to a victim's device and information. It can also be used to eavesdrop on conversations and activity.

Cloning

Cloning, sometimes referred to as SIM swapping, a smart phone occurs when a cybercriminal convinces a network service provider to move a victim's phone number to a new device. To accomplish this social engineering attack the cybercriminal has to know enough information about the victim to impersonate them. Once the number has been assigned to a new phone, the cybercriminal has access to voice messages, texts, photos, and online accounts, including bank accounts and investments.

Signs that a phone has been cloned include the following:

- Receiving text messages asking that the phone be restarted. A restart disconnects the phone from the provider and allows the cloned phone to establish a connection. If an unexpected message requesting that the phone be rebooted is received, ignore the request! Contact the mobile carrier and ask if the phone has to be assigned to a new SIM. If it has, then convince them that you are the true owner and have not requested such a change.
- Unusually high bills for the phone. Any charges or activity fee generated by the cybercriminal will be charged to the existing phone owner.
- All connectivity using the old phone will cease.
- If the old phone was set up with "Find My iPhone" or any other tracking service, the current location will be of the new clone phone.
- Online accounts that the old phone has been associated with may have new passwords preventing the owner from accessing them.

To regain control of a mobile phone that has been cloned the victim needs to do the following:

- Contact the network service provider immediately and explain what happened.
- Change the passwords of all accounts that have been accessed using the phone that was cloned.
- Alert friends and family of the situation so they do not fall for phishing emails from the cybercriminal.
- Perform a factory reset on the device. This can clear any malware that is installed on it.

Default Passwords/Security Codes

Some smart devices, including cell phones, are shipped with default passwords or security codes. These default codes are published on numerous Internet sites. If a user does not change a default password, there is a possibility that a cybercriminal can take advantage of this security flaw.

Jailbreaking

Jailbreaking refers to removing security restrictions built into Apple devices like iPhones. Some owners choose to jailbreak their devices because it gives them greater freedom to customize it and download applications that are not available on the App Store. Another reason for jailbreaking an iPhone is to allow the user to switch network carriers.

Two of the significant dangers associated with jailbreaking an iPhone are greater risks of malware infections and data breaches. It also voids the device's warranty. One last danger is that operating system updates will not be installed automatically on the device.

Malware

Malware is just as significant a threat for smartphones and tablets as it is for PCs and laptops. Examples of malware that mobile device users need to be on the alert for include the following:

- Adware displays ads, some of which lead to malicious Web sites.
- Spyware can gather personal information like banking details, passwords, and Web sites that are visited. This information is then uploaded to a Web site where the cybercriminal can collect it.
- Phishing involves emails, text messages, or appealing links that, if followed, can result in a virus being installed, data being stolen, or ransomware locking up files on the device.
- Smishing is a phishing attack based on SMS (Short Message Service) text messages.
- Trojans are dangerous applications that hide malicious activity.
- Viruses are programs that can damage files, copy data, steal passwords, and other hazardous actions.
- Vishing is a kind of phishing attack that uses voice, i.e., phone calls, to obtain personal information from victims.

QR (Quick Response) Codes

QR codes can be used to visit a Web site or install an application on a mobile device. This type of attack is called *Quishing*, a contraction of "QR" and "phishing."

The danger is that the user does not know whether the Web site or application is malicious or not. There is no way of telling by looking at a QR code whether it is legitimate or dangerous. An analysis by KeepNet found that nearly 2% of scanned QR codes were malicious [KEEP24]. People should only activate QR codes that they have a very high level of confidence are legitimate. QR codes in public places should be avoided.

Social Engineering

Social engineering attacks over the phone can be just as effective as in-person attacks. Specific types of social engineering attacks that use a smart phone include the following:

- Vishing (Voice Phishing): A call, email, or text that appears to come from a legitimate source and requests the victim provide information or take an action that is not in the victim's interest. Frequently, the cybercriminal warns of severe consequences if action is not taken immediately.

- Pretexting: A cybercriminal invents a pretext to persuade the victim to perform an action or give up information that they should not.

Spam Calls

Spam calls are unsolicited calls from unknown parties. They are frequently automated calls informally known as *robocalls*. According to PR Newswire, consumers in the United States received about 3.8 billion robocalls in December of 2023 [PRN24]. Baton Rouge, LA residents had over 38 robocalls per person in December, the most for any US city [PRN24].

The dangers of spam calls and text messages include the following:

- The caller may use social engineering to trick the victim into revealing personal information which can be used for identity theft purposes.

- A spam call or text may attempt to inject malware onto the victim's phone by tricking the victim include clicking on a link or going to a malicious Web site.

- Financial fraud attempts often start with a call or text message from an unknown caller. This type of scam is called *pig butchering*.

- Answering spam calls is a waste of time.

Avoiding Spam Calls

Some ways to avoid spam calls are as follows:

- Do not answer a call unless the caller's number is known. If the call is legitimate, the caller will leave a voice mail that can be listened to later.

- Block or mark unknown numbers as spam.

- Realize that callers can easily disguise their number, so if Caller ID shows your area code that is no guarantee that the call is being made locally.

- Registering with the "Do Not Call Registry" is a positive step, but it is not guaranteed to stop all spam calls.
- Use a call blocking tool like ActiveArmor®, Call Filter®, Scam Shield®, RoboKiller®, or Truecaller® to prevent spam calls from reaching the phone.

Spyware and Stalkerware

Spyware tools are no longer only in the realm of fiction. They are available to the general public at a very low cost. Sometimes the vendor sells these tools as a way for parents to monitor phone usage by their children, but they can be abused by spouses, domestic partners, or employers.

Some of the capabilities of spyware on a mobile phone are as follows:

- tracks the location of the phone
- allows texts to be read
- allows phone calls to be listened in on
- monitors activity on the phone, including every screen viewed and every key clicked
- uses the microphone to listen in on conversations near the phone
- takes photographs of whatever the camera sees at any given time
- reads the calendar on the phone
- accesses the list of contacts on the phone

Signs That a Phone has Spyware

There are a number of signs that malware is running on a mobile device. Some of them are as follows:

- battery life decreases
- higher rate of data usage
- performance is slow or apps take significantly longer to open than normally
- calls or texts sent to numbers that the owner did not contact
- alerts keep popping up
- unusual activity on accounts associated with the phone
- The phone seems warmer or hotter than normal.
- The GPS icon is active when no apps that use it are running.

Third-Party Keyboard Apps

Some users download third-party keyboard apps. These can be easier to use and have more options than standard smartphone keyboards. The danger is they may contain malware. A review of nine vendors' apps performed by the University of Toronto showed that eight had vulnerabilities that could be exploited to track user keystrokes [UNIVT24].

Zero-Click Attacks

A *zero-click attack* is a relatively new attack that allows a cybercriminal to install spyware on iPhones without the user taking any specific action. These attacks are rare and appear to be undertaken by nation-state groups at this time. A successful zero-click installs spyware or other malware on the device. The best defense against this attack is to make sure the device is updated whenever operating systems updates are released.

APPLICATIONS

Smart phone users download and use numerous applications. In 2022, more than 218 billion apps were downloaded to smartphones and tablets [TECH24]. The average smart phone user in 2023 accessed 10 apps every day and 30 apps every month [TECH24].

Apps should only be downloaded from trusted sources. The "gold standard" sources are the Apple Store and Google Play. Both of these sites vet applications before making them available for download. Unfortunately, even this process is not perfect. There have been numerous instances where applications thought to be "safe" did experience problems.

Application Dangers

Applications that are downloaded and installed on mobile devices present a number of dangers.

Some of these dangers are as follows:

- Credential theft: A recent study found malicious Android apps that mimicked well-known vendors like Facebook, Netflix, PayPal, and Snapchat were stealing users' credentials [SC24].

- Data breach or leakage: If the application vendor does not properly handle data, then it can be exposed to the outside world. Examples of data that might be exposed include credit card information, Social Security Numbers, banking details, passwords, and account IDs.

- Malware: Applications that have not been thoroughly vetted can contain malware. Installing such an application on a mobile device can have negative consequences like ransomware, being monitored, and theft of PII.

- Man-in-the-Middle Attacks: Man-in-the-middle attacks occur when a cybercriminal is able to insert himself between the user and Web site the user is accessing. Insecure mobile device applications can allow this type of attack to occur.

- Overprivileged Applications: Applications that request access to more data than they absolutely need are called "overprivileged." An example would be a flashlight application that accesses the mobile device's GPS data or a photo editing application that requests access to the contact list. Neither application requires that data to function. The questions that need to be asked are "Why does the app want to access that data?" and "What is it going to do with the data?"

- Unpatched vulnerabilities: Every application has errors in it. A trustworthy vendor will provide patches for vulnerabilities that are detected in their applications. If patches are not released, then anyone using that app has exposure.

- Weak encryption: Weak encryption of data can occur on both the mobile device and on the application vendor's Web site. Applications that do not properly encrypt user data leave it exposed to cybercriminals.

Protecting Against Application Dangers

The steps that users can take to protect themselves against application dangers are relatively limited. Users must often trust the vendor that wrote the app. Some ways to minimize these dangers are listed here.

- Be extremely cautious of sources that apps are downloaded from. Only download applications from legitimate Web sites.

- Read reviews and evaluations of applications before downloading them. If anyone has posted suspicions about an application, then carefully evaluate whether it is actually needed or not.

- When reviewing the application, pay attention to what is said about the vendor as well. How long has the vendor been in existence? Have any of their other apps had problems? Think twice before downloading applications written by an unknown vendor.

- When installing an application, give it the least possible privileges. Just because an application requests access to the phone's GPS data does not mean that the request has to be approved.

- Even legitimate sources like Apple's App Store and Google Play Apps store have had applications with malware, so always be careful.

HIGH-LEVEL SECURITY CONCERNS

When a cell phone is used, there are dangers at a higher level than the owner's device. While the user has no control over these issues, being aware of them can help the user understand and possibly avoid potential issues. Examples of higher-level security concerns are described here.

Data Erasure

An iPhone can be set to perform a factory reset, i.e., effectively erase all of its data, if the passcode is entered incorrectly 10 consecutive times. This option can be enabled by going to "Settings" then "Face ID & Passcode" and scrolling to the "Erase Data" option. If the phone's data is erased, it can be restored from a backup. If backups are not available, then it will need to be set up again as a new phone.

To prevent brute force passcode attacks on iPhones, there are escalating time delays between attempts to enter the code. There is no delay for the first three attempts, but after that the delays are as listed here:

Attempt Number	Delay
4	1 minute
5	5 minutes
6	15 minutes
7	1 hour
8	3 hours
9	8 hours

Some Android smart phones also have an option like this. Whether it exists depends on the device's manufacturer and the version of Android installed on the phone.

Deciding whether to enable this option is up to the user. It prevents a cyber-criminal from accessing the phone's data, but if the phone has not been backed up, a great deal of data could be lost permanently. Consider the possibilities carefully before setting this option.

Fake Cell Towers

Fake cell towers, also known as Stingrays or IMSI (International Mobile Subscriber Number) catchers, are devices that imitate a cell tower to capture signals from nearby mobile devices. These devices are used both by law enforcement agencies and criminals. They are able to identify who the phone is calling, listen in on cell phone calls, intercept text messages and track the movement of mobile devices.

Determining whether a mobile phone is connected to a fake cell tower is possible, but difficult. Applications are available to do this, but they are not 100% accurate. A signal analyzer is an electronic measuring device that can be used to detect variations in cell towers signals. These variations could be indications that a fake cell tower exists.

The average person's best defense against a fake cell tower is to install a VPN on their mobile devices. This will protect their identity and anonymity. It is advisable to download apps, connect to financial Web sites, perform online shopping and engage in confidential conversations (voice or text) only when connected to a known, secure network.

Malicious Charging Stations (Juice Jacking)

Malicious charging stations, a.k.a. *juice jacking*, is a charging station that is capable of stealing data or installing malware on a mobile device while it is being charged. Setting up a fake charging station or modifying an existing station to allow it to juice jack is not difficult.

Ways to prevent becoming a victim of juice jacking include the following:

- Carry a portable charger so it is not necessary to charge from an unknown device.

- Carry a USB cable and outlet plug so charging can be done directly from a wall outlet.

- Have a USB cable that does not include a data wire. This will prevent cybercriminals from downloading data or uploading malware to the device.

- If prompted to "trust the computer" or accept "sharing data," then unplug the cable and find another charging source.

- Carry a data blocker. This USB based device connects to the USB cable between the outlet and mobile device. It prevents any data transfers across the cable. They can be purchased online for around $10.

Mobile Apps or Mobile Web Sites

To interact with many organizations, consumers have the choice of using a mobile application or a mobile Web site, i.e., a Web site specifically designed to be accessed by a mobile device. Institutions like banks, credit card companies, investment firms, and retail outlets frequently offer both methods of doing business with them. Is either of these methods inherently safer than the other? Is it safer to download an app provided by the bank onto a mobile phone or use the same phone to go to the bank's Web site? Unfortunately, like so many other security-related questions, the answer is different for each user.

To help the reader decide which is best for them, here are some pros and cons of each method.

Mobile Apps Pros

- Users should only download apps from reputable Web sites like the Apple App Store or Google Play. These sites have security measures designed to examine apps on the site and allow ones determined to have no security risks.

- When installing a mobile app, the user general gets to approve its access. For example, the user can prevent the app from accessing the camera, microphone, or location data.

- Mobile apps are more likely to utilize biometric authentication like fingerprints or facial recognition than Web sites.

- Mobile apps generally have better response time than Web sites because the application's software has already been loaded onto the device.

- Mobile apps may offer features not available on an organization's Web site.

Mobile Apps Cons

- The vetting process in mobile app stores is good, but not infallible. Despite this testing, it is possible for mobile apps to contain malicious code. This is relatively rare, but still occurs.

- Mobile apps may attempt to obtain access to data on the phone that is not needed to fulfill their tasks. Device owners must be diligent and careful when granting access to features like the device's camera, microphone, or location data.

- Mobile apps that have not been kept updated can be vulnerable to attacks. It is the responsibility of the device owner to keep the app updated.

Mobile Website Pros

- Mobile Web sites typically have limited or no access to a mobile phone's features like cameras, microphones, and location data.

- Mobile Web sites can be designed to use encryption to protect personal information from being eavesdropped on or stolen.

- The browsers used when connecting to a mobile Web site have extensive security measures built into them. This additional level of security is active for every Web site that the mobile device connects to. Browser security is maximized if the device owner uses a browser that focuses on privacy.

Mobile Website Cons

- Web sites that mimic legitimate sites exist that try to steal consumers' data. Frequently, cybercriminals send potential victims links to these sites.

- Any Web site can potentially display malicious ads designed to infect mobile phones with malware or attempt to steal personal information of the device owner.

- If a public Wi-Fi is used to connect to a mobile Web site it is possible for cybercriminals to steal personal information.

- Not all organizations have optimized their Web sites to run on a mobile device. Web sites that are not designed specifically for mobile devices are not as user-friendly.

- Mobile Web sites have a greater vulnerability of man-in-the-middle attacks than mobile apps have.

- Browsers that have not been kept updated can be vulnerable to attacks. It is the responsibility of the device owner to keep the browser updated.

The security of mobile apps and mobile Web sites are heavily influenced by user actions. The security of each can be acceptable if the user makes good choices. If the user has poor "cyber hygiene," then neither method will be as secure as they should be.

Mobile Phone Thefts

Mobile phones are lost or stolen at an alarming rate. One study estimated that in 2015, a mobile phone was stolen about every 10 seconds in major US cities [OJA15]. The odds of recovering a stolen phone are less than one in three, according to the FCC (Federal Communications Committee) [FCC]. Some steps that can be taken to help maintain a phone's safety are listed here.

- Keep the device updated. Updates frequently include security enhancements.
- Choose a secure PIN, password, or passcode. Easily guessed codes like "123456" will not deter thieves from opening the device.
- Biometrics like fingerprint scans or facial recognition can be used to access mobile devices but be aware that these methods are not infallible.
- If security of the device is imperative, then consider enabling Apple's Lockdown Mode. This mode significantly enhances the device's security.
- Restart your phone regularly; at least once a week is a recommendation made by the National Security Agency [NSA24].
- Enable automatic backups to the cloud service offered by the vendor. If the device is lost, stolen or crashes then its data can be restored to a new device.
- Record the device's serial number and IMEI (International Mobile Equipment Identification) number. If the device is stolen, this will be needed if a police report is filed.
- Enable "Find My Device" or "Find My iPhone" on the device. This can improve the chances of finding it if it is lost or stolen in the future.

Provider Data Breaches

On July 12, 2024, AT&T announced that a data breach exposed call and text records of about 110 million cell phone users [WIRED24]. The exposed data spans the timeframe of May 1, 2022 through October 31, 2022. Having access to it would enable the perpetrators to identify who is talking to whom. Some cell tower identification details were also exposed which would enable perpetrators to have a rough idea of where cell phones were when they made or received calls or sent texts.

This data breach affects not only AT&T users, but also people who subscribed to firms known as mobile virtual network operators (MVNOs) that contracted with AT&T to provide their customers with cell phone service. Examples of potentially affected MVNOs are Consumer Cellular®, Cricket Wireless®, TracFone Wireless®, RedPocket®, and Boost Infinite®.

Retail Tracking

Retailers want to collect data about their customers. They have found a myriad of ways to acquire data about their customers' shopping habits. Some of their methods that involve mobile devices are described here:

- Like other businesses, many retailers have an app that customers can install on their phones to learn about sales, qualify for discounts, and accumulate reward points. If the app was given access to the mobile phone's GPS data, then the retailer knows when a customer is inside or approaching one of their retail outlets.

- Many retailers offer a Wi-Fi network for customers. If a customer connects to the network, then their movement within the store can be tracked.

- Customers carrying mobile devices can be tracked even if they do not connect to the outlet's Wi-Fi using a form of passive tracking. All Wi-Fi enabled devices, i.e., all smart phones, broadcast their MAC (Medium Access Control) addresses regularly. Since MAC addresses are unique, tracker devices in the store can monitor the customer's movements.

- Smart phones and tablets can also be tracked based on their Wi-Fi signal strength. The advantage to the customer is that this method of tracking is more anonymous.

Unsecured Wi-Fi Networks

An unsecured Wi-Fi network is one that does not require a password or authorization to connect with. Examples can be found in public locations like a mall, hotel lobby, coffee shop, restaurant, or airport. Unsecured networks are more likely to attract cybercriminals than secured networks. If it is imperative to connect to an unsecured Wi-Fi network, then a VPN should be used.

BYOD – Bring Your Own Device to Work

BYOD (Bring Your Own Device) - to Work is a policy some organizations have in place that allows employees to use their own electronic devices at work. Some of the advantages of BYOD are as follows:

- cost savings for the organization since the organization does not need to purchase or maintain the devices
- greater productivity because the employee is already familiar with their device
- reduces the number of devices the employee needs to carry

BYOD has disadvantages for both the employee and the organization.

- Will the employee be compensated for providing the device?
- The employee may use applications or online services that are not approved by the organization's IT department such as video conferencing, file storage services, collaboration tools, personal email, and file transfer services. This can make the organization's data more vulnerable.
- What control should the organization have over an employee's device?
- If the employee leaves the organization, how does it guarantee that all its data has been removed from the device?

Finding a Lost Mobile Device

Steps that can be taken to find a lost mobile device are as follows:

- Call the device and listen carefully for its ringing.
- Use iPhone's "Find my iPhone' or Android's "Find My Device" capability from another device to locate the missing mobile phone or tablet. This can only be done if the phone's "find" feature was enabled in advance.
- The mobile carrier might be able to provide the last approximate location of the device before it was turned off or the battery died.
- There are third-party applications that claim they can locate lost or stolen mobile phones. Examples of products like this are Lookout Mobile Security®, Prey®, and CrookCatcher®. These apps, like any others, should be fully researched before installing them on a device.
- Sending a text to the device offering a reward to the finder is one way of finding it. The odds of it succeeding are small, but it is worth trying.

Mobile Payments

Many people are now using mobile devices to make payments. In 2022, global payments in the US were $942 billion [YAHOO24], and the projected amount for 2023 is $2.9 trillion. These statistics may be good news for merchants and the economy, but mobile payments introduce an element of risk for the consumer. The most significant risks are as follows:

- The loss of a mobile phone can result in loss of personal data, fraudulent charges, and other costs to the consumer.
- Data breaches: Every merchant that allows mobile payments stores data about its clients. If that merchant's system is breached details like credit card numbers, bank account numbers, passwords, and PII could be exposed.
- Mobile payments that the consumer claims he did not make, i.e., disputed transactions, can be frustrating and take time to resolve.
- Consumers can be misled and scammed by phishing and social engineering attacks while trying to make payments.

Metadata

Metadata is data about data. Mobile phones contain significant metadata that scammers, merchants, application vendors, and others would like to access. If a device's metadata is breached, the cybercriminal can compile a complete picture of the victim's life. Examples of mobile device metadata include the following:

- Phone calls: Phone metadata includes the numbers that were called, duration of each call, location of the mobile device when each call was made.
- Text messages: Texting metadata includes who texts are sent to, how long the messages are, what times they were sent, and how many times texts are sent to each individual.
- Photographs: Digital photograph metadata potentially includes the type of mobile device that took the photograph, number of pixels in the photo, location where each photo was taken, date and time of each photo, and whether the photograph was edited.
- Social media apps: Social media apps maintain metadata that includes geotagging information. Anyone privy to that data can determine where the user was when a post was made. Other metadata social media apps may store age, gender, what pages a user has viewed or created, and causes supported by the user.
- Browsing: Metadata about Web browsing includes the sites visited.

Mobile Hot Spots

Most, if not all, mobile phones can be used as a mobile hot spot to enable a laptop or tablet to connect to the Internet. The smart phone effectively becomes a personal Wi-Fi network. While this can be a convenient solution for a short-term need it has its drawbacks. Some of the risks are as follows:

- Data can be used at a rate high enough to consume all of the mobile phone's data plan. This can result in unexpected charges on the next bill.
- While acting as a hot spot, the mobile phone's battery is likely drain significantly faster than normal. If it is used as a hot spot for a significant length of time, be prepared to plug the mobile phone into a charger.
- If the connection is not secured properly, a cybercriminal could use a packet sniffer to eavesdrop on the connection between the mobile phone and the Internet or between the mobile phone and the tethered device, i.e., the laptop or tablet, connects to the mobile phone.
- When a hot spot is created, it has an SSID (Service Set Identifier), which is that name of the network that has just been created. The SSID should be changed to a name that is unique and not easily associated with the mobile phone.
- The mobile phone being used should have antivirus software installed on it. Ensure that this is current before using the device as a hot spot.

REMOTELY WIPING A MOBILE PHONE

If a mobile device has been irretrievably lost or stolen, the owner may decide to remotely *wipe* the device instead of allowing a cybercriminal to access its data. Deciding to remotely wipe the device is a difficult decision. If the device was misplaced instead of stolen, then wiping it will be inconvenient or even result in the permanent loss of data. If the decision to wipe is delayed, it could give a cybercriminal more time to break into the device.

Be aware that if a device is wiped, the process cannot be undone. If the stolen phone is later recovered, a restore, potentially from the vendor's cloud backup site, would be needed to restore it to its pre-wiped condition. A restore operation, again potentially from the cloud backup site, could be used to make a replacement phone look like the missing phone before it was wiped. This is a reason to back up the device regularly.

Things to keep in mind when planning to perform a remote wipe are as follows:

- The mobile phone or tablet has to be turned on and connected to a network to receive the wipe command. If the thief powered it down or is preventing it from connecting to the Internet, then a remote wipe cannot be initiated.

- An Apple iPhone can be set to erase all data if the passcode is incorrectly entered ten times. Obviously the "Erase Data" setting must be enabled in advance. After an iPhone has been stolen, it is too late to change this setting.

STEPS TO TAKE IF MOBILE PHONE IS LOST OR STOLEN

If a mobile device is missing, then the first step would be to try and find it. Tips for finding a phone are provided in section "Finding a Lost Mobile Device." If the phone cannot be found and is presumed to be stolen, the following steps should be taken as quickly as possible:

- If the mobile phone is an iPhone, then it can be marked as lost in two ways.

    1. The first is to go to *iCloud.com/find*. Select the iPhone or iPad. Select "Mark As Lost" and follow instructions to leave a phone number and message. The device will be locked.

    2. If the device belongs to a "Family Sharing" group, the "Find My" feature can be used from another iPhone or iPad in that group. Go to the "Find My" screen, select the device, and click the "Mark as Lost" button. The device will be locked with a passcode. Payment cards and passes used with Apply Pay are suspended once the device is locked.

- If the stolen device is an Android phone, sign into *google.com/android/find* to lock the device remotely.

- Change the password used to log onto the device. This can be done by logging into the vendor's Web site, e.g., *appleid.apple.com* or *google.com/android/find*.

- Change the passwords of any online accounts that were stored on the device.

- Call the service provider and report the device as missing. They can disable the SIM card so the account cannot access any networks or data services.

- If the device was used for online banking, then call the bank to prevent account access from that device.

- Shut down any phone wallets, e.g., Apply Pay or Google Pay, associated with the device.

- Alert friends and family that the phone has been lost so they do not fall victim to phishing scams using it.

- If the device is covered by insurance, e.g., AppleCare+ or Samsung Care, then notify the provider. The sooner they are notified, the sooner a payment can be made.

- File a report with local law enforcement. The chances of it being found by law enforcement are small, but it is worth submitting a report that includes the serial number and IMEA (International Mobile Equipment Identity) number. This step may be required by the insurance provider.

TRAVELING WITH MOBILE DEVICES

Traveling with mobile devices introduces a number of potential security risks including the ones described here.

- Will the device function when being used in a foreign country? Will a new SIM card be needed? Make sure these questions are answered before leaving on the trip.

- Mobile devices can be searched for by border control agents. Some countries have numerous restrictions on encryption tools. A laptop or smartphone that contains encryption might be confiscated at the border.

- The potential exists for mobile devices to be subjected to additional malware and automated attack tools in some countries.

- If a mobile device is lost, stolen, or confiscated while traveling, the chances of it being recovered are extremely low. The device should be remotely wiped to avoid any confidential information from being disclosed.

- Communication networks, including Wi-Fi, are regularly monitored in some countries. Be extremely careful when using Wi-Fi networks. If using it is unavoidable, employ a VPN to improve security.

Some suggestions for protecting mobile device while traveling include the following:

- Make sure that all devices have the latest patches installed on them.
- Remove all personal or proprietary information before traveling abroad.
- When traveling to authoritarian countries, it is best to leave personal mobile devices at home and bring a temporary device.
- Always maintain physical control of mobile devices. Never leave them in a hotel room.
- Scan the device for malware once the trip is completed. Consider completely wiping any devices taken abroad and reload the software from scratch.
- Change any account passwords that were used while traveling as soon as the trip is over.

VPNs

Virtual Private Networks were described in Chapter 13. The emphasis was on desktop and laptop devices, but VPNs provide the same privacy and anonymity for mobile devices that they provide for other devices.

WI-FI CONNECTIONS

Be wary of public Wi-Fi networks. An "Evil Twin" site, a.k.a. a fake public Wi-Fi network, can have the same SSID, i.e., name, as a legitimate Wi-Fi network. It is set up by a cybercriminal with better signal strength than that of the real network, hoping that inattentive users will connect to it. This relatively simple scam can allow cybercriminals to monitor all of the victim's traffic as well as harvest credentials and install malware on their mobile devices.

Users can defend against these sites in the following ways:

- Use a VPN.
- Ensure they are connecting to a legitimate Wi-Fi network. If there is any confusion about the name of the legitimate site, then ask someone at the hotel or coffee shop.
- Avoid conducting confidential transactions on a public Wi-Fi network.
- If confidential transactions absolutely must be conducted on a public Wi-Fi network, then change the account's password as soon as possible afterwards.

SAFE MOBILE PRACTICES

- Keep applications updated.
- Enable location tracking via Apple's "Find My" or Android's "Find My Device."
- Set the device to "lock" when it is not actively being used. This can help prevent a thief from accessing the data on it.
- Do not allow mobile devices to automatically join an unfamiliar network.
- Disable automatic Bluetooth pairing when not using it.
- Keep Wi-Fi turned off in unfamiliar locations, e.g., airports, hotels, and convention centers.
- Only download applications from official sites, never from within a browser.
- Do not send confidential information over a Wi-Fi network that you are not convinced is secure.
- Research the vendor or developers before downloading any applications.
- Carefully consider the permissions or privileges being applications, especially new ones.
- Do not set services to "auto-login." It is convenient, but insecure if your device is lost or stolen.
- Periodically delete your browsing history, cookies, and cache.
- Periodically review applications loaded on the device and remove any that are no longer needed.
- Disable GPS location capabilities when not being used.
- Power the device down and restart it on a weekly basis.
- Record the device's serial number and IMEI (International Mobile Equipment Identification) number.
- If the phone service provided allows it, then set a PIN for their SIM card. This can help prevent SIM swapping attacks.
- Keep the mobile device close to you. Be careful not to set it down in a place where it can be stolen. Law enforcement officials say that pickpockets can easily remove a mobile phone that is in the victim's back pocket.

REPLACING MOBILE DEVICES

Eventually every mobile device will need to be replaced. When in use, mobile devices accumulate an enormous amount of information about their owners. To prevent that personal information from being available to a cybercriminal or the next owner, the device needs to have everything erased from it.

Before trading in or throwing away an electronic device, the following steps should be taken.

1. Create a full backup of the device. If the backup is made to the vendor's site or a cloud storage provider, it will be easier to load data onto a replacement device.

2. Remove any credit cards associated with a wallet, Apple Pay, or Google Play Store app.

3. Unpair the phone with any devices it is paired with, e.g., a Fitbit, Apple Watch, headphones, or ear buds.

4. Log out of the Google or Apple account.

5. Delete all the applications that have been downloaded onto the phone.

6. Download a wiping application and run it on the device.

7. Perform a factory reset of the device. This should erase everything in the device's storage.

8. Remove the SIM card from the mobile phone. It can be reused on the new phone or destroyed and thrown away.

REFERENCES

[FCC] "Phone Theft in America," available online at *https://transition.fcc.gov/cgb/events/Lookout-phone-theft-in-america.pdf*, March 2014

[KEEP24] "2024 QR Code Phishing Trends: In-Dept Analysis of Rising Quishing Statistics," available online at *https://keepnetlabs.com/blog/2024-qr-code-phishing-trends-in-depth-analysis-of-rising-quishing-statistics*, January 15, 2024

[NSA24] "Mobile Device Best Practices," available online at *https://media.defense.gov/2021/Sep/16/2002855921/-1/-1/0/MOBILE_DEVICE_BEST_PRACTICES_FINAL_V3%20-%20COPY.PDF*, October 2020

[PRN24] "US Consumers Received Just Under 3.8 Billion Robocalls in December," available online at *https://www.prnewswire.com/news-releases/us-consumers-received-just-under-3-8-billion-robocalls-in-december-according-to-youmail-robocall-index-302029930.html*, Jan 9, 2024

[OJA15] "Wiped, Flashed, and Rekitted: The International Black Market of Stolen Cell Phones," available online at *https://awards.journalists.org/entries/wiped-flashed-rekitted-international-black-market-stolen-cell-phones/*, 2015

[PEW24] Pew Research Center, "Mobile Fact Sheet," available online at *https://www.pewresearch.org/internet/fact-sheet/mobile/*, January 31, 2024

[SC24] SC Staff. "Fake popular Android app versions found stealing credentials," available online at *https://www.scworld.com/brief/fake-popular-android-app-versions-found-stealing-credentials*, May 13, 2024

[TECH24] Laborde, Susan. "Mobile App Download Statistics Everyone Should Know in 2023," available online at *https://techreport.com/statistics/software-web/mobile-app-download-statistics/*, May 28, 2024

[UNIVT24] Knockel, Jeffrey. "The not-so-silent type: Vulnerabilities across keyboard apps reveal keystrokes to network eavesdroppers," available online at *https://citizenlab.ca/2024/04/vulnerabilities-across-keyboard-apps-reveal-keystrokes-to-network-eavesdroppers/*, April 23, 2024

[WIRED24] Newman, Lily Hay. "The Sweeping Danger of the AT&T Phone Records Breach," available online at *https://www.wired.com/story/att-phone-records-breach-110-million/*, July 12, 2024

[YAHOO24] Spherical Insights, LLP. "Global Mobile Payments Market Size to Worth USD 2983.9 Billion By 2032," available online at *https://finance.yahoo.com/news/global-mobile-payments-market-size-150000123.html*, January 30, 2024

16

HOME NETWORKS

If most people were asked to describe their home computer network, the reply would be "What network? I do not have a network." Most people *do* have a home network, and they should carefully consider its security.

Typical Devices on a Home Wi-Fi Network

The variety and number of devices on a home network can be significant. In 2024, the average American household had 17 Internet connected devices according to Parks Associates, a market research and consulting company [BROAD24]. The number of home Wi-Fi enabled devices in the home is projected to triple by 2030, according to Strategy Analytics [FORB24].

The following list of common devices found on home networks is extensive, but not all inclusive.

- desktops
- laptops
- tablets
- smart phones
- intelligent assistants like Siri or Alexia
- printers
- security cameras
- doorbell cameras

- baby monitors
- security systems
- HVAC systems
- large appliances like refrigerators, washing machines, and microwaves
- smart TVs
- smart speakers
- streaming devices like Roku boxes
- gaming consoles

HOME NETWORK TERMS

Some of the terms that are used when describing networks are explained here.

- Access point: connects wireless endpoint devices like laptops and tables to the network by sending and receiving signals to them
- LAN (Local Area Network): a group of computers and other devices connected together within a distinct area like an office
- Modem: translates digital signals from the Internet Service Provider (ISP) so they can be used by local devices in a home
- Router: A router provides access to the ISP's Internet connection to all devices in the home network. Many or most home networks include a wireless router.
- VPN (Virtual Private Network): an encrypted, digital connection between a device and the Internet. Some routers provide VPN functionality for the home network. An alternative is to load a VPN product on a computer or smart phone.
- Wi-Fi (Wireless Fidelity): a brand name created by the Wireless Ethernet Compatibility Alliance, now known as the Wi-Fi Alliance. A home Wi-Fi network allows multiple devices to share an Internet connection without stringing wires to each device.
- Wi-Fi Extender: A device that connects to the existing Wi-Fi network and rebroadcasts the signal so it reaches additional parts of the home. They can be as simple as a small box that is plugged into an electrical outlet.
- Wi-Fi router: a device that combines the functionality of a router with a wireless access point; also called a *wireless router*. Wireless routers are extremely common in homes and small businesses.

▦ SSID (Service Set Identifier): the name of a wireless access point. When setting up a wireless router, the owner will have the option of choosing the SSID name.

ROUTER

A router is a device that connects networks, e.g., an ISP's network and a home network. Most home networks contain a modem and a router. The modem is often provided by the ISP (Internet Service Provider) and is connected to the cable that enters the house or apartment. The router is connected to the modem by an Ethernet cable. Most routers found on home networks are capable of handling Wi-Fi communications.

The number of devices that can connect to a router depends on the make and model of the router, but the theoretical limit is about 250. It also depends on how active the devices are. A mobile phone generates more network activity than a smart thermostat or light bulb does. In practice, most routers can handle up to 40 devices. If a home network has significantly more devices than that, then a Wi-Fi router that supports multiple frequencies (bands) should be considered. Another option be to install a route that allows separate SIDs for the 2.4 GHz (Gigahertz) and 5 GHz frequencies. This would essentially create two separate networks. A final option would be to create a guest network and have some of the wireless devices connect to it. Most wireless routers will support a guest network.

WIRED VS. WIRELESS

The first decision made when setting up or understanding a home network is whether it is wired or wireless. Home networks can be wired, wireless, or a combination of the two. Each setup has distinct advantages and disadvantages. The major points are listed here.

Wired Advantages

▦ Wired connections can be up to ten times faster than wireless, although new variations of the IEEE 801.11 protocol are becoming faster.

▦ more secure than wireless

▦ It still needs a router, but it does not have to be a wireless router.

Wired Disadvantages

- Inflexible. Adding a new location for a desktop computer or moving an existing location requires adding or moving cables. An electrician might be needed to add the new cabling.
- Mobile devices like laptops, smartphones, and tablets cannot easily connect to a wired network.

Wireless Advantages

- There is no need to drill holes in walls or pull cables to add a new location.
- Flexible. Users can walk around the house with a laptop, smart phone, or tablet and never lose connectivity.
- Wireless repeaters can be used to extend the reach.

Wireless Disadvantages

- Slower than a wired network, but improvements are closing this gap.
- Requires a wireless router. These have become common and are more affordable than in the past.
- Coverage can vary depending on the size, shape, and construction materials of the building. This can be overcome with a Wi-Fi extender.
- Broadcast range can extend outside of the home and/or property. The range indoors can be up to 300 feet, and the outdoor range can be 1,000 feet. Either range could allow neighbors or cybercriminals to see and potentially access the network.

Hybrid Network

A hybrid home network can be set up that combines the benefits of both types. Most wireless routers are also capable of connecting to devices by cable. Desktop computers that are not likely to be moved can be connected by cable to the router to take advantage of the higher speed. Other devices, including laptops and tablets, can be connected wirelessly with the router to utilize the flexibility aspect. For many homes, this is a good choice.

SSID (SERVICE SET IDENTIFIER)

An SSID is the name assigned to a Wi-Fi network. This name is broadcast, and any device capable of receiving Wi-Fi signals will list it as a possible network to connect to. Figure 16.1 shows the list of SSIDs that an iPhone has identified.

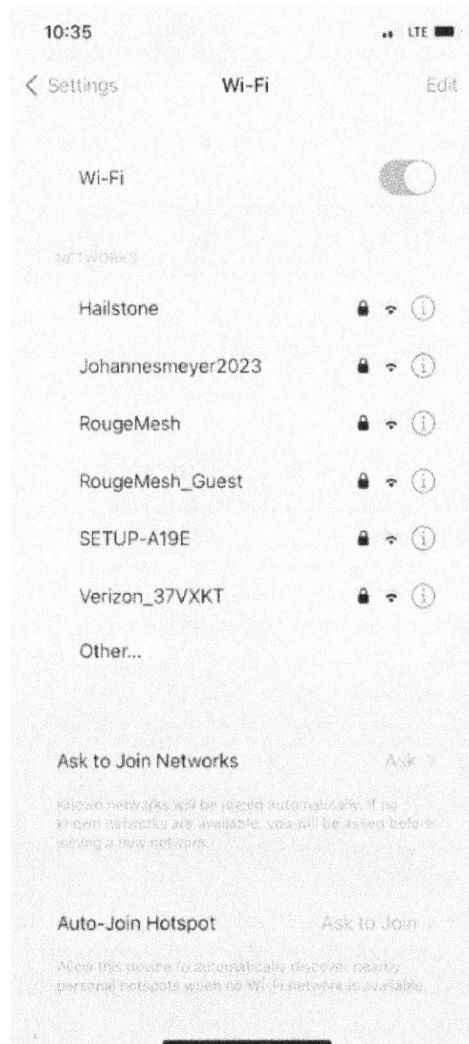

FIGURE 16.1 List of SSIDs

When setting up a wireless router, the owner can keep a default SSID value or create a new value. Keeping the default can provide a cybercriminal with clues about the model and manufacturer of the device. If the make and model are known, then cybercriminals might be able to identify vulnerabilities that the device has.

It is best to choose a new value, but it is also important not to use values that are personally identifiable. Do not use a first or last name as the SSID. Pick a name such that someone wardriving would not be able to recognize who it belongs to.

It is possible to disable SSID broadcasting so it is essentially silent. A Wi-Fi network with a silent or hidden SSID will not appear in a list of wireless networks detected by smart phones, tablets, laptops, or desktops. A potential user would need to know its exact name and enter it instead of simply picking it out of a list. This is likely to stop a neighbor from logging onto a network, but it will not deter a skilled cybercriminal from finding it. A cybercriminal will still be able to "see" a hidden SSID by using a network sniffing tool.

Wi-Fi Network Attacks

Wi-Fi networks can be attacked by cybercriminals to gain entry to networks they should not be able to access. Some of the most common attack types include the following.

- Routers, like software, and other devices have vulnerabilities. Vendors periodically release firmware updates to address potential problems. If the network's owner does not apply the available patches, then the device can be vulnerable to attack.

- Default or weak passwords can easily be guessed by cybercriminals. When setting up a Wi-Fi network, be sure to create strong passwords. If a cybercriminal is able to log onto the network or log in as the router's administrator account, then he can capture passwords, steal data, or install malware on the network.

- Encryption cracking is an attack against the encryption protocol used by the Wi-Fi network. The WEP protocol is no longer secure and should not be used. The WP2 protocol is considered to be secure. WP3 is more secure than WP2 and should be used if it is available.

- *Wi-Fi jamming* is when cybercriminal overwhelms a Wi-Fi network with traffic to prevent legitimate users from accessing it.

▣ Wardriving, also called *access point mapping*, is when cybercriminals literally drive around a location searching for vulnerable Wi-Fi networks. If they are able to log into a vulnerable network with their laptop they will attempt to steal sensitive information like financial data. Wardriving is not as critical a threat as it used to be since the more secure WPA protocol has replaced WEP.

INSTALLING VPNS ON ROUTERS

Chapter 13 describes how a VPN (Virtual Private Network) can be installed on an endpoint device like a desktop, laptop, or smart phone to protect it. The same concept can be applied to protect a router. The advantage of installing a VPN on a router is that not only is the router protected, but so are all the devices that connect to it. Essentially, the VPN provides protection to every device connected to the home network.

Not all routers can have a VPN installed on them. The steps to install a VPN differ based on the router's manufacturer. If this is a process that appeals to the reader, then research will have to be done to confirm that the current router is capable of this. An alternative is that routers are available that already have a VPN built into them. Purchasing a router that has a VPN might be easier than retrofitting an existing router with a VPN.

WI-FI SECURITY

Wi-Fi has security protocols that can be used by the router and the connecting device to encrypt the communications. If the communications were not encrypted, then anyone could eavesdrop on them and be able to capture account IDs, passwords, and other confidential information. The current protocols are WEP and two versions of WPA.

▣ Wired Equivalency Privacy (WEP) is considered obsolete. It should not be used by a router on any network

▣ Wi-Fi Protected Access (WPA): WPA2 is significantly more secure than WEP. WPA3 is more secure than WPA2 and should be selected, if available.

Another step that can be taken to enhance security is *MAC* (Media Access Control) *address filtering*. Every device that connects to the Internet has a unique MAC address. The router's administration can enter a list of MAC addresses into the router. From that point onwards the router will only communicate with devices with those MAC addresses.

MAC whitelisting is a security improvement, but it is not a perfect solution. If cybercriminals can learn what MAC addresses are on the accepted list, they can spoof communication packets so their devices have an accepted MAC address.

WI-FI 802.11 STANDARD

Anyone working with Wi-Fi long enough will eventually see references to IEEE standard 802.11. This refers to a set of frequency standards developed by the IEEE (Institute of Electrical and Electronics Engineers) to make wireless communications in home and office situations possible: 802 is the committee and 11 is the working group within the committee that develops these standards.

Sets of wireless standards have one or two letters appended to 802.11. The specifications that are currently are as follows:

- 802.11g defines transmissions in the 2.4 GHz band.
- 802.11n a.k.a. Wi-Fi4 this boosts the transfer rates in the 2.4 GHz band.
- 802.11ac maximizes transmission rates in the 5 GHz band.
- 802.11ax a.k.a. Wf-Fi6 this deals with both the 2.4 and 5 GHz band and can optionally use the 6 GHz band.

ROUTER ADMINISTRATOR ACCOUNT

To set up or make changes to a router, the user has to log into it using an administrator account.

Some of the tasks that can be performed on the router's admin screens are listed here.

- View router setup details like addresses of the MAC, IP, DNS, and Gateway.
- Confirm SSID, guest network SSID (if it exists), and their passwords.
- Make the SSID visible or hidden.
- Select the security protocol being used.
- Monitor the router's performance.
- Establish parental controls for the router.

- Identify devices that are currently connected to the router.
- Blacklist MAC addresses, i.e., prevent them from connecting to the router.
- Identify if virtual assistants like Alexa or Siri are connected to the router.
- Set the time zone of the router as well as Daylight Saving Time settings.
- Run and review diagnostics for the router.
- Determine if the router's firmware is up to date and perform an upgrade if it is needed.
- Create a backup of the device and restore it from an existing backup file.
- Schedule automatic reboots for the router.
- Set a new password for the router's administrator account.
- View and purge entries in the router's log.
- Initiate traffic statistics logging and review collected statistics.
- Review packet details in the event of a DoS (Denial of Service) attack.

Logging Onto the Router's Admin Page

The following descriptions apply to the TP-Link brand of router. Other brands and models of routers will have similar functionality, but the items may have slightly different names, labels, or locations.

To log onto the router's admin page, open a browser session, and enter the IP address provided in its documentation. The URL address is likely to be 192.168.0.1 or 192.168.1.1. If the documentation is not available, there is frequently a sticker on the back or bottom of the router with this information. This sticker may also list the default username, likely "Admin," and default password.

On the logon page, enter the current password. This will be the default password if it has not been changed or the new password set up during the installation. If the default password is still being used, it should be changed to increase security of the router.

SSID and Guest SSID Values

A series of screens with administrator details are available. On the "Status" page and the "Advanced" tab, the SSID (Service Set Identifier) value and guest network SSID values will be displayed. The SSID is the name by which this wireless network is known. If no guest network has been defined, this value will be blank.

Encryption Protocol

On the page labeled "Wireless" and the tab named "Wireless Settings," settings like the admin account password and encryption settings are displayed. Perhaps the most important setting on this screen is the encryption protocol that is being used. If WEP is listed as a protocol option, it should not be used because it is no longer considered secure. Currently, WPA2 and WPA3 are the most secure protocols. Choose one of these, assuming the router supports them.

Guest Networks

Most wireless routers will support a guest network. This is the network that guests and IoT devices should connect to. If the router supports this, there should be an administrator screen for defining the guest network. The most important fields are its name, password, and the encryption protocol.

Firmware Updates

Like all software, the router's firmware can be updated by the vendor. In many cases, the updates are security related so if an update becomes available, it should be installed. The administrator admin page for the router should include a screen for handling firmware upgrades. On a TP-Link router, this screen can be reached by selecting the "System Tools" page.

To determine whether an upgrade is needed or not, click the "Check for upgrade" button. If "Your firmware is up to date" is displayed, then nothing more needs to be done. If an upgrade is available, then it should be downloaded and installed. The steps to accomplish this differ for each router manufacturer so consult the documentation that came with the device or the maker's Web site.

ROUTER MAINTENANCE

Some tips for keeping a Wi-Fi router up to date are listed here.

- Check every three to six months to see if the router's firmware needs to be updated. Firmware updates include security patches as well as enable the router to work with new software and hardware.
- Rebooting a router regularly helps its performance. A reboot clears the memory cache and can remove malicious code installed by malware. Rebooting every month should be sufficient for most homes. Simply

unplugging the router, waiting a few seconds, and plugging it back in will reboot it. Most routers can be configured to perform reboots automatically at a chosen interval on the administrator Web page.

▪ Experts recommend that routers be replaced every three to five years. Reasons for replacing it include the following:

   • Like all electronic items, routers eventually degrade and fail. This is more likely to occur if it gets poor ventilation and overheats.

   • A new router is almost certain to be faster than the current one. If the Internet seems slower, streaming movies are buffering too frequently, or video games are lagging, then an aging router might be the cause.

   • Newer routers are typically more secure because they support the latest security protocols.

USERS ON THE NETWORK

Another reason a network might be running slower than normal is when an unauthorized person is on it. If someone else is using the Wi-Fi network to watch movies, browse the Web, or play online games, then legitimate users might see a slowdown. It is illegal to steal Wi-Fi access, but the odds of this crime being prosecuted are small. It is better to identify the thief's connection and shut down his access.

Monitoring Connections

There are several ways to see how many connections a router is servicing and find out exactly who is logged into it.

▪ Monitor who is connecting to the Wi-Fi by examining the router's administrator page. Each router's administrator page will be different, but for the TP-Link routers, a list of connections is on the "Status" page and the "Advanced" tab. The list of connections here is called "Wireless Clients," but it might be called "Connected Devices," "Attached Devices," "Wireless Clients," or a similar name on other routers. Make a list of the MAC address of every connected device.

If the connection's details are not displayed, try clicking a right-arrow or ellipses next to a device. Figure 16.2 shows the IP and MAC addresses displayed for a device.

Wireless Clients   Host | Guest

Wireless Clients

IP Address: 192.168.0.146

MAC Address: E6-AB-4C-12-7B-12

Connection Type: 5G

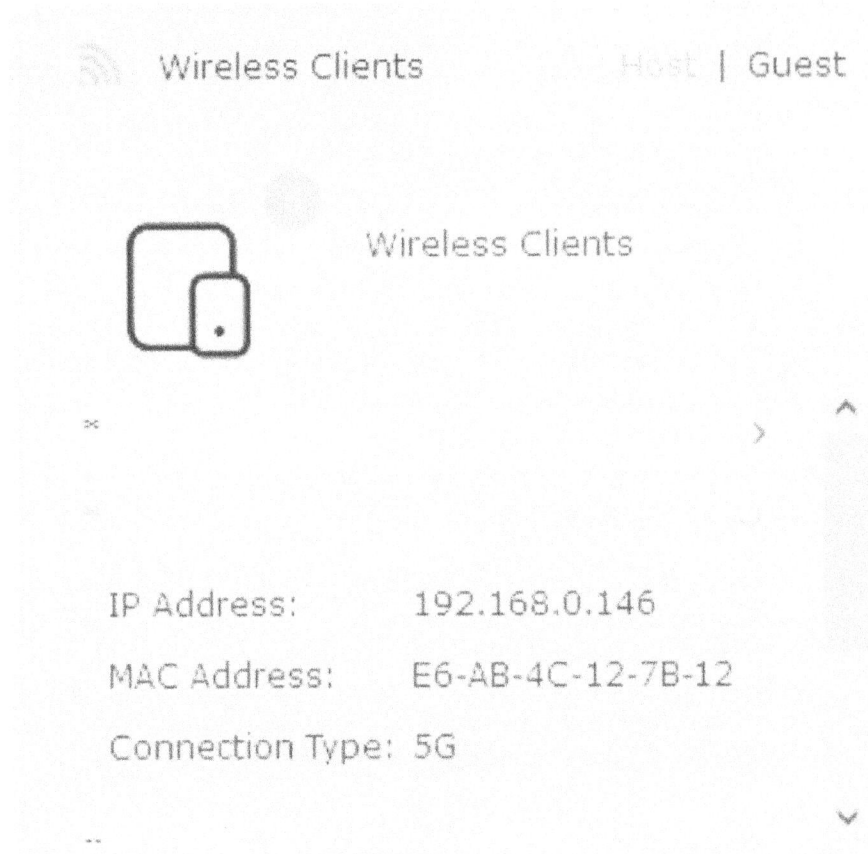

FIGURE 16.2 Searching for a device manufacturer

Obtain the MAC addresses of known devices like smart phones, desktops, laptops, and smart appliances from them. In most cases, this information will be available under a "Settings" screen. Known devices can be removed from the list. If some devices cannot be identified, try visiting the Web site *https:// ipchecktool.com* and entering the MAC address into it. It should identifier the device's manufacturer. The author could not identify a device and used this Web site to learn that the device was a Samsung Smart TV. See Figure 16.3 for a screenshot of this Web page. Any devices that cannot be identified likely belong to an intruder.

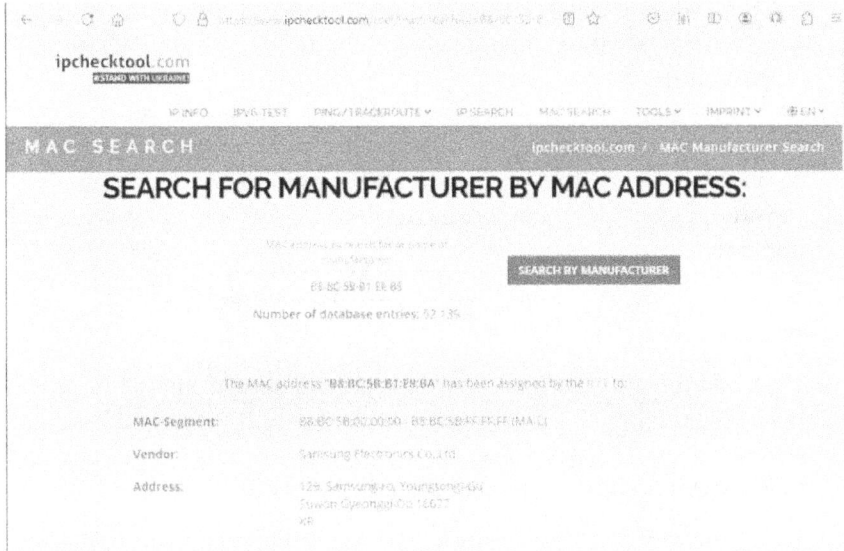

FIGURE 16.3 Searching for a device manufacturer

▓ There are third-party applications that can be loaded on desktop computers or mobile devices that identify devices connected to a wireless network. Examples of this type of tool includes Wireless Network Watcher®, GlassWire®, and Fing®. They can be installed on a smart phone, laptop, or desktop.

Preventing Wi-Fi Theft

Some of the steps that can be taken to kick Wi-Fi freeloaders off the network are as follows:

▓ Change the Wi-Fi network password(s).

▓ Change the network's SSID.

▓ Use a stronger encryption protocol. If WEP is being used, then upgrade to WPA2 or WPA3.

▓ Every device that connects to the Internet has a unique MAC address. Some routers allow the administrator to add MAC filtering so only known devices can connect to the Wi-Fi network. This will be different for every router manufacturer, but the basic elements are to list either the MAC addresses of devices allowed on the network (the *whitelist*) or list MAC addresses of devices that are not allowed on the network (the *blacklist*). For the TP-Link brand wireless router, this functionality is under the "Security" tab.

If freeloaders or cybercriminals connect to the network once, it can happen again. Plan to monitor wireless connections to the network regularly to detect unwanted guests. Repeat the above steps every time a new outsider makes an appearance.

Guest Network

Best practice dictates that very few people should know the admin account password on the router. A "guest" network can be created for other users and their devices. If visitors request wireless access, it is best to give them access to the guest account instead of the admin account.

Being restricted to the guest network should also apply to IoT devices. There is no need for a smart television or thermostat to have access to the admin account. Giving out that access too freely might result in the device being accessed by a cybercriminal.

MEASURES TO PROTECT A WI-FI NETWORK

- Change the default administrator password to a strong password. If possible, change the account name from "Admin" to a more generic name.
- Create a "Guest" network for guest and IoT devices.
- Change passwords periodically, especially if they are given out to numerous people.
- Update the router's firmware whenever a new version is released. Check on this every three to six months.
- Change the SSID name from the default to a generic name. It should not allow cybercriminals to identify the owner or physical location.
- Turn off the Wi-Fi network if it is not going to be used for an extended period of time.
- Use the most secure protocol that is available (WPA2 at a minimum).
- If the router has a hardware firewall, make sure it is enabled.
- Periodically monitor network activity for unwanted users. Take steps to remove them and prevent them from coming back.

REFERENCES

[BROAD24] Clover, Julian. "Average number of connected devices in US Internet households reaches 17," available online at *https://www.broadbandtvnews.com/2024/01/12/average-number-of-connected-devices-in-us-internet-households-reaches-17/,* January 12, 2024

[FORB24] De Nil, Michael. "How Next-Generation Wi-Fi Will Transform the Smart Home," available online at *https://www.forbes.com/sites/forbestechcouncil/2023/03/08/how-next-generation-wi-fi-will-transform-the-smart-home/,* March 8, 2023

CHAPTER 17

ENCRYPTION

Encryption is the process of converting readable data into a format that cannot be read with the ability to return it to its original, readable state. Encryption is used to protect data from being read by an unauthorized person or persons. Individuals, organizations, and governments all have data that needs to be kept confidential. Encryption is used to accomplish that.

WHY ENCRYPT DATA?

If a device is broken into, then encrypted data cannot be used by the cyber-criminals. They may have access to the data, but if it has been encrypted by a reliable cipher using a strong password, they will likely not be able to access it.

Many ransomware attacks now follow up the ransom demand with a threat to sell or leak the victim's data, even if the ransom is paid. Encryption will not protect an individual or organization from a ransomware attack, but if the files have been encrypted, the cybercriminals will not be able to sell or expose it.

One of the more common cybercrimes is identity theft. The impact of identity theft as measured by victims and financial impact is increasing every year. According to an American Association of Retired People (AARP) study, American adults lost $43 billion to identity fraud in 2023 [AARP24]. In Europe, computer-related identity theft reached 682,000 incidents in 2020, up 16% from 2019's count [PAND23]. Data that has been encrypted cannot be used by cybercriminals to perform identity theft attacks.

ENCRYPTION TERMS

Algorithm: a set of steps or instructions to perform a task; in this case, to encrypt data

Cipher: method for performing encryption or decryption

Ciphertext: text or data that has rendered unreadable by encrypting it

Cryptography: the study of encryption

Decryption: process of returning ciphertext back into plaintext, i.e., readable text

Encryption: process of turning plaintext into ciphertext

Encryption key: a value used by an encryption cipher to encode or decode data

Plaintext: text or data that is readable

FOUR FUNCTIONS OF ENCRYPTION

The four fundamental benefits that encrypting data provides are as follows:

- *Confidentiality*: protecting data from being accessed by unauthorized personnel
- *Integrity*: ensuring that the data has not been modified by an unauthorized person.
- *Availability*: The data is always available to authorized personnel.
- *Nonrepudiation*: ability to prove that a message or file came from a specific party. The creator or sender of the data cannot deny that they created or sent it.

A good encryption algorithm ensures that the data it encrypts remains confidential, unmodified, available, and can be definitively traced back to its creator.

ENCRYPTION TYPES

The two most widely used types of encryptions are symmetric and asymmetric.

Symmetric Encryption

Symmetric encryption (a.k.a., secret key encryption) uses a single key to encrypt and decrypt data.

A primary advantage of symmetric encryption is that it is fast. The logic is simpler and requires much less computational power than an asymmetric algorithm. Encryption and decryption can be completed quicker and will work well on less powerful devices.

A disadvantage is that the key must be known to both the creator and recipient of the encrypted file. If the file is encrypted in one location and sent to another location, the recipient needs to have a copy of the key. Getting the key to him or her creates an opportunity for a cybercriminal to obtain the key. The practice of creating and keeping encryption keys secret is called *encryption key management*.

Examples of symmetric encryption algorithms are as follows:

- AES (Advanced Encryption Standard)
- DES (Data Encryption Standard)
- Blowfish
- RCA4 (Rivest Cipher 4) - RCA6

Asymmetric Encryption

Asymmetric encryption, a.k.a. *public key encryption*, has two encryption keys that are mathematically related to each other. Either key can be used to encrypt data and the other key will decrypt it. The public key can be freely distributed while the private key is kept secret.

An example of this type of encryption is as follows: Alice has two keys, a public key and a private key. She can give her public key to all her coworkers or she can post it in a public directory on the Internet. Alice keeps her private key to herself. Anyone that wants to send her confidential data encrypts it using her public key. The only way to decrypt the data is to use Alice's private key, which only Alice has.

If Alice wants to send an encrypted file to Bob, then she needs to know his public key. She encrypts it with his key and sends him the coded file. Only Bob can decrypt her file.

Asymmetric encryption is used to make secure communications with Web sites possible. Websites that have addresses beginning with HTTPS rely on it to ensure all communications between the user and the Web site cannot be understood by anyone else.

Another example of asymmetric encryption shows how it can be used for non-repudiation, i.e., to prove who sent a message. Alice encrypts a message using her private key and sends the encrypted file to Bob. He decrypts it using Alice's public key. If the message can successfully be decrypted using Alice's public key, then it must have been encrypted using her private key. Bob can be assured that Alice sent it.

A significant advantage of asymmetric encryption is that encryption key management is easier. Alice can distribute her public key without worrying that it can be used to decrypt files. Anything encrypted with her public key can only be decrypted with her private key.

The greatest disadvantage of asymmetric encryption is that it is slower than symmetric encryption. This is because the algorithm is computationally intensive. Asymmetric encryption algorithms must be processed on more powerful computers than symmetric algorithms.

Examples of asymmetric encryption algorithms are as follows:

- PGP (Pretty Good Privacy)
- RSA (Rivest-Shamir-Adleman)
- Diffie-Hellman
- ECC (Elliptic Curve Cryptography)

ENCRYPTION KEYS

Encryption keys are a sequence of random digits or characters that when used as input by the encryption algorithm create the encrypted text (a.k.a., *ciphertext*). A weak key can make the best algorithm worthless.

Encryption Key Format

Keys are typically just random numbers that have been created by a random number generator. In general, the longer a key is the stronger it is. Typically, keys have one of several specific lengths: 128, 192, or 256 bits.

Encryption Key Management

Proper management of encryption keys is essential. If they are not properly handled, the chances of them being lost or exposed goes up significantly. Some management suggestions are as follows:

- An organization should have a unique key for every different purpose.
- Keys should be stored securely. They should not be stored alongside the data they are protecting.
- Keys need to be replaced (rotated) periodically. Processes should be in place to securely distribute new keys to the personnel that need them.
- Keys need to be strong (the longer and more random, the better).
- Keys should never be reused.
- Keys that have expired should be destroyed.
- Access to keys should be extremely limited. Insider threats are a real problem. Steps should be taken to ensure that only the necessary personnel have access to keys.

Where to Encrypt

Data has to be stored to be preserved, but it has to be moved between points to be useful. For example, a credit card number might be stored in the consumer's wallet or on her computer, but it has to be given to an online merchant to make a purchase. Encryption can protect data both at rest and in transit.

Data At Rest

Data at rest can be in a structured format like a database or an Excel file. It can also be in an unstructured format like images, audio, video, or text documents. All formats of data need to be protected by encryption.

One method of encrypting data at rest is to encrypt specific files or entire directories using an encryption tool. The drawback of doing this is that it would be easy to overlook data that needs to be protected. This could easily happen if additional data were added to the system after the limited encryption coverage was set up.

Full disk encryption (FDE) and self-encrypting drives (SED) are techniques that encrypt data as it is written to a hard drive or SSD (solid state device) and decrypt it as data is read from the drive. Both of these techniques are transparent to users and applications running on the computer. Depending on the computer, drive, and operating system, there may be a performance impact imposed by encryption.

Bitlocker® is an FDE tool available on Microsoft Windows based computers. Drives on an Apple macOS computer can use FileVault to obtain FDE.

These tools are running by default on the more recent operating system versions. Both of these FDE provide the following benefits:

- They encrypt the entire drive so cybercriminals cannot steal a PC or laptop to remove the hard drive and read its files.
- They protect desktop and laptop computers in the event they are stolen.
- They are integrated into the operating systems so there is no need to add another encryption tool.

Data in Transit

Data that is moving from one device to another is referred to as "data in transit." Examples of this activity includes when an individual is logging into a Web site or application their credentials are sent to that site for verification. Other examples of data in transit include the following:

- uploading data to or downloading it from a Web site
- connecting to or receiving data from a Wi-Fi network
- downloading email from a Web server.
- occurs when an individual enters information into fields on a Web site
- transferring data to another device on an organization's LAN (Local Area Network)
- uploading data to a cloud storage location

Some methods for protecting data in transit are as follows:

- Secure/Multipurpose Internet Mail Extensions (S/MIME) can be used to encrypt email messages.
- Transport Layer Security (TLS) is a security protocol that encrypts communications between Web browsers and the servers they are communicating with. Web sites that use the HTTPS protocol use TLS encryption.
- TLS can also encrypt calls made over the Internet made with the Voice over Internet Protocol (VoIP).

ENCRYPTION IN THE INFRASTRUCTURE

Everyone relies on encryption on a daily basis. Some examples of encryption in everyday life are listed here.

Bluetooth

Bluetooth communications allow devices to communicate over very short distances. Typical examples of its uses include communicating with mice, speakers, keyboards, headphones, ear buds, hearing aids, game controllers, heart rate monitors, printers, and video cameras.

Some uses like speakers and headphones would not need to be secure, but other uses should be protected. The ability for a cybercriminal to eavesdrop on keystrokes, mouse clicks, video feed, and printed documents would be problematic for individuals and organizations.

Cloud Storage

The amount of data stored at rest in "the cloud" is immense and it is growing rapidly. Cybersecurity Ventures predicts that the amount of data in all cloud environments will reach 100 zettabytes by 2025 [CYBER24]. A zettabyte is roughly equivalent to 1 billion terabytes.

To stay in business, all cloud providers protect the data they are storing. Cybercriminals are constantly trying to find ways to access that data. In June of 2023, Toyota stated that the data of about 260,000 customers stored in the cloud was accessed due to a misconfigured environment [CSO23]. Cloud data will continue to be a target of attack.

Communication Apps

Communication apps, like Meta's WhatsApp®, Messenger®, Telegraph®, Slack®, Signal®, Zoom®, and Facebook Messenger® all provide encryption of the conversations or messages they transmit. Most of them provide end-to-end encryption by default so the user does not have to make any changes to have their communications protected by encryption. Others require that the user enable the secure communications option. Before communicating confidential information, the user should determine what level of security is default and what needs to be enabled.

HTTPS Web Sites

HTTPS Web sites encrypt communications by using the TLS protocol. Communications between a browser and the Web site's server are automatically encrypted.

VPN

A virtual private network (VPN) encrypts and protects communications between the user's device and its destination. A VPN can be used to secure communications from a desktop, laptop, or mobile device. VPNs are described in greater detail in Chapter 13 of this book.

Smart Phones

Encryption is used on smart phones like iPhones and Androids to protect all data on the device. A passcode is required to unlock the device. If the device is lost or stolen, the data on it cannot be accessed by a cybercriminal.

Wi-Fi

Wi-Fi communications are encrypted by security protocols WEP (Wired Equivalent Privacy) and WPA (Wi-Fi Protected Access, either WPA2 or WPA3). WEP is the oldest protocol and is no longer considered secure. Any devices that are using this protocol should be upgraded to WPA2 or WPA3.

The protocol being used by a router for a Wi-Fi enabled network can be seen by logging into the router's administrator page. Figure 16.3 provides an example of a wireless router that is using the WPA2 protocol. The router being shown does not offer the WPA3 protocol.

WHAT SHOULD BE ENCRYPTED?

The issue of what data needs to be protected by encryption is a complicated one. One relatively simple approach would be to encrypt everything, and there is nothing wrong with doing that. A better approach would be to understand the types of data that cybercriminals want, so it can be protected wherever that data exists.

Backup Files

Both individuals and organizations should be creating backups regularly. They are the means of recovery in the event of ransomware, natural disasters, hardware failures, or human error.

Backup files can be stored on-site, off-site, or in the cloud. Regardless of their storage location, they must be encrypted. If a cybercriminal could access an unencrypted set of backup files, they could sell the data, extort the victim, engage in identity theft, or attempt account takeover attacks.

An Individual's Data

For individuals, the data that cybercriminals want is their Personally Identifiable Information (PII). Cybercriminals want personal data for a number of reasons:

- Identity theft: If a cybercriminal acquires enough PII, he can impersonate a victim and obtain credit cards or loans in their name.
- Selling: Cybercriminals can sell PII and PHI (Protected Health Information) to other criminals on the Dark Web. Such data can be a quick and easy source of cash for the perpetrator.
- Account takeover: PII can be used to guess account passwords. It can also be used in a social engineering attack against a help desk at an employer, bank, email provider, or mobile phone carrier. If a cybercriminal can guess a victim's password or reset it, they can take over the account and either steal from it or otherwise abuse it.
- Phishing attacks: PII and other information about a potential victim can be used to create legitimate looking phishing emails. For example, if a potential victim collects coins, then an email that refers to his hobby would be viewed with less suspicion than a generic email pitch.
- SIM card takeovers: Cybercriminals can use PII details to convince a wireless carrier to activate a new SIM card for a victim's mobile phone. Once the account has been connected to the new SIM, the cybercriminal will receive MFA codes sent by the victim's bank or credit card provider.
- PHI can be used to submit false medical claims, set up fake prescriptions, or receive medical treatment that the victim will pay for.

Any files or databases that include PII needs to be encrypted. PII includes, but is not limited to, the following.

- Social Security Numbers (SSN)
- credit card information
- date of birth
- driver's license information
- full name

- gender
- mailing address
- passport details
- place of birth
- race

It may seem that individual pieces of PII are not especially valuable. The problem is that if a cybercriminal is able to collect multiple bits of information, then a profile of the individual can be compiled. The profile can be used to accomplish account takeover attacks, SIM swap fraud to get control of a phone, identity theft, and other forms of attacks.

Other individual data that an individual should be encrypting includes the following:

- PHI
- banking / financial documents
- backup files
- images
- videos

An Organization's Data

The types of data that corporations or other organizations need to keep secure include the following:

- employee PII
- financial information, like company credit cards, bank account details, and billing accounts
- salary data, including direct deposit details for employees
- customer data, including their PII, credentials, and methods of payment.
- client and vendor details
- intellectual property (IP), including business plans, future product designs, etc.
- legal information, like contracts and ongoing negotiations
- mergers and acquisitions (M&A) details
- password files

File Types That Need to Be Encrypted

Examples of file types that need to be encrypted are listed below. Some industries and professions, e.g., architects, have specialized file extensions that also need to be encrypted.

- Databases: mdb, db, odb, sql, db3, dbf, and dbs
- Images: jpg, png, gif, tiff, and psd
- Videos: mov, avi, wmv, mp4, and mpeg-4
- Documents: doc, docx, txt, rtf, odt, wps, and pdf
- Spreadsheets: xls, xlsx, and xlsb

DRAWBACKS OF ENCRYPTION

Encryption is critical to ensuring the security of data, but it does have some drawbacks. Some of the more significant disadvantages are described here.

- Encryption is frequently used by criminals. Ransomware uses encryption to prevent the owner of files or entire computers from accessing them unless a ransom is paid. Encryption is also be used by con men, pedophiles, extortionists, terrorists, and nation states to prevent authorities from identifying them.
- It takes CPU power and time to encrypt and decrypt data. This additional computational requirement may make devices run noticeably slower.
- If the encryption key is lost, then the owner cannot access the data. Without the key, the owner is reduced to trying to crack the encryption just like an attacker would.
- Everything related to the encryption process must be done correctly for it to be effective. This includes selecting a good cipher, creating a strong key, encrypting all valuable files, and rotating keys as needed. If any part of this process is done incorrectly, the data will not be properly protected. The owner may assume that all of his files are secure when they are actually not.
- Backups have to be encrypted. This means that the encryption key used to encrypt the backup files also needs to be kept just in case the backup needs to be decrypted. Of course, the key cannot be stored with the backup because that would make it too easy for a cybercriminal to obtain both of them.

※ The encryption cipher chosen cannot have "back doors." After a terrorist shooting in San Bernardino in December of 2015, the FBI desperately wanted to access the terrorists' iPhones to see if additional attacks were planned. Apple told them that no back door existed to bypass the phone's encryption. Many people argue that a back door, even if its use is limited to only the most critical situations, renders the algorithm unusable since it would be a prime target for cybercriminals, nation states, and rogue government agencies.

LEGAL REGULATIONS AND ENCRYPTION

For some types of data, laws and regulations require that it be protected by encrypting it. Examples of data that is covered by laws are as follows:

※ HIPAA (Health Insurance Portability and Accountability Act): This requires protection of all medical records and PHI. HIPPA does not specifically require that covered data be encrypted, but if the data is not encrypted and is exposed, the organization will likely be charged with a violation.

※ PCI DSS (Payment Card Industry Data Security Standard): This defines the security requirements to protect credit card transactions that must be followed by any entity that handles credit card transactions.

※ GDPR (General Data Protection Regulations): Data protection requirements that must be met by any entity that stores data of citizens of the European Union. The GDPR does not mandate data encryption but recommends it.

※ CCPA (California Consumer Privacy Act): This dictates how the personal information of California citizens must be protected.

ENCRYPTION PRODUCTS

There are numerous encryption products available for individuals and organizations. Some of the most prominent ones are listed below:

※ FileVault®: FDE for Apple computers

※ Bitlocker®: FDE protection that comes with the current Windows operating systems

- AxCrypt®: A third-party encryption package that encrypts files and contents of subdirectories.
- PGP® (Pretty Good Privacy): A third-party encryption program that provides excellent security for files, emails, directories, and disk partitions.
- Signal®: This provides encryption for instant messaging, voice calls, and video calls.
- Telegram®: A cloud based instant messaging service that works across platforms and provides end-to-end encryption.

HOW CYBERCRIMINALS CRACK ENCRYPTION

When implemented correctly, encryption protects data from being disclosed to people that aren't authorized to access it. It can be extremely difficult to crack a modern encryption protocol. Unfortunately, criminals have devised methods of defeating encryption.

Obtain the Keys

Encryption keys are needed to decrypt or unlock files that have been encrypted. These keys can be lengthy, 128 and 256 bits are common lengths. Keys must be stored somewhere on the computer. Unfortunately, anything that is stored on a computer can potentially be stolen or exposed. Criminals, knowing how valuable keys are, make efforts to locate and obtain them.

Encryption keys are not static. They need to be changed (rotated) periodically. When they are being changed, it is possible for them to be exposed and stolen. Organizations should have well-established procedures for rotating keys safely.

Social Engineering

The best encryption algorithm in the world cannot keep a file secure if a cybercriminal can trick someone into giving him the encryption key. Social engineering can be used to trick an individual or someone withing an organization into revealing a password or encryption key.

Brute Force Attacks

Even though the number of combinations in a key is astronomical, cybercriminals can still attempt to determine them by trying every possible key combination until the correct one is found. As more powerful computers become available, they make this form of attack feasible against old protocols or short keys. Strong protocols and lengthy keys make this attack difficult. It is estimated that it would take the most modern supercomputer millions of years to crack the AES cipher when it uses a 256-bit key [CLICK24].

Heartbleed and Implementation Weaknesses

If there is a flaw in how encryption is implemented, it can allow cybercriminals to access the data. An example of a vulnerability that was exploited by cybercriminals was Heartbleed. In April of 2017, researchers announced that OpenSSL, an open-source cryptographic library, had a coding error [TECH23]. This bug exposed encrypted data, including usernames and passwords. It was estimated that 66% of all active Web sites on the Internet used code from the OpenSSL library. A patch was developed and released that month. In November of 2020, it was estimated that more than 200,000 computers were still vulnerable to Heartbleed [NORD24].

Cryptanalysis

Cryptanalysis can be used to identify weaknesses in a cipher that may allow it to be broken without resorting to a brute force attack. This form of attack makes it imperative that only strong algorithms be employed.

Quantum Computing

Today's computers use binary electrical signals to represent ones and zeros. Instead of binary logic, quantum computers are powered by subatomic particles called *quantum bits* or *qbits*. Predictions are that quantum computers will be millions or billions of times faster than today's fastest supercomputers.

The speed of quantum computers could allow them to defeat any of today's encryption algorithms in minutes (or even seconds). Fortunately, their arrival is not expected for at least another decade. That may sound like a long time, but it will take an enormous amount of effort to replace all current digital encryption technologies with quantum-based encryption to ensure continued protection of data.

REFERENCES

[AARP24] Ianzito, Christina. "Identity Fraud Costs Americans $43 Billion in 2023," available online at *https://www.aarp.org/money/scams-fraud/info-2024/identity-fraud-report.html*, April 10, 2024

[CLICK24] "How Safe is 256-bit encryption in Modern Times," available online at *https://www.clickssl.net/blog/256-bit-encryption*, April 22, 2024

[CSO24] Venkat, Apurva. "Cloud misconfiguration causes massive data breach at Toyota Motor," available online at *https://www.csoonline.com/article/575483/cloud-misconfiguration-causes-massive-data-breach-at-toyota-motor.html*, June 06, 2023

[CYBER24] Morgan, Steve. "The World Will Store 200 Zettabytes of Data By 2025," available online at *https://cybersecurityventures.com/the-world-will-store-200-zettabytes-of-data-by-2025/*, February 1, 2024

[EFF16] "EFF DES Cracker Machine Brings Honesty to Crypto Debate," available online at *https://www.eff.org/press/releases/eff-des-cracker-machine-brings-honesty-crypto-debate*, August 9, 2016

[NORD24] Einoryte, Aurelija. "What is Heartbleed? The Heartbleed vulnerability explained," available online at *https://nordvpn.com/blog/what-is-heartbleed-bug/*, January 17, 2024

[PAND23] "31 Alarming Identify Theft Statistics for 2024," available online at *https://www.pandasecurity.com/en/mediacenter/identity-theft-statistics/*, January 9, 2024

[PREC22] "AES vs. DES Encryption: Why Advanced Encryption Standard (AES) has replaced DES, 3DES, and TDEA," available online at *https://www.precisely.com/blog/data-security/aes-vs-des-encryption-standard-3des-tdea*, November 14, 2022

[TECH23] Shea, Sharon. "Heartbleed," available online at *https://www.techtarget.com/searchsecurity/definition/Heartbleed*, January 2023

INTERNET OF THINGS

The Internet of Things (IoT) is a network of interrelated devices that connect and exchange data with other IoT devices and the cloud [TECH24]. The term "thing" can refer to devices as dissimilar as heart monitors, tire pressure gauges, chips in cattle, cat litter boxes, smart toilets, toasters, and flip flops.

The first IoT device was considered to be a Coke machine located at Carnegie Mellon University (CMU) in the early 1980s [TECH24]. Programmers at the university connected the machine to the network so they would know whether it had bottles of Coke in it without having to walk down and look for themselves. The concept of IoT devices has advanced significantly since then, but like the first device, they are examples of labor and time savings.

IoT devices can use a number of protocols to communicate using radio frequencies over short ranges. Some communication protocols used are as follows:

- Bluetooth
- Cellular
- LoRaWAN
- NFC
- Wi-Fi
- Z-Wave
- Zigbee

Advantages of IoT Devices

Some of the advantages of employing IoT devices are as follows:

- automation
- convenience
- cost savings
- data collection
- efficiency
- personalization
- productivity
- safety

IoT Devices in Homes

It is estimated that there are over 17 billion IoT devices in homes as of 2024. That number is predicted to reach 29 billion by 2030 [NORD24]. The average US household that has Internet access in 2023 had 17 connected devices [PARK24].

When 5G networks become widely available, it is predicted that the number of IoT devices will increase significantly. The 5G networks have considerable advantages over current networks like 4G. They are faster, can manage more devices, are more energy efficient, and have a lower *latency* (wait times). These advantages will benefit IoT devices in homes, health care, and industry.

Examples of Consumer IoT Devices

The variety of IoT devices in the home continues to grow as more and more makers produce devices to make our lives easier. Examples of what is in many homes include the following:

- appliances like refrigerators, ovens, ranges, microwaves, dishwashers, and coffee makers
- baby monitors
- children's toys
- doorbell cameras
- electronic locks
- fitness tracking wearable devices

- health care devices like heart monitors, CPAP machines, glucose level monitors, and smart pillboxes
- HVAC systems
- lighting systems
- smart TVs
- security cameras

IOT-BASED CYBERATTACKS

Cybercriminals have exploited IoT devices in numerous cyberattacks. There is concern that as more of these devices are installed the number of incidents will grow. Some examples of IoT devices that have been attacked are described in the following sections.

Hacking IoT Devices

Andrew McGill, a reporter at *The Atlantic* magazine, built a virtual toaster and connected it to the Internet [GBH16]. The experiment was to see how long it would take for an unprotected device to be hacked (41 minutes for his toaster). After that first hacking incident, the toaster was hacked a second and third time within an additional 20 and then 30 minutes.

The Mirai botnet was discovered by white hat group MalwareMustDie in August of 2016. This botnet had more than 350,000 devices, including doorbell cameras, printers, wireless modems, routers, and other consumer devices [NORD24]. Other sources estimate the number of zombie devices at over 600,000 [CLOUD17]. Mirai bots were used in a DDoS attack that took down or affected Web sites like Airbnb, Amazon, GitHub, Netflix, Twitter, and Wikileaks [ECO24].

A Las Vegas casino was hacked via a cutting-edge computer-controlled fish tank [BUS18]. The cybercriminals were able to use the IoT thermometer in the fish tank to gain access to the casino's network. Once access to the network was established, they uploaded 10 gigabytes of customer data to a server in Finland [FOR17]. No word is available on whether the fish were harmed during this attack.

A disturbing example of IoT devices being hacked are baby monitors. There have been numerous documented incidents of this happening. A Seattle couple experienced it when a cybercriminal accessed their baby cam and told their three-year-old child, "I love you" [NBC19]. He also rotated the camera by remote control so he could view the entire room.

In 2015, two researchers demonstrated that they were able to take control of a Jeep Cherokee remotely over the Internet while it was being driven by the owner [WIR15]. Some of the actions they were able to perform included controlling the air conditioning, changing radio station and volume, activate the windshield wipers, shift the transmission into neutral, and enable/disable the brakes. The researchers claim to be working on the ability to control the steering of vehicles. Other researchers have been able to remotely control 16 makes of cars in a similar fashion using only the Vehicle Identification Number (VIN) of the target automobiles [SEC23].

Why IoT Devices Are Vulnerable to Cyberattacks

Most IoT devices were not designed with security in mind. For the most part, they were designed to fulfill a specific function and be cheap to mass produce. Some of the specific details that make them vulnerable include the following.

- IoT devices cannot be customized by the consumer so similar devices are essentially identical, i.e., all Model XYZ baby monitors from Acme Industry are functionally identical and all have the same vulnerabilities. If a cybercriminal can break into one of them, then he can break into every one of them worldwide.

- Many IoT devices have default accounts and passwords. A common combination is "admin" and "password." Cybercriminals can easily find these credentials online and log into the admin account. A UK law that took effect in April of 2024 requires IoT manufacturers to set stronger default passwords as well as other security-minded provisions [INFO24].

- Some IoT devices do not encrypt communications. This could enable cybercriminals to eavesdrop on any data they gather.

- The lack of account lockout policies on IoT devices allow unlimited attempts at guessing passwords. Most applications and Web sites allow only a limited number of failed login attempts before locking the account.

- Many vendors never make updates or patches available for their products. Even if a patch is made available, most consumers would not be aware of it. It is common that once an IoT device is installed, the owner largely forgets about it unless it stops functioning.

- Vendors are unlikely to have contact information for consumers who purchased their devices. Even if they wanted to distribute a patch, it would be almost impossible to contact the consumers who purchased them.

- Vendors of low-end IoT products frequently change names, are acquired, or go out of business. It would be difficult (if not impossible) for a consumer to determine what company marketed some products after several years.

HOW CYBERCRIMINALS LOCATE IOT DEVICES

Consumers may think that, although their IoT devices are not secure, no one would be interested in locating them. Unfortunately, this is wrong. Cybercriminals have tools that make it relatively easy to find unprotected IoT devices.

Port Scans

Many IoT devices use a known set of port numbers when communicating with the router or server. Cybercriminals can use scripts and commands to probe the Internet for devices that reply on these ports. One command that can be used is Nmap (Network Mapper). Nmap can be used to scan a range of IP addresses for active hosts (computers), open ports, services running on open ports, and the operating systems running on a host. A scripting tool called NSE (Nmap Scripting Engine) makes it easy for cybercriminals to scan tens of thousands of IP addresses and identify ones that have IoT devices on them.

If a cybercriminal wants to find a pool of potential victims in a specific geographic area, for example a city, it is possible to use IP address ranges to do this. Individuals and organizations get their Internet access from an ISP (Internet Service Provider). ISPs are assigned blocks of IP addresses so there is a rough relationship between IP addresses and physical locations. There is not a perfect correlation between the two, but if a cybercriminal wants to identify the IP addresses in a given city, it can be done.

Vulnerability Scanning Tools

Vulnerability scanning tools search networks looking for hardware, software, firmware, and configuration settings that have known vulnerabilities. These tools are used by white hat hackers to identify and correct problems in their systems before black hat hackers find them. Unfortunately, any tool that has a beneficial use can be applied in detrimental ways. Cybercriminals (black hat hackers) use the same tools to scan networks owned by others to identify and exploit vulnerabilities.

Some scanners specialize in identifying IoT devices with known vulnerabilities. Examples of IoT device vulnerabilities that can be identified include

- default, blank, or commonly used passwords
- missing updates and patches
- misconfigurations
- weak or obsolete communication protocols being used
- open ports
- unsecured data

IoT Search Engines

There are several Web sites that focus on identifying IoT devices that are connected to the Internet. Examples of these sites include the following:

- Censys®
- Shodan®
- Thingful®
- ZoomEye®

Shodan

Shodan is perhaps the most well-known search engine for devices that are connected to the Internet. What Google is to normal searches, Shodan is to IoT and other devices on the Internet. Shodan has Web crawler processes ("spiders") that search the Internet 24/7 looking for devices connected to the Internet.

This tool is publicly available so anyone can access it and it is perfectly legal. The reader needs to understand that searching for devices using Shodan is legal but accessing them without permission is not. It is against federal and state laws to access devices or networks owned by another person or organization without explicit permission.

Shodan allows a wide variety of ways to search for devices on the Internet. Some search criteria are as follows:

- location, including by country, city, and GPS coordinates
- IP address

- port number
- specific types of computers like database servers or Web site servers
- type of device, e.g., camera, router, refrigerator, or HVAC system
- specific operating systems like Windows or Linux
- product, i.e., the name of the product or software
- version of the product. This is useful because cybercriminals can learn which versions have more vulnerabilities.

The author used Shodan to arbitrarily search for a specific brand of wireless video camera. Within a second or two, a list of that make and model of the camera was displayed. Each device that was found included details like its IP address, country, city, and device name. Shodan can also show images that have been taken from IoT cameras found on the Internet.

ABUSING IOT DEVICES

Once a cybercriminal has access to an unprotected or vulnerable IoT device, there are ways they can be abused. Some examples of how they are exploited are described below.

Botnets

Botnet is a combination of the words "robot" and "network." A *botnet* (a.k.a., *a zombie army*) is a network of electronic devices infected with malware that is remotely controlled by a cybercriminal. Often the infected bots are IoT devices. Some of the illegal activities that botnets engage in include the following:

- DDoS attacks can be launched from IoT devices to shut down Web sites until the owner pays the demanded extortion.
- They can use infected routers as a way of masking the source of illegal activities.
- Spam can be launched from compromised IoT devices.
- Phishing emails can be sent from subverted IoT devices.
- Click fraud is a scam where cybercriminals create Web sites that appear legitimate and earn money when ads are displayed on them. Each time a user clicks on an ad displayed on their Web sites, the cybercriminal

gets paid a fee by the company whose ad is displayed. The number of clicks is fraudulently inflated by having bots instead of humans click on the ads. In 2023, the cost of click fraud to businesses was almost $36 billion [CHEQ24].

▨ Brute force attacks to determine account credentials can be launched from IoT devices.

▨ Cryptocurrency mining occurs when a cybercriminal installs mining software on numerous victims' IoT devices. The cybercriminal is using the victim's computers, including IoT devices, to earn cryptocurrency.

▨ They can deliver ransomware to computers on the victim's network.

▨ They can steal login credentials from the victim's network.

▨ They can monitor keystrokes that occur on the victim's network.

One additional negative that can occur if a computer or IoT device becomes part of a botnet is that it can be blacklisted. If an individual's router is flagged as being part of a botnet, it can be added to lists of other infected devices known as blacklists. The result of being blacklisted is that it can be shunned by parts of the Internet. The victim might not be able to send out email or otherwise communicate across the Internet. For a victim working from home or a small business, this could prevent any meaningful work from being performed.

Eavesdropping or Spying

IoT devices like smart televisions, security cameras, baby monitors, and personal assistants have microphones or cameras. If a cybercriminal is able to take control of these devices, they can be used to eavesdrop on or observe occupants in the home or business.

Another form of monitoring is that cybercriminals can potentially identify when the owner is away from home. If IoT cameras show no one is present in the house, the lights have not been turned on, or the smart thermostat is set to a "maintenance" temperature for an extended period, then the criminal can assume that the family has gone on vacation, leaving the house a potential target for robbers.

It is possible for the eavesdropping to be done by an unexpected group of people. Millions of consumers own Echo® speakers and use Amazon's Alexa® digital assistant in their homes. A copy of everything "heard" by Alexa is uploaded to an Amazon server to be transcribed by an artificial intelligence

(AI) application. A small percentage of those recordings are listened to by people employed by Amazon to help improve the AI's accuracy [TIME19]. Would the average consumer be comfortable knowing their conversations are potentially being listened to by one of thousands of Amazon employees?

Toys that spy on children are disturbingly common. In a 2023 report, the US Public Interest Research Group stated that the variety of smart toys in the marketplace is growing [USPIRG23]. The group reports that some of these toys violate the Children's Online Privacy Protection Act (COPPA). Some of the more sophisticated interactive toys upload conversations with the child to speech recognition software on the company's servers. Numerous toys, some discontinued but some still for sale, improperly collected children's voices, images, and other data.

Network Access

If an attacker gains access to an IoT device, his next action might be to move laterally through the network. In one demonstration of this concept, a team of researchers from the University of London and the Universita di Catania uncovered a vulnerability in a smart lightbulb [DIGI23]. Vulnerabilities in the smart bulb and the application that controlled it enabled them to learn the owner's Wi-Fi password.

Knowing the password would allow them to log onto the network as a legitimate user. They could be in a position to control other IoT devices on the network, including door locks, security cameras, and thermostats. It would potentially enable them to monitor unencrypted traffic on the network and obtain personal information on the homeowners.

Ransomware

IoT devices and ransomware can be combined to form two methods of attacking the victims. The first is to use an IoT device as an entry point into an organization's network. Once access to the network is obtained, a conventional ransomware attack against files or computers is carried out. An example of this was the casino ransomware attack already mentioned in this chapter [BUS18].

Another approach is to apply ransomware to the device itself. In January of 2017, 70% of the CCTV devices in Washington DC were infected with a ransomware attack [BITD17]. City officials chose not to pay the $60,000 ransom. To clear the devices of this ransomware, all 123 affected devices were rebooted. This left the system offline and unable to record from January 12th through the 15th.

Future examples of IoT ransomware could include attackers gaining control of IoT devices in homes. Imagine if a cybercriminal was able to gain control of a home's thermostat in January while the homeowner was away. The cybercriminal could turn off the furnace and lock the IoT device to prevent the owner from regaining control of the home's temperature. If outside temperatures were below freezing, the homeowner might be inclined to pay the ransom to avoid frozen pipes and potential water damage.

SECURING IOT DEVICES

IoT devices typically cannot be modified by the consumer to make them more secure. For the most part, these devices are used right out of the box. Until laws are put in place like was done in the UK, consumers have few guarantees that IoT devices purchased will be secure.

Some steps that can be taken by the user to enhance IoT security are listed here.

- If the wireless router has not been replaced in years, it might be time to install a newer, more secure router.
- IoT devices connected to a wireless router have an additional layer of security.
- Replace the default password for the router admin account with a strong, unique one.
- Choose the most secure protocol that the new router supports, optimally WP3.
- If the wireless router has a built-in firewall, make sure it is active.
- Change default passwords immediately when installing an IoT device, if that is a possibility.
- Create a separate network, i.e., a guest network, for IoT devices to run on a home Wi-Fi network. If there are a very large number of IoT devices, then a second wireless router can be installed specifically for them.
- Compile an inventory of IoT devices in the home or business environment. This can help recognize if new, rogue devices are added.
- Research available IoT products to avoid purchasing ones with known security issues

- Install updates of IoT firmware or software whenever they become available
- If the network's wireless router has a built-in VPN, activate it.
- If the IoT device can be updated automatically by the vendor, then enable that option.
- Purchase IoT devices only from established vendors.

REFERENCES

[BITD17] Pascu, Luana. "70% of Washington DC's CCTV cameras infected with ransomware," available online at *https://www.bitdefender.com/blog/hotforsecurity/70-washington-dcs-cctv-cameras-infected-ransomware/*, January 30, 2017

[BUS18] Willians-Grut, Oscar. "Hackers once stole a casino's high-roller database through a thermostat in the lobby fish tank," available online at *https://www.businessinsider.com/hackers-stole-a-casinos-database-through-a-thermometer-in-the-lobby-fish-tank-2018-4*, April 15, 2018

[CHEQ23] Trajcheva, Sanja. "What is Click Fraud? How it Works, Examples and Red Flags," available online at *https://cheq.ai/blog/what-is-click-fraud/*, January 29, 2024

[CLOUD17] "Inside the infamous Mirai IoT Botnet: A Retrospective Analysis," available online at *https://blog.cloudflare.com/inside-mirai-the-infamous-iot-botnet-a-retrospective-analysis*, December 14, 2017

[DIGI23] White, Monica. "How Smart light bulbs could steal your password," available online at *https://www.digitaltrends.com/computing/hackers-can-steal-passwords-through-tp-link-smart-bulbs/*, August 22, 2023

[ECO24] Buchanon, Scott. "Hazards of the Internet of Things," available online at *https://economistwritingeveryday.com/2024/01/16/hazards-of-the-internet-of-things-1-hacking-of-devices-baby-monitors-freezers-hospital-ventilators-in-homes-and-institutions/*, January 16, 2024

[FOR17] Mathews, Lee. "Criminals Hacked a Fish Tank to Steal Data from a Casino," available online at *https://www.forbes.com/sites/leemathews/2017/07/27/criminals-hacked-a-fish-tank-to-steal-data-from-a-casino/*, July 27, 2017

[GBH16] "An Experiment Shows How Quickly the Internet of Things Can Be Hacked." Available online at *https://www.wgbh.org/news/2016-11-01/an-experiment-shows-how-quickly-the-internet-of-things-can-be-hacked*, November 3, 2016

[INFO24] Muncaster, Phil. "New UK Smart Device Security Law Comes Into Force," available online at *https://www.infosecurity-magazine.com/news/smart-device-security-law-today/*, April 29, 2024

[NBC19] Romero, Dennis. "Stranger hacks into baby monitor, tells child, 'I love you.'," available online at *https://www.nbcnews.com/news/us-news/stranger-hacks-baby-monitor-tells-child-i-love-you-n1090046*, November 22, 2019

[NORD24] Zieniute, Ugne. "What is the Mirai botnet, and how does it spread?," available online at *https://nordvpn.com/blog/mirai-botnet/*, April 16, 2024

[PARK24] "Average US Internet Home Had 17 Connected Devices in 2023," available online at *https://www.parksassociates.com/blogs/in-the-news/parks-average-us-internet-home-had-17-connected-devices-in-2023*, January 10, 2024

[SEC23] Arghire, Ionut. "16 Car Makers and Their Vehicles Hacked via Telemetrics, APIs, Infrastructure," available online at *https://www.securityweek.com/16-car-makers-and-their-vehicles-hacked-telematics-apis-infrastructure/*, January 5, 2023

[TECH24] Yasar, Kinza. "Internet of Things (IoT)," available online at *https://www.techtarget.com/iotagenda/definition/Internet-of-Things-IoT*, June 2024

[TIME19] Day, Matt. "Thousands of Amazon Workers Listen to Alexa User's Conversations," available online at *https://time.com/5568815/amazon-workers-listen-to-alexa/*, April 11, 2019

[USPIRG23] Murray, Teresa. "Trouble in Toyland 2023," available online at *https://pirg.org/edfund/resources/trouble-in-toyland-2023/*, November 16, 2023

[WIR15] Greenberg, Andy. "Hackers Remotely Kill a Jeep on the Highway—With Me in It," available online at *https://www.wired.com/2015/07/hackers-remotely-kill-jeep-highway/*, July 21, 2015

REDUCING DIGITAL FOOTPRINTS ON THE INTERNET

The business model of many big tech companies is based on collecting data on consumers and selling it or using it to tailor advertisements to consumers. The amount of information gathered about each of us is significant. An article in *PC Magazine* summed it up succinctly: The title of the article was "What Does Big Tech Know About You? Basically Everything." [PCMAG22]

Data on consumers is frequently sold to marketers, government agencies, and scammers. One estimate is that the value of consumer data being sold will exceed $545 billion by the year 2028 [MONEY24]. According to the Pew Research Center, 81% of Americans feel very or somewhat concerned about how companies use the data they collect on people [PEW24].

Some examples of information about each of us that is somewhere on the Internet include the following:

- web sites visited, including how often and the amount of time spent on each
- name
- Social Security Number
- driver's license number
- gender
- birthdate
- phone number

- address
- email address
- relationship status
- names of individuals in phone's contact list
- education level
- IP address
- income
- cost of house
- credit card numbers
- TV show preferences
- places visited
- photos
- hobbies
- religion
- sexual preferences
- religion
- political affiliation
- organizations associated with
- cars owned
- charities donated to
- type of mobile phones and computers owned
- browser type
- computer operating system
- comments made on Web sites
- searches made on the Internet
- Web sites visited
- videos watched
- online games played
- books purchased and read online
- IoT devices in the consumer's home
- physical locations visited
- reviews posted on products

- emails sent and received
- text messages sent and received
- reviews posted on sites like Yelp and Angi

Reducing the amount of information about themselves should be a goal of everyone. It would be impossible to remove everything from the Internet, but the less information that is available online, the better it is for you.

The Dangers of "Oversharing"

Some of the advice in this chapter may seem to be a little strange. You should choose to implement only the suggestions that seem reasonable and comfortable to you. Never forget the old saying by Patrick Carman: "Just because you're paranoid does not mean there is not somebody watching you."

The world can be a very unforgiving place. Should a photograph or comment posted years or decades ago prevent someone from getting a job, a loan, or admission to their dream university? The author does not think so, but the world we all live in has punished people for less. Even if our digital footprints cannot be deleted, if we are aware of what is out there about ourselves, we can be in a better position to deal with it.

DATA BROKERS

Data brokers aggregate information about consumers from numerous sources. Those sources include public records, social media sites, search engines, banks, cookies, consumer purchases, marketing firms, retailers, surveys, and data scraping.

The top five data brokers in the United States are listed here [ONEREP24]:

1. Experian
2. Equifax
3. Epsilon
4. Acxiom
5. CoreLogic

Selling Consumer Data is Lucrative

Estimates of how much the data broker industry makes annually vary, but the amounts are significant. An article by CNBC estimated that the amount in 2021 was $319 billion [CNBC23]. The same article projected that amount to exceed $545 billion by 2028. An estimate made by Maximize Market Research showed that the data broker market was $252 billion in 2023 and it will grow to $411 billion by 2030 [MMR24]. Regardless of which estimate is closer, it is a significant amount of money.

The Legality of Selling Data

There are very few legal limitations regarding the types of consumer information that data brokers can collect and sell. Even data about children can be collected and sold by data brokers. One limitation is that they cannot sell consumer PII to foreign adversary countries [WILEY24].

Data on the Average American

Data brokers know much about almost all of us. Data brokers compile and sell an average of 1,500 data points per person, according to the World Metrics organization [WORL24]. The same source states that over 80% of all Americans have data in data broker's databases. They hold information about more than 500 million individuals worldwide.

Opting Out

It is possible for individuals to opt out of a data broker's files. In the best case, you can just go to their Web site and fill out a form. Other brokers require the requestor to print out a form, complete it, and then mail it in. Others require a more circuitous route to opt out.

While it is possible to opt out with some companies, the problem is that there are many data brokers that operate in the United States. The Privacy Rights Organization noted that in 2021, there were 540 registered data brokers in the United States [PRIV22]. The Privacy Rights Organization provides a list of all data brokers licensed in the United States at *https://privacyrights.org/ data-brokers*. Unfortunately, there is not a shared form or clearinghouse of opt out requests, so everyone has to submit an opt out request to each and every data broker.

Requesting to opt out is not a one-time action. Data brokers get their data refreshed regularly. The refresh may include data for individuals that have already requested to opt out. To ensure that they continue to be opted out, an individual needs to resubmit their requests periodically, roughly every three months, according to Incogni [INCOG].

INVESTIGATING DIGITAL FOOTPRINTS ON THE INTERNET

Some people may assume that no one would ever bother to investigate his or her digital footprint on the Internet. That assumption is dangerous. Just a few examples of entities that are extremely likely to check a on a person's Internet presence are listed here:

- Human Resources: A company's HR department will check on a person's Internet footprint before hiring them, as well as when making promotion decisions. Up to 90% of employers are reviewing the digital footprints of candidates [CHEEK].
- Landlords: To ensure they not violating restrictions like no smoking or no pets, many landlords review current and prospective tenants' digital footprints.
- Lenders: Mortgage lenders increasingly are reviewing digital footprints of prospective borrowers. The percentage making online checks rose from 6% in 2013 to 34% in 2018 [WILEY22].
- Romantic partners: An Avast study found that 50% of online daters researched their potential dates before meeting them for the first time [PRNE21].
- University admissions: A survey by Kaplan found that 66% of admissions officers accessed the social media accounts of applications [BUS22].
- Visa applications: The United States forms for visas included social media related questions starting in 2019 [JUST23].
- Voters: Individual voters as well as opposing candidates research political candidates' Internet presence.

ADVANTAGES OF MINIMIZING DIGITAL FOOTPRINT

There are many advantages of removing as much personal data from the Internet as possible. One obvious advantage of purging old data is embarrassment: we all become wiser as we age, but may have left behind some photos that were less than appropriate. Other advantages of cleaning up online exposure include the following.

Identity Theft

An excessive amount of personal information online can lead to identity theft. If a cybercriminal can collect personal details like a potential victim's address, phone number, Social Security Number, work history, and educational history, he can take out loans in the victim's name, file bogus insurance claims, and impersonate the victim.

Account Takeovers

The more personal information that is available online, the easier it can be to guess a victim's passwords and challenge question answers. Too many people use easily guessable passwords that are based on schools they went to, pet names, birthdates, and favorite sports teams. If a cybercriminal can find those details from someone's digital footprint, it improves their chances of guessing passwords. Since many people reuse passwords across multiple accounts, the cybercriminal will be able to take over all accounts with the same password.

Phishing Attacks

Phishing attacks rely on convincing the victim that the email sender or caller is authentic. The more the cybercriminal knows about the victim, the more authentic he can seem. If the criminal can find details about the victim's life like hobbies, schools attended, vacation spots, and favorite movies, then tricking the victim will be significantly easier.

Protecting Reputations

A reputation built up over many years can be ruined if a compromising photograph, rash comment, or socially unacceptable statement is found on the Internet. The best protection for this is to never post something like that. The next best protection is to find those artifacts and delete them before anyone else can. Researching yourself periodically can help protect your reputation.

Robocalls

Robocalls are frequently the result of a phone number being associated with a person's footprint on the Internet. Another reason for getting robocalls is that a data breach exposed the telephone number. The best way to deal with robocalls is to ignore them. If the number is not familiar, let it go to voice mail. If it is important, the caller will leave a message.

Spam

Everybody gets some spam in their inbox, but a sudden surge of it should not be ignored. The cause of this increase can be one of several possibilities including the following:

- The recipient is being actively targeted by spammers or other crooks.
- The email address has recently been sold.
- The email address was included in a data breach.
- Someone's email account has been hacked and all names in its contact list are being spammed.
- The email address was scraped off a Web site visited by the victim.
- A previous spam email was opened or replied to.
- An unsubscribe request was made.

The best practice is blocking the email or mark it as "spam" within the email client. This will help to keep the inbox cleaner. Do not open, reply to, or ask to be unsubscribed from an email list. Doing any of these things lets the spammer know he has reached an active account. Frequently, instead of dropping that email address from the list, it will get additional spam.

One way to minimize the amount of spam received is to use a *burner* or disposable email address whenever possible. After creating this dummy account, use it in the following situations:

- when signing up for free trials or services
- to qualify for an online coupon without getting numerous emails from the vendor
- to track the progress of an online purchase delivery
- when registering on social media or forum sites that will only be used a few times
- when responding to a poll or survey
- to leave an anonymous comment or review on a Web site

STEPS TO MINIMIZE INTERNET EXPOSURE

Taking steps to minimize one's Internet exposure should be done by everyone. Some of the more productive steps are listed below. For readers who would rather have an expert manage their digital footprint, suggestions on hiring a company to do this are provided at the end of the section.

Be forewarned that even the best efforts are unlikely to remove every scrap of data about a person from the Internet for several reasons. Not every Web site is willing to remove content from their site. Data on the Dark Web probably will not be found by the average user and certainly is not going to be removed because someone asks that it be done.

A final piece of advice is that even if we are not able to completely remove our existing information on the Internet, everyone can be more prudent about digital footprints they leave from now on.

Alerts

A Google alert can be created so that every time a specific phrase is found by Google, an email will be sent out. It is not a matter of vanity to create an alert triggered by one's name. This tool can be used as a warning to check out and potential deal with information that should be removed from the Internet.

The screenshot in Figure 19.1 shows how to create a Google alert. It is just as easy as entering the topic and clicking the "Create Alert" button.

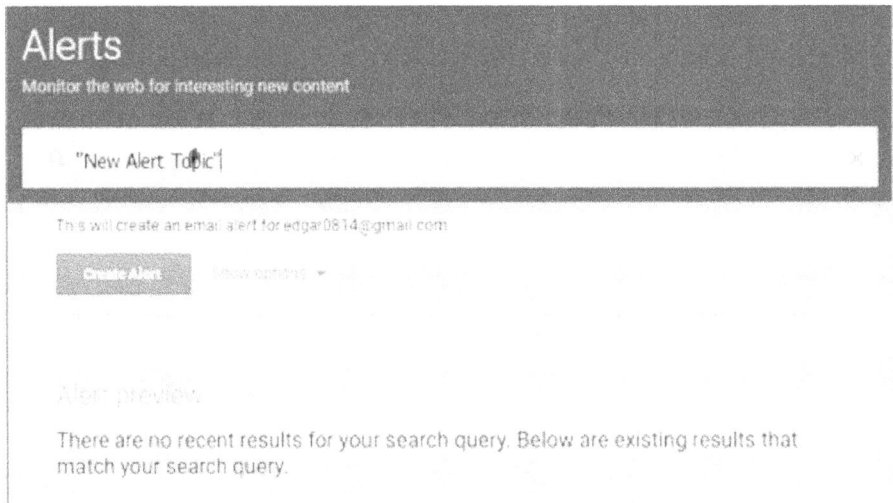

FIGURE 19.1 Creating a Google alert

Figure 19.2 shows the list of Google alerts that the author has created. Once an alert has been created, the options exist to deliver the alerts daily or weekly by clicking on the "Settings" icon to the right of the alerts count. The delivery time of day can also be specified.

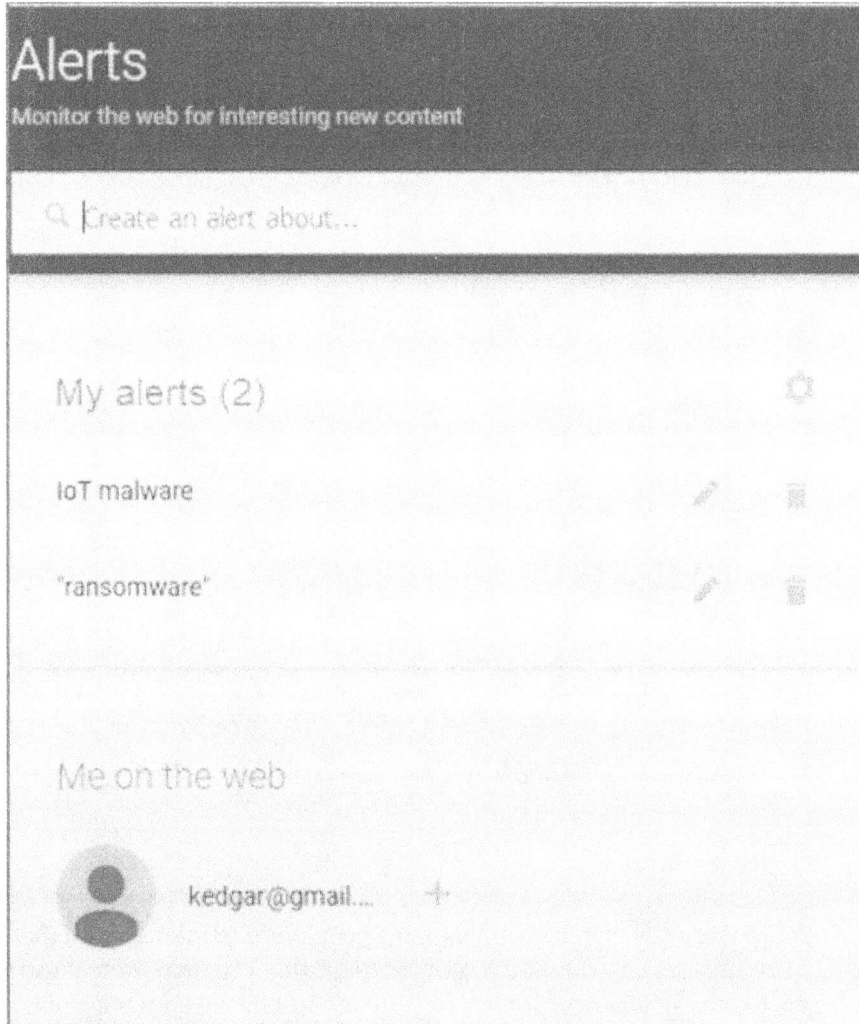

FIGURE 19.2 A Google alert

Figure 19.3 is an example of an email generated by Google alerts on one of my search terms.

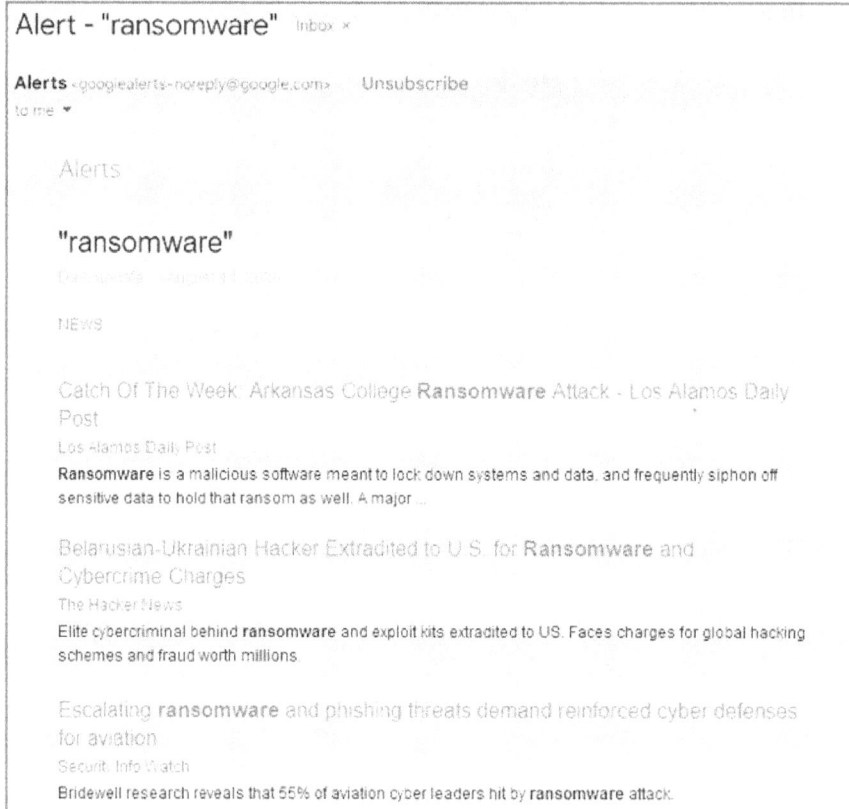

FIGURE 19.3 Example of a Google alert email

Browsers

A browser is the application that most people use to interact with the Internet. Most browsers have useful tools or settings that can help protect us from adding to our digital fingerprints. Here are ways of taking advantage of those tools.

Ad Blocker

Ad blockers should be set up on all Internet browsers. Some of the advantages of using one are

- Blocking pop-up ads, especially video ads, will improve the browser's performance.
- Preventing ads from being displayed ensures that they cannot be accidentally clicked and potentially install malware on the device.
- Web pages will be easier to read without unwanted ads on them.
- Prevent tracking that is associated with Web site ads.

One downside to ad blockers is that some Web sites will not function as designed if ads are blocked. This can be corrected by identifying trustworthy Web sites that should not have ad blocking applied. Another alternative would be to disable ad blocking temporarily if the Web site is important enough.

Browse Incognito

Most browsers have a private or *incognito* setting. Users may think that this allows them to browse and search with total anonymity, but unfortunately that is not the case. Even when going incognito, there are still Internet breadcrumbs following any activity.

At best, browsing in private mode will prevent anyone that uses the same browser later from seeing earlier activity on it. Incognito mode does not prevent activities from being uncovered in the following circumstances:

- Some browser extensions track online activity even when the browser was opened in incognito mode.
- ISPs can see domain names of Web sites visited but not activity on them.
- If mobile phone apps are given permission, they can see the browsing history.
- Web sites visited can track activity on their site via cookies.
- Government agencies can get court orders or warrants to access Internet activity from the ISP.
- Wi-Fi administrators can track online activity.

Clear the Browser's Cache Frequently

A browser cache contains a record of every Web site that has been visited. This can provide a wealth of information to someone who wants to learn about a user and his browsing habits. Periodically clearing the browser's cache can prevent this from happening. In a Firefox browser, click the three horizontal lines in the upper right corner and select the "Settings" option. Then click on the "Privacy & Security" option. Scroll down to the section labeled "Cookies and Site Data" and click the "Clear Data" button.

Figure 19.4 shows the "Clear browsing data and cookies" screen. A dropdown list box next to "When" provides the ability to delete recent activity or everything. To completely clear the browser's cache, click all four checkbox options and select "Everything" for the "When" field. Click the "Clear" button. The steps to accomplish this task in other browsers are similar.

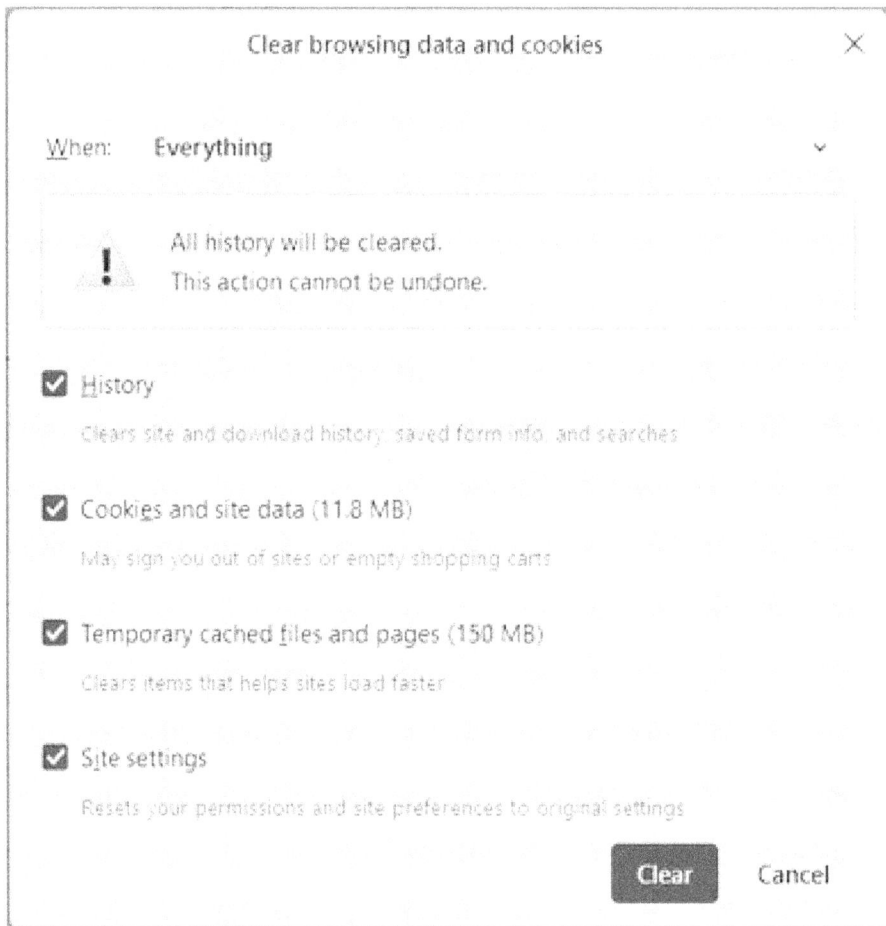

FIGURE 19.4 Clearing the browser cache

An alternative to manually clearing the cache is to set the browser to clear itself every time it is closed. In Firefox, this is the "Delete cookies and site data when Firefox is closed" option shown on Figure 19.5. Microsoft Edge also has settings that allow browsing history to be cleared each time the browser is closed. These settings are found by going to the "Settings" screen. Then select the "Privacy, search, and services" option. Identifying what should be deleted is in the "Delete browsing data" section of the screen.

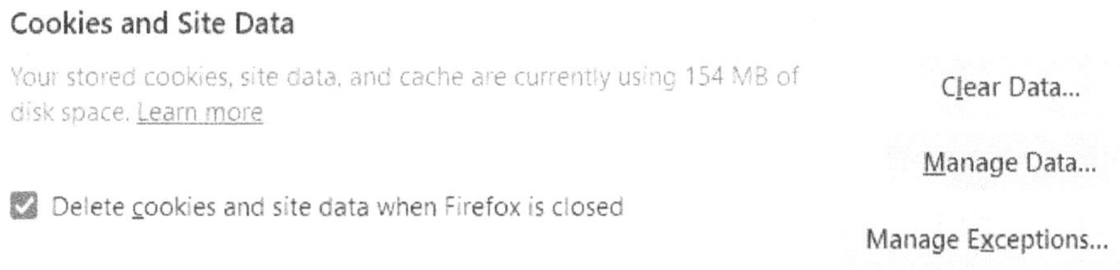

Cookies and Site Data

Your stored cookies, site data, and cache are currently using 154 MB of disk space. Learn more

☑ Delete cookies and site data when Firefox is closed

Clear Data...

Manage Data...

Manage Exceptions...

FIGURE 19.5 Clear the cache when Firefox is closed.

Cookies

Cookies are a way that Web sites and marketers track individuals. Every Web browser provides a way for the user to block cookies. Each browser handles it differently, but the normal way is to go to the "Settings" page then the privacy or security tab. Then select the desired privacy level or option.

When visiting Web sites, a banner may appear listing the site's cookies policy. Do not be reluctant to click the "Reject all cookies" option. If that option is not available, select the option that rejects third-party cookies and only selects first-party cookies.

Do Not Track

Most browsers have a "Do Not Track" setting on their privacy or security page. If this is set, the browser sends a request to Web sites requesting that no tracking of the visitor be done. There is no law that forces Web sites to honor these requests. Adhering to a "Do Not Track" request is entirely up to the Web site designers. There is no harm to enabling this setting so to go ahead and do it.

Safe Browsers

Some browsers are marketed as being safe or secure browsers. They are designed to provide more protection to the user when browsing the Internet. Using a safe browser can reduce a user's Internet footprint. Examples of safe browsers include the following:

- Brave®
- DuckDuckGo®
- Epic Privacy browser®
- Firefox®
- Ghostery Private browser®
- Tor®

Use Multiple Browsers

Every time anyone logs onto a Web site, details about them and their actions are recorded. Web sites are able to determine the computer manufacturer, operating system, time zone, browser, version of the browser, keyboard layout, and many other details to get a unique identification of the user. This might not provide them with the user's name or address, but they will be able to distinguish this user and his device from virtually any other user in the world. This is referred to as *browser fingerprinting*. Even if the user has a VPN installed this form of monitoring cannot be prevented.

If the user alternates between different browsers, it makes it more difficult to uniquely identify them because many of the items being tracked are changing. Some privacy experts recommend that one browser, say Firefox, should always be used for checking email. A second one, say Chrome, should always be used for social media activity. A third one, e.g., Edge, should be used for general Web surfing. This may seem a little extreme, but everyone has to decide how much maintaining their privacy is worth.

Privacy Extensions

A privacy extension is a small software program that modifies the behavior of a browser to enhance security and privacy when browsing. It gives the user additional control over how much data Web sites can collect about the user and his browsing habits. Privacy extensions focus on preventing user Internet activity from being tracked. Examples of privacy extensions include

- AdGuard®
- DuckDuckGo Privacy Essentials®
- Ghostery®
- HTTPS Everywhere®
- Privacy Badger®
- uBlock Origin®

CLEAN UP AFTER YOURSELF

Earlier sections in this chapter explain how one's Internet footprint can be minimized from now on. This section describes how existing details already on the Internet can be removed.

The Web is a difficult place to control. The reality is that even if all of the steps suggested here are taken, it is unlikely that everything about a person will be removed from the Internet. There is also the possibility of having one's data exposed on the Dark Web from a data breach. No advice that anyone can provide will remove all of an individual's data from the Internet.

Privacy Settings

All social media sites allow the user to adjust privacy settings to their preference. This enables them to restrict who can see their posts and other information. Relying on the default privacy settings is not a good idea. Everyone should review all privacy settings on a regular basis.

Examples of privacy type settings include

- who can view the owner's profile?
- who can see the owner's posts? Are they visible to friends, the public, or a selected group?
- what can individuals on the contact list or friend list see vs. what the general public can see?
- whether location data should be shared or not
- whether personal data should be shared or not
- review the friends lists to identify any that can be removed from the account.

- increased privacy settings for accounts belonging to children
- activity status showing the last time the owner was active on the account
- review what is in the owner's profile and whether it needs to be updated.
- review any photos on the site. Should they still be displayed?
- if an "Only Me" setting exists for tagging photographs on the site, consider setting it so photographs of you cannot be tagged. Request that all friends ask for permission before tagging photos of you.
- review all third-party applications connected to social media accounts. Revoke access of apps that are no longer being used.

After modifying the privacy settings to the desired values, the changes should be tested. Log into the media site using a different account. This could be a dummy account based on a dummy email address. Validate that the privacy settings have been modified as desired.

The steps to modify privacy settings differ for each site. Be sure to review and if necessary, change the settings for all social media accounts. Some of the major sites are listed below:

- Facebook
- Instagram
- LinkedIn
- Pinterest
- Reddit
- Snapchat
- TikTok
- Tumblr
- YouTube
- WhatsApp
- X

Metadata on Digital Photographs

Photographs taken with mobile phones or digital cameras can have a significant amount of metadata embedded with the digital image itself or in a separate associated file. Examples of metadata include

- date and time the image was created.
- longitude and latitude coordinates of where the image was created

- direction that the camera was pointed when the image was created
- make and model of the smartphone or camera
- service provider for the smartphone
- ownership details if they have been added to the metadata
- aperture, shutter speed, focal length, and ISO settings of the camera when the image was created

Longitude and latitudes data can especially revealing. Users can enter the coordinates into a mapping Web site and see a map showing the precise location of where the photo was taken. Most people would be extremely uncomfortable if they knew the location of their vacation home, children's favorite playground, or regular hiking trails was available to the general public.

Fortunately, metadata does not have to be exposed. Two ways to eliminate it are listed here:

1. Smartphones can be set to not include metadata when photographs are created. On an iPhone, open the "Settings" app. From there, drill down to the "Privacy & Settings," then "Location Services." Select "Camera" and check the "Never" option. From this point onward, the location information will not be included in the metadata.

   On an Android phone, open the "Camera app Settings" and toggle "Location Settings" to off.

2. Metadata can be removed from images after they have been created. On a Windows computer, right-click on the photo and select "Properties." Select the "Details" tab and click the "Remove Properties and Personal Information" link. The user can remove the metadata fields from the existing image file or create a copy of the image file with metadata fields removed.

   On a Mac computer, metadata can be removed by opening the Photos app. Select the photo to be modified and choose "Image" then "Location." Choose the "Hide Location" option.

Mobile Apps

Mobile apps gather a significant amount of information about the user. When being installed, they often request access to data like that from the GPS, contact list, browsing history, microphone, and camera. According to a *New York Times* investigation, as many as 200 million mobile devices are reporting location data to smart phone apps [TIME22]. Unless there is a very good reason to grant that access, it should be denied.

For apps that have already been installed on a mobile device, it is important to periodically review what access rights have been given to them. On an iPhone, finding which apps have access to GPS location data can be seen by going to the "Settings > Privacy & Security > Locations Services" screen. Identifying which apps have access to the phone's camera and microphone can be done on the "Settings > Privacy & Security > Camera and Settings > Privacy & Security > Microphone" screens. The "Location Services" screen is shown in Figure 19.6.

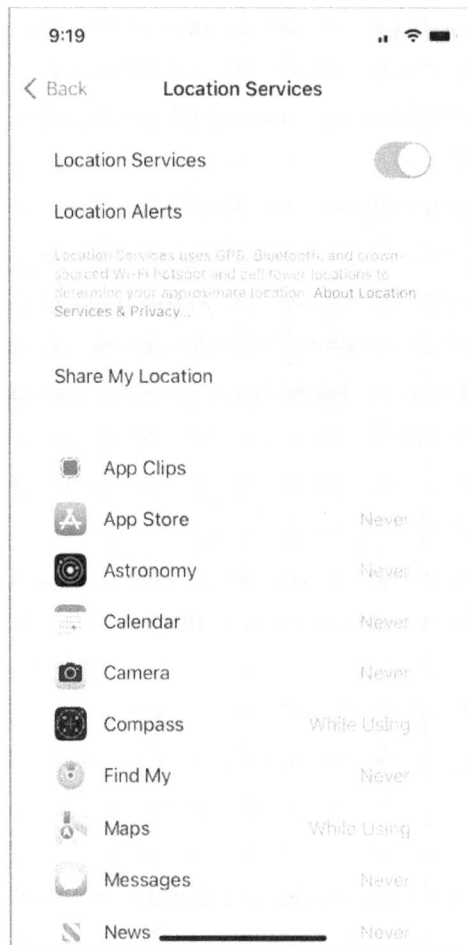

FIGURE 19.6 iPhone location services screen

Loyalty Cards

Grocery stores created loyalty programs to improve their business. These programs are offered by grocery stores, drug stores, fast food restaurants, and casinos. These programs exist for two reasons. First, the "rewards" are an enticement to get customers to come back to that store or chain in the future.

The second reason they exist is that they allow merchants to collect data on customers. When a customer joins, they are required to provide information their name, address, email address, and phone number. Each time a member swipes their loyalty card to get rewards, it enables the store to track what was purchased that visit. Over time, the store compiles an extremely detailed profile of each member's shopping habits. This data can be used to personalize advertising for that customer. This customer data can also be sold to a data broker.

Everyone needs to decide for themselves if the savings offered by these loyalty programs is worth having their shopping history collected.

Remove, Delete, and Close

Everyone should regularly purge old data from their computers, email account, and social media sites. (If something has not been reviewed for years, what are the chances you will use it in the future?) Consider the following list:

- There are many advantages to deleting old emails. One reason is to save space. Purging old emails will make searching for the remaining ones faster and easier. Another reason is that if a cybercriminal gains access to the account, all of those old emails might provide enough personal details to mount an identity attack. One last reason is that any email older than 180 days is considered "abandoned" and the US government does not need a warrant to access them [HOW22].

- Delete old, unused email accounts. If it is not being used it is just one more opportunity for a cybercriminal to learn more about the owner and build a more detailed profile of them.

- Delete old posts, pictures, and videos from Instagram, Flickr, X, and Facebook. (Is it really valuable to keep all old posts, pictures, and videos?) Deleting them will keep them out of the hands of cybercriminals. Additionally, it may prevent a future employer, romantic partner, or landlord from accessing these.

- Delete old accounts associated with rewards programs. If that store is never visited any more, it is better to sever all ties with it.
- Accounts on forums that are never looked at can safely be deleted.
- Unsubscribe from mailing lists that no longer have any value. It will keep your email inbox cleaner and prevent a cybercriminal from learning more about a potential victim.

What Cannot Be Removed from the Internet

Public record information is anything that has been recorded or filed with a public agency. Prior to the advent of online databases, a trip to the courthouse or other government building was necessary to access public information. Much of this information is now available online. Public records cannot be removed from the Internet

Some examples of data that is considered public information in some states and is likely accessible on the Internet includes the following:

- birth and death certificates
- court records
- property tax records
- arrest records for adults
- marriage licenses
- voting registration
- wills are considered public records in some states
- mug shots

Self-Research

Searching for any details available to yourself to see what the Internet holds at least once or twice a year is a good idea. Anything you can find can be found by someone else as well. Anything inaccurate that turns up should be removed as soon as possible.

Uninstall

Every app on a device has a potential vulnerability. The app itself might be collecting data on the user. A cybercriminal may find a way to crack it. The Web site might experience a breach. It might be subpoenaed by the government.

All of these scenarios are possible. One method of minimizing exposure is to uninstall any apps not being used from phones, tablets, laptops, and desktop computers. Be sure to remove any data from the app before uninstalling it.

Use Virtual Credit Cards

Virtual (or *temporary*) credit cards are like regular credit cards except they are not made of plastic. They can be used just like a normal credit card when making online purchases. Their greatest advantage is that they keep the user's PII like email addresses, mobile phone number, and physical credit card numbers private.

Another advantage to them is that if a cybercriminal figures out how to use one, the owner can simply delete it and get a virtual card issued. This is much simpler than getting a physical, plastic card replaced.

Some sources for virtual cards are

- Capital One®
- Privacy®
- Revolut®

If you do not want to go to the trouble of obtaining and using virtual credit cards, that is understandable. It is a new concept and new ideas take time to be accepted. Even if you do not get a virtual credit card, never use debit cards for any online transaction. Credit cards should always be used.

VPN

A VPN provides a great deal of anonymity. It prevents the ISP, Web site, and eavesdroppers from accessing communications and tracking. Use a VPN as much as possible, if not all the time. One should certainly be used when connecting to the Internet via public Wi-Fi.

DIGITAL PROTECTION LAWS

Digital protection laws are being written to mandate protection for citizens' data. Some examples of laws that protect consumers are described here. Hopefully, all consumers will be covered by similar or even stronger laws.

General Data Protection Regulation (GDPR)

The premier example of data protection legislation is the General Data Protection Regulation (GDPR) in the European Union (EU). A survey by Persona shows that 66% of Americans want the US to adopt privacy laws similar to the GDPR [PERS24].

The six principles of the GDPR are as follows [VINCI17]:

1. Data must be treated in a way that is lawful, fair, and transparent.

2. Data should be collected for specified and explicit purposes and not used in a way someone would not expect.

3. It must be clear why the data is being collected and what will be done with it.

4. Reasonable steps must be taken to keep the information up to date and change it if it is inaccurate.

5. Data should not be kept for longer than is needed, and it must be destroyed or deleted when it is no longer used or goes out of date.

6. Data should be processed in a way that ensures the appropriate security, including protection against unauthorized or unlawful processing, loss, damage, or destruction, and it should be kept safe and secure.

California Consumer Privacy Act (CCPA)

In the US, the state of California was the first to enact similar protective legislation. Some of the new privacy rights the CCPA provides include the following [CAAG24]:

- The right to know about the personal information a business collects about them and how it is used and shared.
- The right to delete personal information collected from them (with some exceptions).
- The right to opt out of the sale or sharing of their personal information.
- The right to non-discrimination for exercising their CCPA rights.
- The right to correct inaccurate personal information that a business has about them.
- The right to limit the use and disclosure of sensitive personal information collected about them.

Other states and countries provide varying degrees of protection for consumers' data. Everyone should be aware of the rights that their states or governments have enacted.

REMOVING DATA FROM THE INTERNET

It is possible to have some personal data removed from the Internet, but it is not an easy process. The following sections describe how this can be done.

Even if all the data about you was miraculously removed from the Internet right now, it is likely that new data will be captured about you in the future. If you continue to access the Internet for social media, browsing, sending emails, and online shopping, then data about you will continue to be recorded.

Do It Yourself (DIY)

In 2022, Google provided a "Results about You" tool that can be used to see what information Google has on the requester. If the results are not accurate or the requester would like them removed, then a request for this can be made to Google.

Other Web sites are not so accommodating. Anyone wanting to remove their data will have to locate data about themselves using a search engine. The next step would be to contact the administrator or Webmaster for each site and request that data be removed. Each site is almost certain to have their own contact forms that need to be filled out.

Data Removal Services

If the amount of time and effort it takes to have personal information removed from the Internet seems overwhelming, then you might consider having experts do it. There are several companies that will take on this effort for consumers. Some of the more widely known services are as follows:

- Aura®
- DeleteMe®
- Incognito®
- Norton's ReputationDefender®
- Optery®

FINAL SUGGESTIONS

Some final suggestions for cleaning up your Internet exposure that did not fit into the above categories are as follows:

- If an opt-out or "No Junk Email" option is available when registering an email account, definitely take it.
- Do not provide actual birth dates of other PII on social media sites, if possible.
- Do not store credit card info on store's Web sites. Allowing it to be stored there might be convenient, but if their Web site is breached, all the PII on it, including credit card numbers, will be exposed.
- When signing up for online services, consider using an alternate email address or a pseudonym.
- Do not enter online contests. The odds of winning are abysmal. It is almost certain that personal information required to enter the contest will be sold to data brokers.
- Limit the number of online accounts. Use guest accounts for rarely accessed sites if possible.
- Request that friends and relatives not tag your photographs on their social media sites.
- Use a unique password for every social media account.
- Do not link accounts, i.e., signing into an account via Facebook or Google. Doing this may be convenient, but if the top-level account is compromised, so are all the lower-level accounts.
- Do not use a work computer for personal activities.
- Ignore requests to complete online surveys. There is no personal benefit to completing them. They are just a method of collecting personal information for tracking and marketing purposes.

REFERENCES

[BUS22] "Kaplan Survey: The Percentage of College Admissions Officers Who Say Applications Social Media Content is 'Fair Game' Ticks Up," available online at *https://www.businesswire.com/news/home/20220201005310/en/ Kaplan-Survey-The-Percentage-of-College-Admissions-Officers-Who-Say-Applicants%E2%80%99-Social-Media-Content-is-%E2% 80%9CFair-Game%E2%80%9D-Ticks-Up*, February 1, 2022

[CAAG24] Bonta, Rob. "California Consumer Privacy Act (CCPA)," available online at *https://oag.ca.gov/privacy/ccpa*, March 13, 2024

[CHEEK] Hankel, Isaiah. "Haven't Heard Back from an Employer? Maybe It is Your Digital Footprint," available online at *https://cheekyscientist.com/havent-heard-back-from-an-employer-maybe-its-your-digital-footprint/*, undated

[CNBC23] Burris, Devan. "How grocery stores are becoming data brokers," available online at *https://www.cnbc.com/2023/12/10/how-grocery-stores-are-becoming-data-brokers.html*, December 10, 2023

[HOW22] Hoffman, Chris. "Why You Should Delete Emails Instead of Archiving Them," available online at *https://www.howtogeek.com/709693/why-you-should-delete-emails-instead-of-archiving-them/#in-the-usa-emails-are-abandoned-after-180-days*, March 12, 2022

[INCOG] "Data Broker Opt Out (A: Z)," available online at *https://blog.incogni.com/opt-out-guides/*, undated

[JUST23] "How Social Media Use Can Affect Legal Admissibility to the US," available online at *https://www.justia.com/immigration/social-media-and-visa-applications/*, October 2023

[MMR24] "Data Broker Market is Expected to Grow CAGR of 7.25% Over 2024-2030," available online at *https://www.maximizemarketresearch.com/market-report/global-data-broker-market/55670/*, July 2024

[MONEY24] Osorio, Carolyn. "You've Been Warned: These Companies Are Collecting And Selling Your Data," available online at *https://www.moneydigest.com/1602141/data-broker-companies-that-sell-data-make-ton-money/*, June 13, 2024

[ONEREP24] Shelest, Dimitri. "Top five largest data brokers in America: the hidden impact on privacy and security," available online at *https://onerep.com/blog/largest-data-brokers-in-america*, April 22, 2024

[PCMAG22] Moscaritolo, Angela. "What Does Big Tech Know About You? Basically Everything," available online at *https://www.pcmag.com/news/what-does-big-tech-know-about-you-basically-everything*, January 18, 2022

[PERS24] Bonderud, Doug. "Top GDPR statistics businesses must know," available online at *https://withpersona.com/blog/top-gdpr-statistics-businesses-must-know*, February 2, 2024

[PEW24] McClain, Colleen. "How Americans View Data Privacy," available online at *https://www.pewresearch.org/internet/2023/10/18/how-americans-view-data-privacy/*, October 23, 2024

[PRIV22] "Registered Data Brokers in the United States: 2021," available online at *https://privacyrights.org/resources/registered-data-brokers-united-states-2021*, February 22, 2022

[PRNE21] "50% of Online Dating Services Users Research their Data before their First Face-to-face Encounter," available online at *https://www.prnewswire.com/news-releases/50-of-online-dating-services-users-research-their-date-before-their-first-face-to-face-encounter-301227081.html*, February 11, 2021

[TIME22] Fussell, Sidney. "The Most Important Things to Know About Apps That Track Your Location," available online at *https://time.com/6209991/apps-collecting-personal-data/*, September 1, 2022

[VINCI17] "Six principles of GDPR that you need to know about," available online at *https://vinciworks.com/blog/six-principles-of-gdpr-that-you-need-to-know-about/*, October 25, 2017

[WILEY22] Jayasuriya, Dulani. "The use of digital footprints in the US mortgage market," available online at *https://onlinelibrary.wiley.com/doi/full/10.1111/acfi.12946*, April 12, 2022

[WILEY24] Pozza, Duane. "New Federal Data Broker Law Will Restrict Certain Foreign Data Sales Effective June 23," available online at *https://www.wiley.law/alert-New-Federal-Data-Broker-Law-Will-Restrict-Certain-Foreign-Data-Sales-Effective-June-23*, May 7, 2024

[WORL24] Eser, Alexander. "Global Data Broker Industry Statistics: Revenue Soars, Marketers Embrace Data," available online at *https://worldmetrics.org/data-broker-industry-statistics/*, July 23, 2024

CHAPTER 20

FINAL TIPS

This chapter covers topics that are important but did not fit into any of the preceding chapters and did not justify a chapter of their own. Just because they are covered in the last chapter does not mean that they are not significant.

ATTACK SURFACE

Attack surface is a reference to the number of possible entry points that might allow a cybercriminal to enter a computer or network. Every piece of software installed on a device increases its attack surface. The larger the attack surface, the more ways that a cybercriminal can potentially find as an entry point. The smaller the attack surface of a computer, network, or entire system, the easier it is to protect it.

Reducing the Attack Surface

Taking steps to reduce the attack surface is important for every computer owner. Examples of these steps include the following:

- Manufacturers install a large amount of software, frequently referred to as "bloatware," onto their products. If an application is not going to be used, then it should be removed as quickly as possible so it is not forgotten. Removing as much or all of it immediately after acquiring the device is an excellent step toward reducing the attack surface.
- Remove any software that is no longer needed.

- Delete any accounts that are no longer needed.
- Change the passwords for accounts, especially default accounts, associated with applications on the device.
- Eliminate redundant software. Having two or more applications that do the same thing doubles the ways a cybercriminal can break in without increasing functionality.
- Close any ports that are not being used. Set the firewall to restrict ports that can be accessed by outsiders.
- Use strong passwords for all applications and Web sites.
- Update all software, including applications and operating systems, regularly.
- Use a vulnerability scanner like Nessus Essentials, Wireshark, or OpenVAS to evaluate the attack surface of the computer or environment.

BUYING USED ELECTRONIC DEVICES

There is nothing wrong with trying to save money and re-use an electronic device, but it needs to be done safely. Some of the points to consider before purchasing a previously used device include the following:

- Verify that the device works before purchasing it. Boot it up and perform some basic testing before paying for it.
- Has the device been damaged? Using an electronic device that is damaged could result in an electrical shock or a fire when it is plugged in.
- Confirm that the battery is still working when considering a used laptop. If the battery does not work, a replacement will be expensive or unavailable.
- Confirm that applicable vendors, both hardware and software, still support the device. Specifically, are they still releasing security updates? Without adequate support, any device can quickly become a security liability.
- Determine whether components in it can be upgraded. One of the fastest ways to speed up a computer is to add RAM to it. If RAM cannot be added, the chances of making it faster are limited.
- Be aware that a used computer will not be as fast as a new one. A used computer is unlikely to perform satisfactorily as a gaming system. If the intent is to use it for reading email and general Web browsing, then it may be useful.
- Perform a factory reset before using it to ensure no malware exists on the device.

DATA BREACHES

According to IBM, a data breach is "any security incident in which unauthorized parties access sensitive or confidential information" [IBM24]. Unfortunately, data breaches are a reality in modern life. The *Wall Street Journal* reported that in the US, there were 3,205 data breaches in 2023[WSJ24]. A January 2024 report by *US New and World Report* states that 61% of US citizens learned that their personal data had been compromised or breached at least once [USNEWS24].

Data revealed in data breaches can be used by cybercriminals in many ways. Some of them are as follows:

- Personal details can make phishing and smishing attempts more credible.
- Since many users have the same passwords for multiple accounts breached data can be used for account takeover attacks. This is also referred to as a credential stuffing attack.
- Personal details can be used to apply for loans, credit cards, and mortgages in the name of a victim. The cybercriminal obtains the money and the victim must pay the debt or prove he didn't incur it.
- Leaked personal information can be used to bypass authentication measures. For example, knowing previous addresses or family member names and birthdates could enable a cybercriminal to successfully answer account security questions.

Examples of Data Breaches

A data breach that occurred in December 2023 but did not come to light until August 2024 involved National Public Data (NPD). This company, which collects data for background checks, had an estimated 2.9 billion rows of data leaked [INFO24]. The leaked data included full names, maiden names, Social Security Numbers, email addresses, phone numbers, and mailing addresses of hundreds of millions of Americans [SPY24].

Other significant recent data breaches are listed here [NORD24]:

Victim	Date	Record Count
Yahoo	2013-2016	Over three billion user accounts
Equifax	2017	About 148 million US, 163 million worldwide
Facebook	2019	About 533 million users' records worldwide
Aadhaar	2018	Records of 1.1 billion Indian Citizens

The Increasing Rate of Data Breaches

The number of data breaches is increasing: There were almost 20% more breaches in 2023 than in 2022 [MIT24]. MIT professor Stuart Madnick identified three primary reasons for the increase in personal data theft [MIT24]:

- Cloud misconfiguration: As more data is concentrated in the cloud, it becomes a larger target for cybercriminals. Mistakes made in setting up cloud storage like retaining default settings, not installing software updates, poor authentication, and not encrypting backups make it easier for cybercriminals to access data stored in the cloud.

- Ransomware as a threat is growing and evolving. Criminals with limited technical skills can purchase or rent software that performs ransomware attacks. Current forms of ransomware attacks include downloading the victim data and selling it on the Dark Web as well as demanding a ransom to decrypt the victim's files or devices.

- Attacks on vendors, also known as *supply chain attacks*, enable cybercriminals to attack an organization by penetrating any vendor or supplier that the organization deals with. The Target data breach 2013 occurred when a cybercriminal broke into a third-party vendor that supplied HVAC services for the retailer. They then worked their way onto Target's network [USSENATE14]. Supply chain attacks expand organizations' attack surface geometrically.

Responding to a Data Breach

Individuals cannot prevent data breaches, but they can control how they respond when one occurs. Laws have been enacted that require organizations to notify individuals if their data was or is suspected of being exposed. If an individual receives a data breach notice from an organization the steps that should be taken include the following:

1. Change the passwords on all affected accounts. If those passwords have been used on multiple accounts, then they should be changed in all locations.

2. Contact one of the major credit bureaus requesting that a fraud alert be added to your credit reports. This encourages potential lenders to take additional steps to verify the requestor's identity before issuing new forms of credit.

3. Victims can also apply for a security freeze on their accounts. This limits the access that cybercriminals have to the account, but also prevents legitimate entities like landlords and potential employers from accessing the account as well. A freeze account must be requested from each of the largest US credit bureaus: Equifax, Experian, and TransUnion.

4. Set up multi-factor authentication (MFA) on all accounts.

5. Closely monitor financial accounts and credit reports. Every US consumer can receive one free credit report annually from each of the three major credit bureaus. Free credit reports can be requested at *https://www.annualcreditreport.com*.

6. Be vigilant for phishing and other social engineering attacks that might be based on data exposed in a breach.

DEFENSE-IN-DEPTH

There is no silver bullet for staying safe. No single protection technique is foolproof. The best protection is the concept of "defense-in-depth." The definition of "defense-in-depth" according to the National Institute of Standards and Technology (NIST) is "the application of multiple countermeasures in a layered manner to achieve security objectives. This ensures that attacks missed by one technology are caught by another" [NIST].

A common metaphor when describing the principle of defense-in-depth is a castle. Just as the architects of castles knew that multiple physical levels helped to maximize its security, computer security specialists also design layers of protection. Elements that were included in the overall defense of a castle included:

- open approaches, i.e., nothing for an enemy to hide behind when approaching the castle
- a moat to prevent enemies from nearing the castle walls except by crossing a drawbridge
- strong outer walls that can repel potential invaders
- Arrow slits in the walls from which archers can fire arrows
- watchtowers on the outer wall that provide long distance surveillance and a weapons platform

- battlements on the outer and inner walls allow archers to shoot while minimizing their exposure to enemy fire
- a drawbridge that can be lifted to prevent enemies from crossing the moat
- a portcullis, i.e., a gate, that can restrict entry into the castle once the drawbridge has been crossed
- a gatehouse that provides protection for the drawbridge and portcullis
- inner walls that provide a second line of defense in case the outer walls are breached
- the keep, which is a fortified tower within the castle walls that serves as the bastion of last resort

Examples of Cyber Defense-in-Depth Layers

Examples of actions that are part of a defense-in-depth strategy for an individual's computer environment include the following:

- Strong passwords have been set on all accounts and Web sites. This includes default accounts associated with applications and IoT devices.
- regular application of software patches and upgrades, especially security related patches. Ideally these would be installed automatically.
- installation of antivirus software to protect devices from malware
- user training, so they know not to click dangerous links or open questionable email attachments
- firewalls to control inbound and outbound network traffic.
- email filtering to prevent spam and malware from reaching users.
- creating backups on a regular basis. Ideally multiple backups are stored both on-site and offsite and on different types of media.
- encrypting data so even if a cybercriminal accesses it, he cannot read it or use it for blackmail or extortion purposes.
- using a VPN to prevent cybercriminals from eavesdropping on communications across the Internet.
- limiting online activities, especially transactions, to secure, HTTPS Web sites.

DISPOSING OF ELECTRONIC DEVICES

Eventually, the smart phone or computer that has served so well will need to be replaced. When an electronic device is going to be disposed of, some precautions need to be taken because they can contain a wealth of personal data about their owners. A study of recycled devices by the National Association for Information Destruction found that 40% of resold devices contained personal information [FORB21].

Data That Can Be Exposed by Improper Device Disposal

Examples of data that can be found on devices that are thrown away include the following:

- Social Security Numbers
- passwords
- bank account numbers
- investment fund account numbers
- personal letters or emails
- completed tax forms
- contracts
- health data
- relationship details, i.e., the names of friends and family
- location data

Examples of devices that can retain data include

- desktop computers
- laptop computers
- tablets
- smart phones
- Fitbits
- hard drives
- thumb drives
- external drives
- printers
- copiers
- digital cameras

Steps to Take Before Disposing of Electronic Devices

NIST Special Publication 800-88 "Guidelines for Media Sanitation" provides a complete list of steps that are recommended for government agencies, contractors, NGOs, and other organizations. A summary of steps that consumers should follow are as follows:

- Make a backup of the data on the device. Losing data because it only existed on the device about to be thrown out would be unfortunate.
- Transfer any software licenses that are still needed to the replacement device. Most vendors will allow their product to be transferred to a new device, but some may not. This is especially useful if the replacement device is substantially newer or faster than the old device.
- Deauthorize subscription services like iTunes and Netflix from the device.
- For Apple devices, make sure it will not be found by the "Find My Phone" feature.
- Deleting files is not enough. The standard delete command merely moves files into a trash or recycle bin. They can still be recovered using standard commands or special tools. A secure erase must be done using a tool like File Shredder®, Eraser®, KillDisk®, or BCWipe®.
- If the device is going to be recycled instead of being sold, then its hard drive should be destroyed, possible by a hammer or a drill.
- Perform a factory reset on computers, laptops, tablets, and smart phones that are going to be sold or recycled.
- Remove all SIM cards, SD cards, and DVDs from the device.
- For mobile phones, contact your service provider to remove the device from the account. This should be done whether the device is being thrown away, sold, or recycled.

FREE APPLICATIONS VS. PAID APPLICATIONS

Free seems like the best bargain of all, but that is not always the case. Vendors have to make money somehow. If they are not charging for their product, they may be selling user information or using it for advertising. A saying in the computer security field is "If you're not paying for the product, then *you* are the product!"

Social media sites are a prime example of this concept. It costs a significant amount of money to write the software for their Web sites. Building and operating data centers costs even more. An article posted by Data Center Frontier in 2021 said that Facebook has invested $16 billion to build and operate its data centers in the United States alone [DATA21]. Facebook and other social media sites do not charge users to open an account but instead make their money selling data on users or by selling advertisements on the site. Each of us must decide whether we are comfortable knowing that sites are marketing us.

INCIDENT RESPONSE PLAN (IRP)

An IRP lays out the steps to be taken and who will perform them if a computer or network is compromised. Having a plan can make recovery from an incident faster and easier. It helps ensure that important steps are not overlooked in a crisis.

An IRP for a large organization can be an extremely long and complex document. Some of the points included in the plan would be the following:

- who should be contacted when an incident is identified
- actions to contain the malware
- investigating how widespread the attack is
- steps to maintain business operations until the incident is resolved
- restoring affected hardware and software
- which authorities need to be contacted and who will initiate that contact
- handling the public relation impact of the incident
- handling legal implications if user data has been breached
- determining whether Disaster Recovery (DR) or Business Continuity (BC) plans should be invoked
- identifies who will be responsible for a post-attack forensic analysis
- taking steps to ensure a similar situation does not occur again

It is typical for a business or organization to have an IRP but having one can also be valuable for individuals and families. Of course, a plan for individuals will be much simpler, but having steps laid out will be invaluable if a home computer or laptop gets hacked, stolen, or affected by a natural disaster.

Everyone's needs are different, but steps that should be included in most personal IRP's are listed here:

- Inventory all hardware and software components immediately. It will be challenging to restore the environment if no one remembers details about the devices and what was loaded onto them.

- Compile a list of indicators that the computer has been attacked. It could be as obvious as a message on the screen saying "ALL OF YOUR FILES ARE BEING HELD BY RANSOMWARE" or as subtle as the computer running much slower than usual. If any of these indications occur, then pull out the plan and start working through it.
- Power down the device. Just disconnecting it from the Internet is not sufficient because malware that is already been installed is likely to be affecting files on the device.
- Determine the cause of the problem. Scanning the disk drives of the affected computer should reveal if any malware that has been loaded onto it. The personnel responsible for this can be the owner, a coworker, a relative, or an expert that was previously engaged.
- Remove the malware.
- Re-install software onto the device.
- Restore the data from the most recent backup. Prior to this step make sure that the malware has been completely eradicated. If it still exists on the computer, it can contaminate the backup data as well.
- Identify lessons learned from the incident. This might result in making changes to the IRP, acquiring better antivirus software, using a VPN, or learning not to click on bogus links or open email attachments.

Final IRP Advice

Some file advice on the IRP:

- Write the plan now. No one thinks they will get infected with ransomware, a trojan horse, or other malware but it happens. A study by the University of Maryland found that over 2,200 cyberattacks occur each day in the US alone [EXPL24].
- Review the plan periodically. Annually should be good enough, but it is also wise to review it after acquiring new devices or software.
- Print out the plan. If it is stored on the infected computer, it probably will not be available when it is needed the most.

Not everyone has the experience, skills, or personality to deal with a corrupt computer themselves. There is no shame in having experts handle the technical details of an incident. Contacting an expert or firm in advance, ideally when the IRP is being developed, is advisable. A pre-existing relationship with technical experts will allow them to get involved faster and hopefully resolve the problem more quickly.

ONLINE SHOPPING

Over 81% of the US population and 33% of the world's total population does at least some shopping online [YAG24]. Most online shopping transactions are safe, but unfortunately a small percentage of transactions result in problems. The potential problems range from being scammed out of the payment all the way up to having malware or ransomware installed on the device being used to make the transaction.

Examples of Online Shopping Scams

Examples of online shopping scams include the following:

- The Better Business Bureau (BBB) estimates that at least 80% of links advertising puppies for sale are scams [BBB17]. Those adorable pictures of puppies are copied from other Web sites and the "seller" has no intentions of delivering a puppy [SOPH20]. After the victim pays for the pet, the scam artists may attempt to con the victim for transportation, vet fees, and other additional expenses.

- Fake Web sites that claim to be selling luxury items like purses and jewelry at a steep discount. Somes explain the low prices by saying the store is closing down. Always be wary of prices that seem too good to be true.

- Offers of "free" products including digital ones like movies, audio files, and digital assets used in online video games like Roblox®, Fortnite®, and Apex Legends® can be scams [FSEC]. A study by F-Secure warns that offers of free digital items often result in the victim's login credentials being harvested by the scammers.

- Hard to find, must-have holiday toys are frequently the bait for online shopping scams according to the Better Business Bureau [BBB22]. An Internet search for the toy takes the victim to a Web site that claims to have it, but frequently the site is a scam and the toy will never be shipped.

Steps to Avoid Online Shopping Scams

Steps that the average consumer can take to avoid problems when shopping online include the following:

- Only make purchases from secure Web sites. If the Web site address begins with *HTTPS://*, then it uses encryption to protect the consumer's information. Web sites that begin with *HTTP://* do not have this critical protection.

- Use a credit card instead of a debit card. If a cybercriminal acquires debit card account details, he can potentially steal everything from the account. Consumers are responsible for at most $50 if a credit card is stolen.

- If the merchant never ships the items or they ship the wrong item, the consumer can dispute the charges. Disputed transactions will be removed from the credit card account. If the item was paid for with a debit card, the money cannot be recovered.

- Using a virtual credit card is an even better tactic. If the cybercriminal tries to make charges against it in the future, the card can be cancelled.

- Payment systems like PayPal, Apple Pay®, Google Pay®, or Samsung Pay® for online transactions provide all the advantages of a credit card as well as hiding the consumer's credit card details.

- Only deal with established companies.

- Avoid any conducting transactions over public Wi-Fi. If it absolutely must be done, then use a VPN to ensure a secure Internet connection.

- If the requested payment method is unusual, e.g., money order, wire transfer, or cryptocurrency, there is a good chance that this is a scam.

- If an online search for an unfamiliar company turns up no results, then it is very likely a scam.

- Never forget: If a deal seems too good to be true, then it is probably a scam.

Peer-to-Peer (P2P) Payments

Peer-to-peer payment apps allow users to send and receive money directly to friends, coworkers, relatives, and businesses. The money is withdrawn from or deposited into the user's bank account. Examples of P2P methods include the following:

- Apple Cash®
- PayPal®
- Venmo®
- Cash App®
- Zelle®
- Revolut®

The advantages of these apps are that they are easy to use, quick, and cashless. They run on a user's mobile phone so transactions can be done from anywhere and at any time. Most P2P apps incur fees with each transfer, but some are fee-less.

Besides the fees, the major disadvantage of P2P payment apps is the difficulty getting money back once it has been sent. They do not offer the same protection that a credit card provides. Money can be sent to the wrong party if the wrong name or phone number is entered. In other cases, the merchandise might not be what was promised. Money can also be lost due to a scam.

Examples of P2P scams include the following:

- requests for charitable donations where only a fraction of the funds collected actually goes toward the specified cause
- tech support scams
- fraudulent pet sales
- phishing scams intended to take control of the victim's P2P account
- Accidental transfer scams, where the scammer transfers money into the victim's account and then claims that it was a mistake and asks for it to be transferred back. Later, if the P2P vendor determines that the money was stolen, the innocent victim may have to refund it to the original victim.

Steps to Secure P2P Accounts

Some steps that can be taken to secure P2P accounts include the following:

- Enable MFA to make it more difficult for a cybercriminal to take control of the account.
- Double check that the recipient's name or number is correct before sending money.
- If a fraudulent or questionable transaction appears, notify the P2P app vendor and the bank's customer service department immediately.
- Do not fall victim to phishing calls or emails claiming to be the P2P app's customer service department. Their goal is to trick the victim into revealing the password by stating that the account is suspended or about to be closed unless the user signs in immediately.
- Keep both the application and phone's operating system updated.

REPORTING SCAMS

Typically, victims of any kind of scam do not want to tell anyone about it. The normal reaction is to pretend it never happened. There are at least two reasons for reporting scamming incidents.

The first reason is that it is possible that some of the losses can be recovered. Depending on the method of payment, it is possible that authorities may be able to stop the money from being moved to another country. In 2023, the Federal Trade Commission (FTC) refunded $330 million to consumers [FTC24].

The second reason for reporting scams is to help authorities stop criminals. Information provided to the FTC is shared with the FBI and other law enforcement partners to help them understand the latest techniques and work to stop them. Fraud can be reported online at *https://reportfraud.ftc.gov/*.

SCAMMED AGAIN

Scam victims have a greater chance of being scammed again. Criminals sell lists of victims, called *sucker lists*, to other criminals. Their expectation is that anyone who fell for a scam once is more likely to be deceived a second time. One particularly obnoxious scam is to contact victims and claim they can help recover losses from a previous scam. If anyone requires a fee or upfront payment to help recover losses, then this is definitely a scam.

ADDITIONAL RESOURCES

New information about cyber security comes out regularly. The following sources can be used to stay updated on emerging threats and ways to deal with them.

TABLE 20.1 Additional resources related to cybersecurity

Federal Trade Commission	*www.ftc.gov*
Internet Crime Complaint Center (IC3)	*www.ic3.gov*
National Cybersecurity Alliance	*www.staysafeonline.org*
National Institute of Standards and Technology	*www.nist.gov*
National Coordinator for Critical Infrastructure Security and Resilience	*www.cisa.gov*
Verizon's Data Breach Investigations Report	*www.verizon.com/business/resources/reports/*
FBI	*www.fbi.gov/investigate/cyber*
Department of Homeland Security	*https://www.dhs.gov/archive/science-and-technology/cybersecurity-resources*

THE LAST WORD

The saying goes "freedom is not free." When it comes to the Internet and computers, safety is not free either. It takes knowledge, time, and perhaps some money. Hopefully, this book has given readers the knowledge needed to protect themselves from cyberthreats. It is a dangerous world out there: try to stay safe.

REFERENCES

[BBB17] Baker, Steven. "Puppy Scams: How Fake Online Pet Sellers Steal from Unsuspecting Pet Buyers," available online at *https://www.bbb. org/content/dam/0734-st-louis/puppy-scams-creative/puppy-scams-bbb-study.pdf*, September 2017

BBB22] "BBB Scam Alert: Looking for this season's hot toy? Beware of scams," available online at *https://www.bbb.org/article/scams/16580-scam-alert-looking-for-this-seasons-hot-toy-beware-of-scams*, November 8, 2022

[DATA21] Miller, Rich. "Facebook Showcases its 40 Million Square Feet of Global Data Centers," available online at *https://www.datacenterfrontier. com/hyperscale/article/11427952/facebook-showcases-its-40-million-square-feet-of-global-data-centers*, September 15, 2021

[EXPL24] Howarth, Josh. "How Many Cyber Attacks Occur Each Day? (2024)," available online at *https://explodingtopics.com/blog/cybersecurity-stats*, July 8, 2024

[FORB21] Schafer, Renee. "The Do's and Don'ts of Digital Data Disposal," available online at *https://www.forbes.com/councils/forbesbusinesscouncil/2021/03/05/ the-dos-and-donts-of-digital-data-disposal/*, May 5, 2021

[FSEC] "4 sneaky online shopping scams and how to avoid them," available online at *https://www.f-secure.com/us-en/articles/4-sneaky-online-shopping-scams*, undated

[FTC24] "Data on Refunds to Consumers," available online at https://www.ftc. gov/enforcement/ftc-refund-programs/data-refunds-consumers#Snapshot, undated

[IBM24] Kosinski, Matthew. "What is a data breach?," available online at https://www.ibm.com/topics/data-breach, May 24, 2024

[INFO24] Pallardy, Carrie. "Examining the National Public Data Breach and Risks for Data Brokers," available online at *https://www.informationweek.com/cyber-resilience/examining-the-national-public-data-breach-and-risks-for-data-brokers*, August 22, 2024

[MIT24] Beth Stackpole. "MIT Report details new cybersecurity risks," available online at *https://mitsloan.mit.edu/ideas-made-to-matter/mit-report-details-new-cybersecurity-risks*, April 30, 2024

[NIST. "Defense-in-depth," available online at *https://csrc.nist.gov/glossary/term/defense_in_depth*, undated

[NORD24] Skebaite, Aurelija. "The 20 biggest data breaches in history," available online at *https://nordvpn.com/blog/biggest-data-breaches/*, Aug 21, 2024

[SOPH20] "Coronavirus pandemic coincides with spike in online puppy scams," available online at *https://news.sophos.com/en-us/2020/05/04/coronavirus-pandemic-coincides-with-spike-in-online-puppy-scams/*, May 4, 2020

[SPY24] Johnson, Aurora. "What to Know About the National Public Data Breach—Is it Worthy of the Hype?," available online at *https://spycloud.com/blog/national-public-data-breach-analysis/*, August 22, 2024

[USNEWS24] Lever, Rob. "Digital Privacy Survey Report 2024," available online at *https://www.usnews.com/360-reviews/privacy/digital-privacy-consumer-survey*, January 23, 2024

[USSENATE14] Staff Report. "A 'Kill Chain' Analysis of the 2013 Target Data Breach," available online at *https://www.commerce.senate.gov/services/files/24d3c229-4f2f-405d-b8db-a3a67f183883*, March 26, 2014

[WSJ24] Madnick, Stuart. "What's Behind the Increase in Data Breaches?," available online at *https://www.wsj.com/tech/cybersecurity/why-are-cybersecurity-data-breaches-still-rising-2f08866c*, March 15, 2024

[YAG24] Mosby, Albert. "100+ Online Shopping Statistics 2024 (Worldwide Data)," available online at *https://www.yaguara.co/online-shopping-statistics/*, July 13, 2024

INDEX

www.ingramcontent.com/pod-product-compliance
Lightning Source LLC
Chambersburg PA
CBHW080128220326
41598CB00032B/4997